QUICK COURSE®

in

MICROSOFT®

OFFICE 97

Computer training books for busy people

JOYCE COX

POLLY URBAN

CHRISTINA DUDLEY

AN ONLINE PRESS BOOK

PUBLISHED BY
Online Press Incorporated
14320 NE 21st Street, Suite 18
Bellevue, WA 98007
Phone: (206) 641-3434, (800) 854-3344
Fax: (206) 641-4728
Email: onlinepressinc@msn.com
Web site: http://www.quickcourse.com

Publisher's Cataloging in Publication
(Prepared by Quality Books Inc.)

Cox, Joyce.
Quick course in Microsoft Office 97 / Joyce Cox, Polly Urban.
p. cm.
Covers Word, Excel, Access, PowerPoint.
Includes index.
LCCN: 96-71317
ISBN: 1-879399-69-5

1. Microsoft Office for Windows. 2. Microsoft Word for Windows. 3. Microsoft Excel for Windows. 4. Microsoft Access. 5. Microsoft PowerPoint for Windows. 6. Business—Computer programs. 7. Word processing. 8. Electronic spreadsheets. 9. Computer graphics. 10. Database management. 11. Integrated software. I. Urban, Polly. II. Title. III. Title: Microsoft Office 97.

HF5548.5.M525C69 1997 005.369
QBI96-40551

Printed and bound in the United States of America

1 2 3 4 5 6 7 8 9 O F F I 3 2 1 0

Contents

1 Microsoft Office Basics

Adjust the top margin to make the document sit lower on the page

Right-align the date to balance the page

May 22, 1997

Emma Shakes, President
Tip Top Roofing, Inc.
4239 East Lake Avenue
Lakewood, WA 98403

RE: 1997 CARSON AWARDS

Center text and use bold and underlining for emphasis

Dear Ms. Shakes:

I am pleased to be the bearer of good news! Yesterday, the Carson committee voted unanimously to present one of its 1997 awards to your company, **Tip Top Roofing**. Your efforts during the past year to forge the industry alliances needed for a successful asphalt-shingle recycling program are an impressive demonstration of Tip Top Roofing's ongoing commitment to the environment.

As you know, the prestigious Carson Awards recognize companies who work to ensure that their business practices are environmentally sensitive. This year's awards will be presented at the Carson Gala Dinner on Friday July 25, 1997. I will contact you next week with further details.

Again, congratulations!

Ted Lee

Produce simple documents like this letter, right away

Justify paragraphs to give the letter a formal look

As you probably know, Microsoft Office 97 is a *suite* of applications that are also available as independent programs. Microsoft Office is much more powerful than the sum of its component applications because it "glues" the applications together in such a way that we no longer have to think in terms of applications per se. We can instead focus on the documents (files) we need to work with to accomplish specific tasks. Of course, we still need to know enough about the Office applications to be able to create and manipulate our documents, so let's take a quick look at what's included in the Office suite.

Microsoft Office comes in several editions that include various combinations of primary and secondary applications. The primary applications include the following:

Microsoft Word

- **Microsoft Word.** This award-winning word processor lets us write, edit, and print text documents. We can control the look of the text by changing the font, style, and size of its characters and by setting such elements as indents, line spacing, tabs, and margins. And we can check the accuracy of our words using the built-in spelling and grammar checkers.

Microsoft Excel

- **Microsoft Excel.** This spreadsheet lets us use efficient, built-in functions as shortcuts for performing mathematical, financial, and statistical calculations. These calculations can be as simple as totaling a column or row of values or as complex as figuring the rate of return on an investment under varying circumstances.

Microsoft PowerPoint

- **Microsoft PowerPoint.** This presentation program lets us put together sophisticated slide shows or electronic presentations with professional-looking graphic effects. We can format the slide text in a variety of eye-catching ways and add charts, tables, and pictures for even greater impact.

Microsoft Access

- **Microsoft Access.** This database lets us store and organize information in sets of tables. After creating a database, we can look at the information as a list (in columns and rows), or we can look at each item of information in a form, as though it were recorded on an index card. We can perform calculations and compute statistics such as totals and averages. And we can sort the information, find specific items, and create reports.

- **Microsoft Outlook.** This desktop information management program provides one location for handling our email, calendar, contacts, and task lists.

Microsoft Outlook

In addition to these primary applications, your edition of Office may come with some or all of the following secondary applications:

Supporting programs

- **Microsoft Graph,** which we use to turn tabular data into graphs and charts.
- **ClipArt Gallery,** a collection of ready-made graphics that we can import into any of the primary applications.
- **Microsoft Organization Chart,** which provides the tools for creating diagrams such as organization charts.
- **WordArt,** which enables us to mold text into various shapes for logos and headlines.
- **Equation Editor,** which enables us to correctly format complex equations.
- **Microsoft Map,** which quickly converts appropriate data, such as a worksheet showing Sales by State, to a map format.

Occasionally, Microsoft releases other small applications designed to enhance Office. These are often available for free downloading on the Internet. (Check the product areas of Microsoft's Web site at http://www.microsoft.com.) Microsoft may also include them in future releases of Office. Although these applications are not covered in this book, the techniques you will learn here will allow you to explore them on your own.

This book is a fast-paced introduction to Microsoft Office. We start by covering some of the basic skills used in all the applications. Then we devote two chapters to each of the four primary tools and one chapter to Outlook. Finally, one chapter shows how to recycle information from one application

Microsoft Bookshelf

Microsoft Office 97 comes with Microsoft Bookshelf Basics, a scaled-down version of Microsoft Bookshelf. This integrated, multimedia reference includes the following: a dictionary, a thesaurus, a quotations book, an encyclopedia, an atlas, a world chronology, and an almanac. Bookshelf Basics provides only the dictionary, thesaurus, and quotations book, along with previews of the other components. Inserting the Office CD-ROM and clicking the Bookshelf Basics button on the Office shortcut bar (see page 5) displays a window in which you can pick a topic from a list; search for a topic; list topics that have all types of media, only pictures, only animation or video, or only sound; view a list of all the topics you have already researched; or view a list of the events of the previous year. You can work with all three books at once or with a selected book. For more information, we'll leave you to explore on your own.

to another for maximum efficiency. In 300 pages, we can't hope to cover all the ins and outs of Office and we don't try to. But we don't just skim the surface, sticking with the easy stuff. We focus on the most useful features—the ones most people will use most often and the ones more people would use if they knew how. By the time you finish this Quick Course®, you'll have a firm understanding of the important features of Word, Excel, PowerPoint, Access, and Outlook, and you'll know enough about Office to experiment on your own with the features we don't cover in detail. What's more you'll have created real documents that will serve as models for those you'll need to generate on the job, at school, or for personal use.

Getting Started

Common commands and techniques

Because of all its components, you might think that Office would be difficult to master. Not so. An important aspect of this integrated suite is that you use the same commands and techniques in all the applications to carry out common tasks. Though each application has a particular focus, the techniques for tasks such as editing, formatting, saving, and printing are similar, and the experience you acquire with one application can be applied to another. For the rest of this chapter, we work with Word to create a letter. In the process, you learn basic techniques for working with all the Office applications.

We assume that you've installed Office on your computer and that you allowed the Office Setup program to stash everything in the Program Files/Microsoft Office folder on your C: drive. The Setup program also added items to the Start menu and put various Office components in the StartUp folder so that they are automatically started every time you turn on your computer. We also assume that you've worked with Windows 95 before. If you are new to Windows 95, we recommend you take a look at *Quick Course in Windows 95*, another book in the Quick Course series, which will help you quickly come up to speed.

Creating a New Office Document

Well, let's get going. With Windows 95 loaded, the screen looks something like this:

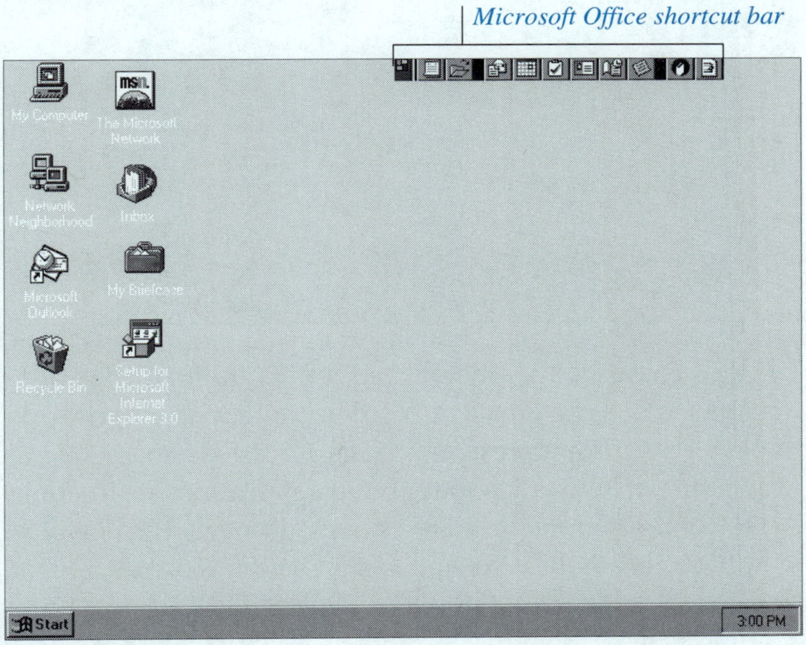

(If the What's New and/or Windows 95 Welcome window is displayed, click the Close button—the button with the X in the window's top right corner—to close each window.)

Notice the string of buttons in the top right corner. These buttons comprise the *Microsoft Office shortcut bar*, which we can use to easily access the tools we need to carry out Office tasks. (If you don't see the shortcut bar, turn to page 258 for information about how to start it, or if necessary, install it before proceeding.) Let's experiment a bit with the shortcut bar:

Microsoft Office shortcut bar

1. Point to each shortcut-bar button in turn, pausing until the button's name appears in a box below the pointer. You can use this helpful feature, which is called *ToolTips*, to identify buttons on toolbars in all the Office applications (see page 10 for more information).

ToolTips

The New Office Document button

2. Click the New Office Document button on the Office shortcut bar to display the dialog box shown on the next page.

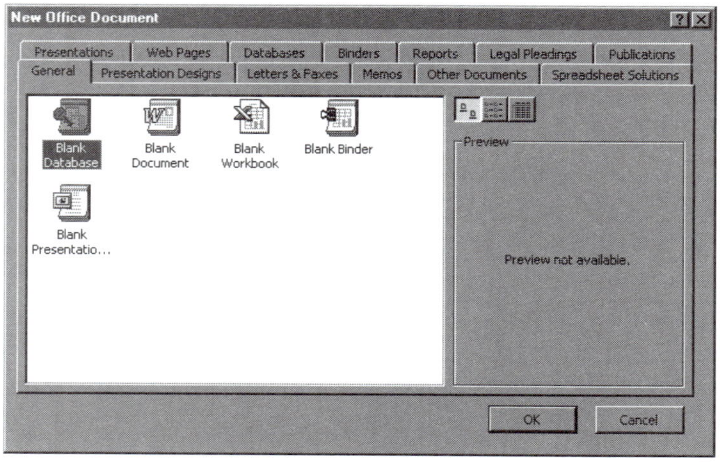

On the dialog box's General tab are icons for the various documents you can create: a Word document, an Excel workbook, a PowerPoint presentation, an Access database, and an Office binder. We talk about giving applications instructions by selecting options in dialog boxes on page 15. For now, simply complete the next step to start a new Word document.

3. Click the Blank Document icon to select it and click OK. Microsoft Word starts and opens a new, blank document. Your screen now looks like the one shown here:

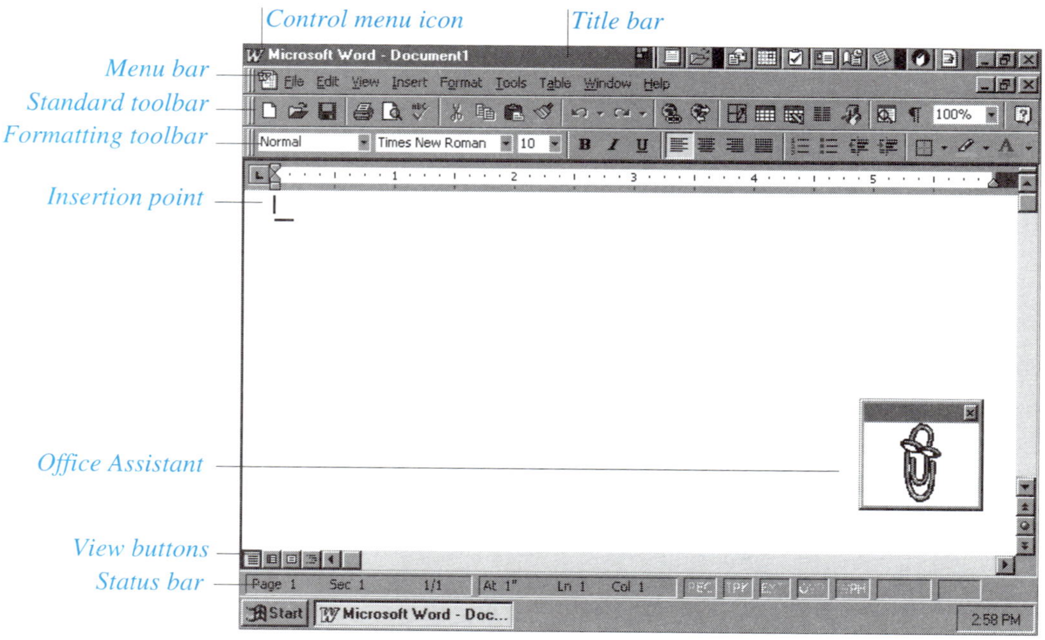

You'll learn what all the labeled parts of the window are as we work our way through this chapter.

4. To reduce screen clutter, turn off the Office shortcut bar by double-clicking the icon at its left end and clicking Yes in the message box that appears so that the shortcut bar will reappear the next time you turn on your computer.

5. If the Office Assistant displays a list of options for you, click the Start Microsoft Word option to start Word. If the Assistant appears by itself, click its Close button (the one with the X) to remove it from the screen. (We'll discuss the Office Assistant in more detail on page 27.)

Entering Text

Let's start by writing a paragraph. Follow these steps:

1. The blinking *insertion point* indicates where the next character you type will appear on the screen. Type the following:

   I am pleased to be the bearer of good news! Yesterday, the Carson Committee voted unanimously to present one of its 1997 awards to your company, Tip Top Roofing. Your efforts during the past year to forge the industry alliances needed for a successful asphalt-shingle recycling program are an impressive demonstration of Tip Top Roofing's ongoing commitment to the environment.

Insertion point

As each line of text reaches the right edge of the screen, the next word you type moves to a new line. This is called *word wrapping*. When entering text in Word and PowerPoint, you don't have to worry about pressing the Enter key to end one line and start another. The applications take care of that chore for you, filling each line with as many words as will fit. (As you follow our examples, don't worry if your word wrapping isn't identical to ours.)

2. Press Enter to end the paragraph. Your screen looks like the one shown on the next page.

Correcting mistakes

All of the Office applications correct some simple typos, such as *teh* (the) and *adn* (and)—we explain how on page 36. If you spell a less common word incorrectly, Word and PowerPoint point out the mistake with a red, wavy underline. We show you some simple editing techniques on page 21, but in the meantime, if you make a mistake and want to correct it, simply press the Backspace key until you've deleted the error and then retype the text.

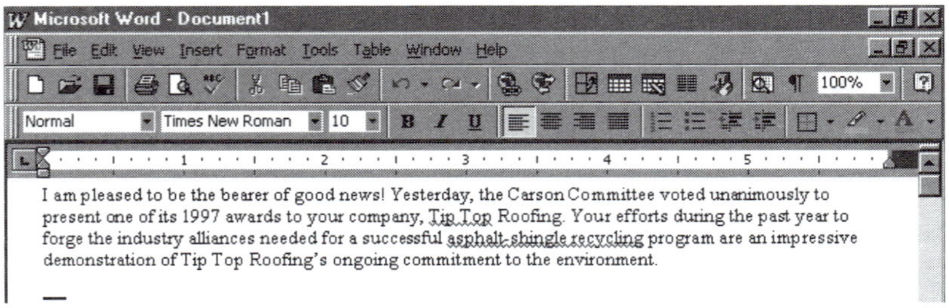

Word flags words and phrases it suspects have grammatical problems with a green, wavy underline. (We discuss Word's grammar feature in more detail on page 48.) Now that we have some text on the screen, let's see what we can do with it.

Selecting Text

Before we start to work on this paragraph, we need to discuss how to select text. In all the Office applications, knowing how to select text efficiently saves time because we can then edit or format all the selected text at once, instead of a letter or word at a time. The simplest way to learn how to select text is to do it, so follow these steps to select some text blocks:

1. Move the pointer to the word *unanimously* and double-click it. The word changes to white on black (called *highlighting*) to indicate that it is selected:

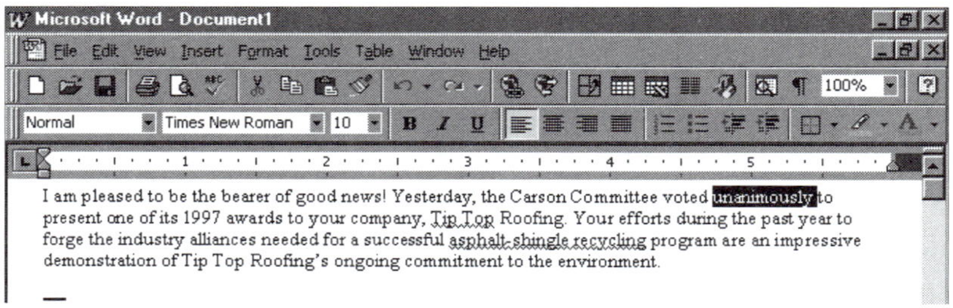

2. Point to the left of *Tip* and click the left mouse button to position the insertion point at the beginning of the word. Then point to the right of *Roofing*, hold down the Shift key, and click the left mouse button. (This action is sometimes referred to as *Shift-clicking*.) Word highlights the words between the two clicks:

Whole word selection

By default, Word selects whole words. For example, if you start a selection in the middle of a word and drag beyond the last character, Word selects the entire word. If you drag to the first character of the next word, Word selects that word, and so on. You can tell Word to select only the characters you drag across by choosing Options from the Tools menu, clicking the Edit tab, deselecting the When Selecting, Automatically Select Entire Word option, and clicking OK.

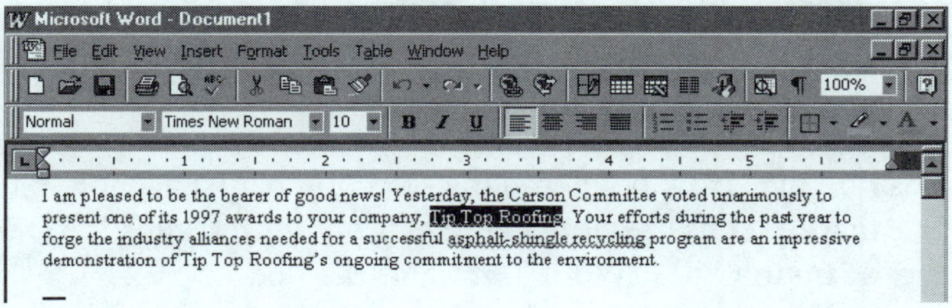

3. Point to the left of the word *recycling*, hold down the left mouse button, drag to the right until *recycling program* is selected, and release the mouse button. Using this technique, you can highlight exactly as much or as little text as you need.

Extending a selection with the Shift key

4. Click an insertion point before the *Y* in *Yesterday*. Hold down the Shift key, press the Right Arrow key until the entire word is highlighted, and release the Shift key.

5. Without moving the selection, hold down the Shift key, press the Down Arrow key, and then press the Right Arrow key until the entire sentence is highlighted, like this:

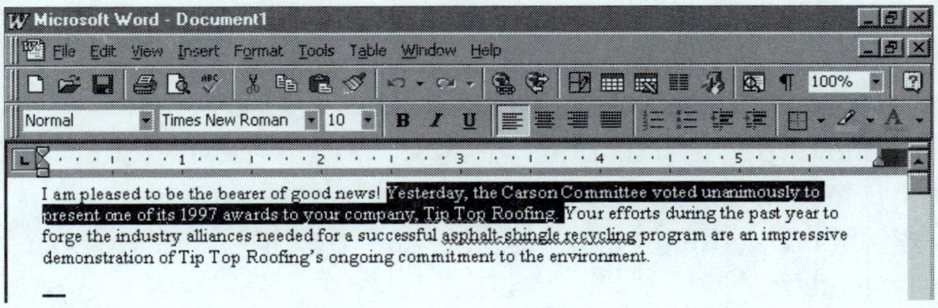

6. Next, try pressing different Arrow keys while holding down the Shift key. As long as you hold down Shift, Word extends the selection in the direction of the key's arrow.

7. Release the Shift key and press Home to move the insertion point to the beginning of the line where the selection starts and also remove any highlighting.

With slight variations, the techniques we've covered so far can be used in all the Office applications. The next selection technique, however, applies only to Word and PowerPoint. Let's run through the steps on the following page.

The selection bar

1. Move the mouse pointer to the far left side of the window. When the pointer changes to a right-pointing arrow, it is in an invisible vertical strip called the *selection bar*.

2. Position the arrow pointer in the selection bar adjacent to the line that contains the words *Tip Top Roofing* and click the left mouse button once. Word highlights the line:

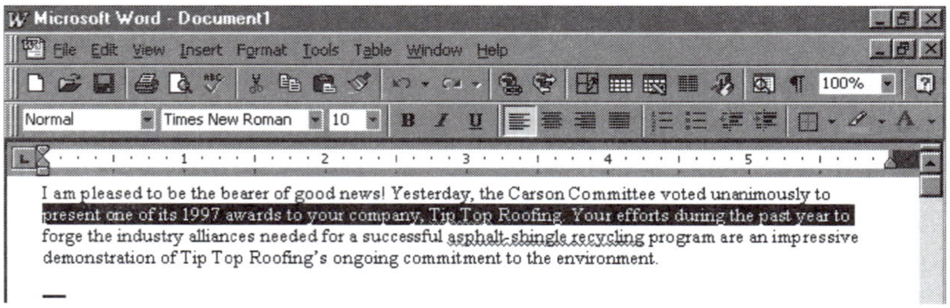

3. Now highlight the entire paragraph by double-clicking in the selection bar next to the paragraph.

We can also drag the pointer in the selection bar to select multiple lines or paragraphs.

Giving Instructions

Now that you know how to select text, let's discuss how we tell the Office applications what to do with the selection. We give instructions by clicking buttons and boxes on toolbars, by choosing menu commands, and by pressing keyboard shortcuts.

Using an IntelliMouse

If you are using the Microsoft IntelliMouse, you can scroll up or down in a file by rotating the wheel between the left and right mouse buttons forward or backward. For continuous scrolling, hold down the wheel button and drag the pointer above or below the origin mark (the dot with the arrows). You can control the scrolling speed by moving the pointer toward or away from the origin mark. To zoom in or out on a page, hold down the Ctrl key as you move the wheel forward or backward.

Using the Toolbars

Each Office application comes with a set of toolbars which provide a simple way of quickly carrying out common tasks. At the moment, Word's Standard and Formatting toolbars are displayed. Once you are familiar with the buttons on these toolbars, you'll recognize many of them on the toolbars of the other applications. More specialized buttons are gathered together on other toolbars, which we can display at any time (see page 15). We can also hide the toolbars if we need to view more of a document at once. Let's explore the toolbars:

1. Familiarize yourself with the buttons and boxes on the two toolbars by moving the pointer slowly over each one so that ToolTips displays its name.
2. Use any of the methods discussed in the previous section to select the first occurrence of *Tip Top Roofing*.
3. Click the Bold button on the Formatting toolbar and then click the Underline button. (You could also add italic formatting by clicking the Italic button.)
4. Press Home to remove the highlighting. As you can see, these two simple changes really make the text stand out:

The Bold, Underline, and Italic buttons

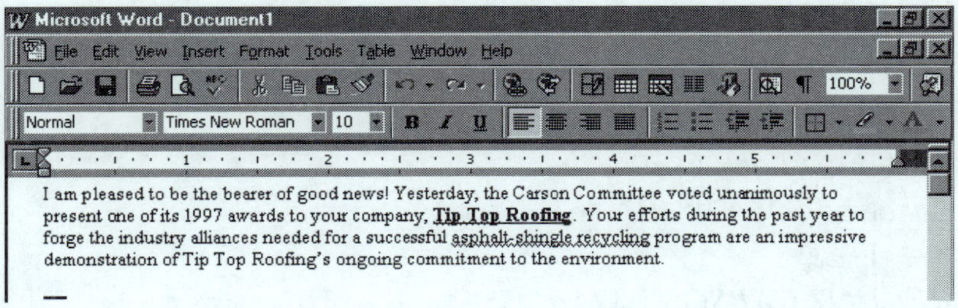

Now let's experiment with the document's font and font size:

1. Select the paragraph and click the arrow to the right of the Font box to display a list of the available fonts.
2. Click Arial in the drop-down list. (If necessary, use the scroll bar on the right side to bring the top of the list into view.) The font of the text changes, and the setting in the Font box now reflects the new font.
3. With the paragraph still selected, click the arrow to the right of the Font Size box and then click 12 in the drop-down list.
4. Now press End so that you can see the results:

The Font box

The Font Size box

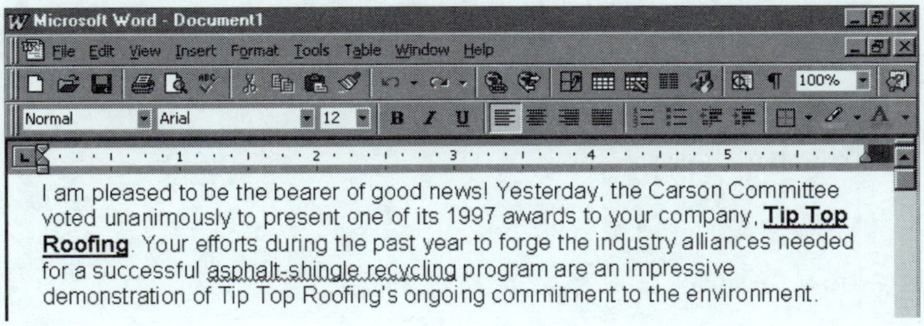

We have just used toolbar buttons and boxes to apply common character formats to a text selection. *Character formats* affect the appearance of individual characters. They can be applied to any number of characters, from one to the whole document. In Word, Excel, and PowerPoint, we can also use toolbar buttons to change *paragraph formats* which affect the appearance of an entire paragraph. Let's see how changing the alignment of a paragraph affects the way it looks:

Character formats

Paragraph formats

Moving to the beginning of a document

1. Press Ctrl+Home to move to the beginning of the document and then type the following, pressing Enter to end paragraphs and create blank lines where indicated:

May 22, 1997 (Press Enter)
(Press Enter)
Emma Shakes, President (Press Enter)
Tip Top Roofing, Inc. (Press Enter)
4239 East Lake Avenue (Press Enter)
Lakewood, WA 98403 (Press Enter)
(Press Enter)
RE: 1997 CARSON AWARDS (Press Enter)
(Press Enter)
Dear Ms. Shakes: (Press Enter twice)

If the Office Assistant appears as you work your way through our examples, click its Close button to turn it off.

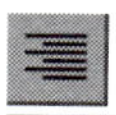

The Align Right button

2. Press Crtl+Home and click the Align Right button to right-align the date.

The Center button

3. Click an insertion point anywhere in the subject (RE:) line and then click the Center button. Here are the results:

Using Menu Commands

Most of the buttons on the toolbars have equivalent commands on the Office application menus, which are arranged on the menu bar that spans the window below the title bar of each Office application. The menus on the menu bar are designed so that once we are familiar with the menu location of the commands in one Office application, we know where to find the same commands in any other Office application. Just as the applications' toolbars have some buttons that are the same and some that vary with each application, the menus have some commands that are the same and some that vary.

Buttons vs. commands

So when do we use a button and when do we use a command? We can always use a command to carry out a particular task, but we can't always use a corresponding button. Clicking the button often carries out its associated command with its predefined, or default, settings without any further input from us. When a command is not represented by a toolbar button, or when we want to use a command with something other than its default settings, we need to choose the command from a menu.

Choosing Menu Bar Commands

Because the procedure for choosing menu commands is the same for all Windows applications, we assume that you are familiar with it. If you are a new Windows user, we suggest that you spend a little time becoming familiar with the mechanics of menus, commands, and dialog boxes before proceeding. Here, we'll run through the steps for choosing a command and do some useful exploring at the same time:

1. Click View on the menu bar to display this menu:

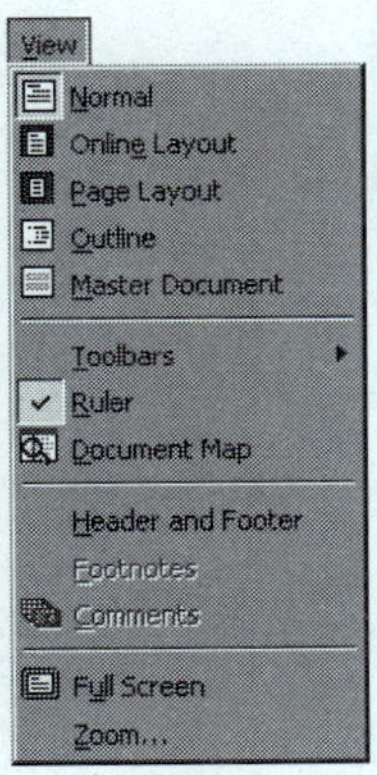

Menu command buttons

You may have noticed that for some menu commands, an icon appears to the left of the command name. The icon simply indicates that a corresponding button exists for this command on one of the application's toolbars.

Mutually exclusive commands

In all the Office applications, the View menu provides commands for customizing the screen display, but the actual commands vary from application to application. Notice that the button icon next to the Normal command appears pressed, indicating that, of the five commands above the first line on the menu, Normal is the command currently in effect. Choosing one of the other five commands puts that command into effect and deactivates Normal.

Turning off the ruler

2. Choose the Ruler command from the View menu by clicking the name to turn off the ruler. Word hides the ruler below the Formatting toolbar. (If your ruler was already turned off, choosing Ruler turns it on. Choose the command a second time to turn it back off.)

3. Click the View menu again and notice that the Ruler command no longer has a check mark next to its name, indicating that the command is turned off. Commands that can be turned on and off are called *toggle commands*. Choosing a checked toggle command turns off the command without affecting the status of any other commands.

Toggle commands

4. Choose the Ruler command to turn on the ruler.

5. Click the View menu again (notice that a check mark has reappeared next to Ruler) and point to the Toolbars command to display this drop-down list:

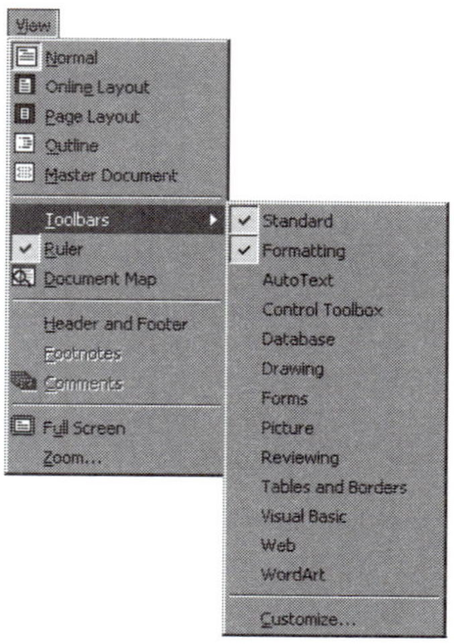

Re-appearing ruler

When the ruler is turned off, you can temporarily display it by pointing to the gray bar below the toolbars. The ruler drops down and remains visible as long as the pointer is over it. When you move the pointer away from the ruler, it disappears.

All of the Office applications have several commands with right-pointing arrowheads next to their names on the menus. Choosing one of these commands displays a *submenu* of additional commands that you can choose simply by clicking them in the usual way.

Submenus

6. Click AutoText to display the AutoText toolbar.

7. Click the View menu again and choose Toolbars and then Customize to display this *dialog box*:

Dialog boxes

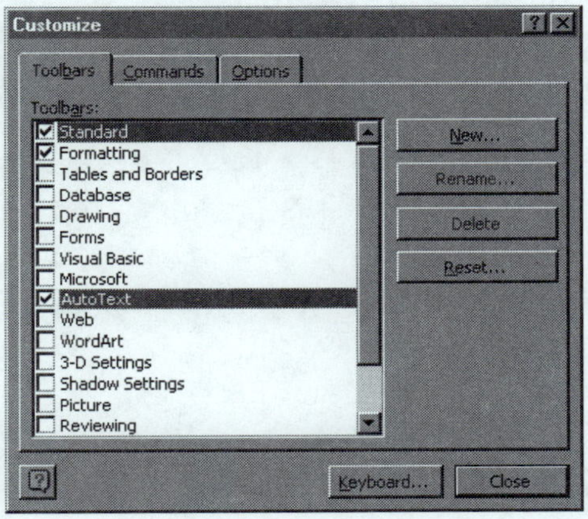

When you choose a command that is followed by an ellipsis on the menu, you have to supply additional information by setting options in a dialog box before an Office application can carry out the command.

Notice that the Customize dialog box is multilayered, with each layer designated at the top of the dialog box by a tab like a file folder tab. The Toolbars tab is currently displayed. (If it's not, click Toolbars at the top of the dialog box.)

8. Click the AutoText check box to turn off that toolbar. Then click the four check boxes below the Formatting check box to turn them on, and click Close. Your screen should look something like the one shown on the next page. Notice that toolbars can appear across the top or bottom of the window, down the sides, or floating over the workspace. (See the tip on the next page for information about toolbars.)

The other Customize options

There are four buttons on the right side of the Toolbars tab in the Customize dialog box that give you more customization options. Click New to create your own custom toolbar. You can then click the Rename or Delete buttons to rename or delete your custom toolbar. (You cannot rename or delete toolbars that come with an Office application.) If you have customized a toolbar and want to return it to its default settings, simply select the toolbar in the Toolbars list and click the Reset button.

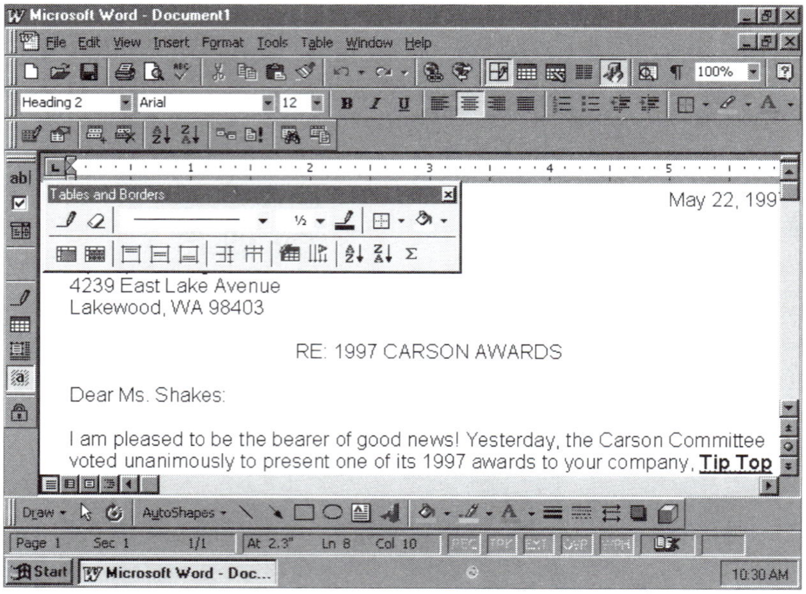

9. Use ToolTips to get an idea of the names and functions of all the buttons on the new toolbars.

More about toolbars

You may have noticed that some toolbars appear "docked" at the top, bottom, or sides of the window while others "float" somewhere in the window. To convert a docked toolbar to a floating toolbar, double-click the left end of a horizontal toolbar or the top of a vertical toolbar. Double-clicking the title bar of a floating toolbar repositions the toolbar in a docked position on the screen. You can also move the floating toolbar to a new position on the screen by dragging its title bar. If you drag to the sides or bottom of the screen, the toolbar arranges itself along the edge of the document window. To return a toolbar to its original location, simply drag it back to that spot and then release the mouse button. You can also customize toolbars by moving, removing, and adding toolbar buttons. For more information, look up "customizing toolbars" in Help. (We discuss the Help feature on page 26.)

Choosing Object Menu Commands

For efficiency, the commands that we are likely to use with a particular object, such as a block of text, are combined on special menus, called *object menus*. Object menus are also available for window elements, such as the toolbars. We access an object menu by pointing to the object and clicking the right mouse button. This action is called *right-clicking*. Try the following:

1. Point to one of the toolbars, right-click to display the toolbar object menu, and choose Database from the menu to turn off the Database toolbar.
2. Right-click a toolbar to display the object menu again. You don't want to repeat step 1 to turn off the toolbars one at a time, so choose Customize from the bottom of the menu to display the dialog box you saw earlier, deselect all the check boxes except Standard and Formatting, and click Close.

Using Keyboard Shortcuts

We can't imagine anyone wanting to work with the Office applications using only the keyboard. Using a mouse makes working with most Windows applications much easier, and Office is no exception. However, if our hands are already on the keyboard, using keyboard shortcuts to access commands can be more efficient. We have already used the Ctrl+Home keyboard shortcut to move to the top of the document now on the screen. Here are a few more examples:

1. Select the subject line (RE: 1997 CARSON AWARDS) and press first Ctrl+B and then Ctrl+U to make the line bold and underlined. (As you know, you can achieve the same effect by clicking the Bold and Underline buttons on the Formatting toolbar.)

2. Now use a keyboard shortcut to change the alignment of the first paragraph you typed. Click an insertion point in the paragraph that begins *I am pleased* and press Ctrl+J to justify it so that its lines are even with both the left and right margins. (Press Ctrl+L to left-align a paragraph, Ctrl+R to right-align it, and Ctrl+E to center it.)

3. Press Ctrl+Home to move the insertion point to the top of the document. Here are the results:

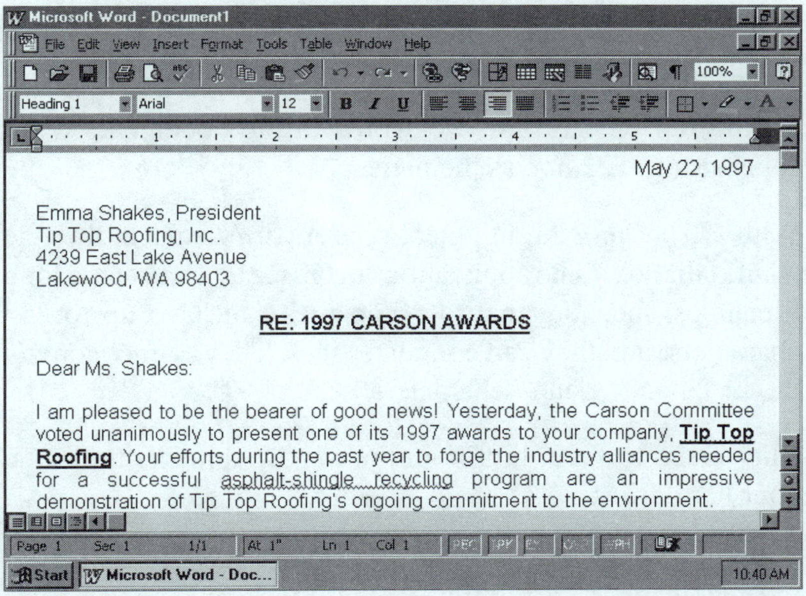

Help with shortcuts

The list of keyboard shortcuts is extensive, and it would take a lot of space to reproduce it here. For more information about keyboard shortcuts, ask the Office Assistant (see page 27) or choose Contents And Index from the Help menu, and on the Index tab, type *keys* in the Type The First Few Letters box. Then click Shortcut Keys in the Check The Index Entry box and click Display. In the Topics Found window, click the entry for the type of task you are interested in and click Display again. (See page 26 for more information about the Help system.)

Saving Files

Until we save the document we have created as a file on a disk, the document exists only in the computer's memory and disappears if the computer is intentionally or unintentionally turned off. To save the document for the first time, we can click the Save button or choose Save As from the File menu to display a dialog box in which we specify a name for the file. Thereafter, clicking the Save button or choosing the Save command saves the file without displaying the dialog box because the file already has a name. Let's save the document now on the screen:

The Save button

1. Choose Save As from the File menu to display the Save As dialog box:

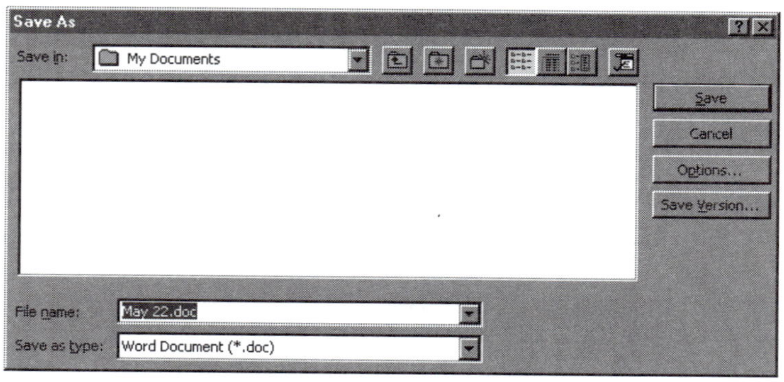

Picking up on the first two words in the document, Word suggests *May 22.doc* as the name.

2. With *May 22.doc* highlighted, type *Award Letter* in the File Name edit box. (The applications in Office 97 can handle long filenames, meaning that the filenames can have up to 255 characters, and they can contain spaces. They cannot contain the : * | \ < > " ? and / characters.)
3. Click Save to save the file in the My Documents folder on your hard drive.

From now on, we can click the Save button any time we want to save changes to this file. Because the application knows the name of the file, it simply saves the file by overwriting the old version with the new version.

Saving in a different folder

The file will be saved in the folder designated in the Save In box. If you want to store the file in a different folder, click the arrow to the right of the Save In box, use the drop-down list to navigate to the folder in which you want the file to be saved, and double-click that folder to display its name in the Save In box before you click Save to save the file. If the folder you want doesn't exist, you can create the folder by clicking the Create New Folder button before you save the file.

More Ways to Create New Files

Part of the magic of a computer is that we can use the same information for different purposes without retyping the information each time. When we have already created one file and we want to adapt it for a different purpose without destroying the original, we can save the file with a new name to create a new file without destroying the old one. Try this:

1. Choose Save As from the File menu, replace the name in the File Name edit box by typing *Tip Top Letter*, and click Save. Word closes Award Letter, and the filename in the title bar changes to Tip Top Letter.

We can create a totally new file at any time without closing any open files. Follow these steps:

The New button

1. Click the New button on the Standard toolbar. Word displays a new file called Document2, completely obscuring Tip Top Letter, which is still open.
2. Type the following paragraph, misspelling the two occurrences of Carson as Carsen (Word—and PowerPoint—will underline possible misspellings with a red, wavy line):

   As you no doubt know, the prestigious Carsen Awards recognize companies who work to ensure that their business practices are sensitive environmentally. This year's awards will be presented at the Carsen Gala Dinner on Friday July 25, 1997. I will contact you next week with more details.

3. Press Enter and then save the document with the name *Carson Dinner*.

Opening Documents

We now have a couple of open documents in separate, stacked windows. For good measure, let's open an existing document:

The Open button

1. Click the Open button on the Standard toolbar to display the dialog box shown on the next page.

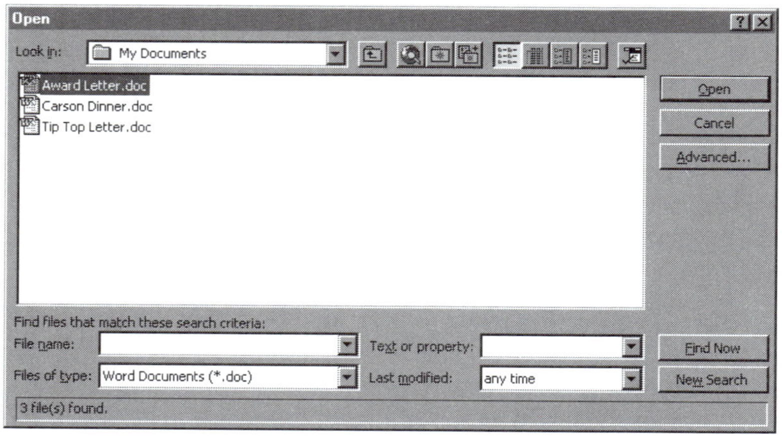

2. With Award Letter selected, click Open.

Manipulating Windows

We'll pause here to review some window basics. Follow these steps to move from one window to another:

1. Choose Tip Top Letter from the list of open files at the bottom of the Window menu. That file comes to the top of the stack of windows.

2. Choose Arrange All from the Window menu. The three open documents arrange themselves so that they each occupy a third of the screen, like this:

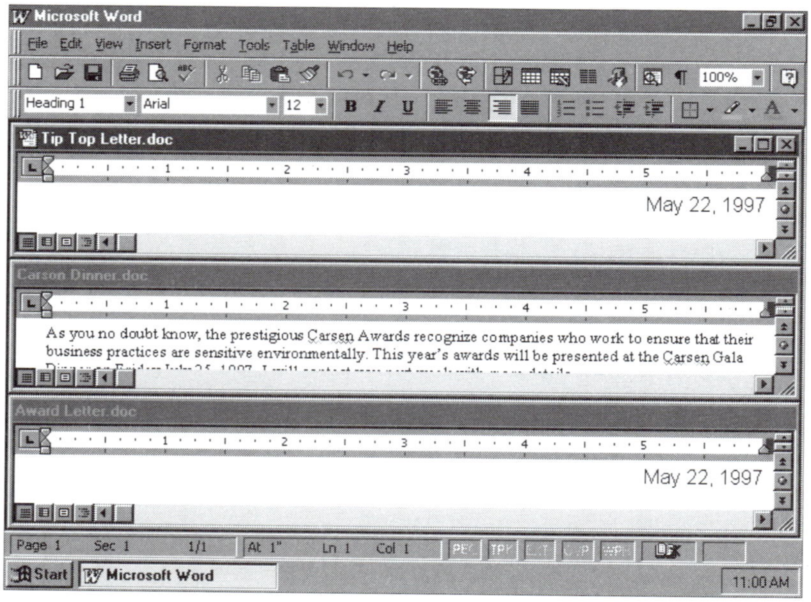

Finding files

At the bottom of the Open dialog box are boxes that provide an easy way of locating the file you need. Suppose you can't remember exactly what you called the Award Letter document or where you stored it. Simply navigate to the folder for your C: drive, click the New Search button, enter *award* in the File Name edit box, and click the Commands And Settings button at the top of the dialog box. Choose Search Subfolders from the drop-down menu to tell Office to look in all the folders on your C: drive. Office searches the specified drive and its subfolders for any Word documents with the word *award* in the filename and displays the one(s) it finds. You can then select the document you want and click the Open button. If you have many files with similar names, you can refine the search by specifying text included in the document or its date of modification, or you can click the Advanced button and specify additional criteria. You can also save searches in the Advanced Find dialog box.

Notice that the title bar of the active window is darker than those of the inactive windows. Any entries you make and most commands you choose will affect only the document in the active window.

3. Click anywhere in Carson Dinner to activate it, and then click the Carson Dinner window's Maximize button (the middle of the three buttons at the right end of the window's title bar). The window expands to fill the screen, completely obscuring Tip Top Letter and Award Letter.

Maximizing a window

Simple Editing

Typically when creating documents, we will start by typing roughly what we want the document to contain and then we'll go back and edit the contents until we are satisfied with them. In this section, we'll quickly cover the editing techniques that we can use in all the Office applications. (Because we are working in Word, we'll be dealing with text, but these techniques can be used with any type of entry.) Other techniques are covered in the chapters about specific applications.

Deleting and Replacing Text

First let's make a few small changes. Follow these steps:

1. Click an insertion point to the left of the *e* in the first occurrence of *Carsen*, press the Delete (Del) key to delete the character to the right, and without moving the insertion point, type *o*. The red, wavy underline that flags the typo disappears.
2. Click an insertion point to the right of the *e* in the second occurrence of *Carsen*, press the Backspace key to delete the character to the left, and again type *o*.
3. Select the words *no doubt* in the first line and press either Delete or Backspace to delete the words.
4. Double-click the word *more* in the last line and with the word highlighted, type *further* as its replacement.
5. Click the Save button to save Carson Dinner.

File management

With Office 97, you can manage your files from within an Office application. You can delete, rename, or move your files from the Open or Save As dialog box. For example, by right-clicking a filename in the Open dialog box, you can choose from several object-menu commands that let you print the file, send a copy of the file to a floppy disk, delete the file, or rename it. You can perform most of these tasks from the Save As dialog box as well.

Moving and Copying Text

We can move or copy any amount of text within the same file or to a different file. Move operations can be carried out in all Office applications using the Cut and Paste buttons on the Standard toolbar. Similarly, copy operations can be carried out using the Copy and Paste buttons. Let's experiment:

The Cut button

1. In Carson Dinner, select the word *sensitive* and click the Cut button. Word removes the text from the document and stores it in a temporary storage place, called the *Clipboard*, in your computer's memory.

The Paste button

2. Click an insertion point to the right of the *y* in *environmentally* and click the Paste button. Word inserts the cut text, preceding it with a space.

Now let's try copying text to a different file:

The Copy button

1. Choose Select All from the Edit menu to select all the text in Carson Dinner, and then click the Copy button.
2. Choose Tip Top Letter from the Window menu to activate the letter.
3. Press Ctrl+End to move to the end of the letter, press Enter to add a blank line, and then click the Paste button to insert the selected paragraph.

As you can see, when we copied the paragraph from Carson Dinner to Tip Top Letter, we copied the formatting of the paragraph as well. We'll reformat the entire letter in a moment.

Undoing and Redoing Commands

For those occasions when we make an editing mistake, the Office applications provide a safety net: the Undo command. Try this:

The Undo button

1. You're not sure you need the paragraph you copied into the letter, so click the Undo button to reverse the paste operation from the previous steps.

The Redo button

2. Change your mind again, and click the Redo button to paste the paragraph back into the letter.

Printing Files

Whether we are writing a letter, generating a budget, producing a slide show, or extracting information from a database, the end product of many of our Office sessions will be a printout. If you can print from any other Windows application, you should have no trouble printing from the Office applications. First, let's finish off the letter:

1. With the insertion point at the end of the letter, type *Again, congratulations!*, press Enter four times, type *Ted Lee*, and press Enter again.
2. Choose Select All from the Edit menu, click the arrow to the right of the Font box on the Formatting toolbar, and change the font to Times New Roman.
3. Change the Font Size setting to 10.
4. Finally, select the second paragraph and click the Justify button on the Formatting toolbar. The letter now looks like this:

The Justify button

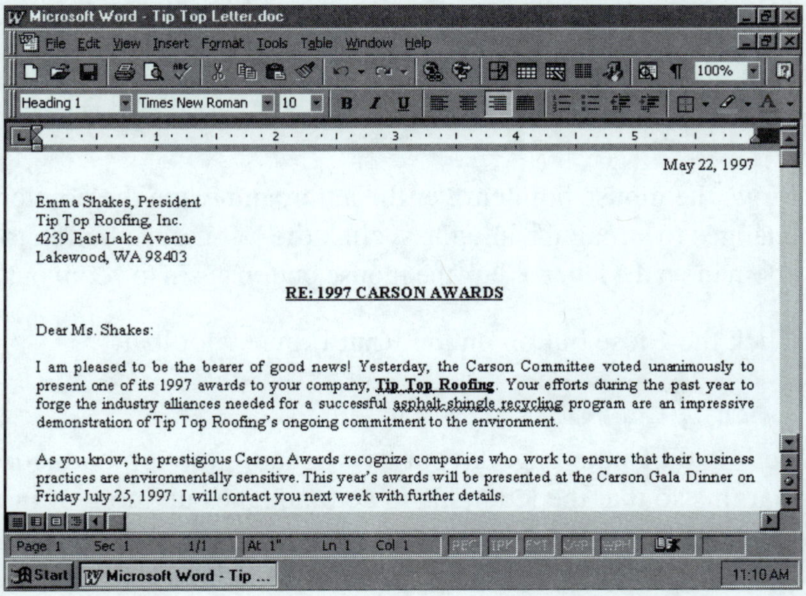

5. Save the letter.

Undoing and redoing multiple actions

In Word, Excel, and PowerPoint, you can undo and redo several actions at a time. Simply click the arrow to the right of the appropriate button and drag through the actions in the list that you want to undo or redo. You cannot undo or redo a single action other than the last one. For example, to undo the third action in the list, you must also undo the first and second.

Previewing Files

The letter we have written is only one page long and it has no header or footer. However, it is worth checking even a file this small in print preview to get an idea of how it looks on the page. Follow these steps to preview the letter:

The Print Preview button

1. Click the Print Preview button on the Standard toolbar to display the entire page like this:

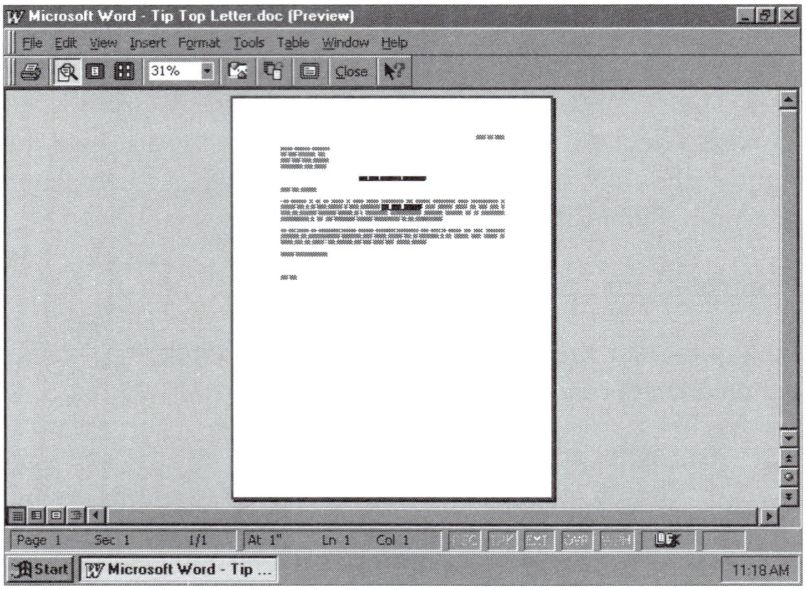

2. Move the mouse pointer over the letter, and when the pointer changes to a magnifying glass, click the left mouse button to zoom in on the letter. Click the mouse button again to zoom out.
3. Click the Close button on the Print Preview toolbar.

> **Editing in print preview**
>
> Suppose you zoom in on a section of a document and notice something you need to change. To edit a document in print preview, click the Magnifier button on the Print Preview toolbar to change the pointer to an insertion point. Make your changes and then click the Magnifier button again. Then click the document to zoom out.

Changing Page Layout

Let's modify the page layout by widening the top and side margins so that the letter sits lower and takes up more of the page. Follow these steps:

1. Choose Page Setup from the File menu to display the dialog box shown at the top of the facing page.

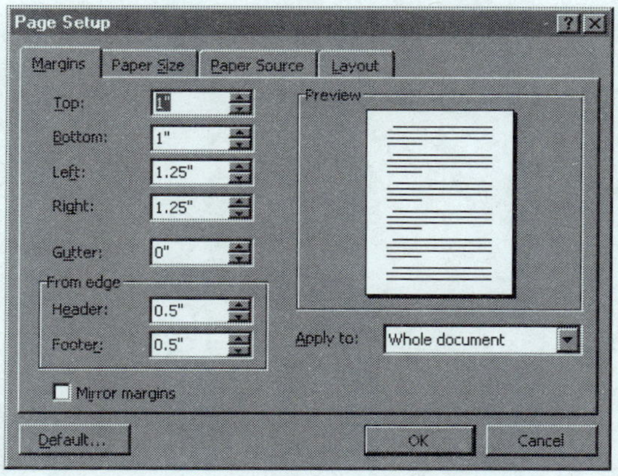

2. With the Top setting highlighted on the Margins tab, type *1.5* and press the Tab key twice to skip over the Bottom setting and highlight the Left setting.

3. Type *1.5* as the new Left setting, press Tab, type *1.5* as the new Right setting, and press Tab again.

4. Notice the effects of your changes in the Preview box on the right and then click OK to return to the letter.

5. Click the Print Preview button to see how the letter looks, and then click Close to return to normal view.

Straightforward Printing

We can print directly from print preview by clicking the Print button on the Print Preview toolbar, but here's how to print a file from normal view:

1. Click the Print button on the Standard toolbar.

The Print button

Word prints the active document with the default settings: one copy of the entire document. To print multiple copies or print selected pages, we must use the Print command on the File menu instead of the Print button on the toolbar. Here's how:

1. Choose Print from the File menu to display the dialog box shown on the next page.

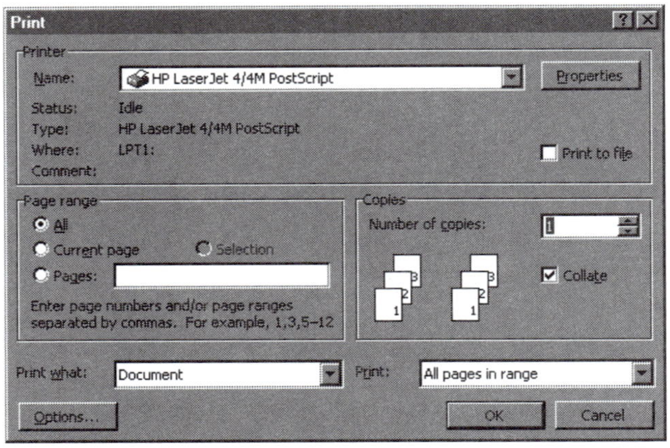

Notice that the Print dialog box tells you which printer Word will use.

Printing multiple copies

2. In the Copies section, type *2* to replace the default setting of 1 in the Number Of Copies edit box.

Printing specific pages

3. Click the Pages option in the Page Range section and type *1-3* in the edit box to tell Word to print pages 1 through 3 only.

4. You aren't actually going to print using these specifications, so click Cancel to close the Print dialog box.

Rather than explain the other printing options in detail here, we'll move on to the next section, where we show you how to get information about these options and other features of the Office applications.

Setting up for printing

When you installed Windows, the Setup program also installed the driver (the control program) for the printer attached to your computer. If you also have access to other printers, you can install their drivers by using the Add Printer Wizard in the Printers folder. (Choose Settings and then Printers from the Start menu.) The installed printers can all be accessed by your Office applications, but only one at a time. To switch printers, choose Print from the File menu, click the arrow to the right of the Name box in the Printer section of the Print dialog box, and select the printer you want to use. Then click OK to begin printing on the specified printer.

Getting Help

Are you worried that you might not remember everything we've covered so far? Don't be. If you forget how to carry out a particular task, help is never far away. You've already seen how the ToolTips feature can jog your memory about the functions of the toolbar buttons. And you may have noticed that the Word, Excel, and PowerPoint dialog boxes contain a Help button you can click to get information about their options. Here, we'll look at ways to get information using the Office Assistant, a new feature of Office 97, which you've probably seen pop up a few times already.

The Office Assistant button

1. Click the Office Assistant button on the Standard toolbar. The Office Assistant appears, giving you several options on how to proceed, as shown here:

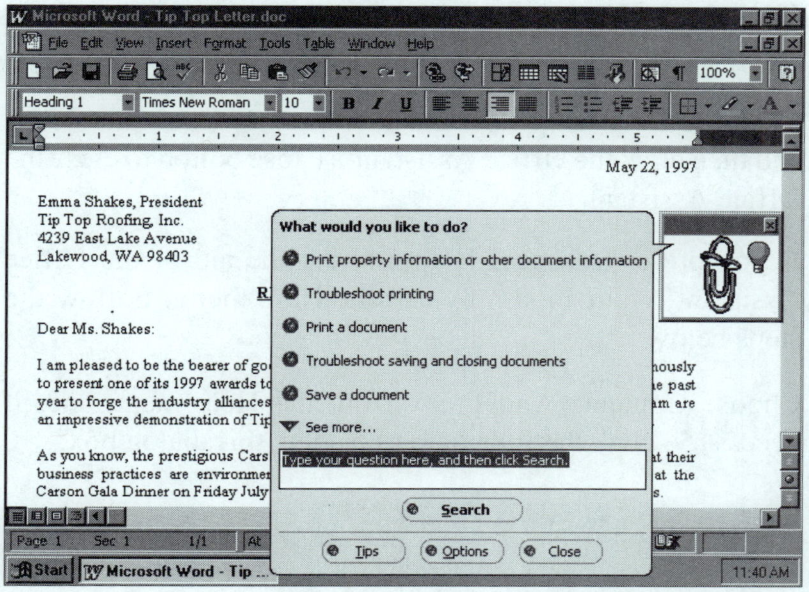

2. Because printing was the last procedure you completed, the Office Assistant's options are currently based on the topic of printing. (If you don't find any of the current options helpful, you can type a question in the Search box and then click the Search button to have the Office Assistant search for topics that most closely match your question.) Click the Print A Document option to display the Help window shown below. (It may take a few seconds while the Help file is being prepared.)

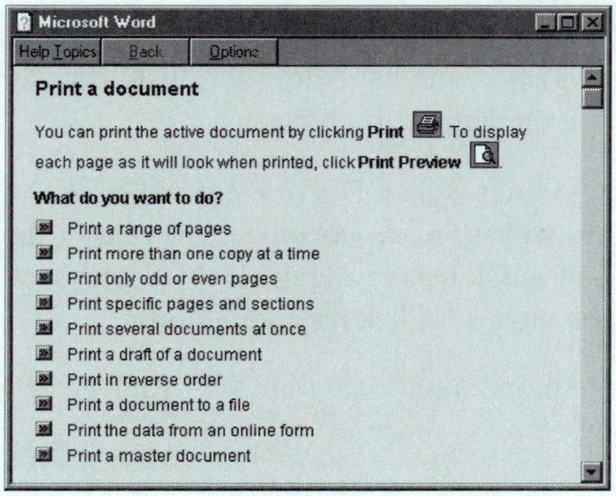

More about the Office Assistant

If the Office Assistant button displays a light bulb, the Office Assistant has a tip for you. Click the button and then click the light bulb in the Office Assistant box to see the tip. If you want to leave the Office Assistant open, you can move it by dragging its title bar, and you can size it by dragging its frame (only two sizes are available). You can then display the search box by clicking the title bar. If having the Office Assistant on the screen bothers you, or if you would like to customize it, you can click the Office Assistant's Options button to open the Office Assistant dialog box. Here, you can select and deselect various options that control when the Office Assistant appears, whether it makes sounds, and what tips it displays. If you want the Office Assistant to appear only when you click the Office Assistant button on the Standard toolbar, deselect the Respond To F1 Key, Help With Wizards, and Display Alerts options in the Assistant Capabilities section on the Options tab. On the Gallery tab, you can click the Next button to scroll through the different animated choices for the assistant (the default is the paper clip) and then click OK to change the assistant. (You will need to insert your Office CD-ROM to complete the switch.)

3. Read through the information and then click the arrow next to the Print A Range Of Pages option to display instructions on how to complete the task.

4. Click the Back button to return to the Print A Document topic, and explore other options.

5. Click the Help window's Close button (the one with the X) and then click the Office Assistant's Close button to close the Office Assistant.

If you prefer to access Help without the aid of the Office Assistant, you can simply use the Help menu. Follow the steps below:

Searching for specific information

1. Choose Contents And Index from the Help menu and, if necessary, click the Index tab to display this dialog box:

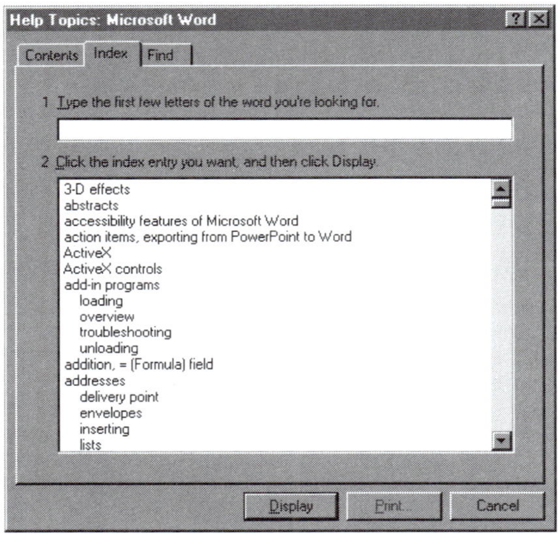

2. In the edit box, type *printi*. The list below scrolls to display topics beginning with the letters you type.

3. In the list of printing topics, select Documents and click the Display button. Then with Print A Document selected in the Topics Found window, click Display again. Help displays the information shown on page 27. Click the Close button.

We'll leave you to explore other Help topics on your own.

Using the Web for help

If you have a modem and are connected to the Internet, you can quickly access Microsoft's Web site to get help or technical support. Simply choose Microsoft On The Web from the Help menu to display a submenu, and then choose the appropriate option.

Quitting

Well, that's it for the basic Office tour. We'll finish up by showing you how to first close a document and then quit an application:

1. Click the Close button at the right end of the menu bar (not the title bar) to close Tip Top Letter.

Closing documents

2. Click Yes to save the changes you have made to the document.
3. To close the Carson Dinner window, choose Close from the File menu and click Yes to save the changes.
4. To close Award Letter, press Alt, press F (for *File*), and then press C (for *Close*).
5. To quit Word, click the Close button at the right end of the title bar.

Quitting applications

Here are some other ways to quit an application:

- Choose Exit from the File menu.
- Press Alt, press F, and then press X.
- Double-click the Control menu icon—in this case, the W—at the left end of the application window's title bar.

2 Word Basics

Assign heading levels and reorganize your documents in outline view

Find and replace text to maintain consistency

Use AutoText and AutoCorrect for often-used text

Check spelling to avoid embarrassing typos

Delete, move, and copy text until it reads exactly right

Redmond Business Environmental Action Team

What is Redmond BEAT?

Redmond BEAT (Business Environmental Action Team) is a local chapter of USA BEAT, a network of companies who are actively working to ensure that their business operations are based on sound environmental practices.

How does it work?

Member companies agree to participate in two ongoing efforts: 1. They pledge to scrutinize their operations and wherever possible, implement procedures that will minimize any adverse effects on the environment. 2. They agree to field-test new "environmentally kind" products and services to evaluate their potential impact on both company costs and the environment.

When was it started?

Redmond BEAT was founded in 1989. USA BEAT, which currently has 210 local chapters, was founded in 1987.

Why was it started?

The chartering of Redmond BEAT was spearheaded by long-time Redmond resident William Henry, President of Creative GlassWorks. Struck by the incongruity between his family's efforts to recycle household waste and the fact that his company was sending several dumpsters of garbage to the Redmond landfill every month, Henry began looking for other ways to dispose of the packaging in which his company received raw materials. His questions caused one of his suppliers, Jordan Manufacturing, to explore alternative packaging methods. The result was less garbage in the Creative GlassWorks dumpsters at no additional cost and negligible other effects for either company. In the meantime, Henry learned about USA BEAT, and a few months of persuasive campaigning later, Redmond BEAT became the newest chapter of a rapidly growing national association.

Who can join?

Membership in Redmond BEAT is open to all companies licensed to do business in the city of Redmond.

Why should my company join?

Current members cite two main reasons for joining. Many companies are managed by people who were attracted to this area by its natural beauty and who want to be part of the effort to preserve it. Other companies stress the potential advantages in today's competitive markets of being perceived as a "green" company by consumers who are increasingly environmentally aware.

How can I find out more?

Come to a meeting. Redmond BEAT meets at 8:00 AM on the last Tuesday of every month at Towne Center. For more information, contact Ted Lee at 555-6789.

In this chapter, we build on what you learned about Microsoft Office and Microsoft Word in Chapter 1. If you haven't read Chapter 1 and are new to Microsoft Word, you should read that chapter before proceeding with this one.

With Word, we can apply fancy formats and add graphics and special effects to increase the impact of a document. But all the frills in the world won't compensate for bad phrasing, bad organization, or errors. That's why this chapter focuses on the Word tools that help us develop and refine the content of our documents. As the example for this chapter, we will create a *frequently asked questions page*, or *FAQ*, for an association called Redmond Business Environmental Action Team (BEAT). FAQs are often distributed in information packages about a company and are usually included as part of commercial Web sites on the Internet.

First let's enter a few headings to establish the basic structure of the document:

1. Start Word by choosing Programs and then Microsoft Word from the Start menu.
2. If necessary, turn off the ruler by choosing Ruler from the View menu. That way, you'll have a bit more room to work.

The Show/Hide ¶ button

3. Click the Show/Hide ¶ button on the toolbar, which displays nonprinting characters such as paragraph marks and spaces.
4. Type *What is Redmond BEAT?* and press Enter. Word enters the heading, inserts a paragraph mark, and moves the insertion point to the next line.
5. Type *Why was it started?* and press Enter.
6. Continue entering the headings shown on the facing page (we've magnified the document to make it easier to read).

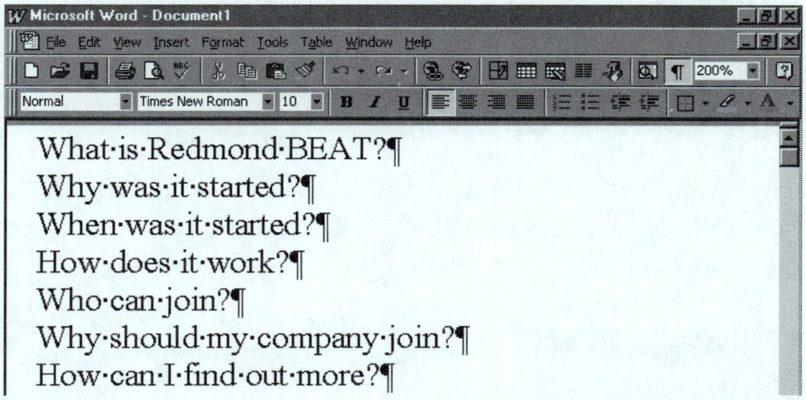

7. Now save the document by clicking the Save button, specifying *Frequently Asked Questions* as the name of the file, and clicking Save.

Let's add some text under a couple of the headings:

1. Click an insertion point between the question mark and the paragraph mark at the end of the *What is Redmond BEAT?* heading, press Enter, and type the following:

   Redmond BEAT (Business Environmental Action Team) is a local chapter of National BEAT, a network of companies who are actively working to ensure that their business operations are based on sound environmental practices.

2. Click an insertion point between the question mark and the paragraph mark at the end of the *Why was it started?* heading, press Enter, and type the following:

   The chartering of Redmond

There's *Redmond* again; that's the third time we've had to type it. Let's look at a couple of ways we can save keystrokes and ensure that the words and phrases we use repeatedly are always entered correctly.

Using AutoText

We use Word's AutoText feature to store text or a graphic so that we can later retrieve it by typing its name and pressing the F3 key. For this example, we'll turn a word we have

Web page creation

For the example document in this chapter, we create an FAQ page, which as we noted earlier is often used in Web pages. If you plan to publish documents for use on the World Wide Web or on intranets, Word 97 can make this process much easier. To turn an existing document into an HTML (HyperText Markup Language) document, simply choose Save As HTML from the File menu. Word saves the file with HTML coding, which formats your document so that it appears in a Web browser the same way it appears in Word. If you want to create a Web page from scratch, you can also use the Web Page Wizard located on the Web Pages tab of the New dialog box. (For more information about wizards, see page 58.)

already typed into an AutoText entry. Follow these steps to simplify the typing of *Redmond*:

1. Right-click one of the toolbars and choose AutoText to display the AutoText toolbar.
2. Select *Redmond*, the word you just typed, and click New on the AutoText toolbar to display this dialog box:

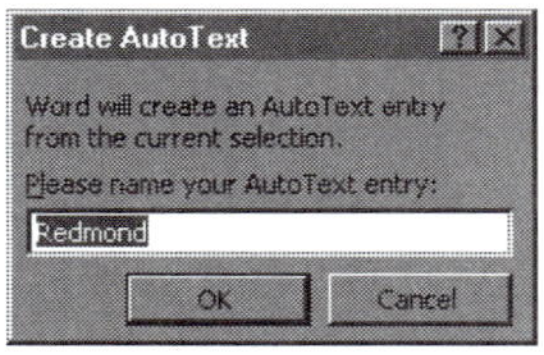

3. Type *red* in the Please Name Your AutoText Entry edit box and click OK.

Now let's use the entry we've just created as we write a few more paragraphs for the FAQ:

1. Click an insertion point after *Redmond* in the paragraph that begins *The chartering of Redmond*, type a space, and then type the following (don't press the Spacebar after *red*):

   BEAT was spearheaded by long-time red

2. Press the F3 key. Word replaces *red* with the *Redmond* entry.
3. Continue typing the following paragraph, using the *red-F3* sequence to insert *Redmond* where indicated. Be sure to type the error marked in bold exactly as you see it so that you will have a mistake to correct later in the chapter. (Word will flag this and any other errors with a red, wavy underline.) Also include the **** characters, which are placeholders for information we'll add later.

   resident William Henry, President of Creative GlassWorks. Struck by the incongruity between his family's efforts to recycle household waste and the fact that his company was sending several dumpsters of garbage to the red-F3 *landfill every month, Henry began looking for other ways to dispose of the packaging in which his company received raw*

AutoComplete

Included in the list of AutoText entries on the AutoText tab of the AutoCorrect dialog box are AutoComplete entries. All these "autos" may seem a bit confusing, but basically AutoComplete allows you to insert items, such as names, dates, and AutoText entries, by typing only the first few characters of the item. For example, if you type *mond*, a box that displays *Monday* appears. If *Monday* is the correct entry, simply press Enter or F3 to insert the word. If *Monday* is not the correct entry, ignore it and keep typing. AutoComplete can automatically complete the date, a day of the week, a month, your name, and AutoText entries. To turn off AutoComplete, deselect the Show AutoComplete Tip option on the AutoText tab of the AutoCorrect dialog box. (When this feature is turned off, you need to press F3 to enter any AutoText entries you have created.)

*materials. His questions caused one of his suppliers, ****, to explore alternative packaging methods. The result was less garbage in the Creative GlassWorks dumpsters at no additional cost and negligible other effects for either company. In the meantime, Henry learned about National BEAT, and a few months of persuasive* ***campaining*** *later,* red-F3 *BEAT became the newest chapter of a rapidly growing national association.*

Suppose we forget the code for an AutoText entry. Does that mean we can't use the entry anymore? Not at all. Try this:

1. Click an insertion point at the end of the *How can I find out more?* heading, press Enter, and type *Come to a meeting* followed by a period and a space.

2. Click the AutoText button on the AutoText toolbar to display the AutoText tab of the AutoCorrect dialog box:

The AutoText button

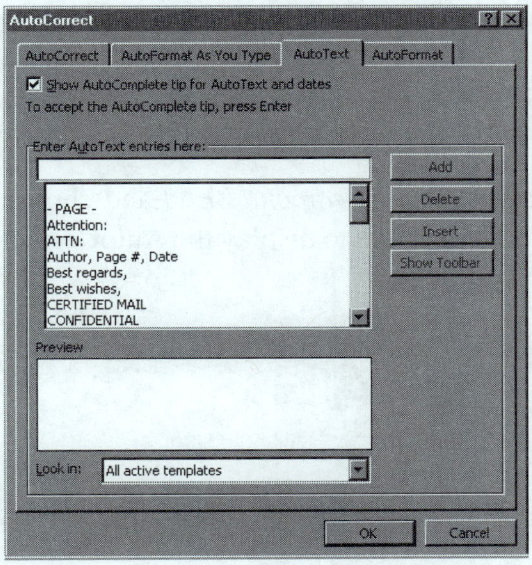

3. Scroll through the list, select *red*, and check the Preview box to see what the entry represents. (The list also includes Auto-Complete entries. See the tip on the facing page.) To insert the selected entry, you could click the Insert button, but instead, click OK to close the dialog box, and we'll show you another way to insert the entry.

Using AutoText to write a letter

You can use the All Entries button on the AutoText toolbar to help you with parts of a letter. When you click All Entries, Word displays seven different categories that are components of many business letters. When you choose one of the categories, Word displays several options for you to choose from. After you select one of the options, Word automatically adds the text to your document. This feature can save you time and offer you choices for sections of your letters that you may not have considered.

4. Click the All Entries button on the AutoText toolbar to display a drop-down list of categories. Select Normal and then *red*. Word inserts the *Redmond* entry at the insertion point.

5. Finish typing the paragraph below:

   BEAT meets at 8:00 AM on the last Tuesday of every month at Towne Center.

6. Turn off the AutoText toolbar by right-clicking it and selecting AutoText from the object menu.

   Now that we've simplified the typing of the word *Redmond*, you've probably noticed some other words that could benefit from the same treatment. How about *National BEAT* and *Redmond BEAT*? To simplify the typing of these entries, we'll use AutoCorrect.

AutoText vs. AutoCorrect

How do you decide when to use AutoText and when to use AutoCorrect? Suppose you own a landscaping business. You know you'd save a lot of time and effort if you could type *aspen* instead of having to type and italicize *Populus tremuloides* (the botanical name for the aspen tree) every time you include this tree in a materials list for your wholesaler. But when you communicate with your clients, you want to be able to refer to the aspen tree by its common name rather than its botanical name. This entry is a prime candidate for AutoText because you can control when Word replaces the name *aspen* with the entry *Populus tremuloides* and when it stays plain old *aspen*. If you use AutoCorrect instead, Word will always replace the name *aspen* with *Populus tremuloides*.

Using AutoCorrect

We use the AutoCorrect feature when we want Word to automatically replace a name with its entry. AutoCorrect names should be unique sequences of characters that we are not likely to use normally in a document. Try this:

1. In the FAQ's first heading, select *Redmond BEAT* and choose AutoCorrect from the Tools menu to display the AutoCorrect tab of the AutoCorrect dialog box:

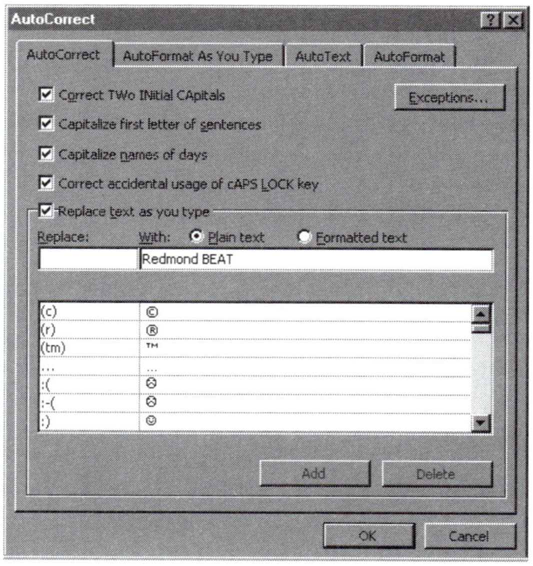

Word is waiting for you to enter the name you want Word to replace with the selected text, which appears in the With edit box. At the bottom of the AutoCorrect dialog box is a ready-made list of words and symbols that Word replaces each time you type them.

2. In the Replace edit box, type *rb* as the name of the entry and click Add. Word adds the name and its replacement to the list.

3. Type *nb* in the Replace edit box, double-click *Redmond* in the With edit box to select it, and type *National*. The entry in the With edit box is now *National BEAT*. Click Add and then click OK to close the dialog box.

Now let's use these AutoCorrect entries so that you can get a feel for what time-savers they can be:

1. Click an insertion point at the end of the *When was it started?* heading, press Enter, and type this:

   nb*, which currently has **** local chapters, was founded in 1987.* rb *was founded in 1990.*

2. Next, click an insertion point at the end of the *Who can join?* heading, press Enter, and type the following (be sure to misspell *the* as *teh*):

   Membership in rb *is open to all companies licensed to do business in* teh *city of* red-F3. *For more information, contact Ted Lee at 555-6789.*

> **AutoCorrect options**
>
> In the AutoCorrect dialog box are several options that take care of common typing "errors." Word can correct two initial capital letters in a word, correct sentences that don't begin with a capital letter, capitalize the days of the week, and correct accidental usage of the Caps Lock key. You can turn any of these options on or off by clicking the corresponding check box. If you click the Exceptions button, you can tell Word not to capitalize the next word following an abbreviation (such as *apt.* for *apartment*). Or you can tell Word not to correct two consecutive initial capital letters in certain instances.

Word Editing Techniques

In Chapter 1, we covered editing techniques that are common to all the Office applications, and you may have already done some simple editing in this chapter if you typed any words incorrectly. In this section, we briefly cover some more ways of revising documents. We'll make a few changes to the FAQ to get a feel for what's involved.

Deleting and Replacing Text

Word provides a few techniques for deleting and replacing text in addition to those covered in Chapter 1. We'll learn these Word-specific techniques as we add a new paragraph to the FAQ:

1. Click an insertion point at the end of the *Why should my company join?* heading, press Enter, and type the following (including the error in bold and the AutoCorrect names, which are not italicized):

   Current members cite two main reasons for joining. Many companies are managed by people who were first attracted to this area by its natural beauty adn *who therefore want to be part of* teh *effort to preserve it. Other companies stress* teh *potential advantages in today's competitive markets of being perceived as a "green"* comapny *by consumers who are increasingly* ***environmently*** *aware.*

Deleting a word to the left

2. Click an insertion point after the last *e* in *therefore* and then press Ctrl+Backspace to delete the word to the left of the insertion point.

Deleting a word to the right

3. Click an insertion point to the left of the *f* in *first* and press Ctrl+Delete to delete the word to the right of the insertion point.

Insert mode

Overtype mode

As you have seen, Word is by default in Insert mode, meaning that when we click an insertion point and begin typing, the characters we enter are inserted to the left of the insertion point, pushing any existing text to the right. Word can also operate in Overtype mode, meaning that when we click an insertion point and begin typing, each character we enter replaces an existing character.

Let's experiment a bit with overtyping. Suppose Redmond BEAT was actually founded in 1989, not 1990. Here's how to make this simple correction:

1. Click an insertion point between the first and second 9s of 1990 under the *When was it started?* heading.

Turning on overtype

2. In the status bar, double-click the overtype box (the fourth box containing the letters *OVR*). The letters *OVR* are highlighted to indicate that you are now in Overtype mode.

3. Type *8*, which overtypes the second 9, and then type *9*, which overtypes the 0, so that the entry now correctly reads *1989*.

4. Double-click the overtype box to turn off Overtype mode. This step is important; you might overtype valuable information if you forget it.

Turning off overtype

Moving and Copying Text

We can move any amount of text within the same document or to a different document. Move operations can either be carried out using the Cut and Paste buttons as discussed in Chapter 1 or by using a mouse technique called *drag-and-drop editing*. Generally, we use drag-and-drop editing when moving text short distances; that is, when the text we're moving and the place we're moving it to can be viewed simultaneously. Try this:

Drag-and-drop editing

1. Select the sentence that begins *National BEAT* under the *When was it started?* heading, including the space after the period.

2. Point to the highlighted text, hold down the left mouse button, drag the shadow insertion point after the period following 1989, and release the mouse button. The selected text moves to the specified location. You have, in effect, transposed the two sentences in this paragraph.

Moving text with drag-and-drop editing

3. Now select the *When was it started?* heading and the following paragraph and move them above the *Why was it started?* heading. (Arrange the screen so that you can see both headings before you drag.)

The procedure for copying text is similar to that for moving text. Try copying some text with the drag-and-drop technique:

1. Use the vertical scroll bar to position the FAQ on the screen so that both the *Who can join?* and *How can I find out more?* sections are visible at the same time.

2. Click an insertion point at the beginning of the sentence that reads *For more information* under the *Who can join?* heading.

Extend-selection mode

You can use extend-selection mode as another way to select text. Click an insertion point where you want the selection to start and then turn on extend-selection mode by pressing F8 or double-clicking the letters EXT in the status bar. You can then click where you want the selection to end and Word immediately highlights all the text between the insertion point and the spot where you clicked. To turn off extend-selection mode, simply press Esc or double-click the letters EXT in the status bar.

3. Select the sentence by holding down Ctrl and Shift simultaneously and then pressing the Right Arrow key until you have highlighted the entire sentence.

Copying text with drag-and-drop editing

4. Point to the selected text, hold down the left mouse button, and drag the shadow insertion point to the right of the last period in the document (after *Towne Center*). While still holding down the mouse button, hold down the Ctrl key (a small plus sign appears next to the mouse pointer), and then release the key and the mouse button together. Immediately, a copy of the selected sentence appears in the location designated by the shadow insertion point, as shown here:

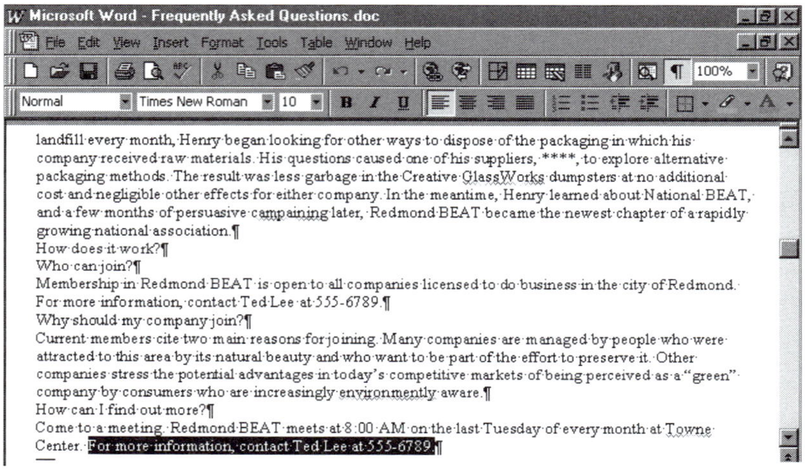

5. Now select the first instance of the *For more information* sentence and press Delete.

Organizing Documents

You have seen how to move text around in a document using cut-and-paste and drag-and-drop editing, but when a document has headings as well as ordinary text, it's often simpler to use Word's Outlining feature to move things around. Most people are accustomed to thinking of outlining as the process that precedes the writing of lengthy documents. With Word, however, outlining is not a separate process but simply another way of looking at a document. Once we use Word's Outlining feature with a particular document, we can switch to outline view at any time to get an overview of our work. In

Smart editing

When you cut or copy and paste text, Word intuits where spaces are needed for the text to make sense. For example, it removes spaces before and adds spaces after punctuation marks. You can tell Word to leave these kinds of adjustments to you by choosing Options from the Tools menu, clicking the Edit tab, clicking the Use Smart Cut And Paste option to deselect it, and clicking OK.

this section, we'll set up the outline for the FAQ and then use it to reorganize the document. Let's get started:

1. Choose Outline from the View menu. Word displays the Outlining toolbar, which allows you to organize your document by assigning levels to the information on the screen. Because Word considers all the headings and paragraphs of the FAQ to be ordinary body text, each one is identified in the selection area to its left by a small hollow square.

2. Move the pointer over the Outlining toolbar, using ToolTips to get an idea of what each button does, and then press Ctrl+End to move to the end of the document.

The Promote button

Heading styles

3. On a new line, type *Redmond Business Environmental Action Team*, and then click the Promote button on the Outlining toolbar. Word moves the heading to the left and makes it bigger to reflect its new status. Notice that Heading 1, the style that Word has applied to the heading, appears in the Style box at the left end of the Formatting toolbar. (See page 72 for more information about styles.) With Word, you can create up to nine heading levels, called Heading 1 through Heading 9. Also notice the large minus icon next to the heading; it indicates that the heading has no subheadings or text.

4. Click an insertion point in the *How can I find out more?* heading and click the Promote button. Repeat this step for each of the other six headings to change them to the Heading 1 style.

The Show Heading 1 button

5. Press Ctrl+Home and click the Show Heading 1 button. Word collapses the outline, and only the level 1 headings are visible:

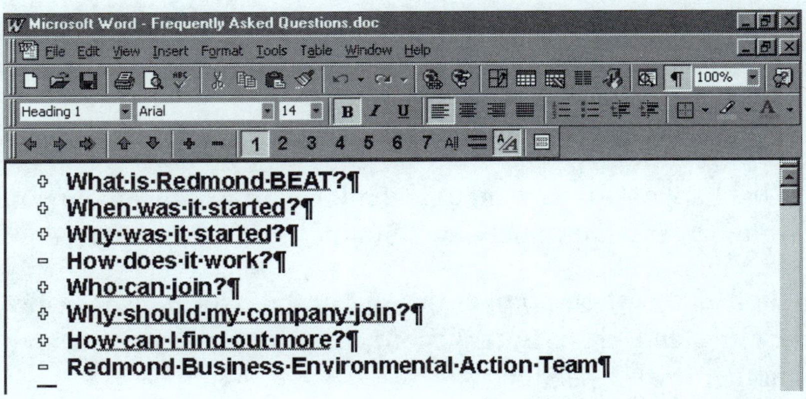

Deleting headings

To delete a heading from an outline, select the heading and press Delete. If you want to also delete the heading's subordinate headings and text, collapse the outline before you make your selection. Otherwise, expand the outline before you select the heading to see exactly which paragraphs will be affected when you press Delete.

Outline symbols

As already mentioned, a minus icon indicates that the heading doesn't have subordinate headings or text; a plus icon indicates that it does. In addition, Word puts a gray underscore below headings whose subordinate information is hidden. Now let's do a little reorganizing:

The Move Up button

6. Click an insertion point in the *Redmond Business Environmental Action Team* heading and click the Move Up button repeatedly until the heading is at the top of the document.

The Move Down button

7. Select both the *When was it started?* and *Why was it started?* headings and then click the Move Down button once to move both headings below the *How does it work?* heading.

The Expand button

8. Click the Expand button to display the body text below the two selected headings. As you can see here, the paragraphs moved with their headings:

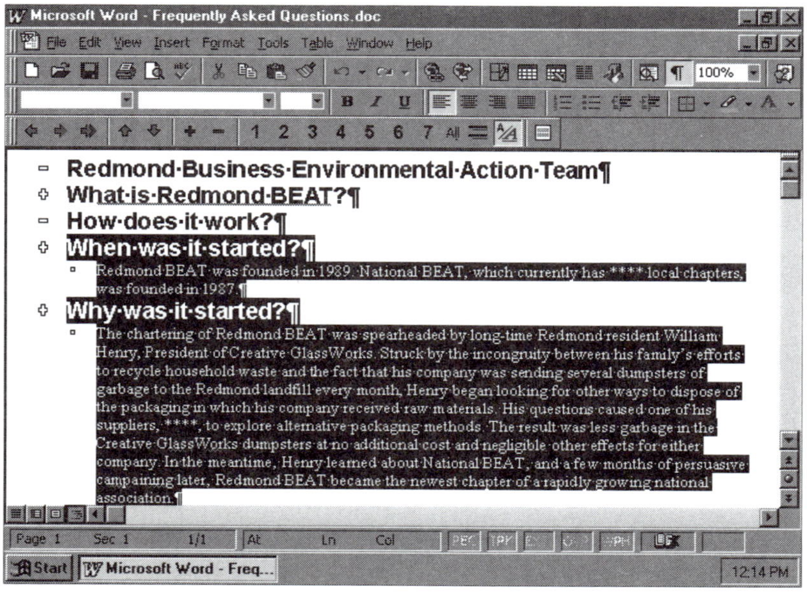

The Collapse button

9. Click the Collapse button to hide the text again.

What happens if we want to add information to the document while we are in outline view? Simple! Follow these steps:

1. Click an insertion point at the end of the *How does it work?* heading and press Enter. Word assumes you want to type another level 1 heading.

2. Click the Demote To Body Text button on the Outlining toolbar and type the following, including the errors in bold:

The Demote To Body Text button

*Member companies agree to participate in two ongoing efforts: 1. They pledge to scrutinize their operations and wherever possible, implement procedures that will minimize any adverse **affects** on the environment. 2. They agree to field-test new "**environmently** kind" products and services to evaluate their potential impact on both company costs and the environment.*

3. Click the Show Heading 1 button to display only the headings.

Notice that all the headings except the first should really be level 2. We have used the Promote button to bump headings up one level. Here's how to bump them down:

1. Select all the headings except the first and click the Demote button on the Outlining toolbar. Word both moves the selected headings to the right so that their relationship to the level 1 heading above is readily apparent, and changes their formatting. In the Style box on the Formatting toolbar, Heading 2 is displayed. The minus icon to the left of the first heading changes to a plus icon, indicating that it now has subordinate headings and text.

The Demote button

2. Click the Show All Headings button to see these results:

The Show All Headings button

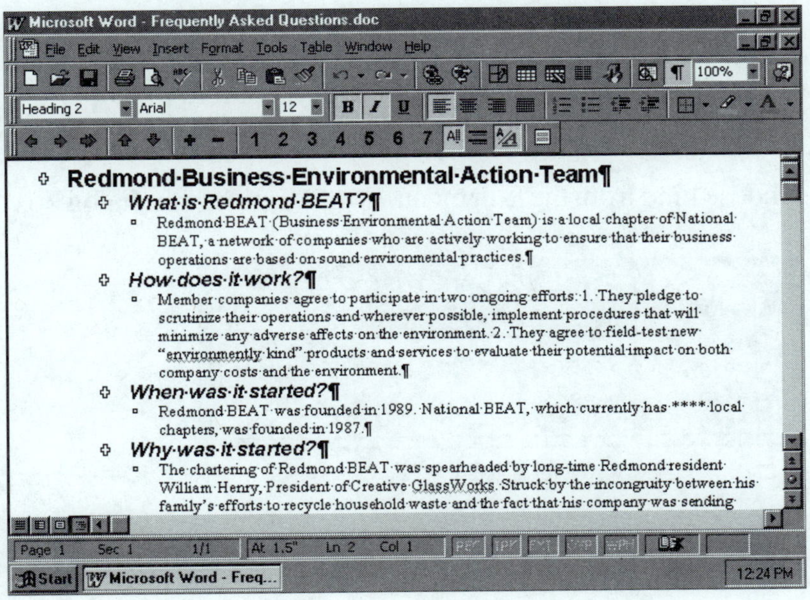

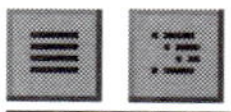

The Normal View and Outline View buttons

Well, after that brief introduction to Word's Outlining feature, we'll return to normal view so that we can move on with the rest of the chapter:

1. Click the Normal View button at the left end of the horizontal scroll bar. Having set up the document's outline, you can return to outline view at any time by simply clicking the Outline View button at the left end of the horizontal scroll bar.
2. Click the Save button to save your work.

Finding and Replacing

With Word, we can search a document for specific characters. We can also specify replacement characters. As you'll see if you follow along with the next example, finding a series of characters is easy.

Finding Text

Recall that while typing the Redmond BEAT FAQ, we left the characters **** as placeholders for information that needed to be added later. Suppose we now need to locate the placeholders so that we can substitute the correct information. In a document as short as the FAQ, we would have no difficulty locating ****. But if the current document were many pages long and several placeholders were involved, we would probably want to use the Find command to locate them. Follow these steps:

1. Press Ctrl+Home to move the insertion point to the top of the document.
2. Choose Find from the Edit menu. Word displays this dialog box:

Editing during a search or replace

You can edit your document in the middle of a search or replace operation without closing the Find And Replace dialog box. Simply click the document window to activate it, make your changes, and then click anywhere in the Find And Replace dialog box to continue your search or replace. You can also click the Cancel button to close the Find And Replace dialog box and instead use the Next Find/Go To and Previous Find/Go To buttons at the bottom of the vertical scroll bar to complete your search without the dialog box in your way.

3. Enter **** in the Find What edit box and click Find Next. Word searches the document, stopping when it locates the first occurrence of ****.

4. Click Cancel to close the dialog box and then type *210* to replace the highlighted placeholder.

The Next Find/Go To and Previous Find/Go To buttons

5. Click the Next Find/Go To button at the bottom of the vertical scroll bar to repeat the Find command with the same Find What text as the previous search. Word locates the second ****. (You can click the Previous Find/Go To button to go back to the previous instance of the Find What text.)

6. Replace the selection with *Jordan Manufacturing*.

Most of our searches will be as simple as this one was, but we can also refine our searches by first clicking the More button in the Find And Replace dialog box to display additional options. We can then use these options or enter special characters (see the tip on page 47). For example, suppose we regularly confuse the two words *affect* and *effect*. We can check our use of these words in the FAQ, as follows:

The Select Browse Object button

1. Press Ctrl+Home to move to the top of the document. Then click the Select Browse Object button at the bottom of the vertical scroll bar to display this palette of options:

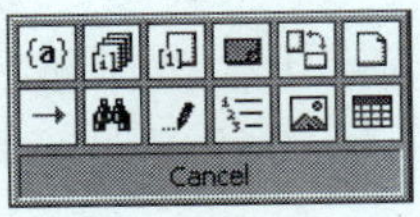

The Find button

2. Click the Find button to display the Find And Replace dialog box again.

3. Click the More button to expand the Find And Replace dialog box, as shown on the next page.

The Select Browse Object options

When you click the Select Browse Object button at the bottom of the vertical scroll bar, Word displays a palette of options that you can use to browse through your document by heading, graphic, table and so on.

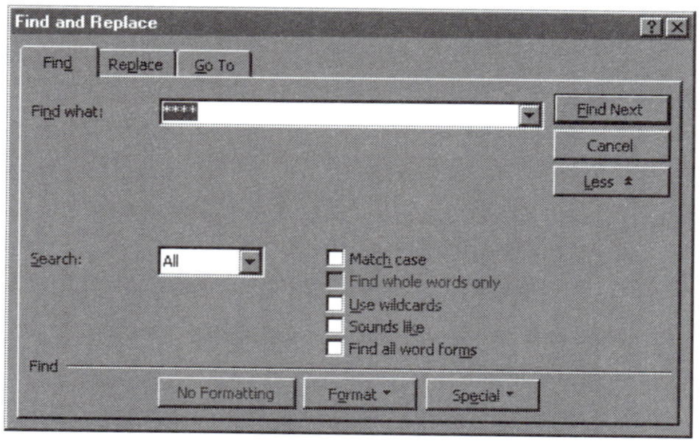

4. Enter *?ffect* in the Find What edit box. The ? is a *wildcard* character that stands for any single character.

5. Check that All is selected as the Search option. Then click Use Wildcards to tell Word to look for a string of characters that matches the Find What text, and click Find Next to start the search. Word stops at the word *affects* in the second paragraph. (You may need to move the dialog box by dragging its title bar so that you can see the text.)

6. This use of *affects* is incorrect, so click Cancel to close the dialog box and change the *a* to *e*.

7. Click the Next Find/Go To button to repeat the search. Word stops at the word *effects*, which is correct.

8. Click the Next Find/Go To button again to ensure that the document contains no other instances of the Find What text, and click No when Word asks whether you want to continue the search.

Finding and replacing formats

To search for text to which you have assigned a particular format, choose Find from the Edit menu, click the More button to expand the Find And Replace dialog box, click the Format button, and then click Font for character formats or Paragraph for paragraph formats. In the Find Font or Find Paragraph dialog box, specify the format you want to find, click OK to return to the Find And Replace dialog box, and click Find Next. Word highlights the next text entry formatted with that format. You can use the Replace command to change a particular format. For example, to change all bold text to bold italic, choose Replace from the Edit menu, click Format and then Font, click Bold in the Font Style list, and click OK. Then click the Replace With edit box, click Format and then Font, click Bold Italic in the Font Style list, and click OK. Back in the Find And Replace dialog box, click either Find Next and Replace or Replace All, depending on whether you want to confirm the replacement of each case of the specified format.

Replacing Text

Often, we will search a document for a series of characters with the intention of replacing them. When we need to make the same replacement more than a couple of times, using the Replace command automates the process. As an example, let's find all occurrences of *National BEAT* and change them to *USA BEAT*:

1. Press Ctrl+Home to move to the beginning of the document, click the Search Browse Object button, click Find, and then click the Replace tab.(You can also use the Replace command on the Edit menu.) Word displays the dialog box shown here:

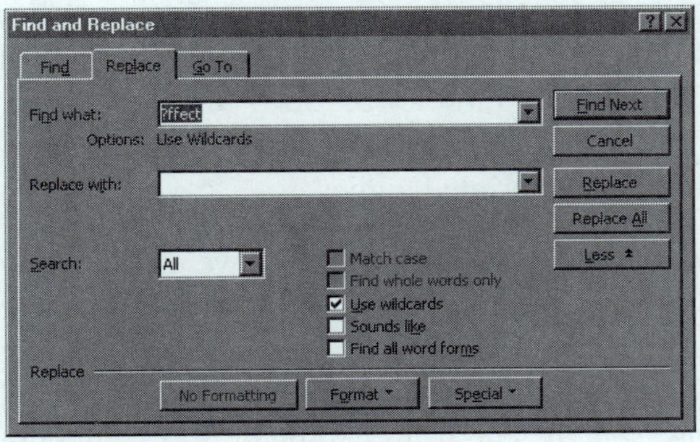

Notice that the text and settings from the last search have been retained.

2. Replace the Find What text by typing *National BEAT*.

3. In the Replace With edit box, type *USA BEAT*. Click the Less button to decrease the size of the dialog box, and press Enter. Word highlights the first occurrence of the Find What text.

4. Click Replace. Word continues the search and highlights the second occurrence.

5. Click Replace All to replace any remaining occurrences, and click OK when Word tells you that two replacements have been made.

6. Click Close to close the Find And Replace dialog box.

As with the Find command, we can use the Match Case, Find Whole Words Only, Use Wildcards, Sounds Like, and Find All Word Forms options to refine the replace procedure. (See the adjacent tip for more information.)

Refining your searches

By using the options available in the Find And Replace dialog box, you can complete more complicated searches in your Word documents. Use the drop-down list of Search options to search forward to the end of the document (Down) or backward to the beginning of the document (Up) from the insertion point, or to search the entire document (All). Click the Match Case option to find only those occurrences of the Find What text with the exact capitalization specified. For example, find the initials *USA* and not the characters *usa* in *usability*. Click the Find Whole Words Only option to find only whole-word occurrences of the Find What text. For example, find the word *men* and not the characters *men* in *mention* and *fundamental*. Click the Sounds Like option to find occurrences of the Find What text that sound the same but are spelled differently. Finally, click the Find All Word Forms option to find occurrences of a particular word in any form. For example, if the Find What text is the word *hide*, Word will also find *hid* and *hidden*. In addition to using the Use Wildcards option for wildcard characters (see page 46), you can also find special characters, such as tabs (enter *^t* in the Find What edit box) and paragraph marks (enter *^p*). For example, find every occurrence of a paragraph that begins with the word *Remember* by entering *^pRemember* as the Find What text.

Checking Spelling

Nothing detracts from a document like a typo. In the past, your readers might have overlooked the occasional misspelling. These days, running your word processor's spelling checker is so easy that readers tend to be less forgiving. For example, resumés and job-application letters with typos will more often than not end up in the recycling bin. The moral: Get in the habit of spell-checking all your documents, especially before distributing printed copies.

Automatic spell-checking

As we created the FAQ in this chapter, we deliberately included a few errors. Because Word flags words it does not recognize with a red, wavy underline, we can simply correct any errors as we create our documents. This feature, called *automatic spell-checking*, can be turned on or off by clicking the Check Spelling As You Type check box on the Spelling & Grammar tab of the Options dialog box. Let's try fixing one of the misspelled words now by following these steps:

1. Point to the word *campaining* in the *Why was it started?* paragraph and right-click it. Word displays this object menu:

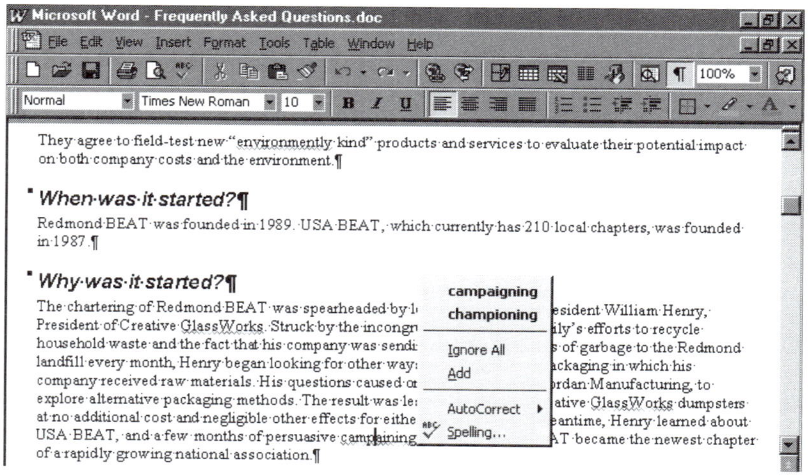

Word displays any words found in its dictionary that come close to the misspelled word. It also gives you the option to ignore the misspelling, add the word to Word's dictionary, create an AutoCorrect entry for the word, or take you to the Spelling & Grammar dialog box for more options.

Checking grammar

When Word's grammar checker is turned on, it works behind the scenes, checking your grammar as you type and underlining suspicious phrases with green wavy lines. Right-clicking underlined phrases displays a dialog box with suggested changes. The usefulness of the grammar checker depends on the complexity of your writing. Only you can decide whether its suggestions are valid and helpful enough to warrant leaving it turned on. See the tip on the facing page to find out how to turn it off.

2. Click *campaigning* to change the word to its correct spelling.

If we prefer to check the spelling of a document all at once, we can use Word's spell-checking capabilities in another way. Follow these steps:

1. Press Ctrl+Home to move the insertion point to the top of the FAQ, and click the Spelling And Grammar button on the toolbar. Word automatically begins checking each word of the document, starting with the word containing the insertion point, against its built-in dictionary. When Word finds a word that is not in its dictionary, it displays this Spelling And Grammar dialog box:

The Spelling And Grammar button

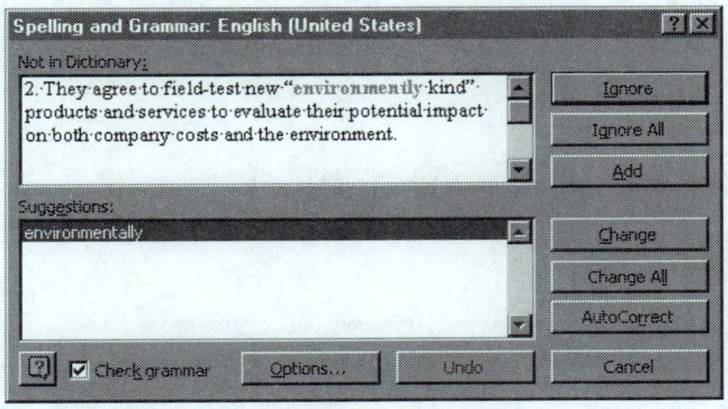

2. As you can see, Word stopped at the word *environmently*. Since this spelling is incorrect, click the Change All button to tell Word that you want to change all occurrences of this misspelling to the suggested spelling.

3. Next Word stops at *GlassWorks*. Click Ignore All to leave all occurrences of this name as they are.

4. Word stops at *Towne*. Possible substitutes appear in the Suggestions list. You have spelled this name correctly and use it often. To prevent Word from flagging it as a misspelling every time, add it to Word's supplementary dictionary, which is called Custom.dic, by clicking the Add button. (You cannot add words to the main dictionary.)

5. When Word reaches the end of the document, it closes the Spelling And Grammar dialog box and displays a message that the spelling and grammar check is complete. Click OK to return to your document.

Spelling and grammar options

Clicking the Options button in the Spelling And Grammar dialog box displays the Spelling & Grammar tab (like the Spelling & Grammar tab in the Options dialog box). Here you can tell Word whether you want it to automatically spell- and grammar-check the current document or hide errors in the document. You can also tell Word to suggest alternatives for the misspellings it finds and to ignore words in capital letters or that contain numbers. In addition, you can create, edit, add, and delete custom dictionaries by clicking the Dictionaries button. If you want to spell-check your documents without using Word's Grammar checker, deselect the Check Grammar As You Type and Check Grammar With Spelling options at the bottom of the Spelling & Grammar tab.

6. Save and close Frequently Asked Questions.

As you create documents and spell-check them, you will start to see that the words you use fall into several categories:

The main dictionary

- Common words that are included in Word's main dictionary.

Document "dictionaries"

- Uncommon words that you use rarely. You will want to tell Word to ignore these words when spell-checking a document. Word will then attach those words to the document in which they are used as a sort of document-specific dictionary and will not flag them as misspellings if you spell-check the document in the future.

The supplementary dictionary

- Uncommon words that you use often in different kinds of documents. You will want to add these words to Custom.dic so that they are not flagged as misspellings.

Custom dictionaries

- Uncommon words that you use with a specific type of document. Instead of adding these words to Custom.dic, you might want to create a custom dictionary for use only with that type of document. To create a custom dictionary, choose Options from the Tools menu, click the Spelling & Grammar tab, click the Dictionaries button, and then click the New button in the

The Thesaurus

You can use the Word Thesaurus to look up synonyms for a selected word by choosing Language and then Thesaurus from the Tools menu. Word displays the Thesaurus dialog box and suggests alternative words for the selected word. To replace the word in your document with one of these alternatives, select the new word in the Meanings list and click the Replace button. You can also select an alternative word and click Look Up to display a list of alternatives for the alternative! Click Cancel to close the Thesaurus dialog box without making any changes.

Smart spelling checks

If your document contains duplicate words, such as *the the*, Word stops at the words and displays them in the Spelling And Grammar dialog box during a spelling check. Clicking Delete removes the duplicate word. Word also stops at strange combinations of uppercase and lowercase letters. For example, Word would stumble over *nAtional* and would suggest *national* as an appropriate substitute. To speed up the checking process, Word's suggestions generally have the same case as a misspelled word. For example, if the misspelling occurs at the beginning of a sentence and therefore starts with a capital letter, Word's suggestions also start with capital letters.

Custom Dictionaries dialog box. Type a name for the dictionary, click Save, and then click OK. Before you can use the custom dictionary, you must open it by selecting it from the Custom Dictionary drop-down list in the Options dialog box and clicking OK. (You can also create and open custom dictionaries on the Spelling & Grammar tab that appears when you click Options in the Spelling And Grammar dialog box.) Then when you check a document's spelling, you can click the Add button in the Spelling And Grammar dialog box to add words to the custom dictionary. (Note that before starting a spelling check, it is a good idea to click the Options button and check which custom dictionary is in effect.)

We can't rely on Word's spelling and grammar checker to identify every error in our documents. Errors of syntax or improper word usage will slip by in a spelling and grammar check. We should always read through our documents to look for any errors that Word might miss.

3

More About Word

Use Word's Fax Wizard to quickly create a professional-looking fax

Create headers to carry page numbers and identifying information

14000 Willows Road
Redmond, WA 98052
Phone: 206-555-6789
Fax: 206-555-1234

Redmond BEAT

Fa

To:

Fax

Pho

Re:

☐ U

•Co
to T
for
Roc

The
are
Frid

Combine two documents to create a new one

Click a button to create a table

AIR POLLUTANT SOURCES
In Millions of Metric Tons

Contributor	Sulfur Dioxide	Carbon Monoxide	Nitrogen Oxides
Transportation	0.9	41.2	8.1
Industrial Emissions	3.4	4.7	0.6
Fuel Combustion	16.4	7.6	10.8
Solid-Waste Burning	--	1.7	0.1
Miscellaneous	--	6.0	0.2

Set first-line indents and the space above and below paragraphs

Tip Top Roofing Wins Carson Award for Recycling Program

Yesterday, the Carson committee voted unanimously to present one of its 1997 awards to **Tip Top Roofing**. The company's efforts during the past year to forge the industry alliances needed for a successful asphalt-shingle recycling program are an impressive demonstration of Tip Top Roofing's ongoing commitment to the environment.

The prestigious Carson Awards recognize companies who work to ensure that their business practices are environmentally sensitive. This year's awards will be presented at the Carson Gala Dinner on Friday July 25, 1997.

REDMOND BUSINESS ENVIRONMENTAL ACTION TEAM

Dress up headings with borders and shading

What is Redmond BEAT?

Redmond BEAT (Business Environmental Action Team) is a local chapter of USA BEAT, a network of companies who are actively working to ensure that their business operations are based on sound environmental practices.

How does it work?

Member companies agree to participate in two ongoing efforts:

1. They pledge to scrutinize their operations and wherever possible, implement procedures that will minimize any adverse effects on the environment.
2. They agree to field-test new "environmentally kind" products and services to evaluate their potential impact on both company costs and the environment.

Click a button to create numbered and bulleted lists

When was it started?

Redmond BEAT was founded in 1989. USA BEAT, which currently has 210 local chapters, was founded in 1987.

Why was it started?

The chartering of Redmond BEAT was spearheaded by long-time Redmond resident William Henry, President of Creative GlassWorks. Struck by the incongruity between his family's efforts to recycle household waste and the fact that his company was sending several dumpsters of garbage to the Redmond landfill every month, Henry began looking for other ways to dispose of the packaging in which his company received raw materials. His questions caused one of his suppliers, Jordan Manufacturing, to explore alternative packaging methods. The result was less garbage in the Creative GlassWorks dumpsters at no additional cost and negligible other effects for either company. In the meantime, Henry learned about USA BEAT, and a few months of persuasive campaigning later, Redmond BEAT became the newest chapter of a rapidly growing national association.

Who can join?

Membership in Redmond BEAT is open to all companies licensed to do business in the city of Redmond.

Why should my company join?

Current members cite two main reasons for joining. Many companies are managed by people who were attracted to this area by its natural beauty and who want to be part of the effort to preserve it. Other companies stress the potential advantages in today's competitive markets of being perceived as a "green" company by consumers who are increasingly environmentally aware.

How can I find out more?

Come to a meeting. Redmond BEAT meets at 8:00 AM on the last Tuesday of every month at Towne Center. For more information, contact Ted Lee at 555-6789.

Turn formatting combinations into styles

Use multicolumn formats to vary document designs

Chapter 2 showed you some ways to edit, reorganize, and polish the content of your Word documents. In this chapter, we will explore ways to create useful documents with Word's ready-made templates and wizards. We'll then discuss Word features that can give our documents a really professional look.

Using Word's Templates

A Word template is a pattern that includes the information, formatting, and other elements used in a particular type of document. Unless we specify otherwise, all new Word documents are based on the Blank Document template. Word comes with quite a few other templates that we can use as is or modify; or we can create our own templates (see the tip on page 57).

Installing templates

Depending on the type of setup you selected, you may or may not have included all of Word's templates when you installed Office on your computer. To install Word's templates, close any open applications (including the shortcut bar) and choose Settings and then Control Panel from the Start menu. Double-click the Add/Remove Programs icon in the Control Panel window and click the Install button on the Install/Uninstall tab. When the Install Wizard's first dialog box appears, follow the instructions and then click Next. The wizard searches your floppy drive and CD-ROM drive for an installation program and then enters the program's pathname in its final dialog box. Click Finish to display the Microsoft Office 97 Setup dialog box, and then click the Add/Remove button. Select Microsoft Word in the Maintenance dialog box; click Change Option; select Wizards And Templates; click Change Option; select More Wizards; click OK twice; and then click Continue to proceed with the installation.

As part of the Microsoft Office installation procedure, a number of sample templates were copied to the Templates subfolder of the Program Files/Microsoft Office subfolder on your hard drive. To preview these templates, follow the steps below:

1. With Word open, check that the ruler (choose Ruler from the View menu) and nonprinting characters (click the Show/-Hide ¶ button) are displayed.
2. Choose New from the File menu to display the multi-tabbed dialog box shown below. (We have installed all the Word templates, so our dialog box may have more tabs than yours. See the adjacent tip if you want to install more templates.)

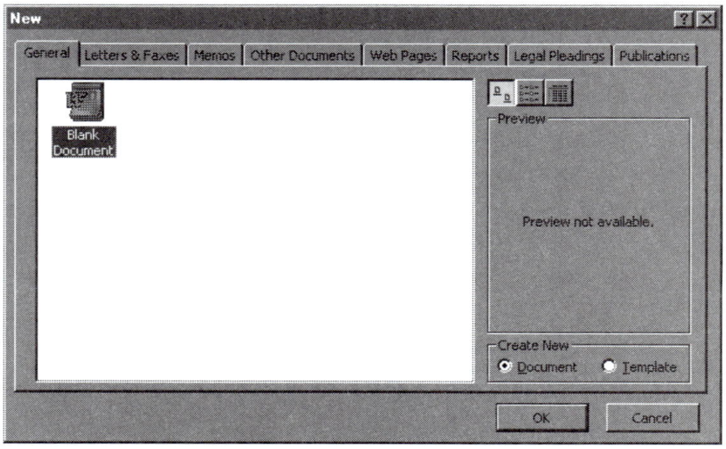

Word separates the templates into different categories as you can see by reading the names of the various tabs. The default selection (which is available even when the other templates haven't been installed) is Blank Document on the General tab.

3. Click the Letters & Faxes tab and click the Fax Wizard once to highlight it. The Preview box on the right side of the dialog box displays a preview of the highlighted item.

4. Click other templates on the Letters & Faxes tab and then switch to some of the other tabs. As you can tell from their names and previews, the templates provide the basis for many common business documents.

5. When you are ready, click Professional Memo on the Memos tab and either press Enter or click OK. Word switches to page layout view and displays this memo form on your screen:

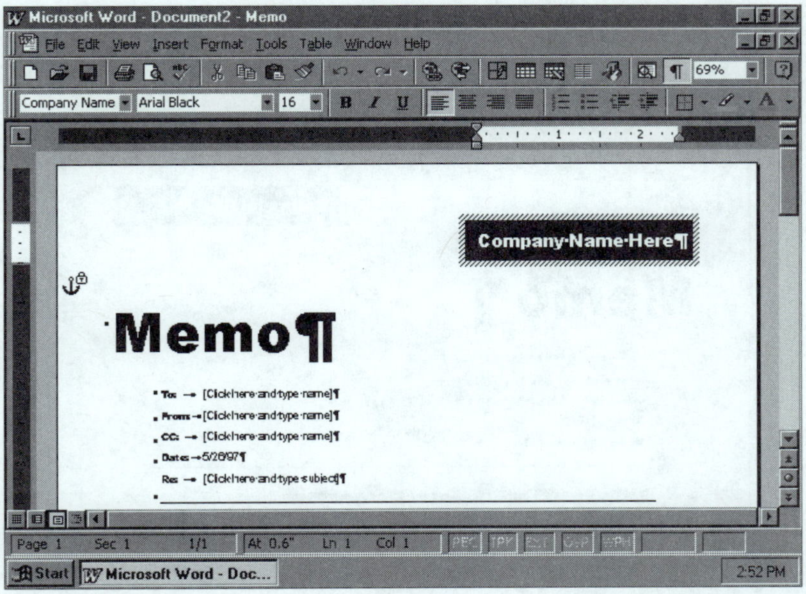

As you can see, all the common elements of a memo have placeholders within square brackets, and Word has entered the current date (using the date stored in your computer—see the tip on page 56). Let's fill in the memo now:

1. In the black box on the right, select *Company Name Here* but not the paragraph mark, and replace it by typing *Redmond*

Page layout view

Page layout view is a cross between normal view and print preview. In this view, we can see the layout of our pages at a size that allows efficient editing and formatting. For example, the pages appear with headers and footers visible on the screen.

BEAT. (If you ax a paragraph mark by mistake, immediately click the Undo button on the toolbar to reinstate it.)

2. In the To section, click the placeholder text to select it, and type *Sandra Peters, Northwest BEAT*.
3. In the From section, type *Ted Lee* and in the CC: section, type *Nathan Chou, Washington BEAT*.
4. Finally, in the Re: section, type *Carson Awards*.
5. Now select the title *How to Use This Memo Template* but not the paragraph mark, and replace it with *Tip Top Roofing Wins Carson Award for Recycling Program.*

Take a moment to admire your work. Without adding any formatting of your own, you've created a professional-looking header for a memo, as shown here:

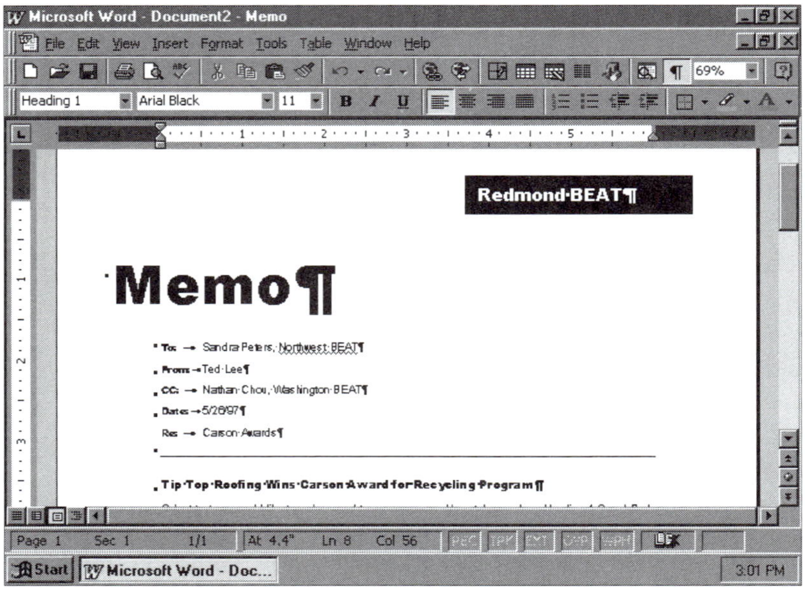

6. Choose Save As from the File menu and save the document with the name *Memo*.

Below the memo title, we need to enter the text of the memo. This information is essentially the same as that contained in

Date fields

Word automatically enters the date stored by your system's clock/calendar when you open a document based on the memo template. Why? Because the document contains a special code called a *field*. Fields can contain a variety of information; this particular field is an instruction to get the current date and display it in the field's location. If you do nothing to this field, Word will insert the current date each time you open the document. If you want to "freeze" the current date, click the field to select it, and then press Ctrl+Shift+F9. The field is converted to normal text that will not be updated and that can be edited. To insert a date field in your document, choose Date And Time from the Insert menu, and in the Date And Time dialog box, select a date format, click the Update Automatically option to select it, and then click OK.

the letter we wrote in Chapter 1. The beauty of a word processor like Word is that instead of retyping the information, we can borrow it from the letter and edit it to suit the purpose of the memo. Here's how:

1. Select the text of the main paragraph (but not the paragraph mark) and press the Delete key.
2. Now click the Open button on the toolbar, and in the Open dialog box, double-click Tip Top Letter to open the letter from Chapter 1 in its own window.
3. Select just the two paragraphs of the letter, including the paragraph mark between them, and click the Copy button.
4. Choose Memo from the bottom of the Window menu and make sure the insertion point is in front of the blank paragraph.
5. Click the Paste button to insert the copied text.
6. Edit the text of the memo so that it looks like the one shown below. (We've magnified the memo so that the text is more readable.)

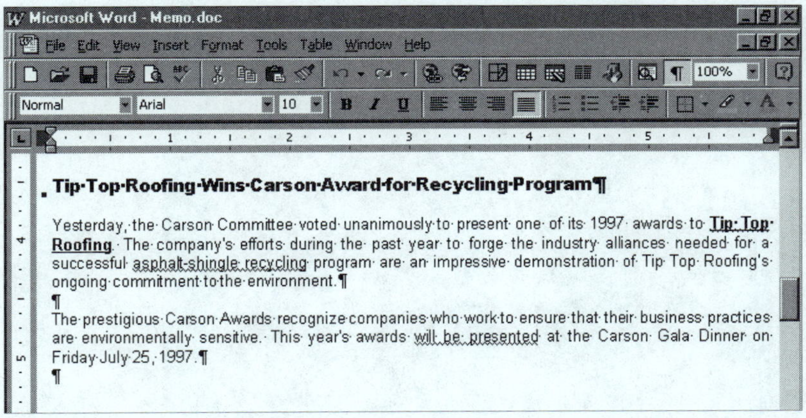

7. Print and save the document, and then close it.
8. Close Tip Top Letter, clicking No if Word asks whether to save any changes.

Creating custom templates

You can save any document as a template and then open a new document based on that template every time you need to create that type of document. To save one of your documents as a template, choose Save As from the File menu. Click the down arrow to the right of the Save As Type box and select Document Template. Word displays the contents of the Templates subfolder. Double-click the folder in which you want to store the new template. Assign a name to the template in the File Name edit box and click Save. To use the new template, choose New from the File menu and select the template the same way you would select any of Word's sample templates.

Using Word's Wizards

When we create a new document based on a wizard, the document we see depends on our answers to questions the wizard asks. Let's use the Fax Wizard to create a fax to announce Tip Top Roofing's recycling award:

Creating a fax

1. Choose New from the File menu, click the Letters & Faxes tab, and double-click Fax Wizard to display the wizard's first dialog box:

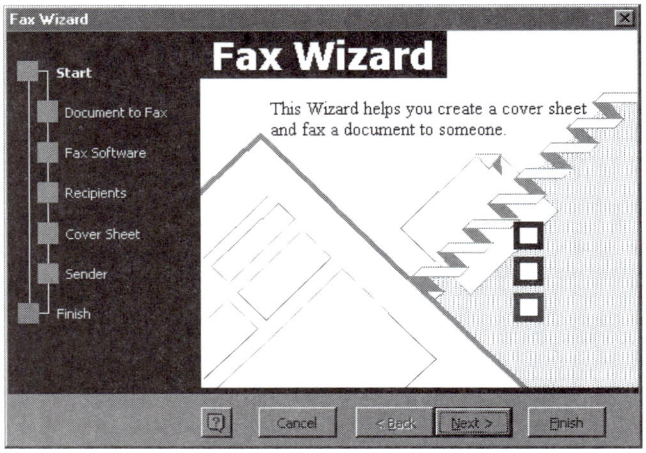

2. Click Next to display the second dialog box:

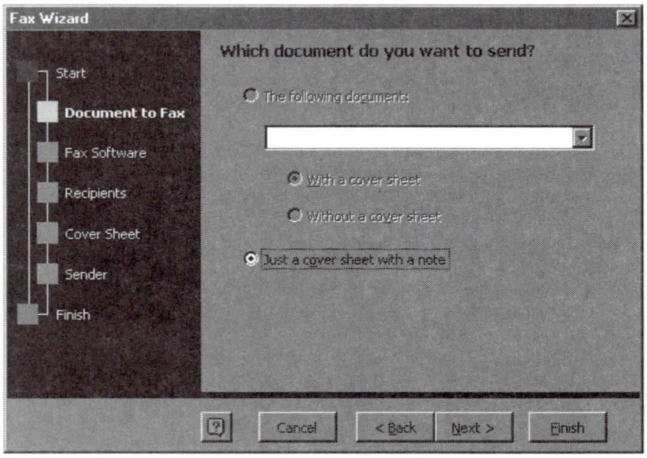

3. Be sure the Just A Cover Sheet With A Note option is selected and then click Next to display the wizard's third dialog box:

Wizards

Wizards are tools that are incorporated into all of the Microsoft Office applications to help you accomplish specific tasks. They work in the same basic way, regardless of the task or the application. They all consist of a series of dialog boxes that ask you to provide information or select from various options. You move from box to box by clicking the Next button, and you can move back to an earlier box by clicking the Back button. Clicking Cancel cancels the entire procedure.

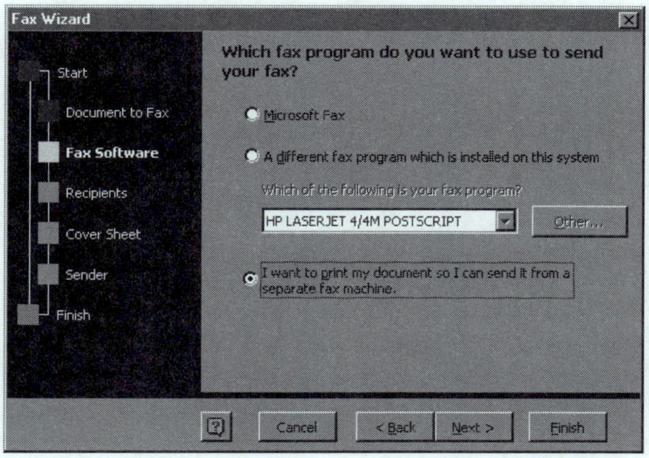

4. Click the third option so that you can print out the document and send it from a separate fax machine. Then click Next to display this dialog box:

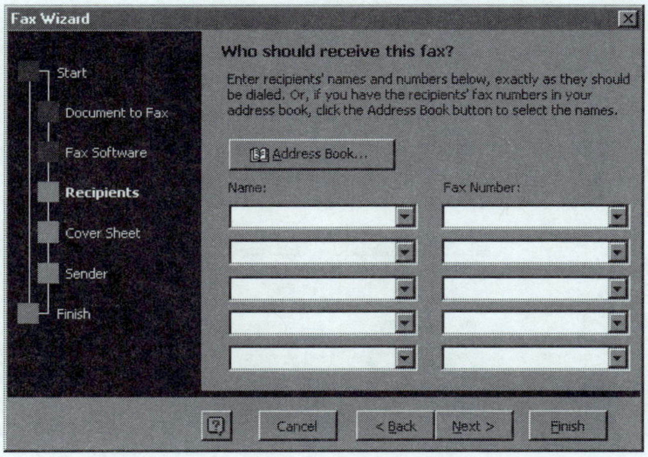

Here, you can select names and numbers from your address book (see page 244 for more information about the Address Book), or you can type in the names and numbers manually. (If the Fax Wizard has been used before, the names of recent fax recipients may appear in the drop-down lists.)

5. With the insertion point located in the top Name box, type *Sandra Peters*, press Tab, type *360-555-7778*, and click Next to display the dialog box shown on the following page.

More Fax Wizard options

If you plan to send a fax to several people at once, you can do so using the Fax Wizard. Simply fill in the names and numbers in the fourth dialog box (or use the Address Book—see page 244 for more information about the Address Book). After you've completed all of the wizard's dialog boxes, Word displays the fax along with the Mail Merge toolbar. The names and numbers you included are now merge fields. To view the fields, click the View Merged Data button and then cycle through the faxes by clicking the Next Record or Previous Record buttons on the Mail Merge toolbar. To print the faxes, click the Merge To Printer button on the Mail Merge toolbar. (We discuss the topic of mail merge more in Chapter 11.) If you want to send your faxes directly from your computer, you must have a modem connected and turned on. Then select Microsoft Fax (a program that comes with Windows 95) or a different fax program in the third Fax Wizard dialog box. When Word displays your fax, you can complete the document and click the Send Fax Now button on the Fax Wizard toolbar. Word then walks you through the steps for sending your fax.

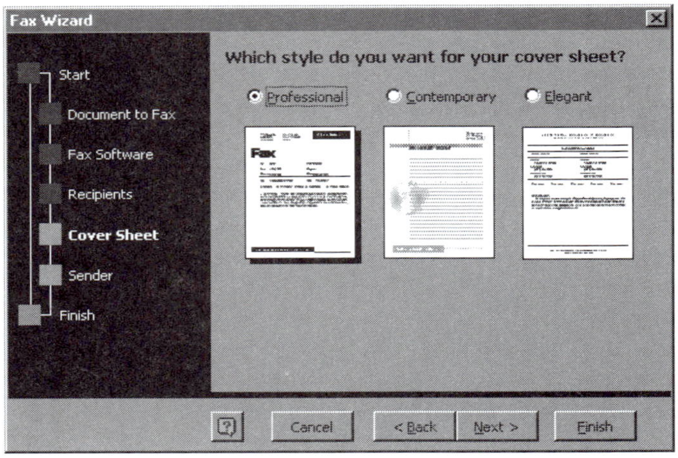

6. With the Professional option selected, click Next to display this dialog box:

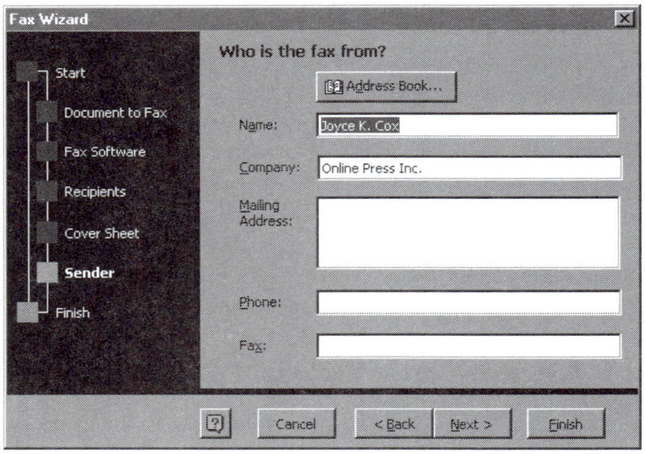

7. In the Name box, type *Ted Lee* and press Tab. Then continue entering the information shown below, pressing Tab to move from box to box:

Company:	*Redmond BEAT*
Mailing Address:	*14000 Willows Road*
	Redmond, WA 98052
Phone:	*206-555-6789*
Fax:	*206-555-1234*

8. Finally, click Finish to display the fax shown here (we've turned off the ruler so you can see more of the document):

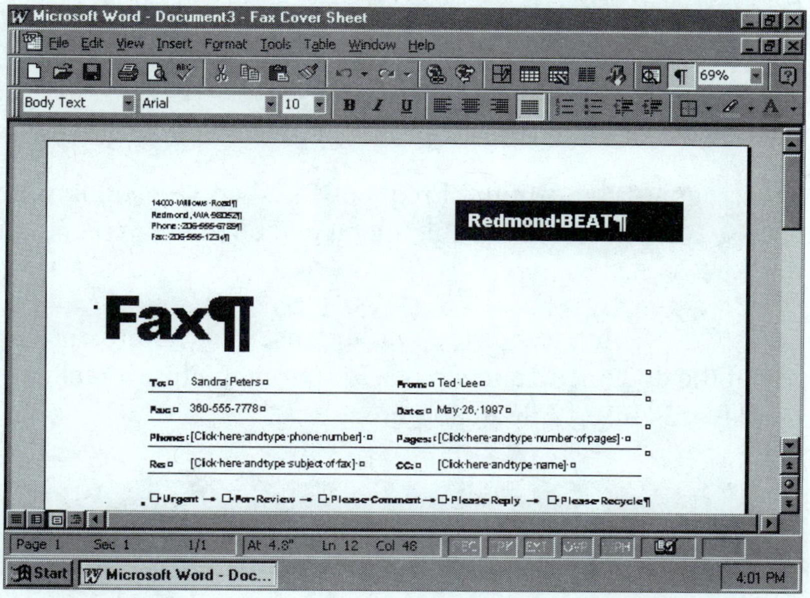

Now let's insert the text:

1. Select the [Click here and type any comments] placeholder text and then open Memo (the document you created in the last section).

2. Select the two main paragraphs, click the Copy button, and then close Memo.

3. With the placeholder text still selected in the fax, click the Paste button.

4. Save the fax with the name *5-26-97 Fax* (or the date of your fax) and then print and close it.

More About Formatting

As you saw in the previous chapter, a well-designed document uses formatting to provide visual cues about its structure. For example, a report might use large bold type for first-level headings and smaller bold type for second-level headings. Summary paragraphs might be indented and italic. In this section, we'll explore some more formatting techniques as we combine the FAQ page from Chapter 2 and the memo we created earlier in this chapter to make a flyer. Follow the steps on the next page.

Painting formats

If you want to format a block of text with a set of formats that you have already applied to another block of text, you can copy all the formatting in a simple three-step procedure. Select the text whose formats you want to copy, click the Format Painter button on the Standard toolbar, and then select the text you want to format. Word duplicates the formatting for the new selection.

1. Starting with a blank window, click the Open button on the Standard toolbar, and with the contents of the My Documents folder displayed, double-click Frequently Asked Questions to open it.

2. To safeguard the original Frequently Asked Questions file, choose Save As from the File menu and change the name of the version now on your screen to *Flyer*.

Merging documents

3. Press Ctrl+Home to be sure that the insertion point is at the top of the document, and choose File from the Insert menu to display this Insert File dialog box:

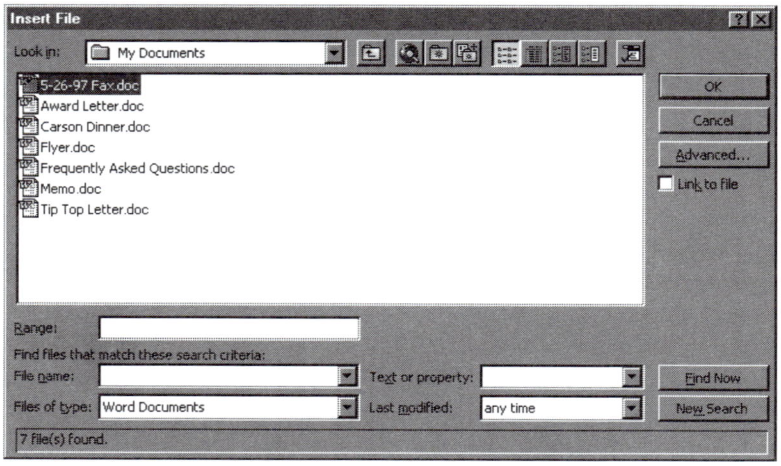

4. Select Memo and click OK to merge the file with Flyer.

5. Press Ctrl+Home to move to the top of the combined document, and select and delete everything from the memo except the title and the two paragraphs (don't forget to delete the blank paragraph at the end of the memo).

6. Click the Save button on the toolbar to save the combined document, which should look like the one shown at the top of the facing page.

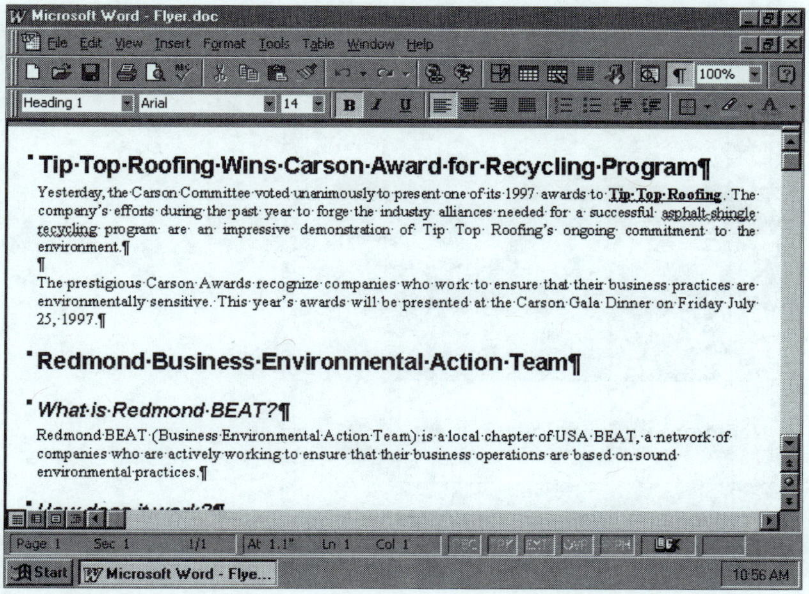

Notice that the Heading 1 style applied to the heading in the memo has adopted the Heading 1 style characteristics used in the FAQ. (We discuss styles in more detail on page 72.) From now on, we won't tell you when to save the flyer, but you should do so at regular intervals to safeguard your work.

Making Titles Stand Out

As you know, we apply character formatting when we want to change the appearance of individual characters. Here we'll focus on the titles of the two "articles" in the new flyer. Let's get started:

1. Move to the top of the document, select the title of the memo, click the Center button on the Formatting toolbar to center the title, change the font to Times New Roman, and then change the size to 16 points.
2. Now select *Redmond Business Environmental Action Team*, the title of the FAQ. Center the title and change the font to Times New Roman and the size to 16 points.
3. With the title still selected, choose Font from the Format menu. Word displays the dialog box shown on the next page.

Rebreaking titles and headings

As you create titles and headings for your Word documents, you may find that some of them would be more aesthetically pleasing if they broke to multiple lines or in a different spot. To rebreak a title or heading (or any other line of text), click an insertion point where you want the break to occur and press Shift+Enter. Word then inserts a line break, which it designates on the screen with a broken-arrow symbol.

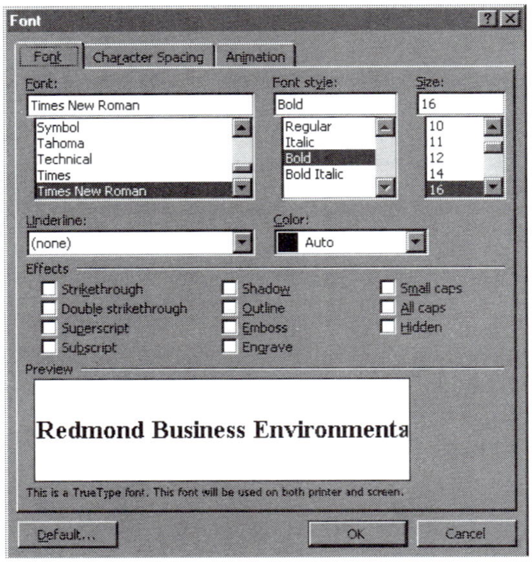

As you can see, the dialog box reflects the character formatting of the selected title. It also provides several formatting options not available on the Formatting toolbar.

Small capital letters

4. Click Small Caps in the Effects section to format the title in small capital letters with large initial capital letters, and then click OK.

If you want, you can experiment with some of the other options in the Font dialog box before moving on.

Adding Borders and Shading

To emphasize particular paragraphs, we can draw lines above and below or to the left and right of them, or we can surround the paragraphs with different styles of boxes. Let's box the FAQ title by following these steps:

1. With the title still selected, choose Borders And Shading from the Format menu to display the Borders And Shading dialog box shown here:

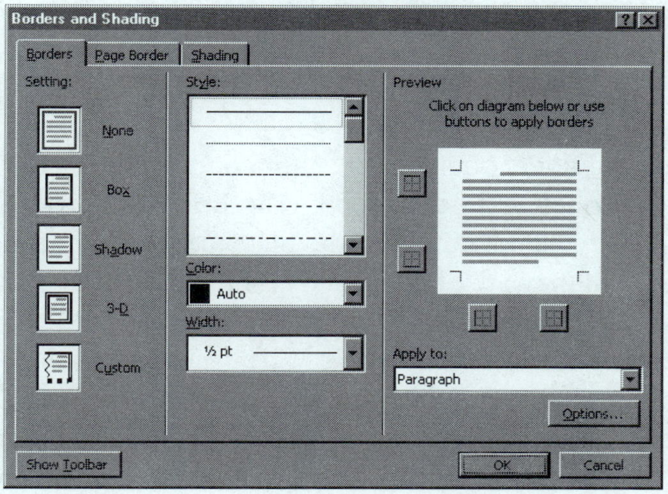

2. Click the arrow to the right of the Width box and select the 1 ½ pt single-line option.

Changing line styles

3. Click the Box setting. Word displays a preview on the right side of the dialog box.

Adding a border

4. Next click the Shading tab and in the Fill section, click Gray-25% (the third box in the second row) to fill the box around the title with a light gray color. Then click OK.

Adding shading

5. Click anywhere to remove the highlighting to see this:

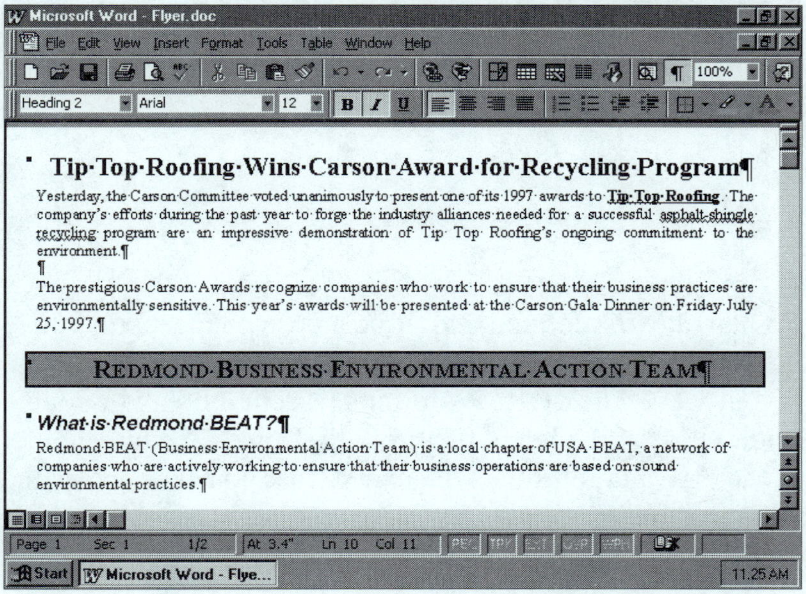

6. If you want, experiment with the other possible border and shading options.

Setting Up Multiple Columns

Newsletters and flyers often feature multicolumn layouts like those of magazines and newspapers. These layouts give us more flexibility when it comes to the placement of elements on the page, and they are often visually more interesting than single-column layouts. With Word, setting up multiple columns for an entire document couldn't be easier. We simply click the Columns button on the toolbar and select the number of columns we want. And as you'll see if you follow these steps, when we want only part of a document to have a multicolumn layout, we select that part of the document before clicking the Columns button:

1. Select the text from *What is Redmond BEAT?* to the period following the telephone number in the very last sentence.

The Columns button

2. Click the Columns button. Word drops down this grid of columns:

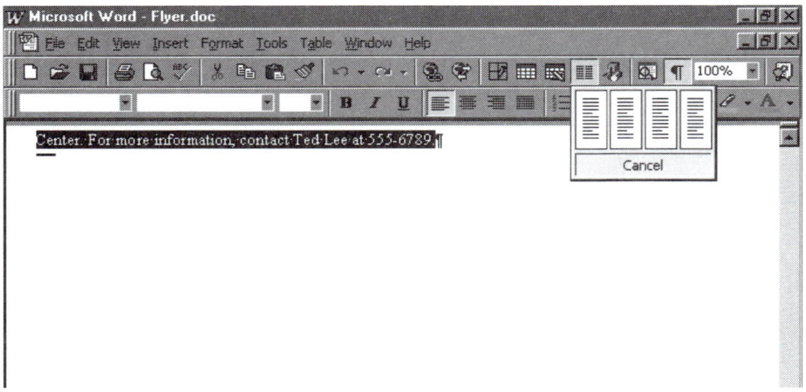

3. Point to the first column, move the mouse pointer across three columns, and click. When Word asks you to switch to page layout view, click OK. Word puts a section break (a double dotted line) at the beginning of the selected text and another at the end, and reformats the text so that it snakes across the page in three columns. The document now looks something like this:

Document sections

When applying different formatting, such as different numbers of columns or different margins, to only part of a document, Word designates the beginning and end of that part with section breaks. You can insert section breaks manually by choosing Break from the Insert menu, selecting an option in the Section Breaks section, and then clicking OK. You can have the new section start at the top of the next new page, the next even page, or the next odd page; or you can have the new section continue immediately after the old section.

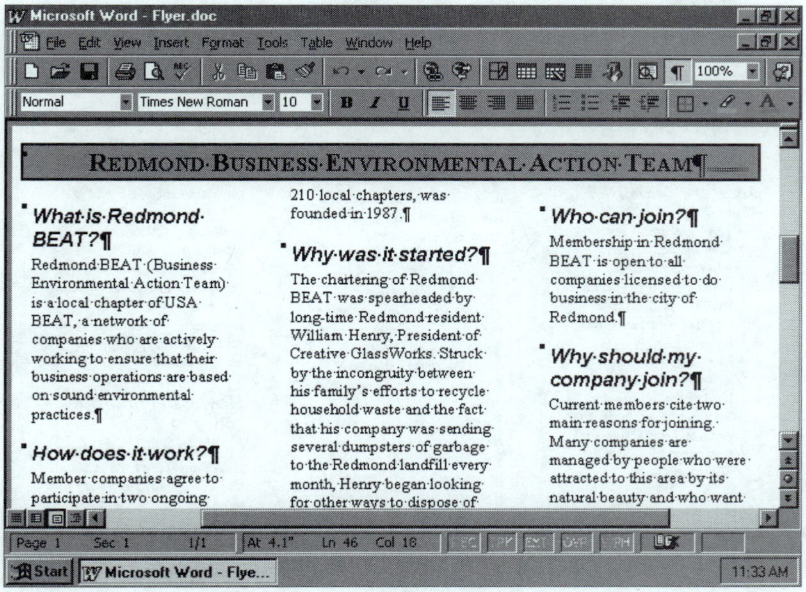

Creating Lists

The second paragraph of the FAQ contains two numbered items that would stand out better if they were set up as a list. Word has two built-in list formats: one for numbered lists and one for bulleted lists. Here's how to implement the numbered list format (the bulleted list format works the same way—see the tip on page 68 for more information):

1. Use the scroll bar to move to the second paragraph, click an insertion point to the left of the number 1, and press Enter.
2. Click an insertion point to the left of the number 2 and press Enter. Word recognizes that consecutive paragraphs starting with numbers comprise a numbered list, and responds by adding a 2 and a period in front of the new paragraph and giving both numbered paragraphs a hanging-indent format. This capability is called *AutoFormat As You Type* (see the adjacent tip).
3. Delete the extra 2, the period, and the space in the second numbered paragraph. The results are shown at the top of the next page.

AutoFormat As You Type

By default, Word automatically formats certain elements of your documents, such as numbered lists. If you want to turn this feature off, choose AutoCorrect from the Tools menu and click the AutoFormat As You Type tab to view the settings available with this option. In the Apply As You Type section, deselect any of the features you want to turn off. In the Replace As You Type section, you can tell Word to turn straight quotes (" ") to smart quotes (“ ”), use superscript with ordinals (1st), use fraction characters (½), change symbol characters, apply formatting, and create hyperlinks for Internet and network paths. In the Automatically As You Type section, you can control the treatment of lists and styles.

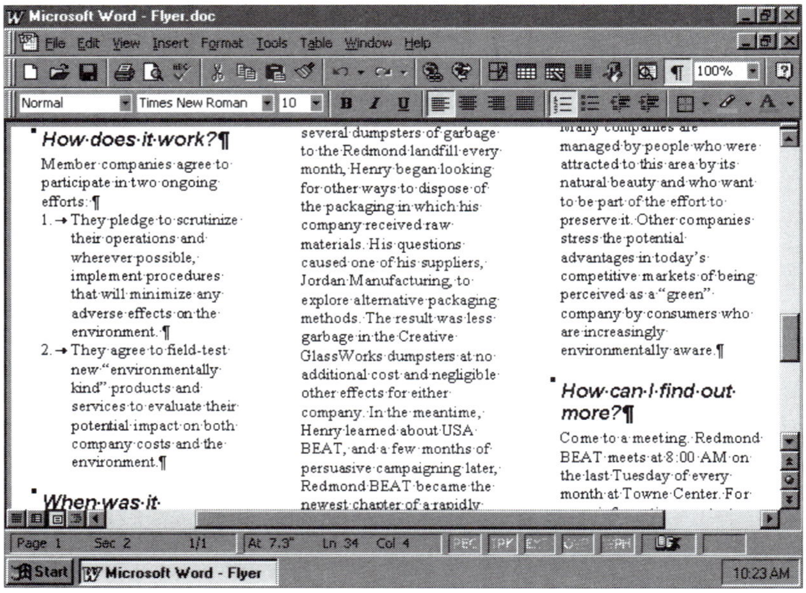

Creating numbered lists from scratch

If you want to type a numbered list from scratch, you can type 1, a period, and a space, and then press Enter after typing your text. Word then automatically formats the next paragraph as the next item of the numbered list. To return to regular paragraphs, click the Numbering button to turn the list off. (To turn off AutoFormat As You Type options altogether, see the tip on the previous page.)

You can also quickly convert existing text paragraphs to numbered lists by selecting the paragraphs and clicking the Numbering button.

> **Bulleted lists**
>
> To create a bulleted list, you select the paragraphs you want to be bulleted and click the Bullets button on the Formatting toolbar. You can also type an asterisk (*) and a space and Word will convert the paragraph to a bulleted list as soon as you press Enter. (See the previous tip for more information about the AutoFormat feature.) By default, Word precedes each paragraph with a large, round dot. You can change the bullet symbol by choosing Bullets And Numbering from the Format menu, and on the Bulleted tab, selecting one of five other standard symbols. You can modify the format of both bulleted and numbered lists by clicking the Customize button on their respective tabs, making your changes, and clicking OK.

Adding Headers and Footers

The flyer is currently only one page long. For documents that are longer than one page, we'll usually want to add a header or footer, so we'll show you how to do that next.

Headers are printed in the top margin of the page, and footers are printed in the bottom margin. With Word, we have many header and footer options. For example, we can create identical headers and footers for every page, a different header and footer for the first page, different headers and footers for left (even) pages and right (odd) pages, or different headers and footers for each section of a document.

Suppose we want a header to appear on all pages of the flyer except the first. To create this type of header, we need to add at least one more page to the flyer, like this:

1. Press Ctrl+End to move to the end of the document, and then choose Break from the Insert menu to display this dialog box:

Inserting page breaks

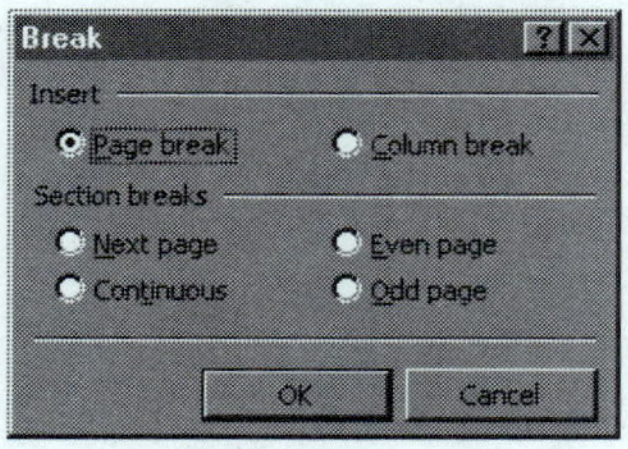

2. Accept the default Page Break option by clicking OK.

3. Now insert another page break using a different method: Press Ctrl+Enter. Your document has three pages.

4. Press Ctrl+Home to move to the top of the document.

Now let's tackle the header:

1. Choose Header And Footer from the View menu. Word dims the text of the document, outlines the space in which the header will appear with a dotted box, and displays the Header And Footer floating toolbar, as shown here:

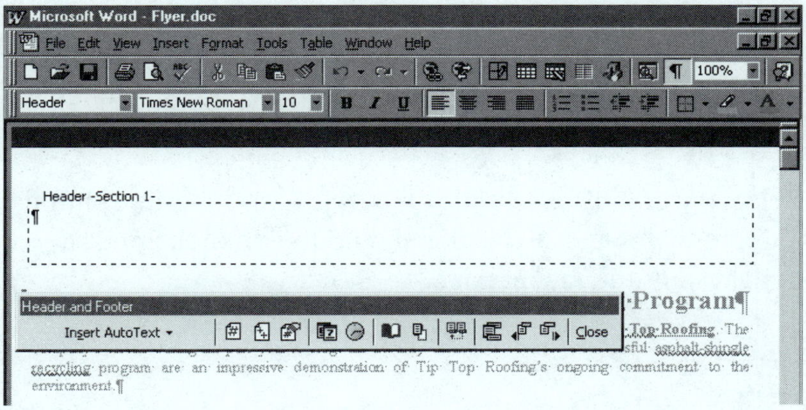

2. Click the Page Setup button on the Header And Footer toolbar to display the dialog box shown on the next page.

The Page Setup button

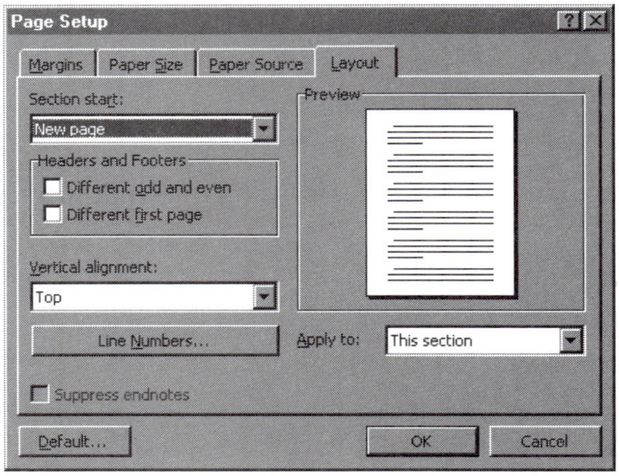

If necessary, click the Layout tab to display its options.

3. In the Headers And Footers section, select the Different First Page option and click OK. Word changes the header designation to read *First Page Header - Section 1*.

The Show Next button

4. We're going to leave the first page header blank, so click the Show Next button on the Header And Footer toolbar to move to the next page, which begins section 3. (Section 2 is the three-column section on page 1.)

The Same As Previous button

5. Click the Same As Previous button to toggle it off, thereby indicating that you want this header to be different from the first one.

The Insert Page Number button

6. Now type *Redmond Business Environmental Action Team*, press the Tab key twice, type *Page* and a space, and click the Insert Page Number button.

7. Select the entire header, click the Bold and Underline buttons, and press Home. The header should look like the one shown at the top of the facing page.

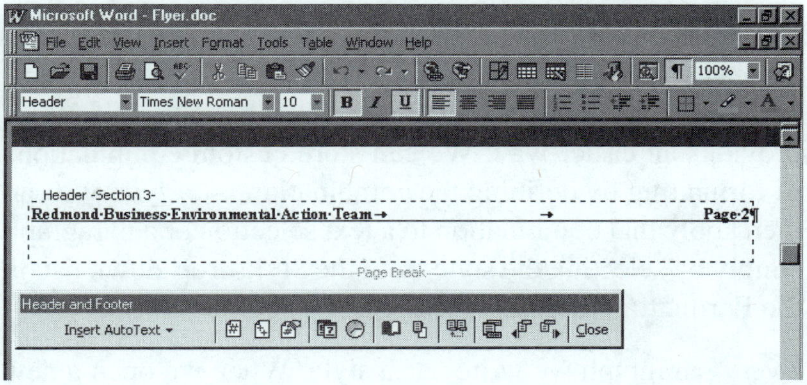

8. Click the Close button to return to page layout view.

Let's take a quick look at the flyer in print preview:

1. Click the Print Preview button. Then click the Multiple Pages button on the Print Preview toolbar to drop down a grid of "pages," and drag through the left and center "pages" in the top row. Word displays the first two pages of your document side by side, as shown here:

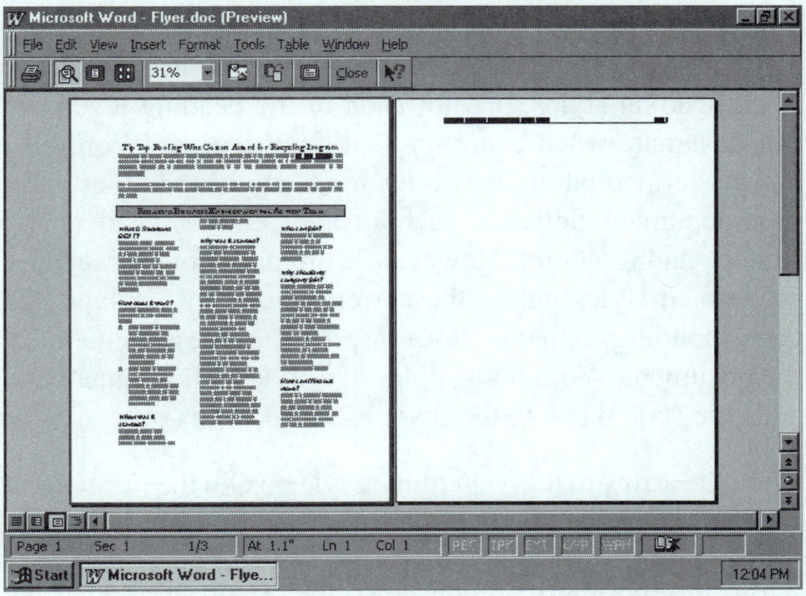

2. Press Page Down to see the third page, and then click the Close button on the Print Preview toolbar.

More about page numbers

If you want your headers or footers to contain nothing but page numbers, you don't have to create a header or footer. You can have Word perform this chore for you. Choose Page Numbers from the Insert menu, and in the Page Numbers dialog box, specify if the page numbers should appear at the top or bottom of the page, how they should be aligned, and whether a number should appear on the first page, and click OK. Word then inserts page numbers in the document's header or footer. Whether you add page numbers this way or by clicking the Insert Page Number button on the Header And Footer toolbar, you can format them by clicking the Format button in the Page Numbers dialog box. You can select from five numbering schemes: Arabic numbers (1, 2, 3), lower/uppercase letters (a, b, c/A, B, C), and lower/uppercase Roman numerals (i, ii, iii/I, II, III). You can also specify whether chapter numbers should be included and select a starting number.

Formatting with Styles

We can work through a document applying formats to headings and other special paragraphs one by one, but Word provides an easier way: We can store custom combinations of formatting by defining the combination as a *style*. We can then apply that combination to a text selection or a paragraph simply by selecting the style from the Style drop-down list on the Formatting toolbar.

The Normal style

Every paragraph we write has a style. When we open a new blank document, it is based on the Blank Document template, and Word applies the Normal style to all paragraphs unless instructed otherwise. The Normal style formats characters as 10-point regular Times New Roman and paragraphs as left-aligned and single-spaced. When we base a document on a template other than Blank Document, the styles included as part of that template become available, and as you saw earlier in this chapter, we can then create documents like the memo simply by filling in the paragraphs of the template.

Using Word's Predefined Styles

As you learned in Chapter 2, Word comes with nine predefined heading styles, one for each of the heading levels we can designate when using the Outlining feature. Word also has predefined paragraph styles for a number of other common document elements, such as index entries, headers and footers, and footnotes. However, Word does not list the other predefined styles unless the current document contains the corresponding elements. If we insert one of these elements in the document, Word both applies the style to the element and adds the style name to the Style list. Check this out:

1. Click the arrow to the right of the Style box on the Formatting toolbar to drop down the Style list.
2. Scroll through the list. You'll see that Word has added the styles from the memo template, as well as a style for the headers you just created.

The style name is displayed in the format it would appear if you applied it to the selected paragraph. To the right of the

Character styles vs. paragraph styles

Character styles affect only the selected text and apply their formats on top of any paragraph formats applied to the selected text. Paragraph styles affect the entire paragraph containing the insertion point. For example, you can apply a paragraph style that makes the font and size of an entire paragraph 12-point regular Arial and then select the first word and apply a character style that makes the font and size of just that word 18-point bold italic Arial.

style name, Word displays the paragraph alignment, the font size, and whether the style is a paragraph style or a character style. (Paragraph styles are indicated with a paragraph mark, and character styles are indicated with the letter *a*.)

3. Press the Esc key to close the list.

When Word applies one of its built-in styles to an element, it uses the predefined formatting for that element. Once the style is available on the Style list, we can apply the style to other paragraphs. We can also redefine the style to suit the document we are creating, and we can create entirely new styles.

Creating Custom Styles

Although Word does a good job of anticipating the document elements for which we will need styles, we will often want to come up with styles of our own. For example, the spacing between the first two paragraphs of the flyer is controlled by a blank paragraph mark, and the paragraphs have no first-line indent. Let's create a style that specifies the spacing following the paragraphs (a more flexible way of controlling spacing), indents the first line of each paragraph, and makes the size of the characters slightly larger:

1. Delete the paragraph mark between the first and second paragraphs.

2. Click an insertion point in the first text paragraph and choose Paragraph from the Format menu to display this dialog box:

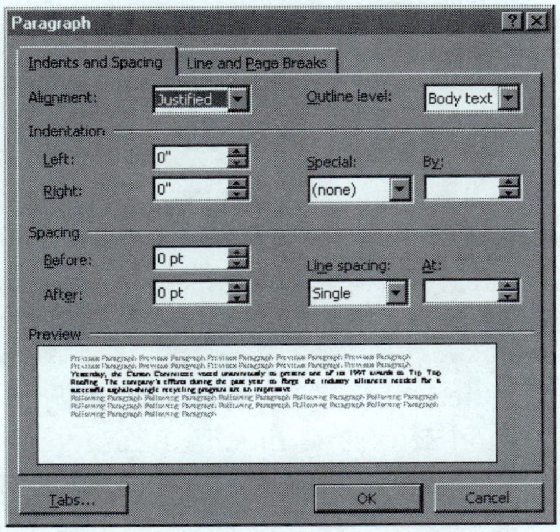

The Style dialog box

You can manage the available styles and create new ones by choosing Style from the Format menu. You can click the New button to define a new style, the Delete button to remove the selected style, and the Modify button to display a dialog box in which we can change the selected style. (See the tip on page 75 for another way to modify styles.) If styles occur in a particular sequence in a document, you can specify that one style should automatically follow another by selecting the first style, clicking the Modify button, and selecting a style from the Style For Following Paragraph drop-down list.

Notice that you can control alignment, indentation, the space above and below paragraphs, and line spacing (single-spaced, double-spaced, and so on), all from this one dialog box.

Indenting the first line

3. In the Indentation section, select First Line from the Special drop-down list. Word enters 0.5" in the By edit box as the default first-line indent and shows in the Preview box below how your text will look with this setting.

4. Change the setting in the By edit box to *0.15* and then change the After setting in the Spacing section to *6*. Click OK.

5. Now select the paragraph (including the paragraph mark) and select 12 from the Font Size box on the Formatting toolbar. Then click the paragraph to see these results:

Now follow the steps below to assign a different name to the new style:

1. With the insertion point located in the first paragraph of the flyer, click the Style box to highlight the name in it.

2. Type *Indented Paragraph*, the name you want for this style, and press Enter. Word adds the style name and displays Indented Paragraph in the Style box to indicate that it is applied to the current paragraph.

3. Click an insertion point in the second paragraph of the flyer, drop down the Style list, and select the Indented Paragraph

Transferring styles to other documents

Once you have created a style for use in one document, you don't have to recreate it for use in others. You can simply copy the style to the new document. Or if you want the style to become a part of the set of styles available with a particular template, you can copy the style to that template. Simply choose Style from the Format menu, and in the Style dialog box, click the Organizer button. The Styles tab shows a list of styles available in the current document. Select the style you want to copy and click the Copy button. Word copies the style to the template selected in the Styles Available In box.

style. Word changes the style of the second paragraph so that its formatting is consistent with the first paragraph.

Now let's turn our attention to the FAQ part of the flyer. Suppose we want to justify these paragraphs and add a little space before each one. (Paragraphs with space before them are called *open paragraphs*.) Follow these steps:

Open paragraphs

1. Click an insertion point in the first text paragraph of the FAQ and choose Paragraph from the Format menu.
2. In the Spacing section, change the Before setting to *3 pt* and click OK.
3. Now click Normal in the Style box to highlight it, type *Open Paragraph* as this style's name, and then press Enter.
4. In turn, select each text paragraph of the FAQ (including the numbered paragraphs) and then select Open Paragraph from the Style list to apply that style.

Modifying styles

To modify one of Word's default styles or one of your own, you first select text that uses the style you want to change and make the formatting changes. Then to redefine the style to include the changes you have made, select the style in the Style list. When Word displays the Modify Style dialog box, you can select the Update option to modify the existing style or the Reapply option to reapply the style's existing formatting to the paragraph. Click the Automatically Update check box if you want the style to be updated whenever you make a change to text that uses the style. (To turn off the Automatically Update option, choose Style from the Format menu, click Modify, deselect the Automatically Update check box, and click OK and then Close.) Click OK to implement your choices or click Cancel to close the dialog box, leaving your formatting changes intact without redefining the style. Once you redefine the style, all other occurrences of that style in your current document are updated as well.

Hyphenating a document

By hyphenating some words, you can really improve the looks of justified columns, such as those in the FAQ. To hyphenate a document, press Ctrl+Home to move to the top of the document, choose Language and then Hyphenation from the Tools menu, and select Automatically Hyphenate Document in the Hyphenation dialog box. Deselect Hyphenate Words In CAPS so that Word does not hyphenate words in capital letters, such as BEAT. Change the Limit Consecutive Hyphens To setting to *2* and click OK. Word quickly hyphenates the document, thus eliminating many of the large spaces between words.

The Numbering button

5. Now go back and select the second and third paragraphs under the *How does it work?* heading and click the Numbering button on the Formatting toolbar to apply the numbered-list format "on top of" the Open Paragraph style. Here are the results:

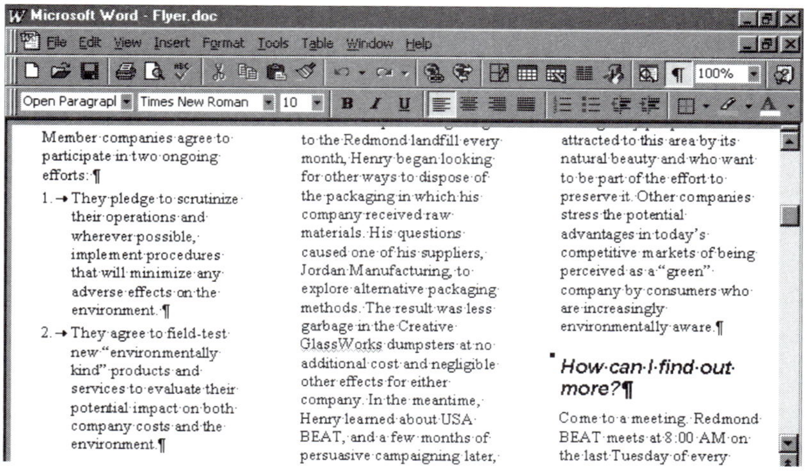

Now check the layout of the pages:

1. Click the Print Preview button and then press Page Down to view all the pages.

2. If the text from the first page now runs onto the second page, click Close and choose Page Setup from the File menu.

3. On the Margins tab, change Bottom to *0.5*, select Whole Document from the Apply To drop-down list, and then click OK.

4. Check the document in print preview again to verify that all the text now fits on the first page.

Creating Tables

Creating tables in Word is a simple process. We specify the number of columns and rows and then leave it to Word to figure out the initial settings. To demonstrate how easy the process is, we'll add a table to the flyer:

1. Press Ctrl+End to move to the end of the flyer and press Backspace to delete one of the blank pages.

2. Type *AIR POLLUTANT SOURCES* as the table's title, press Enter, type *In Millions of Metric Tons*, and press Enter twice. Make the title bold and 14 points and make the subtitle bold and italic. Center both lines.

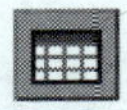

The Insert Table button

3. Press Ctrl+End, click the Insert Table button to drop down a column/row grid, and point to the top-left cell (the intersection of the first column and the first row).

4. Hold down the mouse button and drag the pointer across four columns and down six rows. The grid expands as you drag beyond its bottom edge, and Word shows the size of the selection below the grid. When you release the mouse button, Word inserts this table structure:

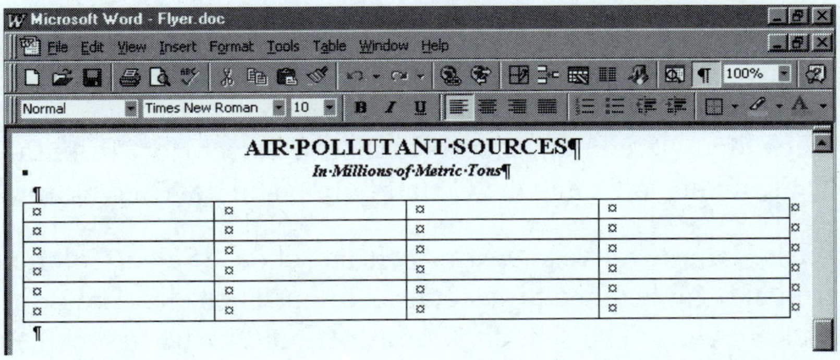

The table has four equal columns that together span the width of the document's text column. The insertion point is in the first cell. To make an entry in this cell, all we have to do is type, like this:

1. To enter column headings, type *Contributor* in the first cell and press Tab. The insertion point moves to the cell to the right. Type *Sulfur Dioxide* and press Tab to move to the next cell. Type *Carbon Monoxide* and press Tab. Finally, type *Nitrogen Oxides* and press Tab. (Pressing Tab at the end of the first row moves the insertion point to the first cell in the second row.)

2. Type the entries shown on the next page, pressing Tab to move from cell to cell. (You can also use the Arrow keys or mouse to move around.)

Changing column width

You can adjust column widths in three ways: by moving the markers designated with grids on the ruler, by dragging column borders, or by using the Cell Height And Width command. To use the ruler, click an insertion point in the table and move the pointer over the grid marker to the left of the column you want to adjust on the ruler. When the pointer changes to a two-headed arrow, drag to the right or left until the column is the width you want it. To drag a column border, simply point to the vertical column border and drag the two-headed pointer to the left or right until the column is the desired width. Or choose Cell Height And Width from the Table menu and enter exact width measurements on the Column tab of the Cell Height And Width dialog box.

Transportation	*0.9*	*41.2*	*8.1*
Industrial Emissions	*3.4*	*4.7*	*0.6*
Fuel Combustion	*16.4*	*7.6*	*10.8*
Solid-Waste Burning	*- -*	*1.7*	*0.1*
Miscellaneous	*- -*	*6.0*	*0.2*

3. After typing *0.2*, press Tab. Word adds a blank row to the table.

The Tables And Borders button

4. Type *TOTAL*, press Tab, and then click the Tables And Borders button to display the Tables And Borders toolbar. (If necessary, double-click the toolbar's title bar to dock the Tables And Borders toolbar below the Formatting toolbar.)

The AutoSum button

5. Click the AutoSum button on the Tables And Borders toolbar. Word looks at the values above the current cell and totals them.
6. Press Tab and click the AutoSum button again. Then repeat this step for the final column.
7. Click anywhere in the first row, choose Select Row from the Table menu, and click the Center button and the Bold button.
8. Press Home to move to the first cell, and choose Select Column from the Table menu to select its column. Then click the Bold button twice. (The first click turns off bold in the first cell.)
9. To center the values, point to the left of the 0.9 entry in the Sulphur Dioxide column, drag through all the cells containing values to select them, and click the Center button.
10. Press Home to see these results:

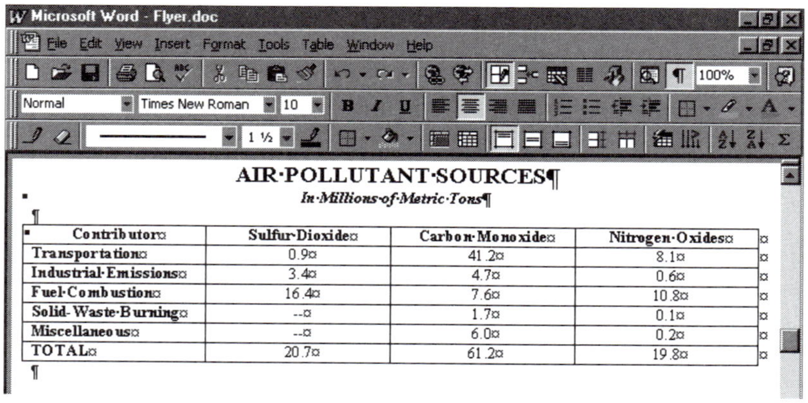

Deleting rows and columns

To delete one or more rows or columns, select the rows or columns and choose Delete Rows or Delete Columns from the Table menu. (If you don't select rows or columns first, the command is named Delete Cells, and choosing this command displays a dialog box in which you can specify what you want to delete.) To delete the entire table, select the table and then choose the Delete Rows command.

Before we wrap up this section, let's add gridlines to the cells and put a border around the whole table:

1. With the insertion point anywhere in the table, choose Select Table from the Table menu.

2. Check that the Line Weight box is set to the 1 ½ pt single-line option.

The Line Weight box

3. Click the arrow to the right of the Border button on the Tables And Borders toolbar and select All Borders from the palette of options (the first option in the second row). Then press Home to see these results:

The Border button

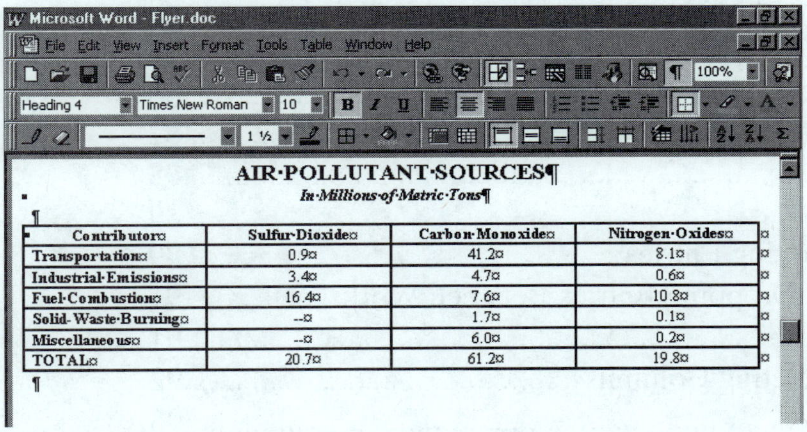

Contributor	Sulfur·Dioxide	Carbon·Monoxide	Nitrogen·Oxides
Transportation	0.9	41.2	8.1
Industrial·Emissions	3.4	4.7	0.6
Fuel·Combustion	16.4	7.6	10.8
Solid-Waste·Burning	--	1.7	0.1
Miscellaneous	--	6.0	0.2
TOTAL	20.7	61.2	19.8

4. Look over the flyer in print preview and then click the Print button. Your flyer should look like the one shown at the beginning of this chapter.

5. Click Close, click the Tables And Borders button to turn off the Tables And Borders toolbar, and then save and close the Flyer document.

With the features we have explored in these first few chapters, you should have no trouble using Word to create useful documents for your work.

4 Excel Basics

Add a header to identify the worksheet

Add a border and shading to a selected range

1997 Job Log

Preliminary Income Analysis

1997

Invoice Total	$48,406.33
Average Invoice	$4,033.86
Largest Invoice	$11,300.22
Smallest Invoice	$1,325.75
Profit Margin	25%
Estimated Profit	$12,101.58

Set up a calculation area to group important results

Use functions and names to simplify calculations

Job Number	Date Completed	Amount of Invoice
019704A	2/2/97	$1,576.18
0197260	3/29/97	$4,744.57
0297150	5/10/97	$11,300.22
039717A	4/29/97	$7,940.62
0397270	6/12/97	$2,632.00
049719A	6/25/97	$3,514.93
0697070	8/14/97	$6,233.78
0797240	8/22/97	$1,898.46
0897250	9/26/97	$2,576.59
0997040	10/4/97	$1,325.75
109710A	11/27/97	$2,910.00
1197030	12/10/97	$1,753.23
		$48,406.33

Enter numbers as text

Use the AutoSum button to total values

Display values (dates, currency, etc.) consistently using the Cells command

Microsoft Excel, the spreadsheet component of Microsoft Office, is tailor-made for performing calculations on our data. If you want to maintain lists of information that you can summarize in reports, you should use Access rather than Excel. But if you need to analyze sales, calculate budgets, figure out loan or stock information, or compare two financial situations, Excel is the place to be. In this chapter, we give you an overview of Excel as we create a simple worksheet for Tip Top Roofing. Follow these steps:

Starting a new workbook

1. Choose Programs and then Microsoft Excel from the Windows Start menu.

2. If necessary, close the Office Assistant and maximize the window. Your screen now looks like this:

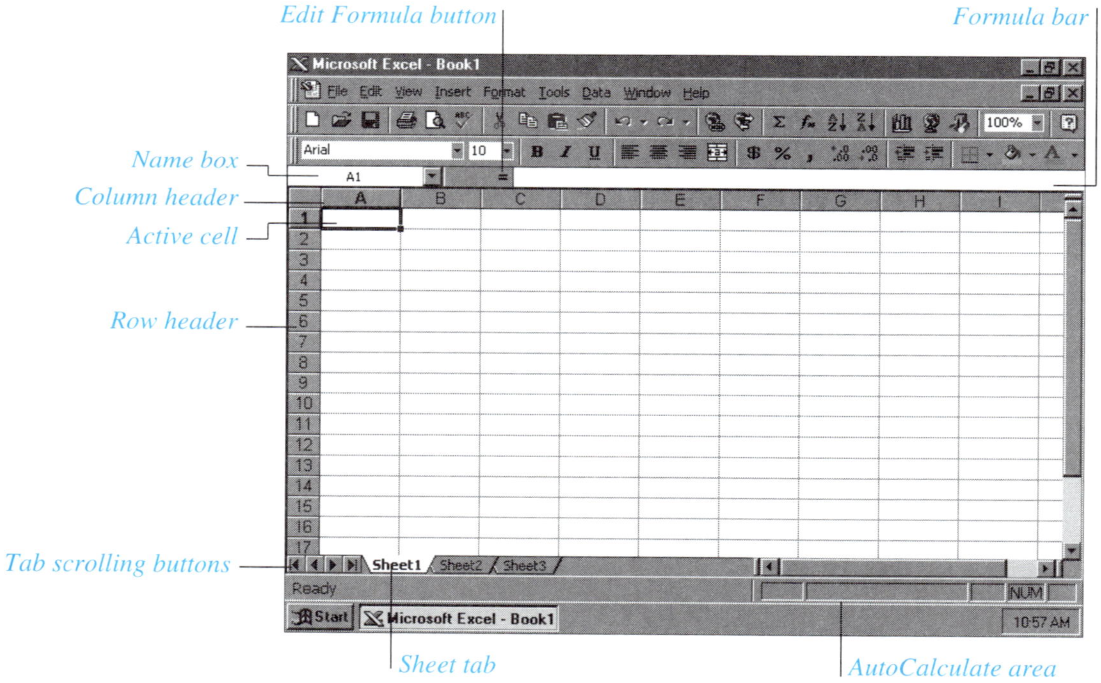

Taking up the majority of the screen is a blank *worksheet*, which as you can see, is laid out in a grid of *columns* and *rows* like the ledger paper used by accountants. There are 256 columns, lettered A through IV, and 65,536 rows, numbered 1 through 65536. (When you drag the horizontal or vertical scroll box, Excel displays the letter of the current column or the number of the current row, respectively.) The rectangle at the junction of each column and row is called a *cell*. To identify each of the 16 million plus cells on the worksheet, Excel uses an *address*, or *reference*, that consists of the letter at the top of the cell's column and the number at the left end of its row. For example, the reference of the cell in the top left corner of the worksheet is A1. The *active cell*—the one we're working with—is designated on the worksheet by a heavy border. Excel displays the reference of the active cell in the *name box* at the left end of the formula bar.

Cell addresses

The active cell

The *status bar* at the bottom of the window includes an *AutoCalculate area*, where Excel displays the sum of the entries in the selected cells. For more information about the AutoCalculate area, see the tip on page 96.

An Overview of Workbooks

The worksheet on the screen is just one *sheet* in the current file, which is called a *workbook*. By default, each new workbook contains three sheets. However, a single workbook file can contain many sheets of different types including worksheets, chart sheets (where we can create graphs of our data), and macro sheets (which store automated ways of manipulating the data or the workbook). This workbook format allows us to store related data on separate sheets but in a single file.

For each sheet in a workbook, Excel displays a *tab*, like a file folder tab, above the status bar at the bottom of the screen. These tabs are handy for moving from sheet to sheet. Let's see how to use them to move around the workbook:

Sheet tabs

1. Click the Sheet2 tab. Excel displays that sheet.

2. Click the Sheet3 tab to display that sheet and finish by selecting Sheet1.

Although you haven't entered any data in your workbook yet, let's go ahead and save it with the name 1997 Jobs. As you'll see if you follow the steps on the next page, saving workbooks is just like saving other Microsoft Office files.

The tab scrolling buttons

The number of sheets in the workbook may exceed the number of tabs Excel can display at the bottom of the worksheet window. You can use the tab scrolling buttons to the left of the Sheet1 tab to bring the tabs for hidden sheets into view, without changing the active sheet. Click the First Sheet or Last Sheet button to display the tabs for those sheets and the Previous Sheet or Next Sheet buttons to move tabs into view one at a time.

Saving workbooks

1. Click the Save button. Because you have not yet assigned the workbook a name, Excel displays the Save As dialog box (see page 18).
2. Be sure the My Documents folder appears in the Save In box and then type *1997 Jobs* in the File Name edit box.
3. Leave the other settings in the dialog box as they are for now and click Save.

   From now on, you can save this workbook by simply clicking the Save button.

Entering Data

Most worksheets consist of blocks of text and numbers in table format on which we can perform various calculations. To make our worksheets easy to read, we usually enter text as column and row headings that describe the associated entries. Let's try entering a few headings now:

Entering text

1. With cell A1 selected, type *Job Number*. As you type, the text appears in both the cell and the formula bar, and a blinking insertion point in the cell tells you where the next character you type will be inserted. A Cancel button (✕) and an Enter button (✓) appear between the text and name box. Meanwhile, the indicator in the status bar changes from Ready to Enter because the text you have typed will not be recorded in cell A1 until you "enter" it.
2. Click the Enter button to complete the entry. Excel enters the Job Number heading in cell A1, and the indicator changes to Ready. The entry is left-aligned in its cell. (Unless you tell Excel to do otherwise, it always left-aligns text.)
3. Click cell B1 to select it. The reference displayed in the name box changes from A1 to B1.
4. Type *Date Completed*, but instead of clicking the Enter button to enter the heading in the cell, press the Tab key. Excel completes the entry in cell B1 and selects cell C1.

When you need more sheets

If you need to add sheets to a workbook, simply choose Worksheet from the Insert menu. Excel inserts a new sheet to the left of the active sheet and makes the new sheet active. If you frequently create workbooks with more than three sheets, you can change this default number by choosing Options from the Tools menu, and on the General tab, increasing the Sheets In New Workbook setting.

5. Type *Amount of Invoice* and click the Enter button. Here's how the newly entered row of headings looks in the worksheet:

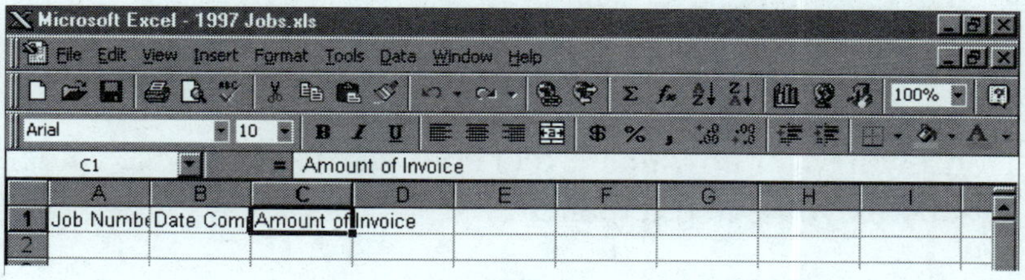

Notice that the headings are too long to fit in their cells. The Job Number and Date Completed headings are still intact, however. (If you're skeptical, click either cell and look at the formula bar.) After we have entered more information, we'll adjust the column widths to accommodate long entries (see page 94).

As you'll see in the next section, you can complete entries in several different ways, which we've summarized here:

To do this...	Use this...
Stay in the same cell	Enter button
Move down	Enter key or Down Arrow
Move up	Shift+Enter or Up Arrow
Move right	Tab key or Right Arrow
Move left	Shift+Tab or Left Arrow

Entering numeric values is just as easy as entering text. Follow along with these steps to enter the amount of each completed roofing job in column C:

1. Click cell C2 to select the first cell in the Amount of Invoice column and type *1576.18*. Press Enter to complete the entry, which Excel right-aligns in its cell.

2. Enter the amounts shown below and at the top of the next page in the indicated cells, pressing Enter after each one:

C3	*4744.57*
C4	*11300.22*
C5	*7940.62*
C6	*2632.00*
C7	*35149.30*
C8	*6233.78*

Correcting mistakes

If you make a mistake, you can click the cell containing the error and simply type the new entry. If you want to correct part of an entry, click its cell and press F2, or double-click the cell so that you can edit the entry directly in the cell. You can then press Home or End to move the insertion point to the beginning or end of the entry and press Right Arrow or Left Arrow to move the insertion point forward or backward one character. Press Backspace to delete the character to the left of the insertion point or Delete to delete the character to the right of the insertion point. Then type the correction and click the Enter button.

C9	*1898.46*
C10	*2576.59*
C11	*1325.75*
C12	*2910.00*
C13	*1753.23*

Don't worry for now that Excel does not display these values exactly as you entered them.

Entering Numbers as Text

Now we're ready to enter the job numbers in column A. Normally, we want Excel to treat ID numbers as text rather than as values on which we might want to perform calculations. If the "number" includes not only the digits 0 through 9 but also letters and other characters (such as hyphens), Excel recognizes it as text. However, if the number consists of only digits and we want Excel to treat it as text, we have to explicitly tell Excel to do so. Follow these steps to see how Excel treats two types of job numbers:

1. Click cell A2, type *019704A*, and press Enter. This job number consists of digits and a letter, so Excel treats the entry as text and left-aligns it.
2. In cell A3, which is now active, type *0197260* and click the Enter button. This job number consists of only digits, so Excel treats the entry as a value and right-aligns it. (Note that Excel also removes the first zero.)

How do we tell Excel to treat an entry that consists of only digits as text? We begin the entry with an apostrophe ('). Follow these steps:

1. In cell A3, type *'0197260* and press Enter. (When you type the new entry, Excel overwrites the old entry.) Because of the apostrophe, Excel now recognizes the new entry as text.
2. Enter the job numbers shown on the facing page as text in the indicated cells, preceding those that end in 0 with an apostrophe.

Long numeric values

Excel allows a long text entry to overflow into an adjacent empty cell and truncates the entry only if the adjacent cell also contains an entry. However, Excel treats a long numeric value differently. By default, Excel displays values in scientific notation, and values with many decimal places might be rounded. For example, if you enter 12345678912345 in a standard width cell (which holds 8.43 characters), Excel displays 1.23457E+13 (or 1.23457 times 10 to the 13th power). And if you enter 123456.789 in a standard width cell, Excel displays 123456.8. In the latter case, Excel leaves the underlying value unchanged, and you can widen the column to display the value in the format in which you entered it. (Adjusting the width of columns is discussed on page 94.) Excel tries to automate the column-adjustment process by estimating the width needed for long numeric values so that they are fully displayed. If the program can't make the necessary adjustment, it displays pound signs (#) instead of the value you entered to indicate that the value is too large to display in the cell.

A4 *'0297150*
A5 *039717A*
A6 *'0397270*
A7 *049719A*
A8 *'0697070*
A9 *'0797240*
A10 *'0897250*
A11 *'0997040*
A12 *109710A*
A13 *'1197030*

Entering Dates and Times

For a date or time to be displayed correctly, we must enter it in a format that Excel recognizes as a date or time. Excel then displays the entry as we want it but stores it as a value so that we can perform date and time arithmetic (see the tip below). Let's see how Excel handles different date formats:

1. Enter the following dates in the indicated cells, pressing the Enter key after each one:

B2 *Feb 2, 1997*
B3 *3/29/97*
B4 *5/10/97*
B5 *Apr 29, 97*
B6 *12-June-97*
B7 *6/25/97*
B8 *aug 14, 97*
B9 *8/22/97*
B10 *26-Sep-97*
B11 *10-4-97*
B12 *11/27/97*
B13 *December 10, 1997*

Again, don't worry if Excel displays the dates differently from the way you enter them. Later, we'll come back and make sure all the dates appear in the same format. As you can see on the next page, we've now completed all the columns of this simple worksheet.

Date and time arithmetic

Each date you enter is internally recorded by Excel as a value that represents the number of days that have elapsed between that date and the base date of January 1, 1900, which is assigned the value 1. As a result, you can perform arithmetic with dates—for example, you can have Excel determine whether a payment is past due. Similarly, each time you enter is internally recorded as a decimal value that represents the portion of the day that has elapsed between that time and the base time of 12:00 midnight.

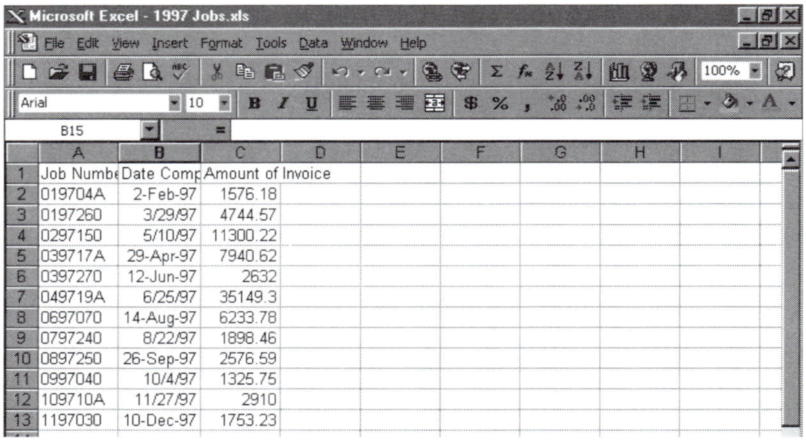

Selecting Ranges

Ranges

Range references

In Chapter 1, we covered some techniques for selecting text. Here, we'll select blocks of cells, called *ranges*. Any rectangular block is a range, whether it includes two cells, an entire row or column, or the entire worksheet. *Range references* consist of the address of the cell in the top left corner of the rectangular block and the address of the cell in the bottom right corner, separated by a colon. For example, A1:B2 consists of cells A1, A2, B1, and B2. Follow these steps to select various ranges:

Selecting with the mouse

1. Point to cell A1, hold down the left mouse button, and drag to cell C13. As you drag, the reference in the name box indicates the number of rows and columns in the selected range.
2. Release the mouse button when A1:C13 is highlighted. As you can see here, cell A1 (where you started the selection) is white, indicating that it is the active cell in the range:

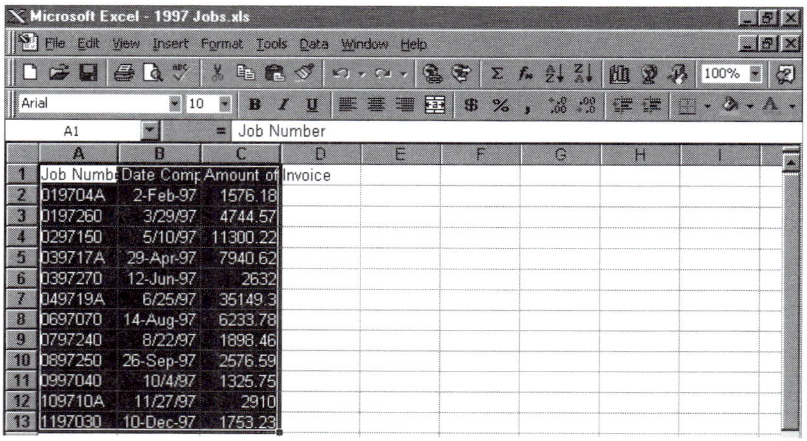

Selecting entire columns and rows

You can select all the cells in a column by clicking the column header (the gray box containing the column's letter). Similarly, you can select all the cells in a row by clicking the row header (the gray box containing the row's number).

Next, try selecting ranges with the keyboard:

Selecting with the keyboard

1. Select cell B6, hold down the Shift key, press the Right Arrow key once and the Down Arrow key twice, and release the Shift key. The range B6:C8 is selected.

2. Press Ctrl+Home to deselect the range and activate cell A1.

Editing Entries

In this section, we briefly cover some simple ways of revising worksheets. Up to now we have been working with one worksheet. In one of the following examples, we will copy data from one worksheet to another in the same workbook. But first let's see how to change individual entries.

Glancing at the Amount of Invoice column in 1997 Jobs, suppose we notice that the amount in cell C7 should be 3514.93, not 35149.3. To correct the entry without having to retype the whole thing, follow these steps:

1. Double-click cell C7 to select the cell and position an insertion point in the current entry.

2. Point between the 4 and 9 in the cell and click the left mouse button to reposition the insertion point. Then type a period.

3. Press the Right Arrow key once and press the Delete key to delete the second period.

4. Press Enter to confirm the corrected entry.

Copying and Moving Entries

You can copy an entry or group of entries anywhere within the same worksheet or in a different worksheet using the Copy and Paste buttons on the Standard toolbar or the Copy and Paste commands on the Edit menu. Similarly, moving entries is a simple cut-and-paste operation. Try this:

1. Select A1:C13 and click the Copy button.

2. Click the Sheet2 tab at the bottom of the worksheet window to display Sheet2, and with cell A1 selected, click the Paste button.

Selecting more than one block

A range can consist of more than one block of cells. To select a multiblock range, select the first range, hold down the Ctrl key, select the next range, and so on.

Excel faithfully pastes in a copy of the range from Sheet1. (Notice that you don't have to select the entire paste area.)

We can also use a simple mouse operation called *AutoFill* to copy and paste cells. Follow these steps:

Copying with AutoFill

1. With A1:C13 selected in Sheet2, move the pointer to the bottom right corner of the selected range. The pointer changes to a black cross, called the *fill handle*.
2. Hold down the left mouse button and drag the outline of the selection over the range D1:F13. As you drag, a small box adjacent to the mouse pointer displays the headings of columns that will be copied when you release the mouse button.
3. Release the mouse button. Excel pastes a copy of the selected cells into the designated paste area.

The result of dragging a copy is similar to using the Copy and Paste buttons or the equivalent commands, except that Excel doesn't place a copy of the selected range on the Clipboard.

We can also drag a selection to move it. Here's how:

1. Select D1:F13 and point to the right border of the selection.
2. Hold down the left mouse button and drag the outline of the selection over the range F1:H13. (Excel displays the range reference in a box adjacent to the mouse pointer.)
3. Release the mouse button. Excel moves the entries to their new location, like this:

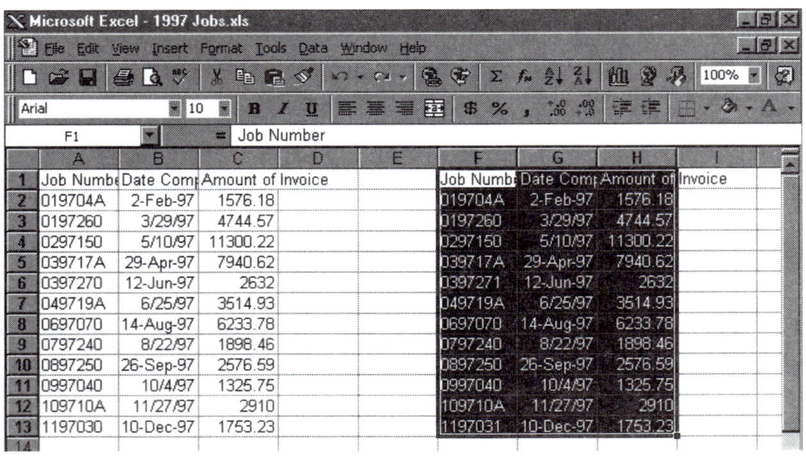

Checking spelling

If your worksheets will be seen by other people, you will probably want to spell check them. You can easily accomplish this task by clicking the Spelling button on the Standard toolbar. Excel then performs a spelling check similar to the one Word performs (see page 48). If you don't want to spell check the entire worksheet, select the cells you want to check and then click the Spelling button.

Dragging and Dropping Entries Between Worksheets

As you've already seen, you can copy and move entries between worksheets using the Copy, Cut, and Paste buttons (or the Copy, Cut, and Paste commands). You can also use drag-and-drop editing to copy and move entries between worksheets. Follow these steps:

1. Select F1:H13 in Sheet2 and point to the bottom border of the selection.
2. Hold down the Alt key and the left mouse button and drag the outline of the selection to the Sheet3 tab. Sheet3 opens.
3. While still holding down the Alt key and the left mouse button, drag the outline of the selection over the range A1:C13 and then release the Alt key and the mouse button. Now Sheet1, Sheet2, and Sheet3 all contain the same information.

To copy rather than move entries between worksheets using drag-and-drop editing, hold down Ctrl+Alt and the left mouse button.

Clearing Cells

Clearing cells is different from cutting entries. Cutting entries assumes we want to move the entries somewhere else, whereas clearing cells simply erases the entries. Follow these steps:

1. Click the column A header on Sheet3—the gray box containing the letter *A*—to select the entire column, and then choose Clear from the Edit menu. Excel displays this submenu:

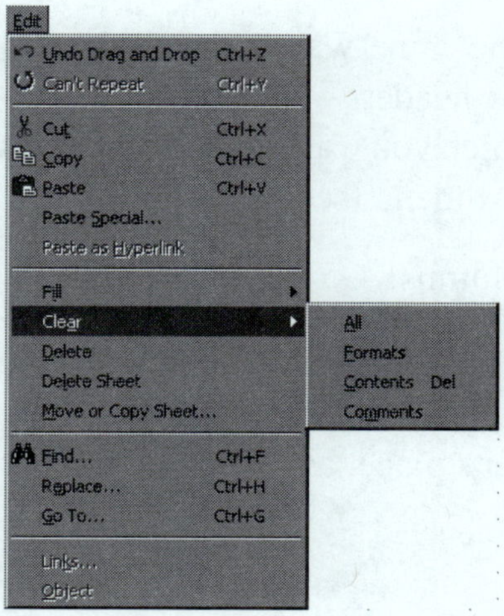

Attaching comments to cells

You might want to attach a comment to a cell for a variety of reasons (to explain a formula or remind yourself to check an assumption, for example). Simply select the cell, choose Comment from the Insert menu, and type the comment in the text box that appears. (The comment is "signed" with the name entered when Excel was installed on your computer. You can edit or delete this signature.) Click anywhere outside the cell and text box to enter the comment. Excel then places a red marker in the top right corner of each cell with a comment attached. To see a comment, just point to the red marker. To edit or delete a comment, right-click the cell and choose either Edit Comment or Delete Comment from the object menu. (You can also remove comments attached to a selected cell by choosing Clear and then Comments from the Edit menu.)

The All option clears both the formats and contents of the selected cells. Formats clears only formats, and Contents clears only contents. Comments clears any comments attached to the selected cells (see the tip on page 91), leaving the formats and contents intact.

2. Choose All. The entries in the column disappear.
3. Now select B1:C13 and clear the cells by pressing the Delete key. (When you press Delete, Excel leaves any formats and comments intact.)
4. Next click the Sheet2 tab, select A1:C13, point to the selection, and click the right mouse button to display the selection's object menu. Choose Clear Contents to clear the selected cells.
5. Move to Sheet1 by clicking its tab.

Inserting and Deleting Columns

It is a rare person who can create a worksheet from scratch without ever having to tinker with its design—moving this block of data, changing that heading, or adding or deleting a column here and there. In this section, we'll show you how to insert and delete columns. Follow these steps:

1. Point to the column C header, hold down the left mouse button, and drag across the column D header to select the two columns.
2. Choose Columns from the Insert menu. Excel inserts two blank columns in front of the Amount of Invoice column, one for each column in the selection.

Inserting rows works exactly the same way as inserting columns. You simply select the row headers—the boxes containing the row numbers—above which you want to insert the rows and choose Rows from the Insert menu (see page 96).

Now let's see how to delete columns:

1. Click the header for column D and choose Delete from the Edit menu. Excel deletes the column and moves the Amount of Invoice column over to take its place, as you can see here:

Inserting and deleting cells

Rather than insert an entire row or column, you can insert a specified number of cells. Simply select a cell or range of cells and choose Cells from the Insert menu. When the Insert dialog box appears, select the Shift Cells Right or Shift Cells Down option and click OK. Excel then inserts the cell(s), shifting the selected cell(s) to the right or down. (You can also insert an entire row above the selection or an entire column to the left of the selection using the last two options in the Insert dialog box.) Deleting cells is similar to inserting them except that you choose the Delete command from the Edit menu and make selections in the Delete dialog box.

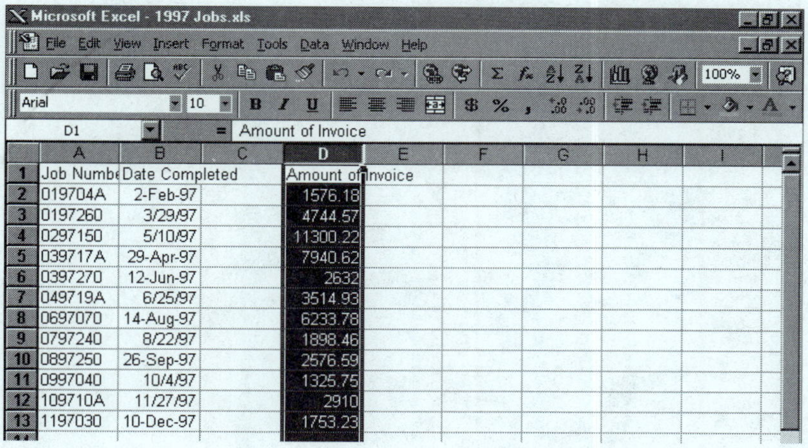

You can leave the empty column C where it is for now—we'll use it later.

Formatting Entries

Excel offers a variety of formatting options that let us emphasize parts of a worksheet and display data in different ways. For example, we can use a different font or style to distinguish different categories of information in the worksheet. Try this:

1. Select A1:D1, the range that contains the headings.
2. Click the Bold button and then change the font size to 12.

As you know, by default Excel left-aligns text and right-aligns numeric values. We can override the default alignment by using the alignment buttons. Here's how:

1. With A1:D1 still selected, click the Align Right and Align Left buttons, noting their effects.
2. When you're ready, click the Center button, which is a typical choice for headings.

Changing the Display of Numbers

Earlier, we entered dates in column B in a variety of formats. Now we'll show you how to change the date format to reflect the needs of the worksheet. Follow the steps on the next page.

AutoFormats

An autoformat is a predefined combination of formatting that works well with certain kinds of worksheets. To apply an autoformat to a worksheet, first select the range of cells you want to format and choose the AutoFormat command from the Format menu. When the AutoFormat dialog box appears, select an option from the Table Format list (an example of your selection is displayed in the Sample box) and click OK. You can also customize an autoformat by clicking the Options button in the AutoFormat dialog box and selecting or deselecting the options in the Formats To Apply section. It's worth setting up a worksheet and experimenting with autoformats so that you know what is available and which kinds of worksheets can take advantage of this one-stop formatting feature.

Formatting dates

1. Use the mouse or keyboard to select the range B2:B13, which contains the dates.

2. Choose Cells from the Format menu to display this dialog box:

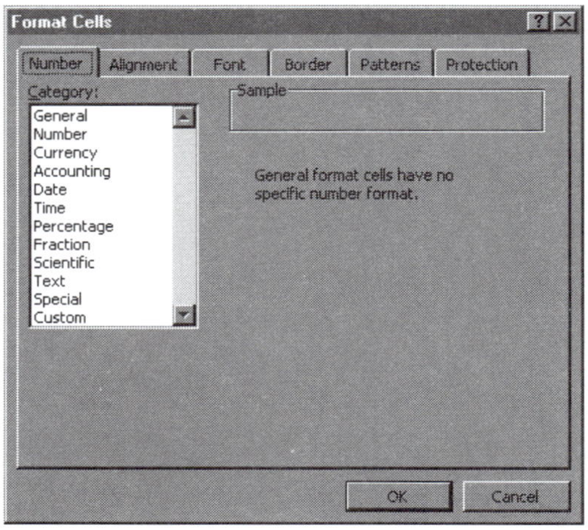

3. On the Number tab, select Date in the Category list, select 3/4/97 in the Type list, and click OK.

Next let's display the column D entries as currency:

Displaying numbers as currency

1. Select D2:D13, right-click the selection, and then choose Format Cells from the object menu to display the Format Cells dialog box.

2. On the Number tab, select Currency in the Category list.

3. Accept the default settings by clicking OK. (Don't worry if Excel replaces some entries with # signs; see the tip on page 86.)

Column width shortcuts

To adjust the width of a column to fit its longest entry, select the column and choose Column and then AutoFit Selection from the Format menu, or double-click the column header's right border. To change the standard width, choose Column and then Standard Width, type a new value in the Standard Column Width edit box, and click OK. (Columns whose widths you have already adjusted retain their custom widths, but all the other columns are now the new standard width.)

Changing Column Widths

As a finishing touch for this worksheet, let's adjust the widths of columns A, B, and D so that all the entries are visible and the headings fit neatly in their cells:

1. Move the mouse pointer to the dividing line between the headers of columns A and B. The pointer shape changes to a vertical bar with two opposing arrows.

2. Hold down the left mouse button and drag to the right until column A is wide enough to display the Job Number heading.

(As you drag, the width is displayed in a box above the pointer.) Release the mouse button when you think that the heading will fit.

3. Change the width of column B using the same method. Move the mouse pointer between the headers of columns B and C. Then hold down the mouse button and drag to the right until column B is wide enough to display its heading.

Now we'll widen column D using a different method:

1. Select D1 and choose Column and then Width from the Format menu. Excel displays this Column Width dialog box:

2. Type *20* and press Enter. Here are the results:

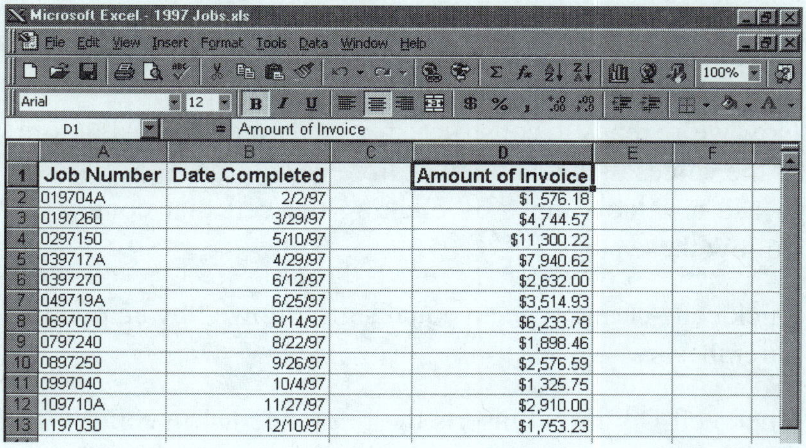

	A	B	C	D	E	F
1	Job Number	Date Completed		Amount of Invoice		
2	019704A	2/2/97		$1,576.18		
3	0197260	3/29/97		$4,744.57		
4	0297150	5/10/97		$11,300.22		
5	039717A	4/29/97		$7,940.62		
6	0397270	6/12/97		$2,632.00		
7	049719A	6/25/97		$3,514.93		
8	0697070	8/14/97		$6,233.78		
9	0797240	8/22/97		$1,898.46		
10	0897250	9/26/97		$2,576.59		
11	0997040	10/4/97		$1,325.75		
12	109710A	11/27/97		$2,910.00		
13	1197030	12/10/97		$1,753.23		

3. Save the worksheet.

We can adjust the height of rows the same way we adjust the width of columns. Simply drag the bottom border of the row header up or down or choose Row and then Height from the Format menu to make the row shorter or taller.

AutoComplete

You don't have to repeatedly type the same text entry in a column. When you type the same first character or two of the next entry in the same column, Excel's AutoComplete feature completes the entry for you. For example, if the entry in cell A1 is *North*, the instant you type *N* in cell A2, Excel enters *orth*. (You can either enter Excel's suggestion in the cell or continue typing your own entry.) You can also right-click the next cell in a column of text entries and choose Pick From List from the object menu to display a drop-down list of the entries you've already typed. You can then simply select the next entry from the list rather than typing it.

Simple Calculations

The whole purpose of building worksheets is to have Excel perform calculations for us. Excel has many powerful functions that are a sort of shorthand for various mathematical, logical, statistical, and financial calculations. However, the majority of worksheets involve simple arithmetic.

Doing Arithmetic

Formulas

In Excel, we begin a *formula* (Excel's term for an *equation*) with an equal sign (=). In the simplest formulas, the equal sign is followed by a set of values separated by +, –, *, or /, such as =5+3+2. If we enter this formula in any blank cell in the worksheet, Excel displays the result 10.

Let's experiment with a few formulas. We'll start by inserting a couple of blank rows:

Inserting multiple rows

1. Select the headers for rows 1 and 2 to select the two rows, and choose Rows from the Insert menu. Excel inserts two blank rows above the table, moving the table down so that it begins in row 3.

Now we're ready to construct a formula in cell A1, using some of the values in the Amount of Invoice column. We tell Excel to use a value simply by clicking the cell that contains it. Follow these steps:

1. Click cell A1 and type an equal sign followed by an opening parenthesis.
2. Click cell D4. Excel inserts the reference D4 in cell A1 and the formula bar.
3. Type a plus sign and click cell D5. Excel adds the reference D5 to the formula.
4. Continue to build the formula by typing plus signs and clicking cells D6, D7, and D8.
5. Type a closing parenthesis, type / (the division operator), and then type *5*. The formula now looks like this:

AutoCalculate

You can use the AutoCalculate area at the right end of the status bar to instantly see the results of certain functions. Right-click the AutoCalculate area to display a menu of functions, and choose the function you want. (The default function is SUM.) Next select a range of values on your worksheet. The result of the function you selected appears instantly in the AutoCalculate area. For example, if you choose the AVERAGE function and then select a range of values, the average of the values appears in the AutoCalculate area.

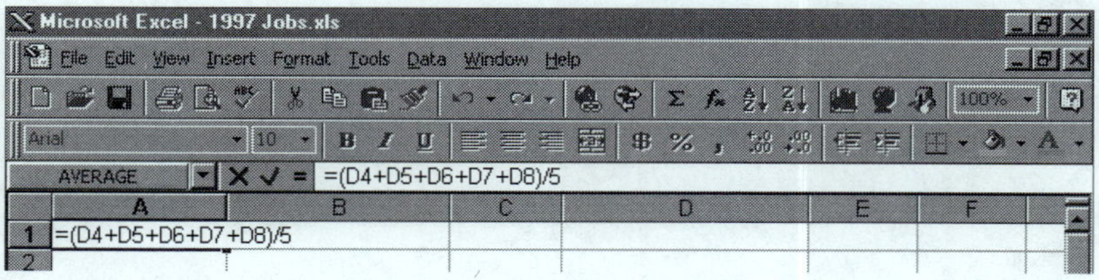

This formula tells Excel to first add the amounts in cells D4, D5, D6, D7, and D8 and then divide the result by 5, to obtain the average of the five amounts.

6. Click the Enter button. Excel displays the result of the formula, 5638.718, in cell A1.

We can use this technique to create any simple formula. Start by typing an equal sign, then enter a value or click the cell that contains the value, type the appropriate arithmetic operator, enter the next value, and so on. Unless we tell Excel to do otherwise, the program performs multiplication and division before addition and subtraction. If you need parts of the formula to be carried out in a different order, use parentheses as we did in this example to override the default order.

Order of precedence

Totaling Columns of Values

Although this method of creating a formula is simple enough, it would be tedious to have to type and click to add a long series of values. Fortunately, Excel automates the addition process with a very useful button: the AutoSum button.

Using the AutoSum Button

The AutoSum button will probably become one of your most often-used Excel buttons. In fact, using this button is so easy that we'll just show you what to do:

The AutoSum button

1. Click cell D16 and then click the AutoSum button. Excel looks first above and then to the left of the active cell for an adjacent range of values to total. Excel assumes that you want to total the values above D16 and enters the SUM function in cell D16 and in the formula bar. Your worksheet looks as shown on the next page.

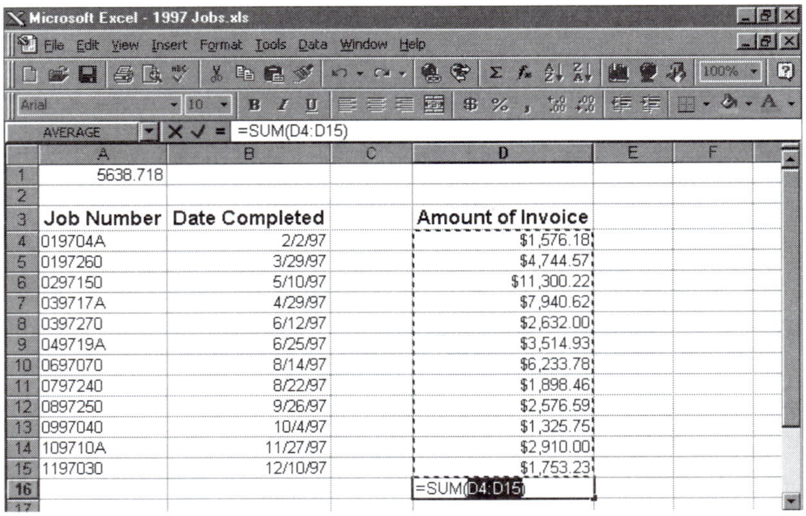

2. Click the Enter button to enter the formula in cell D16. Excel displays $48,406.33—the sum of the values in D4:D15.

That was easy. The AutoSum button serves us well whenever we want a total to appear at the bottom of a column or to the right of a row of values. But what if we want the total to appear elsewhere on the worksheet? Knowing how to create SUM functions from scratch gives us more flexibility.

Using the SUM Function

Let's go back and dissect the SUM function that Excel inserted in cell D16 when we clicked the AutoSum button so that we can examine the function's components.

With cell D16 selected, you can see the following entry in the formula bar:

=SUM(D4:D15)

Like all formulas, the SUM function begins with an equal sign (=). Next comes the function name in capital letters, followed by a set of parentheses enclosing the reference to the range containing the amounts we want to total. This reference is the SUM function's *argument*. An argument answers questions such as "What?" or "How?" and gives Excel the additional information it needs to perform the function. In the case of SUM, Excel needs only one piece of information—the references of the cells we want to total. As you'll see later, Excel

Displaying formulas

By default, Excel displays the results of formulas in cells, not their underlying formulas. To see the actual underlying formulas in the worksheet, choose Options from the Tools menu, display the View options, select Formulas in the Window Options section, and click OK. Excel widens the cells so that you can see the formulas. Simply deselect the Formulas option to redisplay the results.

might need several pieces of information to carry out other functions, and we enter an argument for each piece.

Creating a SUM function from scratch is not particularly difficult. For practice, follow these steps:

1. Press Ctrl+Home to move to cell A1 and type this:

   =SUM(

2. Select D4:D15 on the worksheet in the usual way. Excel inserts the reference D4:D15 after the opening parenthesis.
3. Type a closing parenthesis and click the Enter button. Excel displays in cell A1 the total of the values in the Amount of Invoice column—$48,406.33.

Referencing Formula Cells in Other Formulas

After we create a formula in one cell, we can use its result in other formulas simply by referencing its cell. Try this:

1. Select cell B1 and type an equal sign.
2. Click cell A1, which contains the SUM function you just entered, type / (the division operator), and then type *12*.
3. Click the Enter button. Excel displays the result—the average of the invoice amounts—in cell B1.
4. Press the Delete key to erase both the experimental formula and its result from cell B1.

Naming Cells and Ranges

Many of the calculations that we might want to perform on this worksheet will use the total we have calculated in cell A1. We could include a copy of the SUM function now in cell A1 in these other calculations, or we could simply reference cell A1. The latter method seems quick and simple, but what if we subsequently move the formula in A1 to another location? Excel gives us a way to reference this formula no matter where on the worksheet we move it. We can assign the contents of

Function names

When you type a function name, such as SUM, in the formula bar, you don't have to type it in capital letters. Excel capitalizes the function name for you when you complete the entry. If Excel does not respond in this way, you have probably entered the function name incorrectly.

cell A1 a name and then use the name in any calculations that involve the total.

We assign a name by using the Name command on the Insert menu. Follow these steps:

1. Select cell A1 and click the name box at the left end of the formula bar.
2. Type *Total* and press Enter. The name box to the left of the formula bar now refers to the cell by the name you just entered, instead of by the reference A1. You can use either designation in formulas.

To see how Excel uses assigned names, try this:

1. Click cell D16, which currently contains the SUM function you inserted earlier in the chapter.
2. Type =*Total* and click the Enter button. The worksheet does not appear to change, but now instead of two SUM functions, the worksheet contains only one. You have told Excel to assign the value of the cell named Total, which contains the SUM function, to cell D16.

Name conventions

Certain rules apply when you name cells or ranges. Names can have up to 255 characters and can include capital letters. Although you can use a number within the name, you must start the name with a letter or an underscore. Spaces are not allowed within the name; instead you should use underscore characters to represent spaces. For example, you cannot use 1997 or Totals 1997 as a name, but you can use Totals_1997. Cell references can't be used as names, and you can't have two names that are distinguished only by their capitalization.

We can also assign names to ranges. Let's use a different method to assign the name Amount to the cells containing amounts in column D:

1. Select D4:D15 and choose Name and then Define from the Insert menu. Excel displays the dialog box shown here:

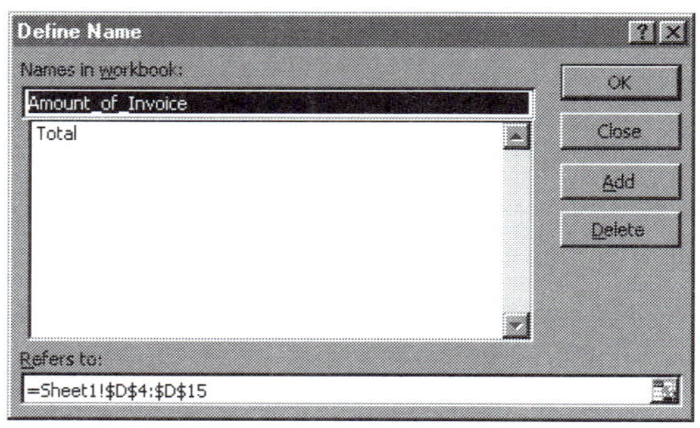

Notice that the Names In Workbook list now displays Total, the name you assigned earlier. The range reference

Sheet1!$D$4:$D$15 is displayed in the Refers To edit box. This absolute reference points to the selected range on Sheet1 of the current workbook. (For an explanation of absolute references, see page 118.)

2. Replace the name Excel suggests in the Names In Workbook edit box, Amount_of_Invoice, with *Amount* and click OK.

Now let's replace the range reference in the SUM function in cell A1 with the new range name:

1. Click A1 to select it and display its contents in the formula bar.
2. Drag through the D4:D15 reference in the formula bar to highlight it.
3. Choose Name and then Paste from the Insert menu to display this dialog box:

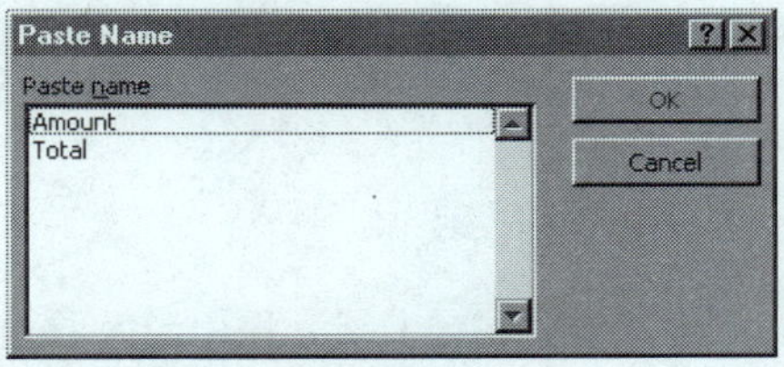

4. Click Amount and then click OK. Excel replaces the range reference with the assigned name, and the formula now reads *=SUM(Amount)*.
5. Click the Enter button to redisplay the results of the SUM function in A1.

Efficient Data Display

Usually when we create a worksheet, we are interested not so much in the individual pieces of information as in the results of the calculations we perform on the pieces. So before we discuss other calculations we might want to perform with this worksheet, let's look at ways to format our information to make the results of our calculations stand out from our data. It's a good idea to design worksheets so that the results are easily accessible and in a predictable location. For these

Calculation area advantages

Creating a calculation area at the top of your worksheet is a good habit to get into and offers the following advantages:

- You don't have to scroll around looking for the totals and other results.
- You can print just the first page of a worksheet to get a report of the most pertinent information.
- You can easily jump to the calculation area from anywhere on the worksheet by pressing Ctrl+Home to move to cell A1.

reasons, we leave room in the top left corner of our worksheets for a calculation area.

Let's create an area at the top of Sheet1 of the 1997 Jobs workbook for a title and a set of calculations. We'll start by freeing up some space at the top of the worksheet:

1. Select A1:D16 and click the Cut button.
2. Select A10 and click the Paste button to move the selection to A10:D25.

Now let's enter a title for the worksheet:

1. In cell A1, type *Preliminary Income Analysis* and click the Enter button.
2. Format the title by clicking the Bold button on the Formatting toolbar, and then clicking 10 in the Font Size box, typing *22*, and pressing Enter. The height of row 1 increases to accommodate the larger font.
3. In cell A2, type *1997* and click the Enter button.
4. Format the subtitle by clicking the Bold and Italic buttons and by selecting 14 from the Font Size list.

The Merge And Center button

5. To center the title above the calculation area, select A1:D1 and click the Merge And Center button. Excel centers the title over the selected area and merges the four cells, but the title is still stored in cell A1.
6. Repeat step 5 for the subtitle using the range A2:D2.

Next, we'll set off the calculation area. With Excel, we can get really fancy, using borders and shading to draw attention to calculation results. Try the following:

Adding a border

1. Select A1:D9 and choose Cells from the Format menu.
2. In the Format Cells dialog box, click the Border tab.
3. In the Line section, select the last option in the first column of the Style box, and then select Outline in the Presets section.

4. Finally, click the Patterns tab, select a light gray square in the color palette (we selected the last square in the fourth row), and click OK. Excel surrounds the calculation area with a border and fills it with a light gray shade.

Adding shading

Now that we've created a calculation area, let's move the calculation in cell A10. Follow these steps:

1. Select cell A4, type *Invoice Total*, and press Enter.
2. Select cell A10 and use the Cut and Paste buttons to move the formula to cell B4. (We'll show you how to quickly restore the gray shading to cell B4 in a moment.)

Moving formulas

Now let's add another touch:

1. Select A4:A9 and click the Bold button.

Preformatting cells

Why did we tell you to select the empty cells below Invoice Total before applying the Bold style? Try this:

2. Select cell A5, type *Average Invoice*, and click the Enter button. The new heading is bold because you already applied the Bold style to cell A5.
3. Choose Column and then AutoFit Selection from the Format menu to widen column A so that the headings fit within the column. From now on, adjust the column width as necessary to see your work.

We can also save time by applying number formats to empty cells. Here's how:

1. Select B4:B9 and choose Cells from the Format menu.
2. Click the Number tab, select Currency in the Category list, and select the third option in the Negative Numbers list. Be sure the Decimal Places setting is 2 and then click OK. Excel formats the selected cells with a dollar sign, a comma, and two decimal places.
3. To see the Currency format for negative values, select cell B5, type *–1234*, and click the Enter button. As you can see,

Underlying vs. displayed

After you apply a format, the value displayed in the cell might look different from the value in the formula bar. For example, 345.6789 is displayed in its cell as $345.68 after you apply the Currency format. When performing calculations, Excel uses the value in the formula bar, not the displayed value.

Excel displays the negative value in parentheses, aligning the value with the positive value above it.

The Format Painter button

4. With cell B5 selected, click the Format Painter button on the Standard toolbar and then click cell B4 to transfer the formatting of B5 to B4. Here's the result of all your formatting:

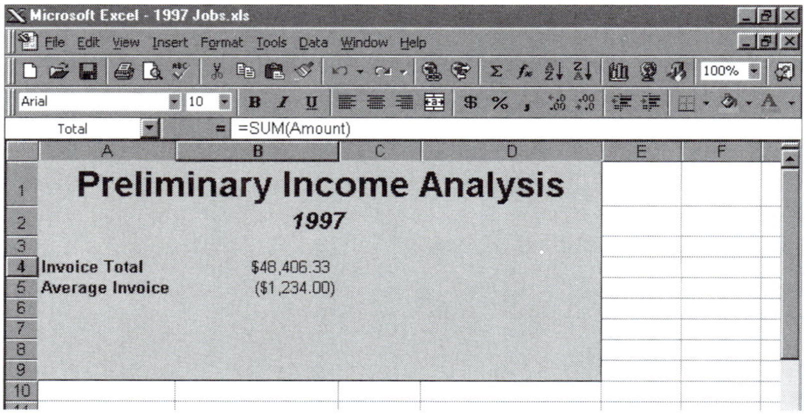

More Calculations

Now let's perform some more calculations on the data in 1997 Jobs, starting with the average invoice.

Averaging Values

To find the average amount for the invoices we've entered in this worksheet, we'll use Excel's AVERAGE function. We'll use the Paste Function button on the Standard toolbar to avoid errors, and to make sure we include all the arguments Excel needs for the function. Here are the steps:

The Paste Function button

1. Select cell B5, press Delete, and click the Paste Function button. Excel displays this Paste Function dialog box:

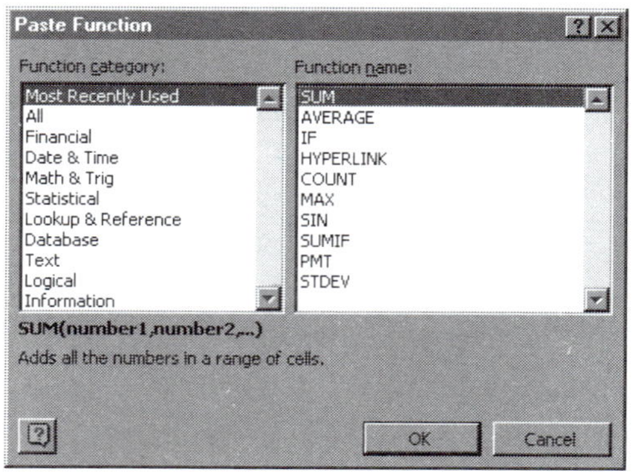

2. Select AVERAGE in the Function Name list and click OK. Excel displays this dialog box:

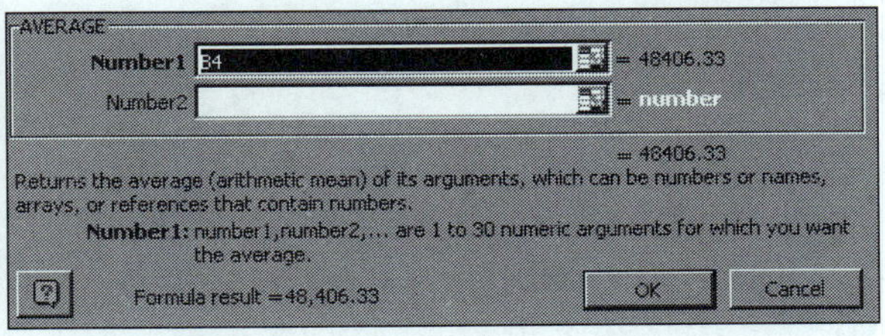

The dialog box contains a definition of the function and its arguments. In the Number1 edit box, you can enter a number, cell reference, name, formula, or another function.

3. Click the button with the red arrow at the right end of the Number1 edit box to shrink the dialog box. Then select D13:D24 in the worksheet to add its reference to the formula selection.

4. Click the button with the red arrow again to enlarge the dialog box, as shown here:

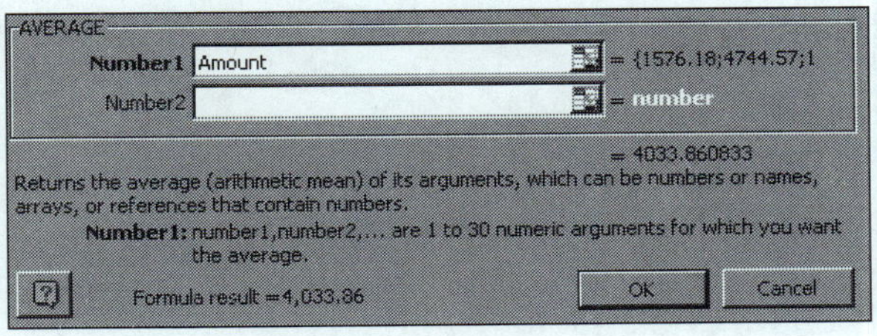

5. Click OK to enter the formula in cell B5 and press Ctrl+Home to see the results. Excel displays $4,033.86 in cell B5.

Identifying Largest and Smallest Invoices

Excel provides two functions that identify the largest and smallest values in a group. To understand the benefits of these functions, imagine that 1997 Jobs contains data from not 12 but 112 invoices! Let's start with the largest invoice:

1. Select cell A6, type *Largest Invoice*, and press the Tab key to confirm the entry and select cell B6.

2. Click the Edit Formula button on the formula bar (the equal sign to the left of the formula bar). Then click the arrow to the

Conditional formatting

To monitor the activity of a worksheet, you can use conditional formatting, which highlights a cell or cells that meet certain criteria. For example, you can change the color of the value in a particular cell to magenta when it falls between 100,000 and 200,000. To apply this type of formatting, first select the cell or cells and choose Conditional Formatting from the Format menu. In the Conditional Formatting dialog box, select a condition from the second drop-down list and enter the conditional parameters in the appropriate edit boxes. For example, select Between from the drop-down list and enter *100,000* and *200,000* in the adjacent edit boxes. Finally, click the Format button, select the formatting you want to use to highlight the cell (such as a color), and click OK twice. When the value in the selected cell meets the condition(s) you've set, Excel highlights the cell with the formatting you selected. To delete conditional formatting from a cell, select the cell and choose Conditional Formatting from the Format menu. Click the Delete button, select the condition you want to delete, and then click OK twice.

right of the function box, which has replaced the name box at the left end of the bar. Select MAX from the drop-down list.

3. Type *Amount* in the Number1 edit box and click OK. Excel enters the largest invoice amount, $11,300.22, in cell B6.

Now for the formula for the smallest invoice, which we'll type from scratch:

1. Select cell A7, type *Smallest Invoice*, and press Tab.
2. Type *=MIN(Amount)* and press Enter. Excel displays the result, $1,325.75, in cell B7.

Calculating with Names

The last calculation we'll make with this set of data involves the Invoice Total value from cell B4. As a gross indicator of how well Tip Top Roofing fared in 1997, let's calculate the estimated profit:

1. First insert a couple of new rows in the calculation area by dragging through the headers for rows 8 and 9 and choosing Rows from the Insert menu.
2. In cell A8, type *Profit Margin* and press Tab.
3. Type *20%* and click the Enter button.
4. With cell B8 still active, click the name box, type *Profit_Margin*, and press Enter.

Now for the formula that will calculate the profit margin:

1. Select cell A9, type *Estimated Profit* and press Tab.
2. With cell B9 selected, type the formula *=total*profit_margin* and press Enter. Excel multiplies the value in the cell named Total (B4) by the value in the cell named Profit_Margin (B8) and displays the result, $9,681.27, in cell B9. (Notice that Excel displays the result of the formula in the Currency format. When you inserted two rows earlier, those rows assumed the formatting of the selected rows.)

A function for every task

Excel provides many functions for common business and financial tasks—some of them quite complex. To get more information about a function, choose Contents And Index from the Help menu. Then type *worksheet functions* on the Index tab and double-click List Of to display the Topics Found dialog box, which lists categories of worksheet functions. Double-click the category you are interested in (such as About Financial Functions), scroll the Help window, and then click a specific function (such as RATE). Excel displays a description of the function, its syntax, and any other pertinent information.

3. Now select cell B8, type *25%*, and click the Enter button. Instantly, the value in cell B9 changes to reflect the new profit margin, as shown here:

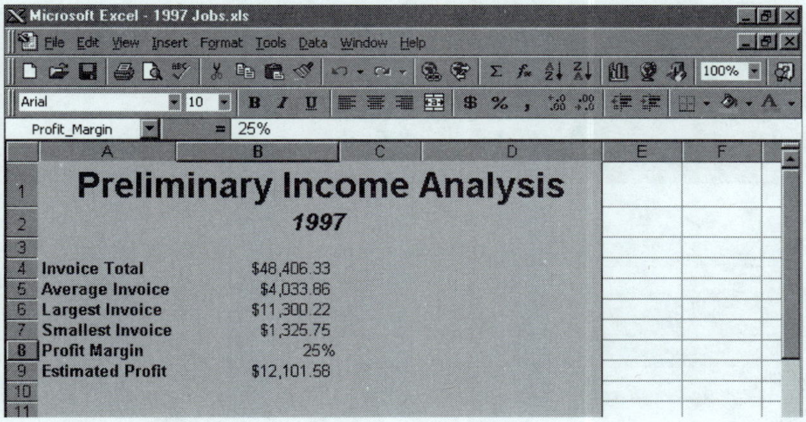

If a hundred calculations throughout the worksheet referenced the cell named Profit_Margin, Excel would adjust all their results to reflect this one change!

Printing Worksheets

Usually, we'll want to preview worksheets before we print them to make sure that single-page documents fit neatly on the page and that multipage documents break in logical places. Follow these steps to preview the worksheet:

1. Click the Print Preview button on the Standard toolbar. The Print Preview window opens, with a miniature version of the printed worksheet displayed.

2. To examine part of the page in more detail, move the pointer over that part, and when the pointer changes to a magnifying glass, click the mouse button. Excel zooms in on that portion of the page. Click again to zoom out.

By default, when Excel prints a worksheet, it does not print any header or footer text. We can add a header and footer by opening the Page Setup dialog box. Follow the steps on the next page.

1. Click the Setup button on the Print Preview toolbar to display the Page Setup dialog box. (When you're not in print preview, you can access this dialog box by choosing Page Setup from the File menu.)
2. Click the Header/Footer tab to display these options:

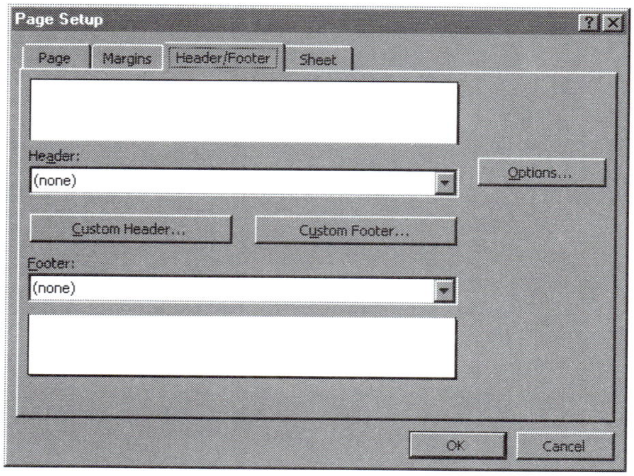

3. Click the Custom Header button to display the Header dialog box shown here:

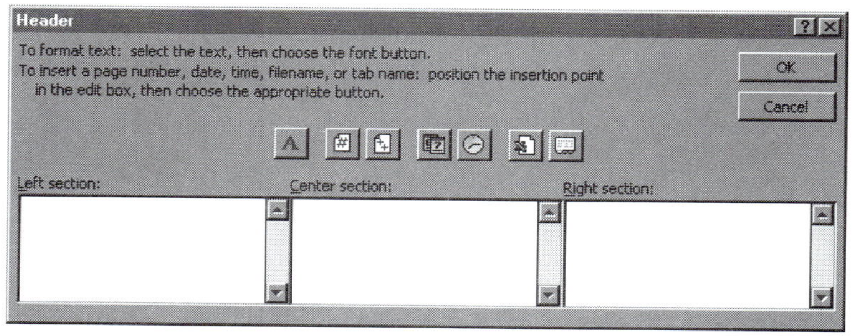

To add a header, you enter text and codes in the appropriate boxes and click the buttons in the middle of the dialog box. (For a list of header and footer codes, see the adjacent tip.)

4. Click an insertion point in the Center Section box and type *&b1997 Job Log*. The &b code tells Excel the text is bold.
5. Click OK to return to the Header/Footer tab.
6. Now click the Margins tab of the Page Setup dialog box to display these options:

Header and footer codes

The buttons in the Header and Footer dialog boxes add codes that do the following:

&[Page]	Adds current page number
&[Pages]	Inserts total number of pages
&[Date]	Adds current date
&[Time]	Adds current time
&[File]	Adds filename
&[Tab]	Adds sheet name

Here are some formatting codes:

&b	Prints following characters in bold
&i	Italicizes following characters
&u	Underlines following characters

You can also format headers and footers by selecting the text you want to format and clicking the Font button (the capital A).

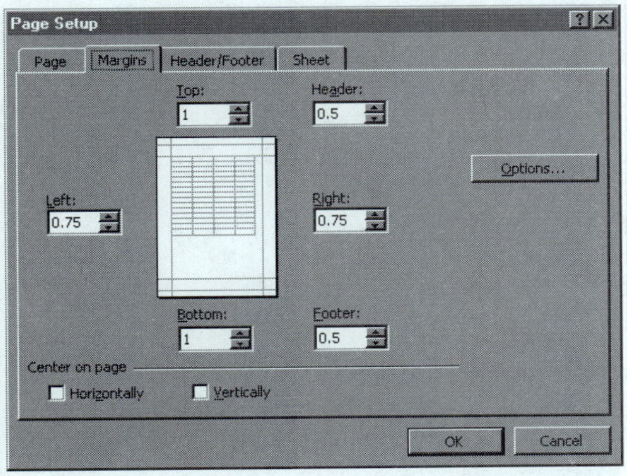

7. In the Center On Page section, click Horizontally to center the worksheet horizontally on the page. The worksheet diagram shows you the effects of your changes.

Centering on the page

8. Click OK to enter your selections. Here's the finished product:

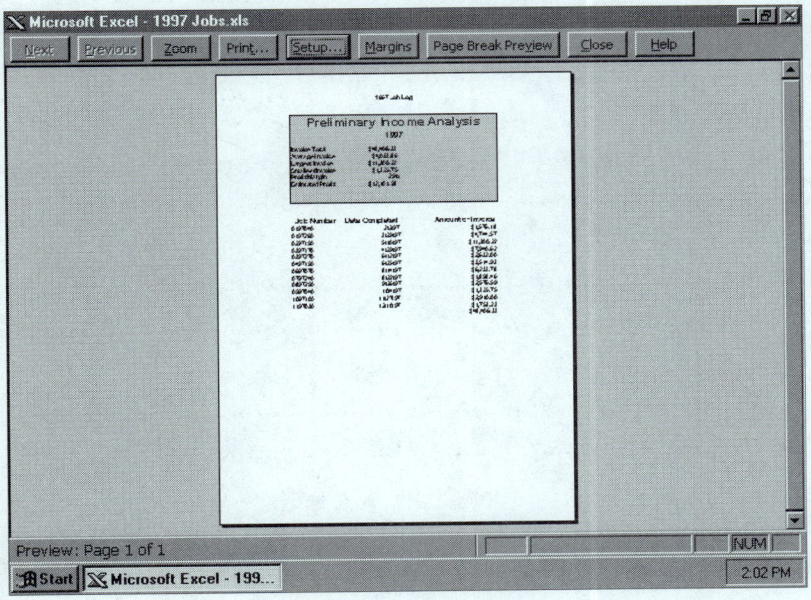

9. When you're ready, click the Print button on the Print Preview toolbar and then click OK in the Print dialog box to print the worksheet.

10. Save the workbook and quit Excel.

5

More About Excel

1997 Job Log

Preliminary Income Analysis

1997

Invoice Total	$48,406.33
Average Invoice	$4,033.86
Largest Invoice	$11,300.22
Smallest Invoice	$1,325.75
Profit Margin	25%
Estimated Profit	$12,101.58

Consolidate data in a worksheet by category

Quarter	Amount of Invoice
1	$1,576.18
1	$4,744.57
2	$11,300.22
2	$7,940.62
2	$2,632.00
2	$3,514.93
3	$6,233.78
3	$1,898.46
3	$2,576.59
4	$1,325.75
4	$2,910.00
4	$1,753.23
	$48,406.33

Change an invoice amount, and links update the other sheets

Quarterly

Quarter	Total
1	$6,320.75
2	$25,387.77
3	$10,708.83
4	$5,988.98

Annual

1997 INCOME

	1st Quarter	2nd Quarter	3rd Quarter	4th Quarter	Total
Income	$6,320.75	$25,387.77	$10,708.83	$5,988.98	$48,406.33
Expenses	$5,372.64	$21,579.60	$9,102.51	$5,090.63	$41,145.38
Net Income	$948.11	$3,808.17	$1,606.32	$898.35	$7,260.95

Link quarterly income amounts to quarterly consolidations

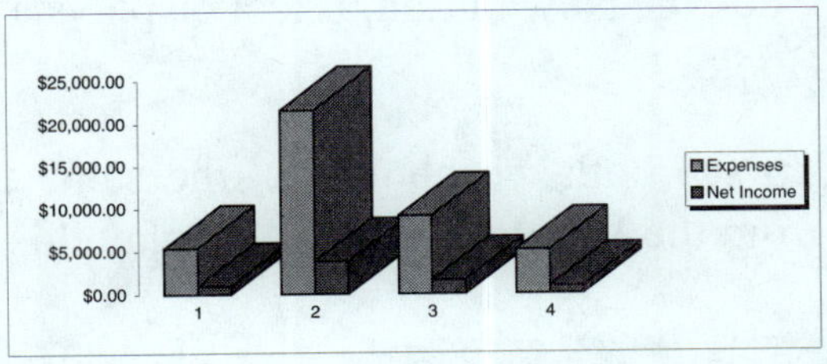

Create an embedded graph that is also linked to the source invoice data

We covered a lot of important ground in Chapter 4, and you now have a feel for some of the power of Excel. In this chapter, we introduce you to more Excel techniques, such as how to work with multiple workbooks and how to create a link between two worksheets. We also give you lessons in consolidating and graphing.

Working with Workbooks

In Chapter 4, we moved a range between two worksheets. Excel also allows us to transfer data between two workbooks to compare the information in one workbook with that in another. For example, if Tip Top Roofing kept their 1997 invoice analysis in one workbook and their 1998 invoice analysis in another workbook, they could quickly determine which year was more profitable by simply opening both workbooks side by side on the same screen.

Let's start by opening an existing workbook and a new one:

1. Start Excel, click the Open button on the Standard toolbar, and double-click 1997 Jobs to open that workbook. Because you have made no changes to the default Book1 workbook, Excel automatically closes it.
2. Click the New button. Excel displays a new workbook called Book2.
3. To see both workbooks at the same time, choose Arrange from the Window menu to display this dialog box:

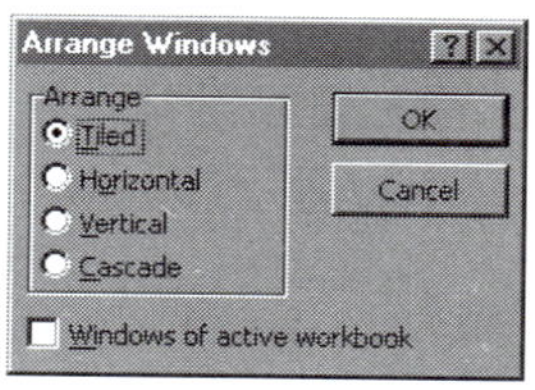

4. Click OK to accept the default Tiled option. Excel arranges Book2 and 1997 Jobs side by side on your screen.

Copying sheets

You can copy a sheet within your current workbook or to another workbook. Select the sheet you want to copy and choose Move Or Copy Sheet from the Edit menu. In the To Book edit box of the Move Or Copy dialog box, specify the destination workbook. In the Before Sheet box, select the sheet that will follow the copied sheet. Then select the Create A Copy option and click OK.

Copying Entries Between Workbooks

In addition to using the Copy and Paste buttons (or the Copy and Paste commands) to copy information between workbooks, you can also use drag-and-drop editing. Try the following:

1. Activate 1997 Jobs by clicking its title bar.
2. Select A14:D26 and point to any border of the selection. (We scrolled the window and pointed to the top border.)
3. Hold down the Ctrl key and the left mouse button (a plus sign appears next to the pointer). Then drag the outline of the selection until it is over the range A1:D13 in Book2.
4. Release both the Ctrl key and the mouse button. Here's the result:

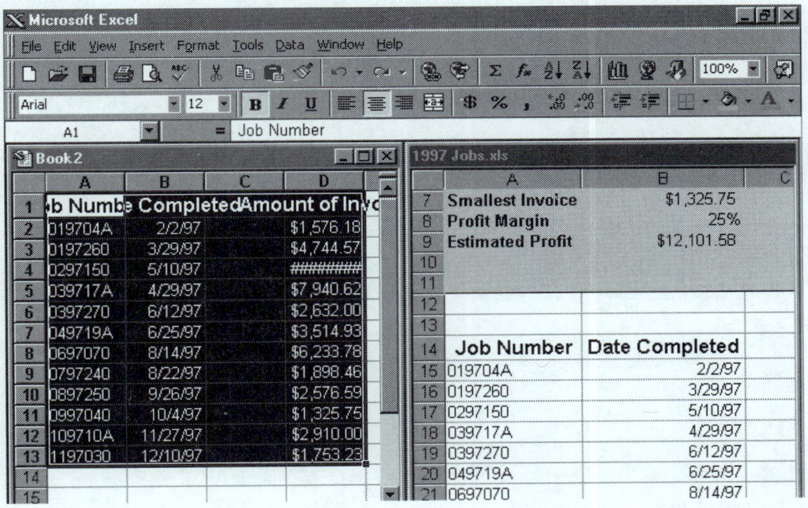

To move rather than copy entries between workbooks, you simply hold down the left mouse button.

5. Press Ctrl+Home to move to cell A1.

Moving Sheets Between Workbooks

A sheet can easily be moved within a workbook or from one workbook to another. For this example, we'll move a worksheet from Book2 to 1997 Jobs, but first let's rename a couple of the worksheet tabs so that we can easily identify the worksheet we're going to move. Follow the steps on the next page.

Renaming sheets

1. Activate the 1997 Jobs window and then double-click the Sheet1 tab to select its name.

2. Type *Invoices 1997* and press Enter. Excel displays the new name on the tab.

3. Activate the Book2 window, double-click the Sheet1 tab, and enter *Invoices 1998* as the name.

Moving sheets

4. Point to the Invoices 1998 tab and hold down the left mouse button. The pointer becomes an arrow with a sheet attached to it.

5. Drag the sheet pointer until it sits between Invoices 1997 and Sheet2 of the 1997 Jobs workbook. Excel indicates with an arrowhead where it will place the selected sheet.

6. Release the mouse button. The Invoices 1998 sheet now appears in 1997 Jobs, as shown here:

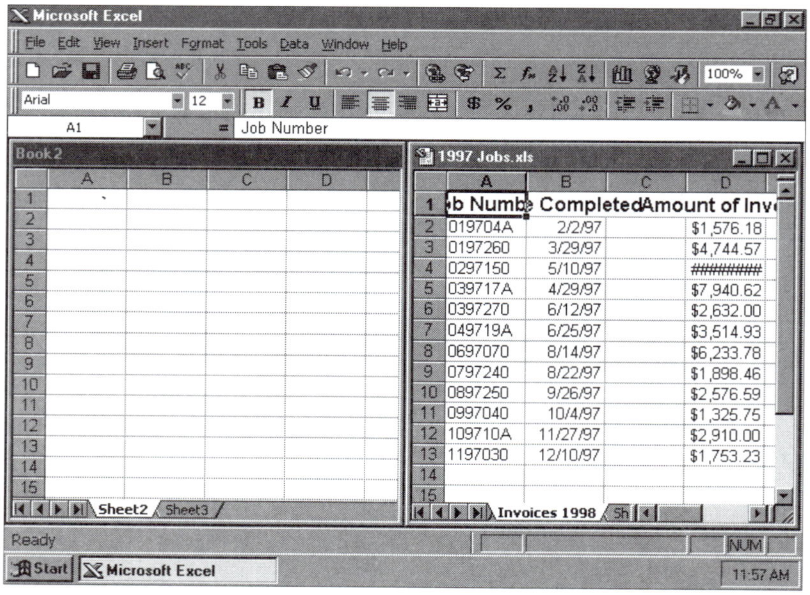

Deleting Sheets

Before deleting a sheet from a workbook, you should always display it. Excel permanently deletes the sheet, so it is wise to do a quick visual confirmation before sending a sheet into oblivion. In this example, we'll delete the sheet we just moved to 1997 Jobs and then close Book2. Follow these steps:

1. With the Invoices 1998 sheet active, choose the Delete Sheet command from the Edit menu. Excel warns you that the sheet will be permanently deleted.

2. Click OK. Excel removes the Invoices 1998 sheet from the 1997 Jobs workbook.

3. Activate Book2 and close it by clicking the Close button at the right end of Book2's title bar. When Excel asks whether you want to save your changes to Book2, click No.

4. Maximize the 1997 Jobs window, display the Invoices 1997 worksheet (if necessary, click the Previous Sheet button—see the tip on page 83), and press Ctrl+Home.

Formulas That Make Decisions

There will be times when we want Excel to carry out one task under certain circumstances and another task if those circumstances don't apply. To give this kind of instruction to Excel, we use the IF function.

In its simplest form, the IF function tests the value of a cell and does one thing if the test is positive (true) and another if the test is negative (false). It requires three arguments: the test, the action to perform if the test is true, and the action to perform if the test is false. We supply the arguments one after the other within the function's parentheses, separating them with commas (no spaces). Try this:

1. Select cell D4, type the following, and then press Enter:

   =IF(B4=0,"TRUE","FALSE")

   Excel checks whether the value in cell B4 is zero (the test), and because it isn't zero, it ignores TRUE (the action to perform if the test is true) and displays FALSE (the action to perform if the test is false) in cell D4.

2. Double-click cell D4, drag through *=0* to highlight it, type *<100000*, and press Enter. The entry in cell D4 instantly changes from FALSE to TRUE because the value in cell B4 is less than one hundred thousand; that is, the test is true.

Text values as arguments

When entering text values as arguments in a formula, you must enclose them in quotation marks. Otherwise, Excel thinks the text is a name and displays an error message. For example,

=RIGHT("Excel",2)

gives the value "el," but

=RIGHT(Excel,2)

results in an error—unless the name Excel happens to be assigned to a cell on the worksheet.

In this example, the test Excel performed was a simple evaluation of the value in a cell. However, we can also build tests that involve other functions. Suppose that the last character of the job numbers in column A of the worksheet indicates whether the roofing job is a contract (A) or subcontract (0) job, and we want to assign Contract and Subcontract entries to each job number so that we can compare the contributions of the two types of jobs to the Tip Top Roofing income. Follow these steps:

1. Delete the entry in D4.
2. Insert a new column between columns A and B by selecting B3:B26 and choosing Columns from the Insert menu. (The first two cells in column B have been merged to accommodate the title and subtitle, so you must exclude those cells.)
3. Enter the heading *Type of Job* in cell B14. Then use the Cut, Paste, and Format Painter buttons to restore the entries now in C4:C9 to B4:B9.
4. Select cell B15, type the following, and click the Enter button:

   =IF(RIGHT(A15,1)="A","Contract","Subcontract")

   You have told Excel to look at the character at the right end of the value in cell A15 and if it is A, to enter *Contract* in cell B15. If it is not A, Excel is to enter *Subcontract*. Here is the result:

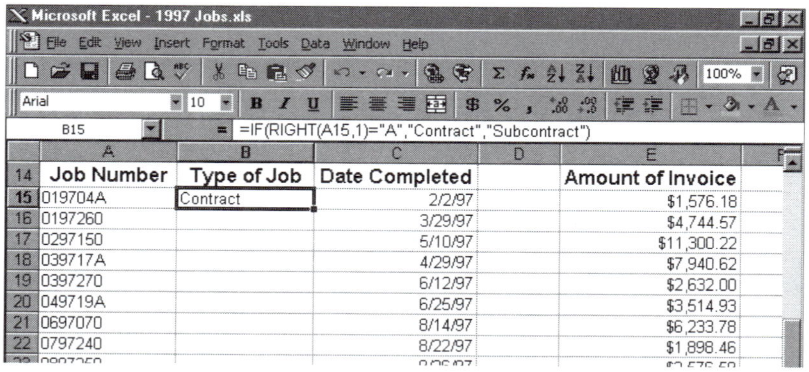

Using Nested IF Functions

When constructing decision-making formulas, we can use IF functions within IF functions. Called *nested functions*, they

Logical operators

Here is a list of operators you can use with the IF function:

= <> <> >= <=

You can also use AND and OR to combine two or more tests. The function

=IF(AND(B4=0,B5>0),"Yes","No")

displays Yes only if both tests are true. The function

=IF(OR(B4=0,B5>0),"Yes","No")

displays Yes if either test is true.

add another dimension to the complexity of the decisions Excel can make. Here's a quick demonstration:

1. Select cell D14 and enter the column heading *Quarter*.
2. Select column D, choose Cells from the Format menu, and double-click General on the Number tab of the Format Cells dialog box.
3. Now select cell D15 and type this formula all on one line:

   =IF(MONTH(C15)<4,1,IF(MONTH(C15)<7,2,
   IF(MONTH(C15)<10,3,4)))
4. Check your typing, paying special attention to all the parentheses, and then click the Enter button.

You have told Excel to check the month component of the date in cell C15. If it is less than 4 (that is, before April), Excel is to display 1 in the corresponding cell in the Quarter column. If the month is not less than 4 but is less than 7 (that is, before July), Excel is to display 2 in the Quarter column. If it is not less than 7 but is less than 10 (that is, before October), Excel is to display 3. Otherwise, Excel is to display 4. If you have typed the formula correctly, Excel enters 1 in cell D15.

Copying Formulas

The IF functions we just entered are arduous to type, even for good typists. Fortunately, we don't have to enter them more than once. By using AutoFill, we can copy the formula into the cells below, like this:

1. Select B15 and position the pointer over the bottom right corner of the cell. The pointer changes to the black fill handle.
2. Hold down the mouse button and drag down to cell B26. Excel copies the formula from B15 into the highlighted cells.
3. Select cell D15, point to the bottom right corner of the cell, hold down the mouse button, and drag down to cell D26. The worksheet now looks like the one on the next page.

The Fill command

You can use the Fill command to copy entries into a range of adjacent cells. Select the cell(s) whose contents and formats you want to copy, drag through the adjacent range, and choose Fill from the Edit menu. How Excel copies the cell(s) is determined by the shape of the selection and the command you choose from the Fill submenu. For example, selecting cells below an entry and choosing Down copies the entry down a range; selecting cells to the right of an entry and choosing Right copies the entry to the right; and so on. Three related commands are also available on this submenu: Across Worksheets copies entries to the equivalent cells on a group of selected worksheets (to select the worksheets, hold down Ctrl and click each sheet's tab); Series fills the selection with a series of values or dates; and Justify distributes the contents of the active cell(s) evenly in the cells of the selected range.

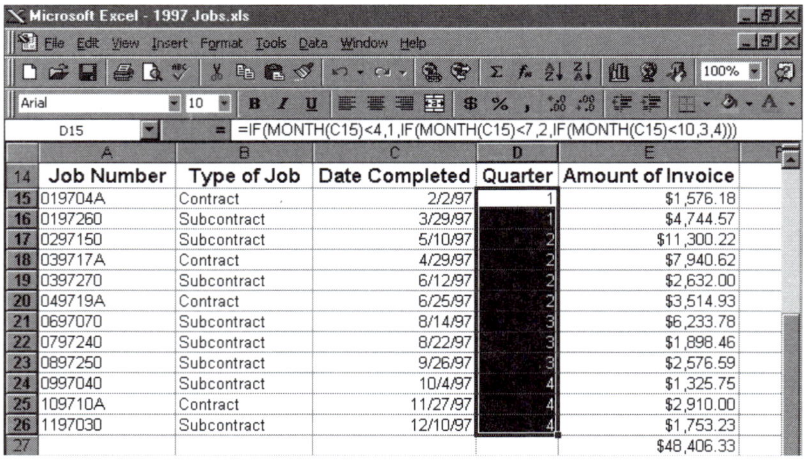

4. Select cell B16 and look at the formula in the formula bar. Excel has changed the original formula

=IF(RIGHT(A15,1)="A","Contract","Subcontract")

to

=IF(RIGHT(A16,1)="A","Contract","Subcontract")

Excel changed the reference so that it refers to cell A16 as its argument, not A15. Why?

Relative references

By default, Excel uses *relative references* in its formulas. Relative references refer to cells by their position in relation to the cell containing the formula. So when we copied the formula in cell B15 to cell B16, Excel changed the reference from A15 to A16—the cell in the same row and one column to the left of the cell containing the formula. If we were to copy the formula in cell B15 to E15, Excel would change the reference from A15 to D15 so that the formula would continue to reference the cell in the same relative position.

Absolute references

When we don't want a reference to be copied as a relative reference, as it was in the examples, we need to use an *absolute reference*. Absolute references refer to cells by their fixed position in the worksheet. To make a reference absolute, we add dollar signs before its column letter and row number. For example, to change the reference C4:C9 to an absolute reference, we would enter it as \$C\$4:\$C\$9. We could then copy a formula that contained this reference anywhere on the worksheet and it would always refer to the range C4:C9.

Mixed references

References can also be partially relative and partially absolute. For example, $C3 has an absolute column reference and a relative row reference, and C$3 has a relative column reference and an absolute row reference.

Consolidating Data

We can use Excel's Consolidate command to summarize data in a variety of ways. In this section, we'll show you how to use the Consolidate command to total the invoice amounts in 1997 Jobs by quarter, enter the totals in a separate worksheet, and create a link between the totals and their source data. Follow these steps:

1. First name the destination worksheet by double-clicking the Sheet2 tab in 1997 Jobs, typing *Quarterly* as the name, and pressing Enter.
2. In cell A1 of the Quarterly sheet, type *Quarter*, and in cell B1, type *Total*. Make the headings bold, size 12, and centered.

Now for the consolidation:

1. Select cell A2 in the Quarterly sheet and choose Consolidate from the Data menu to display this dialog box:

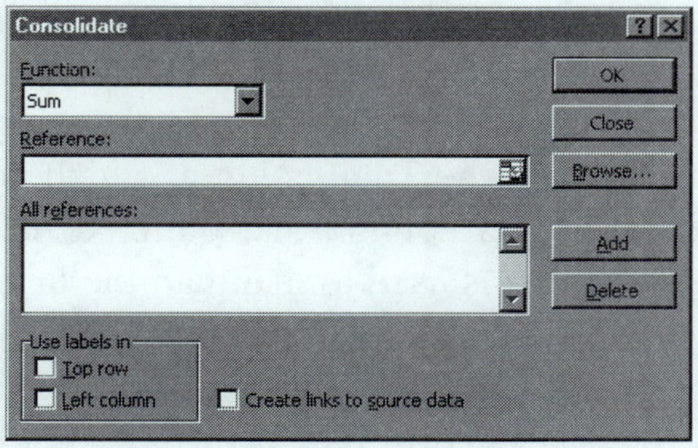

2. Click the Invoices 1997 tab to move to the source worksheet. Excel enters the name of the worksheet in the dialog box.

3. Click the button with the red arrow (at the right end of the Reference edit box) to shrink the Consolidate dialog box, and then select D15:E26. Excel enters an absolute reference to the selected range in the dialog box.

4. Click the button with the red arrow again to redisplay the entire dialog box.

5. If Sum does not already appear in the Function edit box, select it from the Function drop-down list.

6. In the Use Labels In section, select the Left Column option to tell Excel to use the entries in the Quarter column as labels in the destination worksheet. (Excel returns you to the Quarterly sheet at this point.)

7. Select the Create Links To Source Data option to link the data in the Quarterly sheet to the data in the Invoices 1997 sheet, and then click OK to perform the consolidation. Here are the results after we widen columns A and C:

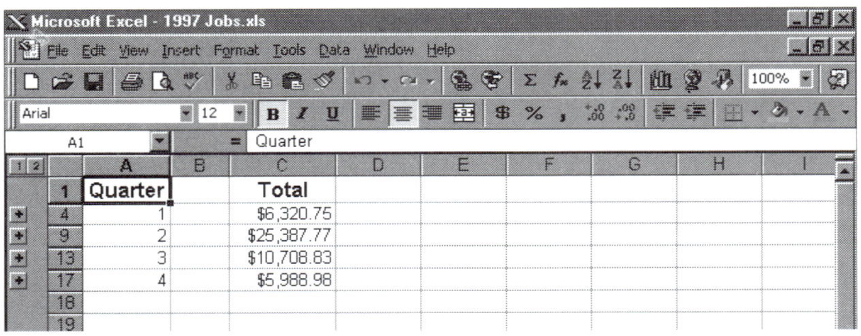

As you can see, Excel enters the column labels in the Quarter column and the quarter totals in the Total column, which is now column C. Excel inserted a column and outlined the worksheet to hide the mechanisms used to maintain the link between the totals and their source data. (The topic of outlining is beyond the scope of this book, but if you're interested, you might want to read the adjacent tip.) When you have time, you can practice consolidating data from several worksheets and use some of the other functions available in the Consolidate dialog box. In the meantime, let's use the consolidated quarterly totals in another worksheet.

Outlining worksheets

Excel's outlining feature lets you view as little or as much of a worksheet as you want to see. To outline a worksheet, select all the cells containing data and choose Group And Outline and then Auto Outline from the Data menu. Excel searches for what it considers to be the most important information (for example, the totals) and uses this information to create different row and column outline levels. Initially, an outlined worksheet displays all its levels. You use the Row Level buttons and Column Level buttons in the top left corner of the window to expand and collapse the outline. For example, clicking the 2 Row Level button displays only the first and second levels and hides any lower levels. You can also click the Hide Detail buttons (marked with minus signs) above and to the left of the worksheet to collapse an outline level. Excel deduces that the last row or column of a section is the "bottom line" of the collapsed section and displays only that row or column. Conversely, you can click the Show Detail buttons (marked with plus signs) to expand collapsed levels. Choose Group And Outline and then Clear Outline to exit outline mode.

Setting Up a Summary Income Statement

Before we can move on, we need to set up the following summary income statement for Tip Top Roofing:

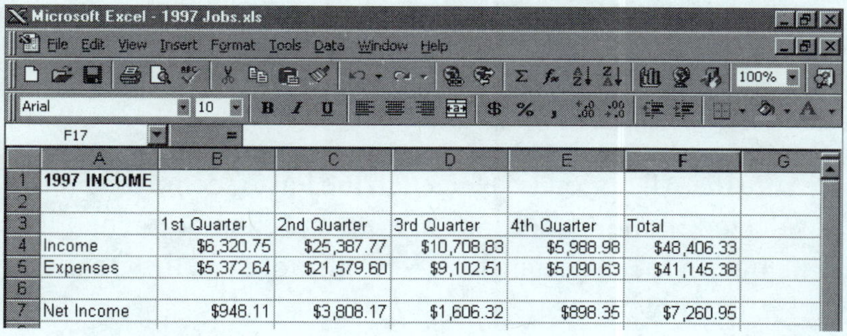

	A	B	C	D	E	F	G
1	**1997 INCOME**						
2							
3		1st Quarter	2nd Quarter	3rd Quarter	4th Quarter	Total	
4	Income	$6,320.75	$25,387.77	$10,708.83	$5,988.98	$48,406.33	
5	Expenses	$5,372.64	$21,579.60	$9,102.51	$5,090.63	$41,145.38	
6							
7	Net Income	$948.11	$3,808.17	$1,606.32	$898.35	$7,260.95	

Follow these steps:

1. Double-click the Sheet3 tab of 1997 Jobs and enter *Annual* as the sheet name.
2. In cell A1, type *1997 INCOME*, click the Enter button to enter the title, and click the Bold button to make the title bold.
3. In cell B3, type *1st Quarter* and click the Enter button. Using AutoFill, drag the fill handle to cell E3 (see page 117 and the adjacent tip for more information about AutoFill). Excel fills C3:E3 with the labels 2nd Quarter, 3rd Quarter, and 4th Quarter. Enter *Total* in cell F3 and *Income* in cell A4.
4. Select A3:F4, choose Cells from the Format menu, and double-click General on the Number tab.

To link the quarter totals on the Quarterly sheet to those on the Annual sheet, follow these steps:

1. Click the Quarterly tab, select C4 (the first quarter total), and click the Copy button.
2. Click the Annual tab, select B4, and choose Paste Special from the Edit menu to display the dialog box shown on the next page.

More about AutoFill

You can copy information from one area of your worksheet to an adjacent area using three methods: AutoFill, dragging, and copy and paste. These methods produce similar results unless the entry you are copying contains a number that can be incremented, such as in the 1st Quarter heading, or the cell contains an entry from a custom list. If the cell contains a number that can be incremented, using AutoFill copies the entry and increments the number—for example, 1st Quarter becomes 2nd Quarter, 3rd Quarter, and so on. If the cell contains an entry from a custom list, using AutoFill fills the cells with other entries from that list. You define a custom list by choosing Options from the Tools menu, clicking the Custom Lists tab, clicking NEW LIST in the Custom Lists box, and typing the list's entries in the List Entries box. After you click OK, you can enter the list in consecutive cells of any worksheet by typing one of the entries and dragging the fill handle. This feature is invaluable if you frequently create worksheets involving lists of the same entries, such as part numbers or employee names.

Excel templates

Excel offers several templates that you can use to create documents such as invoices and purchase orders. To open a template, choose New from the File menu, click the Spreadsheet Solutions tab of the New dialog box, and double-click a template icon. (If you performed a Typical installation, you may need to run Setup again to install all of Excel's templates.) If the template contains Excel macros, a dialog box may appear, asking you to enable them. (This precaution protects you against macro viruses that may infect workbooks obtained from unreliable sources.) After the template opens, you can use the buttons on the template's toolbar to help you complete the document. (You can even click the Display Example/Remove Example button to see an example of a completed document.) In addition, you can point to one of the red markers on the template to get help with a particular item. If you want to customize a template—add a company logo or address, for example—click the Customize button in the top right corner of the template, and when the Customize Your Invoice sheet opens, enter the information you want to include in your custom template. To save a custom template, click the Lock/Save Sheet button, select the Lock And Save Template option, and click OK. Then enter a name for your template in the Save Template dialog box and click Save.

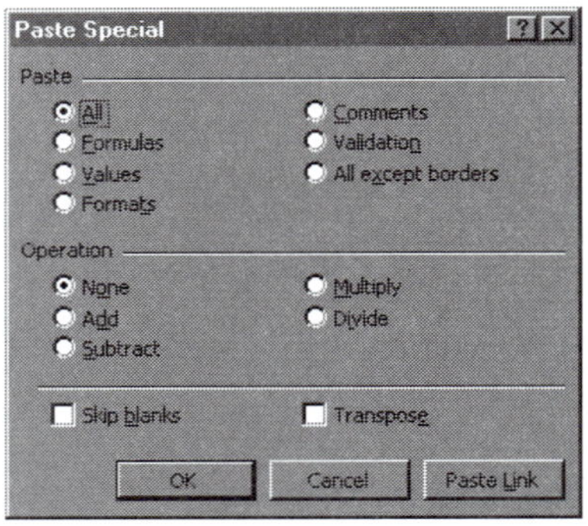

3. Be sure the All option is selected in the Paste section and None is selected in the Operation section, and then click the Paste Link button to create a link between the totals in the Quarterly and Annual worksheets.
4. Repeat steps 1 through 3 for the 2nd, 3rd, and 4th Quarter totals in the Annual sheet.

Let's tackle the expenses by following these steps:

1. Enter the following information in the indicated cells:

A5	*Expenses*
A7	*Net Income*
B5	*= .85*B4*

2. Select B4:F7 and assign the Currency format (see page 94).
3. Use AutoFill to copy the formula in cell B5 to C5:E5.
4. Widen column A so that all its labels fit. Then drag through the headers for columns B through F, choose Column and Width from the Format menu, type *12* in the Column Width edit box, and click OK. The selected columns take on the new width.

Now, let's compute the Total column and Net Income row:

1. Select cell F4, click the AutoSum button, and click the Enter button.
2. Use AutoFill to copy the formula in cell F4 to cell F5.
3. In cell B7, type *=B4–B5* and click the Enter button. Excel enters the result, $948.11 as the 1st Quarter's net income.
4. Use AutoFill to copy the formula in cell B7 to C7:F7.

Voila! Your worksheet should look like the one shown earlier.

Testing Links

Earlier, when we consolidated the quarter totals, we created a link between the Quarterly sheet and the Invoices 1997 sheet. In the previous section, we used the Paste Special command to create a link between the Annual sheet and the Quarterly sheet. With these links in place, we can change the data in the original source worksheet—the Invoices 1997 sheet—and Excel will automatically update the data in the destination worksheets—the Quarterly and Annual sheets. To test the links we created, try the following:

1. Click the Invoices 1997 tab, select E22, type *100000*, and click the Enter button. The total in cell E27 is $146,507.87.
2. Next click the Quarterly tab and, if necessary, widen column C. The third quarter total in cell C13 is now $108,810.37.
3. Finally, click the Annual tab and note the changes Excel has made in the summary income statement.

As you can see, creating links between worksheets can really save us time because when we update the source worksheet, Excel updates any linked worksheets for us. Obviously, links help cut down on typographical errors, too.

Creating Graphs

Excel shares the graphing program, Microsoft Graph, with the other members of Microsoft Office. If you're new to Graph, this section will serve as a good introduction to the features and flexibility of this graphing program.

With Excel, we can create graphs in three ways: on the current worksheet, as a separate sheet in the current workbook, or in another workbook. In this section, we show you how to quickly plot a graph on the current worksheet. The advantage of this method is that we can then print the graph and the underlying worksheet on the same page. Let's create a column graph based on the income and expenses data in the Annual sheet by following the steps on the next page.

Noncontiguous ranges

1. Select A5:E5 in the Annual sheet. Then hold down the Ctrl key and select A7:E7.

The Chart Wizard button

2. Click the Chart Wizard button to display the first of four dialog boxes that lead you through the process of creating and customizing a graph. (If the Office Assistant appears, click its Close button.)

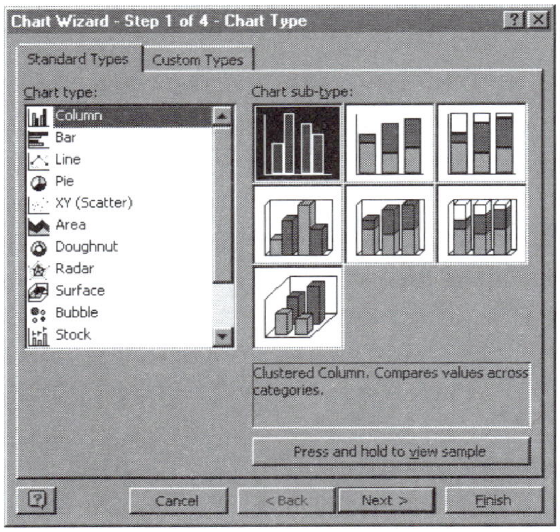

3. Select 3-D Clustered Column as the graph type (the first option in the second row) and click Next to display this dialog box:

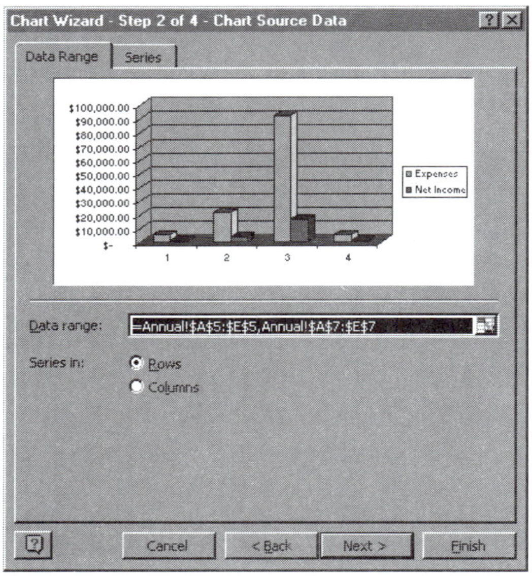

Graph displays how the selected range will look as a graph, with all labels and other information in place.

Creating graphs on chart sheets

To create a graph on a separate chart sheet, first select the data and then click the Chart Wizard button. Build the graph in the Chart Wizard's dialog boxes as usual. When you reach the fourth Chart Wizard dialog box, select the As New Sheet option and click Finish. Excel places a sheet named Chart1 in front of the worksheet containing the selected data and plots a graph on the Chart1 sheet. To quickly build a graph in the default format on a separate chart sheet, simply select the worksheet data you want to plot and press the F11 key.

4. Accept the default settings and move to the third dialog box by clicking Next. (At any point, you can click the Back button to move back to a previous dialog box, so you can always select a different format if you change your mind.)

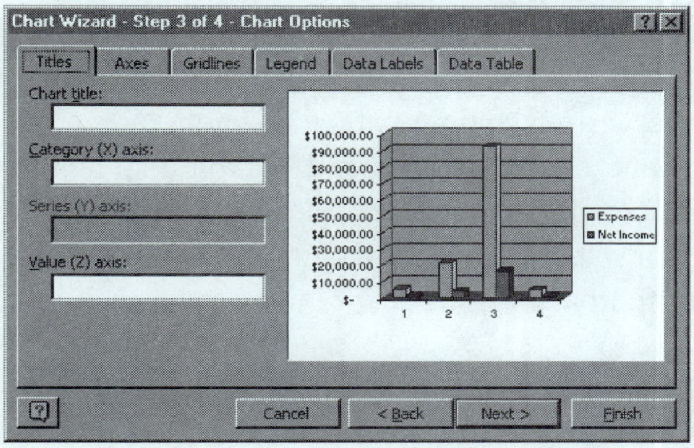

Here you can add and change titles, axes, gridlines, and so on.

5. Click Next to accept the settings and display this dialog box:

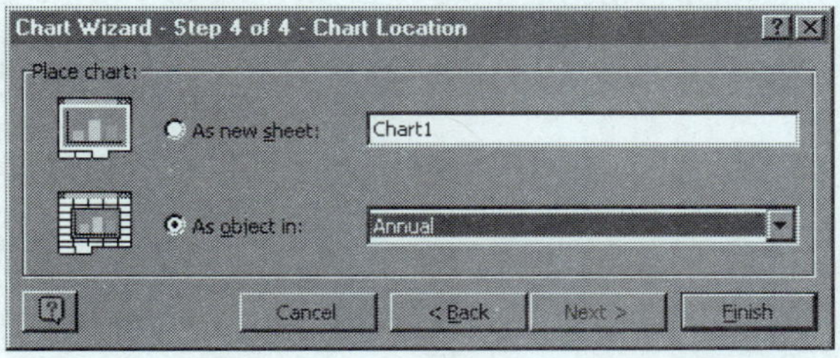

6. Click Finish to insert the graph in the Annual sheet, like this (we dragged the Chart toolbar below the Formatting toolbar):

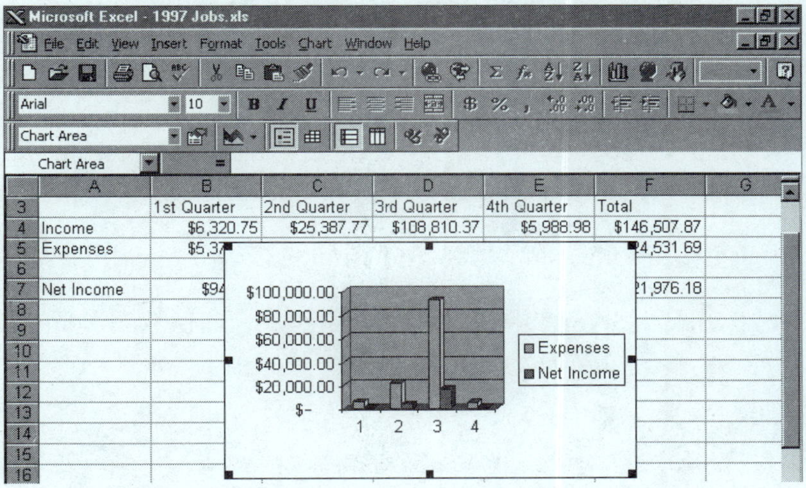

The default graph format

Initially, Graph creates a graph in its default format, which is a two-dimensional column graph. To change the default format, choose Chart Type from Graph's Chart menu and select a different type on the Standard Types or Custom Types tab of the Chart Type dialog box. Then click the Set As Default Chart button at the bottom of the dialog box, and when Excel displays a message box to confirm your default graph selection, click Yes. After you click OK in the Chart Type dialog box, the new default graph type takes effect immediately and remains in effect until you change it.

Data markers

As you can see, four groups of columns, called *data markers*, represent the four quarters of data you selected. Within each group, one data marker represents the expenses category and the other represents the net income category. The data markers are identified in the legend by the labels from column A of the selected range: Expenses and Net Income. Before moving on to the next section, take a moment to familiarize yourself with the various elements of the graph. When you point to an element, such as the legend, Graph displays the element's name in a box. (To select a specific element, you can click it once or select it from the Chart Objects drop-down list on the Chart toolbar.)

Sizing and Moving Graphs

Handles

You don't have to worry about the precise size and location of a graph when you create it because you can always adjust it by dragging the small black squares, called *handles*, around the graph's frame. Try this:

1. Point to the middle handle on the left side of the frame and drag it to the left to increase the graph's width.
2. Drag a corner handle diagonally outward to increase both the height and the width proportionally.
3. Move the entire graph below the data of the Annual sheet by pointing inside its frame and dragging in the direction in which you want to move. (If you click too near the chart area, you'll move the chart within the frame instead.)

Adding values to an existing series

If you add values to a set of data in a worksheet and want to update a graph you created earlier to reflect the new values, you can select the values and drag the selection to the graph. When you release the mouse button, Graph displays the Paste Special dialog box. Click New Point(s) and Rows or Columns and then click OK to add the additional data points along the category axis. To add values to a graph located on a separate chart sheet, you can select the values, click the Copy button, move to the chart sheet, select the graph, and click the Paste button.

Updating Graphs

Graph has actively linked the graph to its underlying data, so if we change the data, Graph will redraw the graph to reflect the change. To demonstrate graph updating, let's restore the original amount in cell E22 of the Invoices 1997 worksheet:

1. Click the Invoices 1997 tab and enter *1898.46* in cell E22.
2. Next click the Annual tab. The updated graph looks like this:

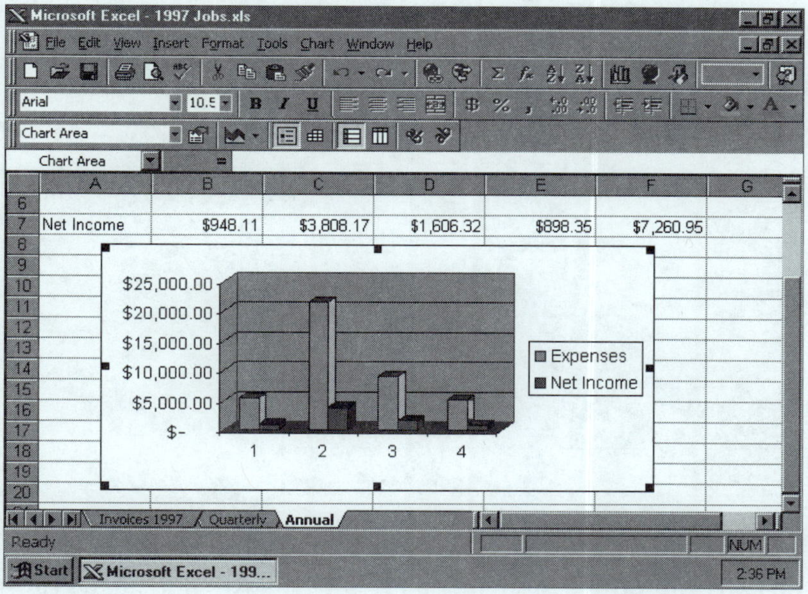

3. To view the graph in a separate window, without the clutter of the worksheet, choose Chart Window from the View menu. Choose Chart Window again to return to worksheet view.

Changing the Graph Type

No matter what type of graph you need—area, bar, pie, line, and so on—Graph has a format that will probably do the job. You can always come up with impressive visual support for a worksheet by carefully selecting from among Graph's many predefined graph types. Let's try changing the type of the graph currently on your screen so that you can see some of the possibilities:

1. Be sure the graph is selected (surrounded by handles). If it isn't, click anywhere within the graph to select it. Note that when the graph is selected, the Microsoft Graph program modifies the menus on the menu bar to accommodate the commands appropriate for working with graphs.

2. Choose Chart Type from the Chart menu to display the dialog box shown on the next page.

X axis and y axis

Graph uses the terms *x axis* and *y axis* in some of its dialog boxes. For clarification, here are a couple of definitions: The x axis shows the information categories—for example, expenses and net income; the y axis shows the data points (plotted values).

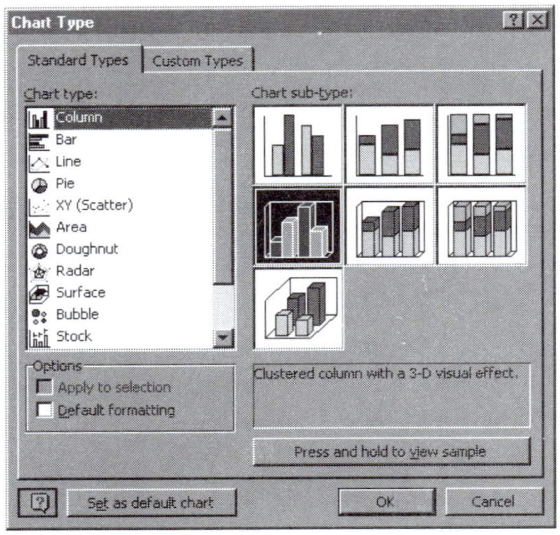

3. In the Chart Type list, select the Line option and click OK. Graph draws this graph, in which the expenses and net income data are represented as two separate lines on the graph:

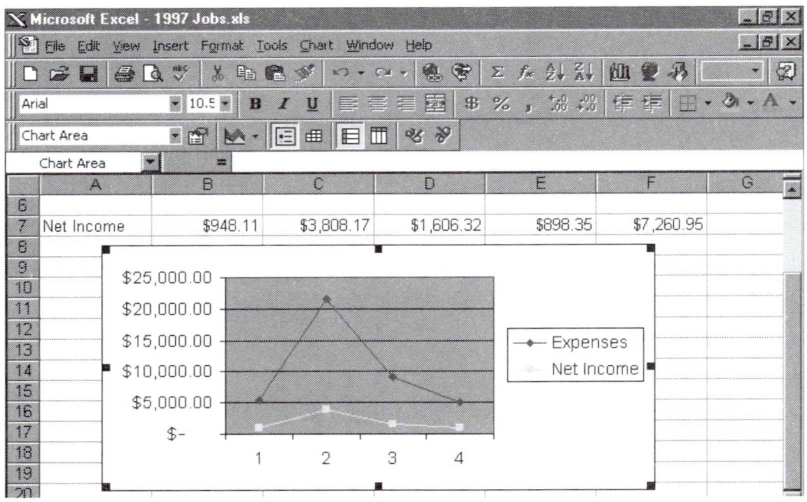

4. Click the Undo button to restore the previous type.

The Chart Type button

5. Now click the arrow to the right of the Chart Type button on the Chart toolbar to display this drop-down palette of graph types:

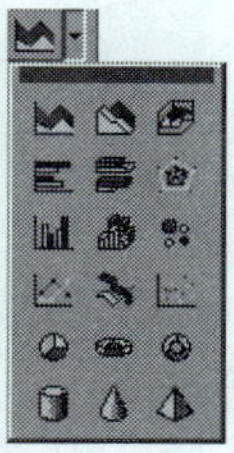

6. Select the 3-D Pie Chart option (the second option in the fifth row). The four quarters of expenses data are represented as colored wedges in a three-dimensional pie graph, as shown below. (You no longer see the net income data because a pie graph can display only one set of data.)

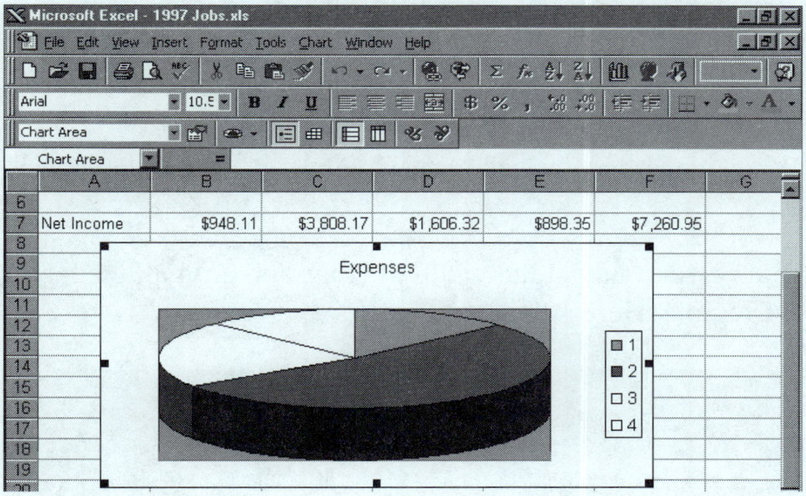

7. Select other graph types from the Chart Type dialog box or the Chart Type palette to get an idea of what's available. Then finish up with a simple two-dimensional column graph.

Using Custom Graph Types

Often, selecting one of the options on the Standard Types tab of the Chart Type dialog box will produce exactly the graph we need, but sometimes we might want something slightly different. Before spending time adjusting the format of a graph type, it's worth exploring Graph's custom types. Follow these steps:

1. With the graph selected, choose Chart Type from the Chart menu and click the Custom Types tab to display the options shown on the next page.

Adding notes

To add explanatory notes to a graph, select the graph, click an insertion point in the formula bar, type the note, and press Enter. Graph displays a text box containing the note in the middle of the graph. You can use the frame and handles around the text box to reposition it or resize it. To format the text box and the note it contains, choose Text Box from the Format menu and make your selections on the tabs of the Format Text Box dialog box.

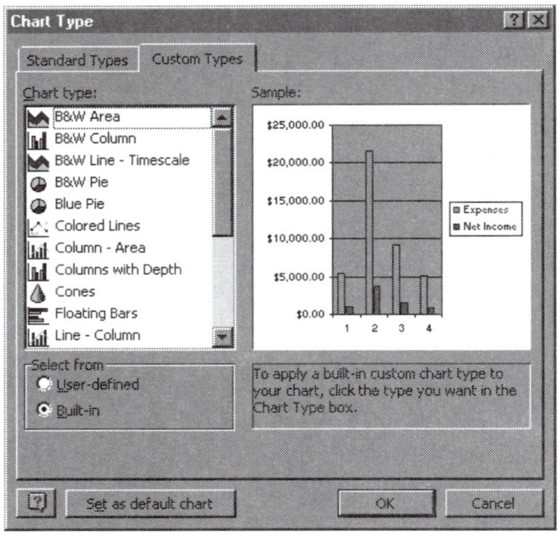

2. In the Chart Type list, select the graph types that interest you and then check the results in the Sample box.

3. When you are ready, select the Columns With Depth type and click OK.

4. If necessary, adjust the width of the graph until all the labels are legible. Here's the result:

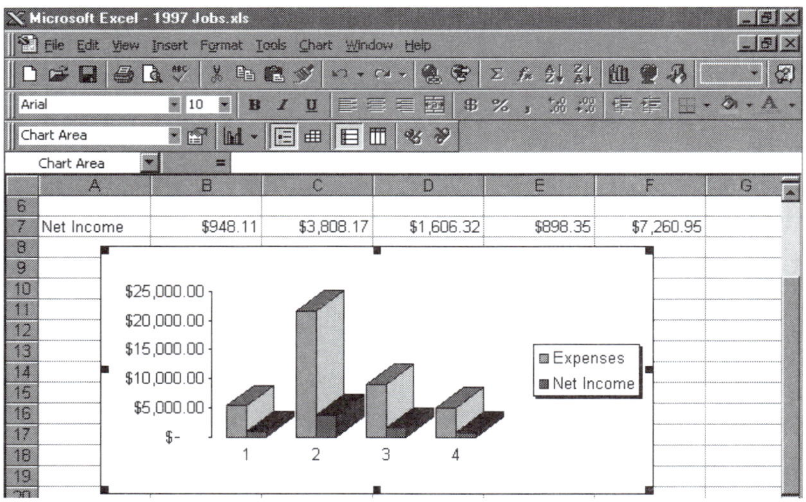

You might want to continue exploring some of the other available custom graph types. In particular, try creating a combination graph, which plots one type of graph on top of another as an "overlay" (see the adjacent tip).

Combination graphs

To create a combination graph, select one of the combination graph types (for example, Line-Column) on the Custom Types tab of the Chart Wizard or Chart Type dialog box. You can plot your data as one graph type overlaid by another graph type—for example, a column graph overlaid by a line graph. If your data includes series that span widely divergent ranges of values, you can plot the data against two y axes of different scales—for example, one series against a y-axis scale on the left of the graph ranging from 0 to 100 and another series against a y-axis scale on the right of the graph ranging from 100,000 to 1,000,000.

Previewing and Printing Graphs

Previewing and printing graphs is much like previewing and printing worksheets. We can preview and print the worksheet data and graph together or just the graph. Follow these steps:

1. Click anywhere outside the graph to deselect it, click cell A1, and then click the Print Preview button. As you can see, one or two adjustments would improve the look of this page.
2. Click the Close button to return to the Annual worksheet. Adjust the position and size of the graph so that it is centered on columns A through F and separated from the worksheet entries by about five rows of blank cells (see page 126).
3. Deselect the graph, click the Print Preview button again, and then click the Setup button on the Print Preview toolbar.
4. Click the Margins tab, change the Top setting to *1.5*, and in the Center On Page section, select the Horizontally option.
5. Click OK to implement your changes. Here are the results:

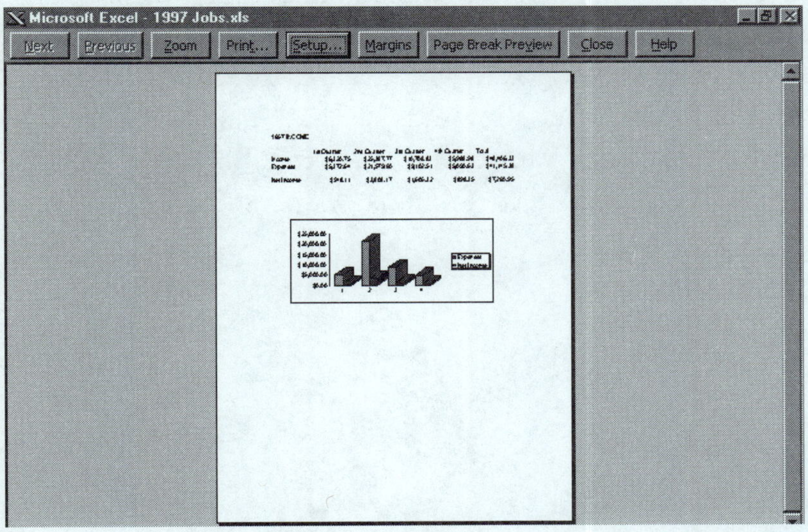

If you want, you can now click the Print button to create a paper copy of your graph.

Chapters 4 and 5 have given you a quick overview of Excel. Don't be shy about exploring the program further on your own and using its many features to create more sophisticated worksheets.

Printing graphs only

To print a graph without its underlying worksheet, click the graph to select it, and click the Print button on the Standard toolbar. (Or choose Print from the File menu, be sure the Selected Chart option is selected in the Print dialog box, and click OK.)

6 PowerPoint Basics

Include the subject, speaker, and company on the title slide

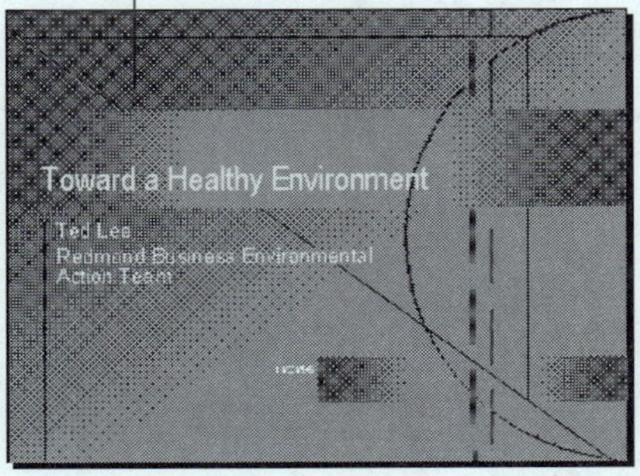

Use bulleted list slides to make your points succinctly

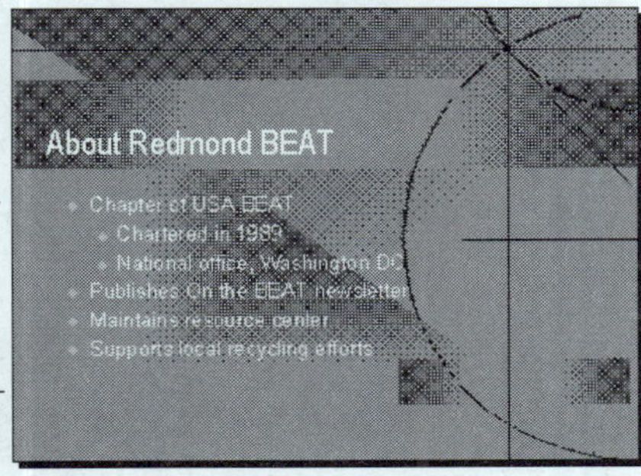

Add subordinate bullets for secondary items

Create two presentations and then merge them

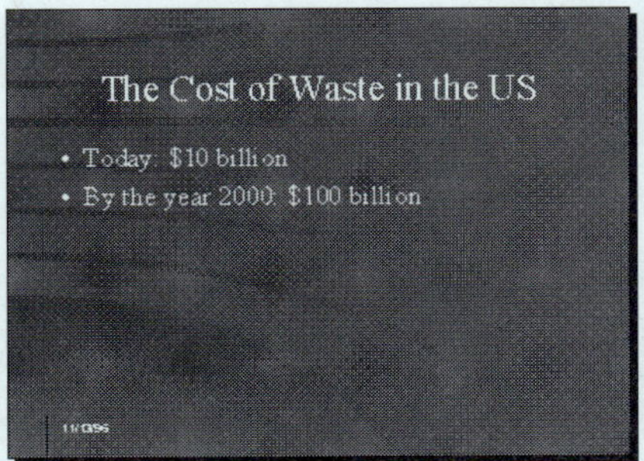

Make a bigger impact by using just a few bulleted items

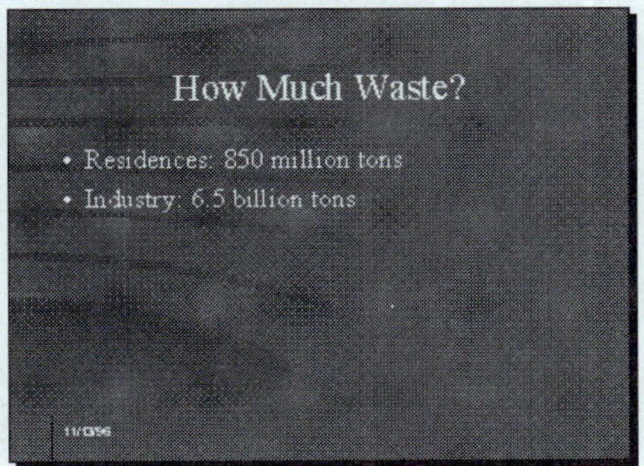

Change the look of a presentation by changing its template

PowerPoint is the presentation component of Microsoft Office, and it's packed with all sorts of tools to simplify the task of creating presentations. From good old reliable transparencies to electronic slide shows with "flying bullets," PowerPoint does it all.

In this chapter, we cover the basic steps for developing PowerPoint presentations. First we introduce you to the AutoContent Wizard, which helps you decide on the text of a presentation. Then we show you how to get just the look you want by creating a presentation based on one of PowerPoint's design templates.

Using the AutoContent Wizard

For our first presentation, we're going to let the AutoContent Wizard be our guide. The AutoContent Wizard asks a few questions to get the ball rolling and then lets us select one of several sample presentations as a starting point. Follow these steps to start PowerPoint from the Windows Start menu and use the AutoContent Wizard:

Starting Microsoft PowerPoint

1. Click the Start button and choose Programs and then Microsoft PowerPoint from the Start menu.

2. If the Office Assistant appears, click the Start Using Microsoft PowerPoint option to close the assistant. Your screen should look something like this:

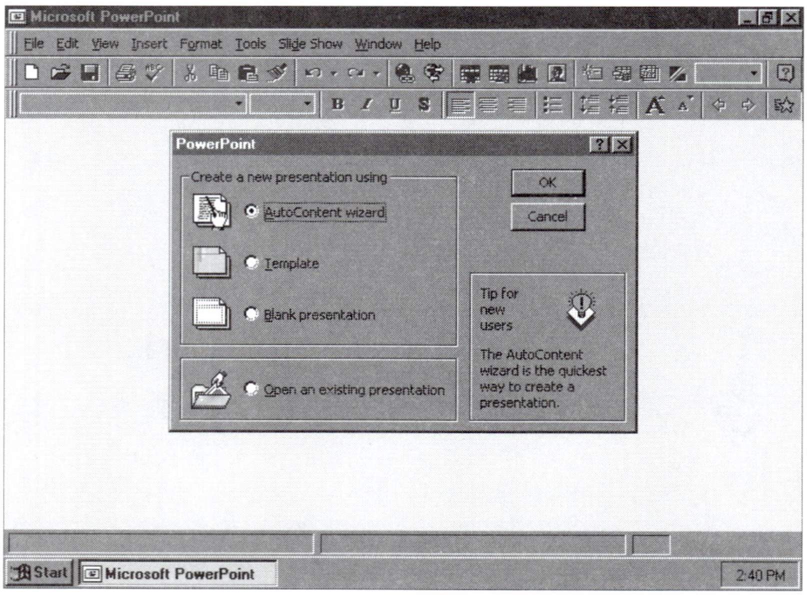

As you can see, you can start a new presentation in one of three ways, or you can open an existing presentation.

3. With the AutoContent Wizard option selected, click OK to display the first AutoContent Wizard dialog box. (If the Office Assistant reappears, click the second option to turn it off.)

4. Read the information in the dialog box and then click Next to move to this dialog box, where you select the type of presentation you want to create:

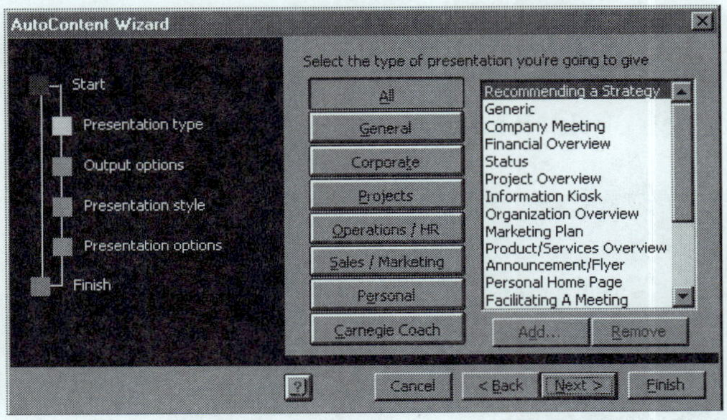

5. Click the buttons in the middle of the dialog box to see the Presentation types in each category. When you're ready, click the General button, select the Recommending A Strategy presentation type, and click Next to display this dialog box:

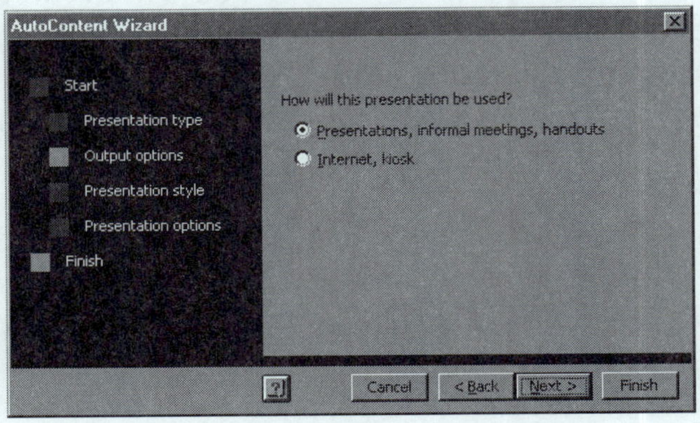

6. Click Next to accept the default option for how the presentation will be used and to display the dialog box shown on the next page.

Bypassing dialog boxes

While going through the AutoContent Wizard, as well as other wizard's dialog boxes, you can bypass sections of the wizard. On the left side of the dialog box, click the colored square next to the name of the dialog box you want to display. You can also move backward to a previous dialog box using this method.

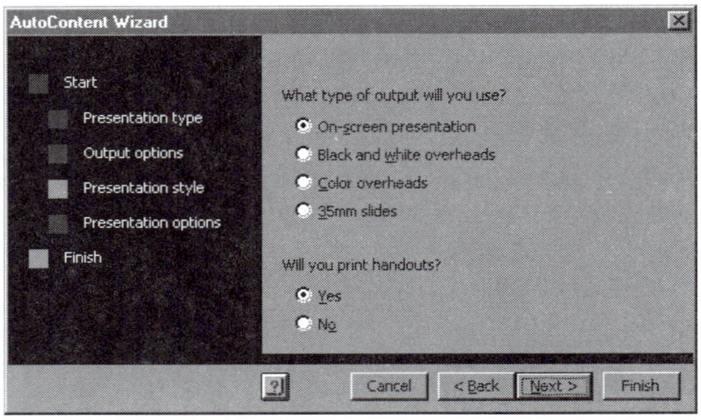

7. Check that On-Screen Presentation is selected as your output option and that No is selected in the Will You Print Handouts section, and then click Next to display this dialog box:

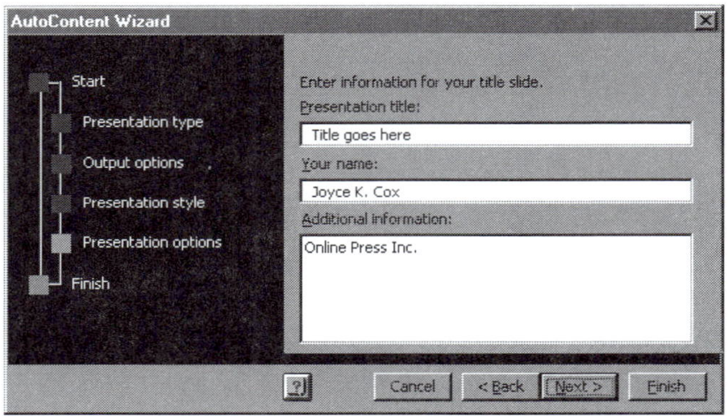

The information you enter in this dialog box will become the first slide, called the *title slide*, of the presentation. In the middle and bottom edit boxes, PowerPoint may have entered the name and company name used when the program was installed.

8. Type *Toward a Healthy Environment* in the top edit box, type *Ted Lee* in the middle edit box, and type *Redmond Business Environmental Action Team* in the bottom edit box. Click Next to display the AutoContent Wizard's final dialog box as shown on the facing page.

Presentation do's and don'ts

Using a program like PowerPoint won't ensure that your presentations will be successful. You have to use some common sense, too. Here are some tips for creating clear, concise presentations:

- Know as much as possible about your audience before you start creating your presentation and tailor its tone, words, and graphics appropriately.
- What points do you want your audience to remember after your presentation? Come up with an overall theme that you can reinforce throughout the presentation.
- Make each slide convey only one main idea that can be interpreted at a glance.
- Cut the verbage on each slide to the essentials. Never have more than six bulleted items on a slide. The more bulleted items you have, the fewer words you should use in each item.
- Make sure your capitalization and punctuation are consistent. On any one slide, don't mix complete sentences and partial sentences.
- Above all, don't expect your slides to carry the entire weight of the presentation. To hold the attention of your audience, you must be poised and confident, and you must express your ideas clearly and persuasively.

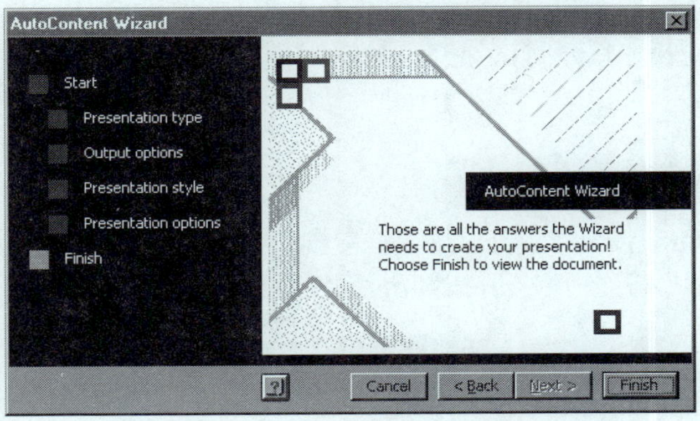

9. Click Finish. PowerPoint opens the presentation window:

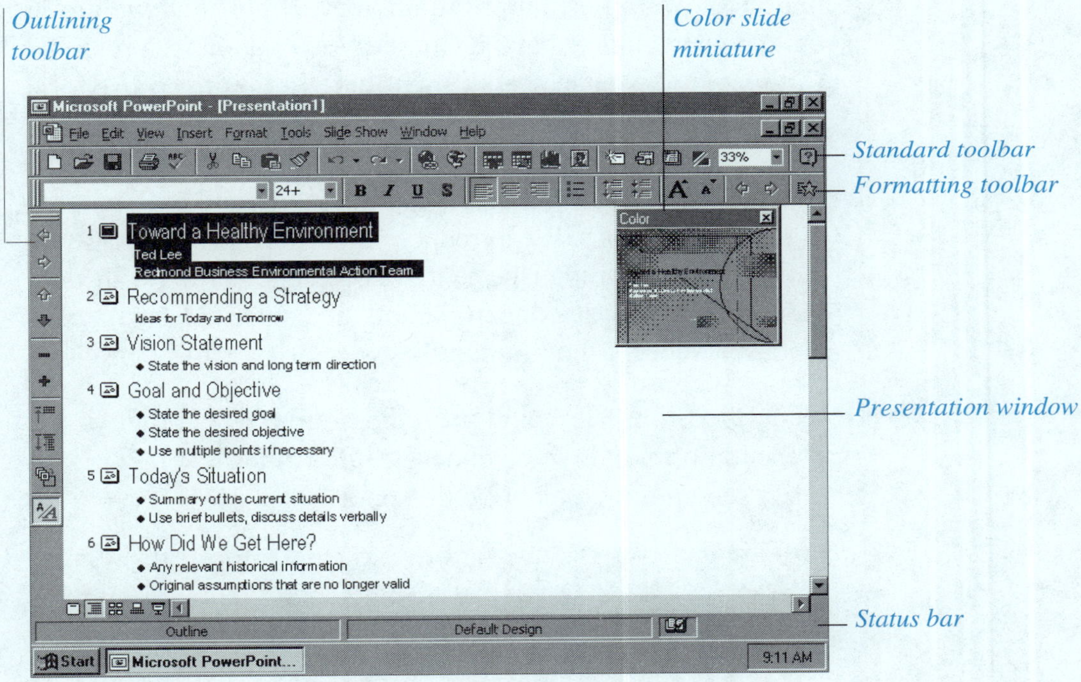

Taking up most of your screen is your new presentation, which PowerPoint displays in *outline view* in the *presentation window*. The first topic is the title-slide information you entered in the fifth AutoContent Wizard dialog box. The remaining topics are PowerPoint's suggestions as to the items you might want to cover when recommending a strategy. Each topic supplied by PowerPoint is designated by a number and a small slide icon to indicate that the topic will appear as the title of a slide. Subtopics are indented and bulleted to indicate that they will appear as bulleted items on their respective slides. Also on your screen is a color slide miniature, which displays the default design template for the presentation.

Before we go any further, let's save the presentation:

1. Click the Save button to display the Save As dialog box, type *1 Redmond BEAT* in the File Name edit box and click Save.

Switching to Slide View

Above the status bar in the bottom left corner of the presentation window is a row of buttons that we use to switch from one view of a presentation to another. Right now we are in outline view; notice that the Outline View button is "pressed." In this view, we can see all the topics and bulleted lists of a presentation in outline form. We can enter and edit text in this view, but, as we discuss on page 142, we'll probably use outline view mainly for reorganizing the topics and bulleted text of our presentations. We introduce you to the other views as you work your way through the next two chapters, starting with *slide view*, where we can concentrate on the content of the presentation one slide at a time. Follow these steps to switch to slide view:

The Slide View button

1. Click the Slide View button in the bottom left corner of the presentation window, or choose Slide from the View menu. Your screen now looks like this one:

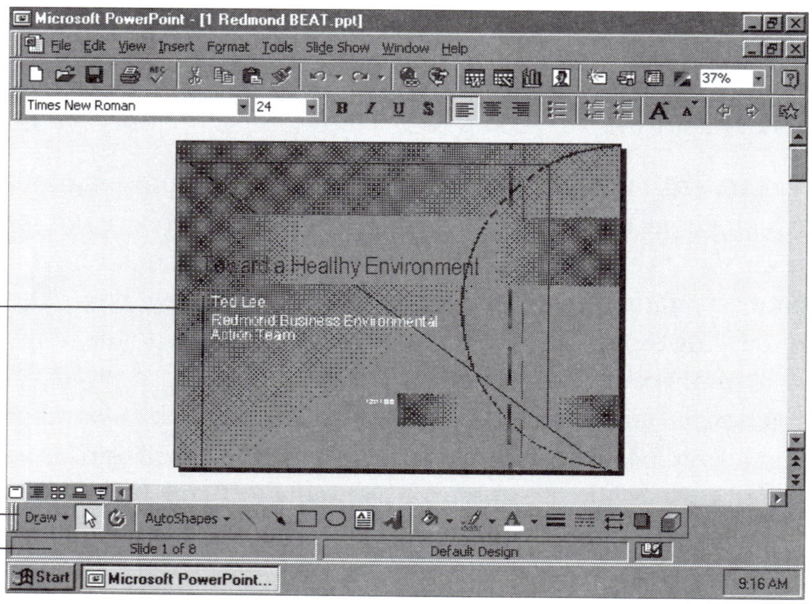

Slide

Drawing toolbar

Slide indicator

Occupying the window is a representation of the title slide of your presentation displayed with PowerPoint's default *template*, which controls the appearance of the slide (see page 145 for more information about templates). The right scroll bar has acquired a Previous Slide button and a Next Slide button, which you can click to move backward and forward through the presentation's slides.

Editing Text in Slide View

As you'll soon discover, we can work on different aspects of a presentation by viewing it in different ways. When it comes to editing the text of a presentation, slide view and outline view are our best bets. We show you how to reorganize the slides in outline view on page 142. In this section, we concentrate on editing text in slide view. Follow these steps:

1. With the title slide of 1 Redmond BEAT displayed, click the Next Slide button twice to move to Slide 3, as shown here:

The Next Slide button

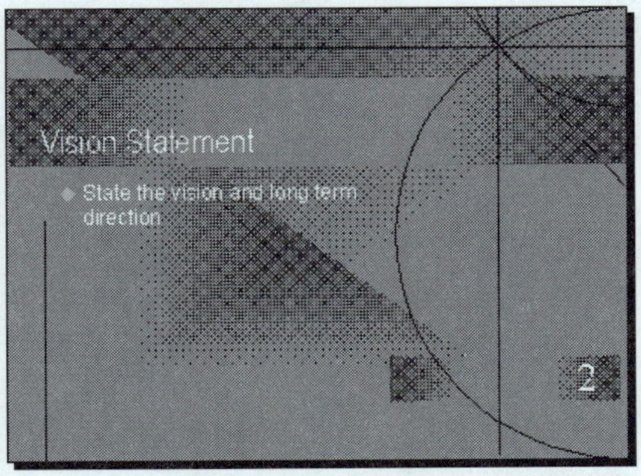

Don't worry that the numbers on the slides aren't accurate, we will delete the numbers later.

2. On Slide 3, activate the "object area" of the slide by clicking an insertion point in the bulleted item. PowerPoint surrounds the area with a shaded border and highlights the bulleted item.
3. Select the text to the right of the bullet and type this text:

By the year 2000, all Redmond companies will have evaluated their business practices and implemented any changes necessary to promote a healthy environment

Moving among slides

In addition to the Previous Slide and Next Slide buttons, you can use the Page Up and Page Down keys to move from one slide to another. You can also use the scroll bar by simply dragging the scroll box up or down. As you drag, PowerPoint displays the number and title of the slide that will appear when you release the mouse button at that point.

4. Save your changes.

   Slide 3 looks pretty good, so let's move on to the next slide.

1. Click the Next Slide button to display Slide 4.
2. Activate the "title area" of the slide by clicking an insertion point after *Goal*.
3. Type an *s* to turn *Goal* into *Goals*, and then delete *and Objective*.
4. Activate the object area of the slide by clicking anywhere in the slide's bulleted list.
5. Select the text of the first bulleted item and type *Encourage win-win solutions*.
6. Repeat step 5 to replace the second bulleted item with *Stop waste* and the third bulleted item with *Reduce the nation's garbage bill*.
7. Press Enter. PowerPoint moves the insertion point to a new line, preceded by a bullet.
8. Type *Increase business awareness*. Here are the results:

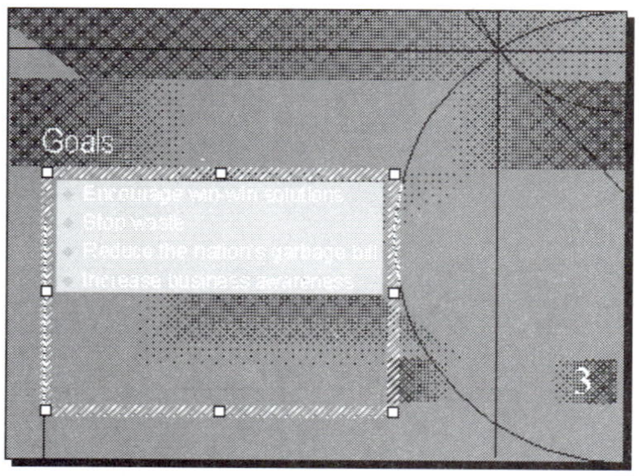

The fewer bulleted items the better

The default slide template allows you to enter eight single-line bulleted items on a slide, but eight is really too many. As we said in the tip on page 136, you will stand a better chance of getting your point across to your audience if you limit the number of bulleted items to no more than six single lines. The more bullets you have on a slide, the harder it is for your audience to focus on any one of the points you are trying to make. If you have many bulleted items, try to find ways of breaking them up into logical groups and use a different slide for each group.

Adding Subordinate Points

To get a point across, we will sometimes need to add subordinate points below a main bullet. Let's add some subordinate points now by following these steps:

1. Click the Next Slide button to move to Slide 5, click the title to activate the title area of the slide, select *Today's Situation*, and type *About Redmond BEAT*.

2. In the object area, change *Summary of the current situation* to *Publishes On the BEAT newsletter* and press Enter to create a new bullet.

3. Type *Supports local recycling efforts* and press Enter.

4. Type *Chapter of USA BEAT* and press Enter.

5. Now click the Demote button on the Formatting toolbar. PowerPoint indents the line to show that this point is subordinate to the preceding bullet.

The Demote button

6. Type *National office, Washington DC*, press Enter to create a new subordinate point, type *Chartered in 1989*, and press Enter.

7. To stop adding subordinate points and create a new main bulleted item, click the Promote button. PowerPoint moves the line back out to the margin.

The Promote button

8. Type *Maintains resource center* as the fourth first-level bullet.

9. Finally, delete the *Use brief bullets* item by selecting the text and pressing the Delete key. Slide 5 now looks like this:

Deleting bulleted items

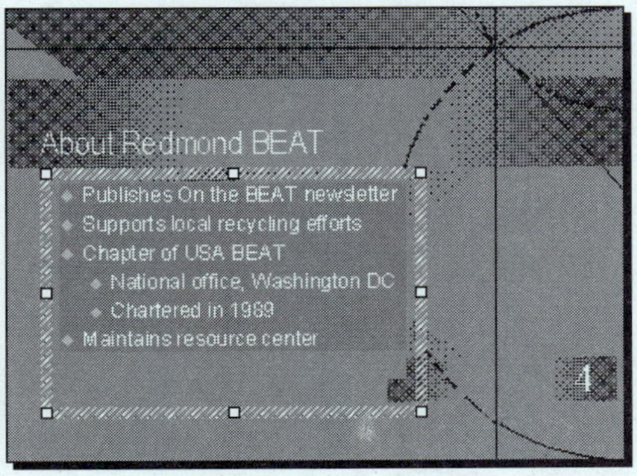

(We resized the object area to make every bullet point fit on one line; see the adjacent tip for more information.)

Deleting Slides in Slide View

Because we'll create the next four slides using a design template, we need to dispose of Slides 2, 5, 6, and 7 which were provided by the AutoContent Wizard. Follow the steps on the next page to delete Slides 2 and 5 (we'll take care of Slides 6 and 7 in a moment):

> **Resizing slide areas**
>
> You can resize any area of a slide. Click the area once to select it, point to a middle handle and drag to resize the frame. If you drag a corner handle, the height and width change proportionally.

1. Click the Previous Slide button until you see Slide 2, which contains the title *Recommending a Strategy*.

2. Choose the Delete Slide command from the Edit menu.

3. Move to Slide 5, which bears the title *How Did We Get Here?* and repeat step 2 to delete that slide.

4. Press the Page Up and Page Down keys to be sure the slides have truly been deleted.

5. Now delete the numbers from the bottom right corner of Slides 2 through 6 by clicking the number to select it (it will be surrounded by handles), highlighting the number, and then pressing the Delete key.

Working in Outline View

In outline view, we can see all the topics and bulleted lists of the presentation in outline form. We can edit slide text in outline view, but this view really shines when it's time to organize a presentation. Organizing is often a trial-and-error process. We start by evaluating the major topics, add and delete a few subtopics, and then move items around and change their levels. This task is easiest to accomplish in outline view because the Outlining toolbar puts the tools needed for organizing a presentation close at hand. Try this:

The Outline View button

1. Click the Outline View button to switch to outline view. Your screen should look like to the one shown earlier on page 137.

2. Close the color slide miniature by clicking its Close button.

3. If the Outlining toolbar is turned off, right-click one of the displayed toolbars and select Outlining from the object menu.

4. If necessary, scroll the outline until you can see all the bulleted items under the *About Redmond BEAT* topic, and then click the bullet to the left of *Maintains resource center*.

The Move Up button

5. Click the Move Up button on the Outlining toolbar until the selected item sits above *Supports local recycling efforts*.

The Move Down button

6. Now click the bullet to the left of *National office, Washington DC* to select the item, and click the Move Down button once. The two subordinate points effectively switch places.

Selecting a bulleted group

7. Click the bullet to the left of *Chapter of USA BEAT*. PowerPoint selects not only the text adjacent to the bullet but also its two subordinate points.

8. Click the Move Up button three times. PowerPoint moves the main bullet and its subordinate points to the top of the *About Redmond BEAT* list, which now looks like this:

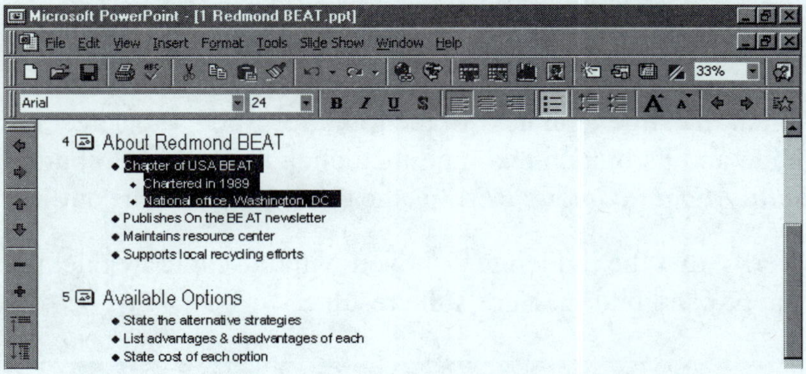

Here's another way to rearrange bulleted items:

Reorganizing by dragging

1. Under the *Goals* topic, click the bullet to the left of *Increase business awareness*.

2. Point to the selected text, hold down the left mouse button, drag the shadow insertion point until it sits to the left of the *E* in *Encourage*, and release the mouse button. PowerPoint moves the selection to its new location at the top of the bulleted list.

As you scroll through the outline of the presentation, you might notice a slide or two that would work better in a different location. However, if the outline is too long to fit on the screen all at one time, it is sometimes hard to decide on a precise order for the slides. The solution is to collapse the outline so that only the main topics are visible. Follow the steps on the next page.

The Collapse All button

1. Click the Collapse All button on the Outlining toolbar and then scroll to the beginning of the presentation. All of the bulleted items are hidden and a gray line appears under each topic to indicate the presence of hidden information, as shown here:

2. Click the slide icon next to the topic for Slide 4 to select the slide and its hidden text, and then click the Move Up button until *About Redmond BEAT* is the second topic in the outline.

The Expand and Collapse buttons

3. Verify that the hidden text moved with the topic by clicking the Expand button. Here's the result:

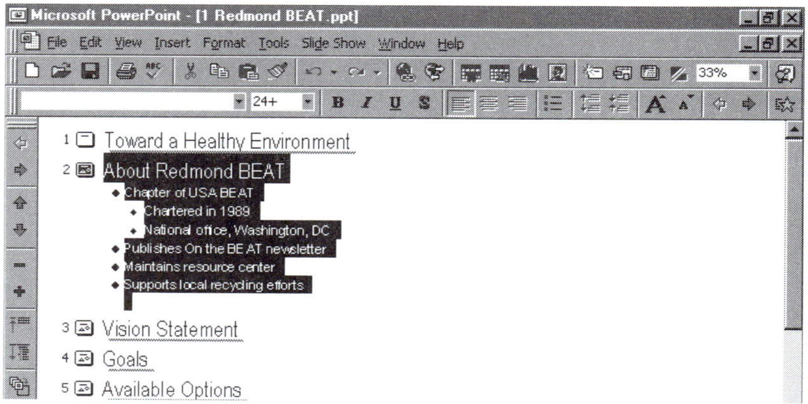

4. Click the Collapse button to once again hide the bulleted items.

> **Selecting parts of a slide**
>
> You can use many of the standard Office text-selection techniques when editing text in both outline and slide views. For example, you can double-click a word to select it. In outline view, you can click a bullet to select the bulleted item and its subordinate bullets. Also in outline view, you can click the slide icon to the left of a topic to select the topic and all of its bulleted items. In slide view, you can select an entire text object, such as a bulleted list, by clicking the object and then either choosing Select All from the Edit menu or pressing Ctrl+A.

Deleting Slides in Outline View

Deleting a slide in outline view is a simple editing process. Let's delete the last two slides in the presentation:

1. Click the slide icon next to the topic for Slide 5, hold down the Shift key, and click the icon for Slide 6 to select both Slides 5 and 6.

2. Press Delete and then click OK in the message box to delete the slides.

3. Click the Expand All button to display the entire outline. Then save and close the presentation.

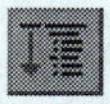

The Expand All button

Using a Design Template

If we know exactly what we want to say but we need a little help coming up with a design for our presentation, we can bypass the AutoContent Wizard and start a presentation based on one of PowerPoint's design templates. And, if we have trouble selecting a design, we can easily switch to a different template with just a few mouse clicks (see page 150). Follow the steps below to create a second presentation using a design template:

1. Choose New from the File menu to display the New Presentation dialog box and then click the Presentation Designs tab, which looks like this:

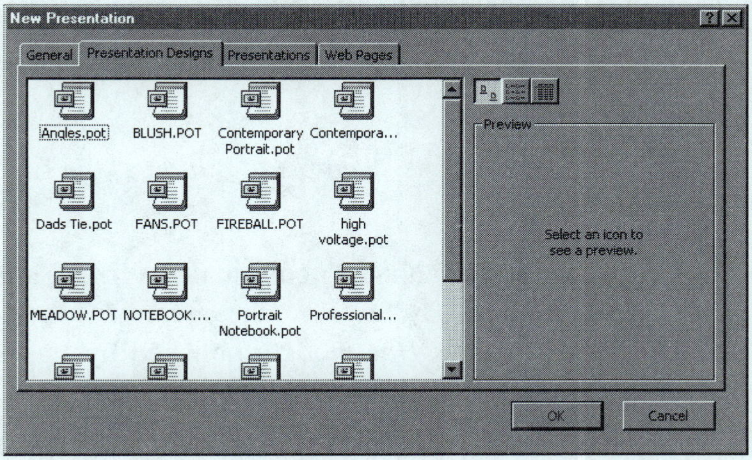

2. Click any template icon and then check the Preview box on the right to see a sample of the template. Click other template icons, noticing their different designs.

3. When you're ready, double-click the Pulse icon. PowerPoint opens the New Slide dialog box shown on the next page.

Black and white view

To see how your presentation looks in black and white, you can click the Black And White View button on the Standard toolbar. A color miniature of the current slide is also displayed in the presentation window. (You can display a slide miniature at any time by choosing the Slide Miniature command from the View menu.) Click the Black And White View button again to return to color view. (Click the slide miniature's Close button or choose Slide Miniature from the View menu to close the miniature.)

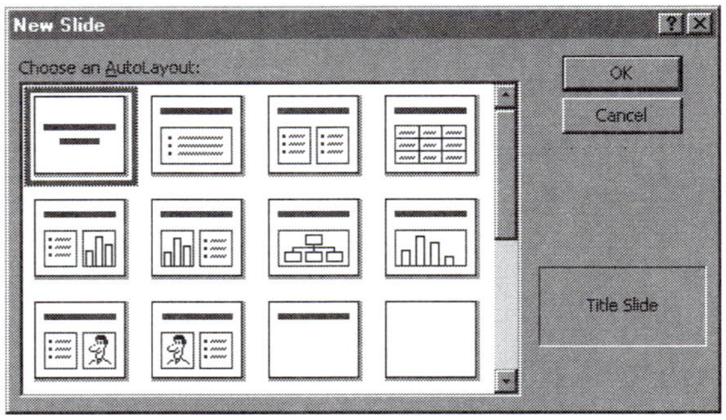

Autolayouts

PowerPoint provides 23 predefined slide layouts, called *auto-layouts*, plus one blank slide that you can use to design a slide layout of your own. You can scroll the other autolayouts into view by using the scroll bar to the right.

4. Click the second autolayout in the top row and click OK to create a bulleted list slide.
5. Save the presentation with the name *2 Redmond BEAT*.

Slide 1 is now ready and awaiting our input. Follow these steps:

1. Click the title area and type *The Cost of Waste in the US* as the slide's title.
2. Click the object area and type *Today: $10 billion* as the first bulleted item.
3. Press Enter to start another bulleted item and then type *By the year 2000: $100 billion*. (By the way, the source for these statistics is *The Recycler's Handbook*, published by Earth Works Press in Berkeley, California.)

Adding Slides

When we create a presentation based on a design template, PowerPoint provides only the initial slide. To add three more slides to the presentation, follow these steps:

The New Slide button

1. Click the New Slide button on the Standard toolbar to display the New Slide dialog box.
2. With the Bulleted List autolayout selected, click OK to add a second slide to your presentation.

3. Click the title area of Slide 2 and type *How Much Waste?*

4. Type *Residences: 850 million tons* as the first bulleted item and *Industry: 6.5 billion tons* as the second bulleted item, pressing Enter to start the second bulleted item.

5. Repeat steps 1 and 2 to add a new bulleted list slide and then type *Where Do I Start?* as the title.

6. Click the object area of Slide 3 and type these bulleted items:

- *Join Redmond BEAT*
- *Attend meetings at 8:00 AM on the last Tuesday of every month*

7. Add a fourth bulleted list slide and type *What Can I Do?* as the title. Then type the following bulleted items:

- *Start a recycling program*
- *Educate employees*
- *Buy post-consumer products*
- *Call Ted Lee at 555-6789 for more suggestions*

Moving Text Between Slides

If you take a look at Slide 4, you'll notice that the fourth bulleted item might be better suited for Slide 3. We can move the text to Slide 3 using a little cutting and pasting, like this:

1. With the object area of Slide 4 activated, select the text of the fourth bullet.

2. Click the Cut button to remove the text from the slide and store it temporarily on the Clipboard.

3. Click the Previous Slide button to move to Slide 3, click an insertion point at the end of the second bulleted item, press Enter to create a new bullet, and then click the Paste button to paste the bulleted text onto Slide 3, which looks like the one shown on the next page.

Repositioning text objects

You can use the mouse to reposition text objects on a slide. For instance, if you want to shift the title up a bit, click the title area to select it, point to the frame surrounding the area, hold down the left mouse button, and then drag the frame upward. You can use this same technique to reposition the object area on a slide. In addition, you can resize text objects by dragging the handles that appear when an object is selected.

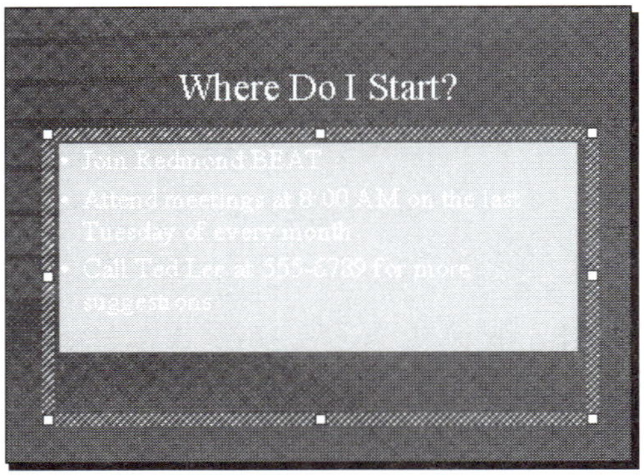

Merging Presentations in Slide Sorter View

Thumbnails

In slide sorter view, we can see the slides of a presentation laid out visually. Sketches, called *thumbnails*, display the slides in enough detail that we can get a pretty good idea of how they look. We can then make adjustments to the presentation by adding or deleting slides or changing their order. Slide sorter view is also a good place to merge presentations because we can see and control the merging process. Follow these steps to merge 2 Redmond BEAT with 1 Redmond BEAT:

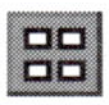

The Slide Sorter View button

1. Click the Slide Sorter View button in the bottom left corner of the presentation window. Your screen looks like this:

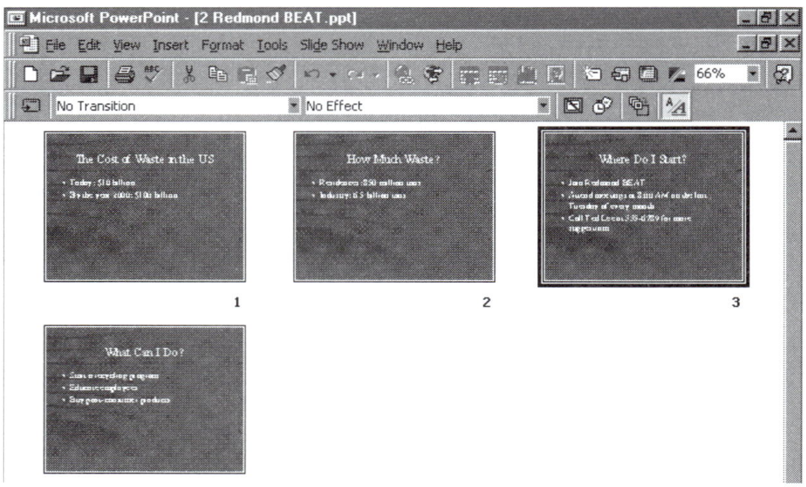

2. Now choose 1 Redmond BEAT from the bottom of the File menu and click the Slide Sorter View button. (If 1 Redmond

Changing the bullet character

PowerPoint's Bullet command allows you to change the character preceding the bulleted text on a slide. Just select the bulleted items and choose Bullet from the Format menu. When the Bullet dialog box appears, select a font in the Bullets From drop-down list and then select a character and click OK. If you want to change the color or size of the bullet, use the Color and Size options in the Bullet dialog box.

BEAT is not one of the four most recently opened files, use the Open command to open the file.)

3. Choose the Arrange All command from the Window menu to place the presentations side by side.

   The small slide icons below each slide in 1 Redmond BEAT indicate that a transition effect has been added to each slide (part of the Recommending A Strategy presentation type). We discuss transitions and other effects in the next chapter.

4. To decrease the size of the slide thumbnails so that you can see all the slides of both presentations at the same time, click the arrow to the right of the Zoom box on the Standard toolbar of the active window and select 25% from the drop-down list. Then do the same thing in the other window. Here are the results:

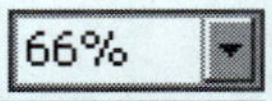

The Zoom box

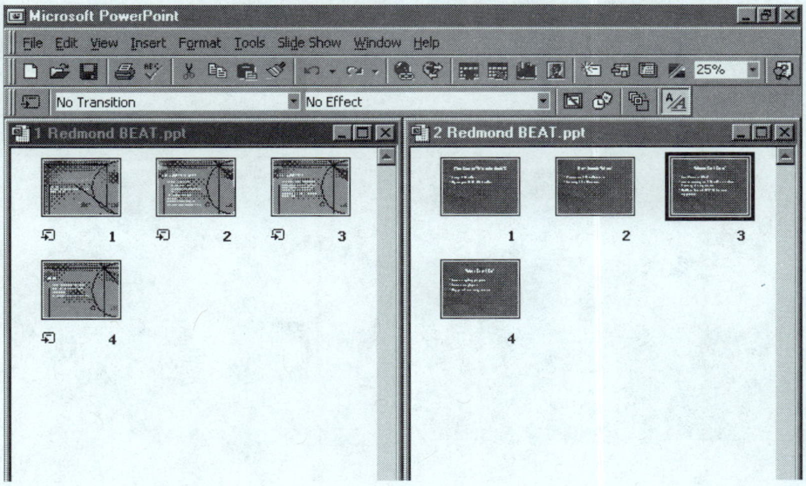

Now we can combine the two presentations:

1. Select all of the slides in the active 2 Redmond BEAT presentation by choosing Select All from the Edit menu.
2. Point to any one of the selected slides, hold down the left mouse button, and drag the vertical marker to just after Slide 4 in the 1 Redmond BEAT presentation.
3. Release the mouse button to drop the 2 Redmond BEAT slides into place. PowerPoint renumbers the merged slides and

The Show Formatting button

The Show Formatting button is the last button at the right end of the Slide Sorter toolbar. When you click this button, PowerPoint removes the formatting, as well as the design template, from the current slides, leaving only the slide titles. Removing the formatting and design template can be a real time-saver because PowerPoint does not have to "redraw" the slides every time you make a change to your presentation in slide sorter view. To restore the formatting and design template, click the Show Formatting button again.

overwrites the design template of 2 Redmond BEAT with that of 1 Redmond BEAT.

4. Close the 2 Redmond BEAT window, clicking No when PowerPoint asks whether you want to save your changes.

Reordering Slides in Slide Sorter View

Now that we've merged the two presentations, suppose we decide that Slides 7 and 8 need to be transposed. Here are the steps for reordering slides in slide sorter view:

Increasing the thumbnail size

1. Maximize the 1 Redmond BEAT window and select 50% from the Zoom drop-down list to increase the size of the slide thumbnails.

2. Click Slide 8 to select it, hold down the left mouse button, and drag the vertical marker to the left of Slide 7. When you release the mouse button, Slides 7 and 8 switch places, like this:

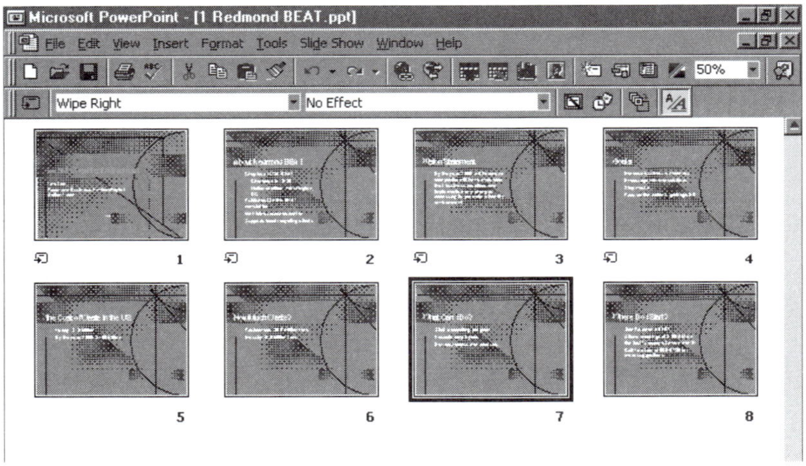

Adding comments

The Comment command lets you add comments to your slides. First display the slide in slide view and choose Comment from the Insert menu. When the comment text box appears, type your comment in the box. The Reviewing toolbar is displayed automatically when you add a comment to a slide. You can use the buttons on this toolbar to insert additional comments and to show or hide existing comments. To change the location of a comment on a slide, click the comment to select it, point to its frame, and drag it to a new location. To change the size of a comment, drag its handles in the desired direction. Although comments appear in slide show view, you can always hide them by clicking the Show/Hide Comments button on the Reviewing toolbar or by choosing the Comment command from the View menu.

Applying Templates

The appearance of a presentation is controlled by the template we select. As a result, we can change the entire look and feel of a presentation by simply switching to another template. As you saw in the New Presentation dialog box shown on page 145, PowerPoint offers a wide variety of design templates to choose from. Follow these steps to see how easy it is to reapply the Pulse template:

1. With 1 Redmond BEAT displayed on your screen in slide sorter view, click the Apply Design button on the Standard toolbar to open this dialog box:

The Apply Design button

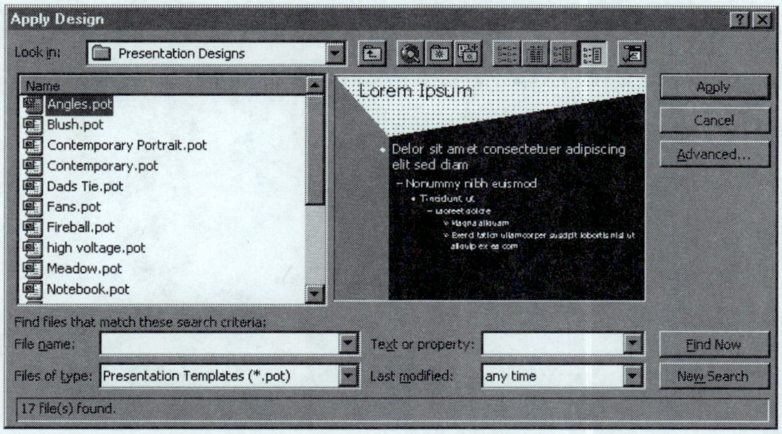

2. Scroll the Name list until you can see the Pulse template. Then double-click its icon to apply that template to your presentation, like this:

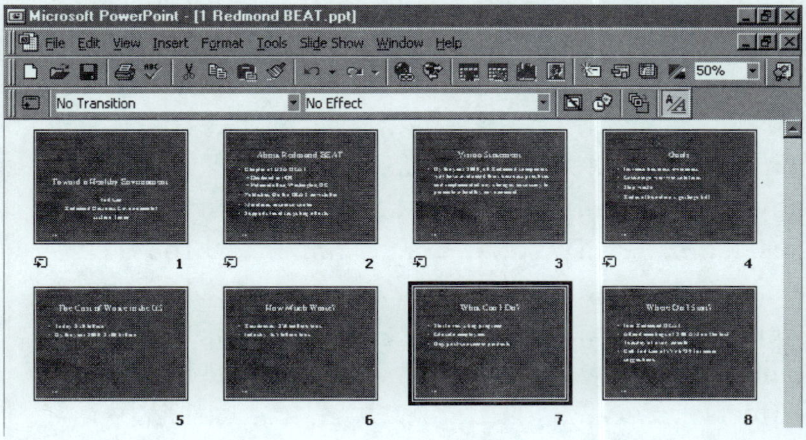

3. Save and close the presentation, and then close PowerPoint.

Now that you've learned how to create presentations using the AutoContent Wizard and a design template, you're ready to start exploring ways of enhancing presentations. In the next chapter, we show you how to add graphs, organization charts, and special effects to your presentations so that you can wow your audiences with visual information.

Customizing your presentation

You can manipulate the components of a template in a variety of ways to come up with a custom design. For example, you can add a company logo to the background or change the template's default fonts and colors. (Or, if none of PowerPoint's templates fit the bill, you can also create a design from scratch.) PowerPoint provides two master slides for customizing a presentation: the Title Master and the Slide Master. As their names suggest, the Title Master controls the title slides in your presentation, and the Slide Master controls the other slide types, such as bulleted list slides. When you make changes to a master slide, all of the related slides in a presentation are affected. For example, to change the font and color scheme of all the title slides in your presentation, switch to slide view, choose Master and then Title Master from the View menu, select the text of the title placeholder, and change the font in the usual way. Then choose Slide Color Scheme from the Format menu, select a color scheme in the Color Scheme dialog box, and click the Apply button to apply the new color scheme to the title slide(s). Click the Close button on the floating Master toolbar to return to slide view.

7

More About PowerPoint

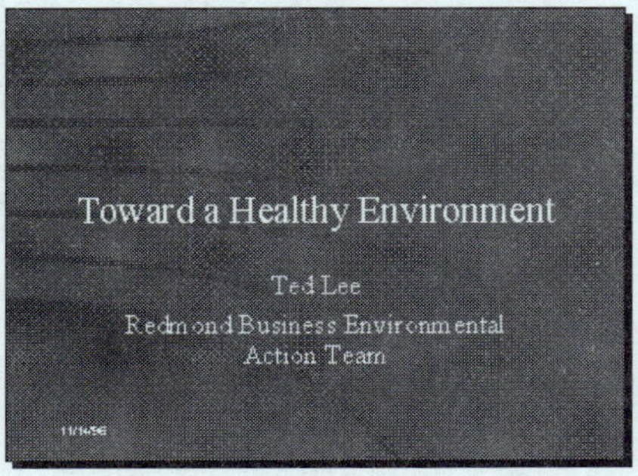

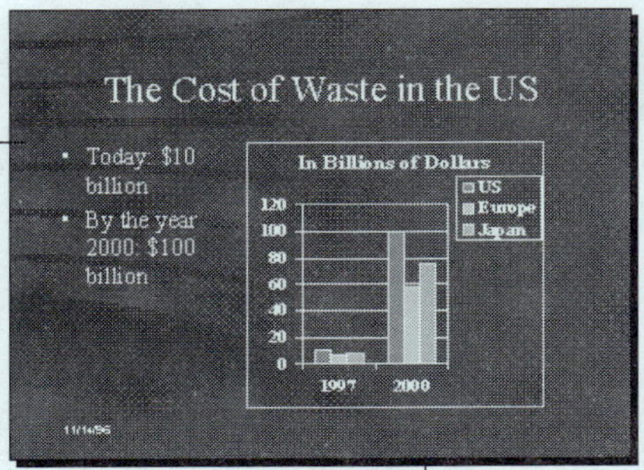

Adjust the size and position of the object area

Create and format a graph to visually present numeric data

Create an organization chart to illustrate a company hierarchy

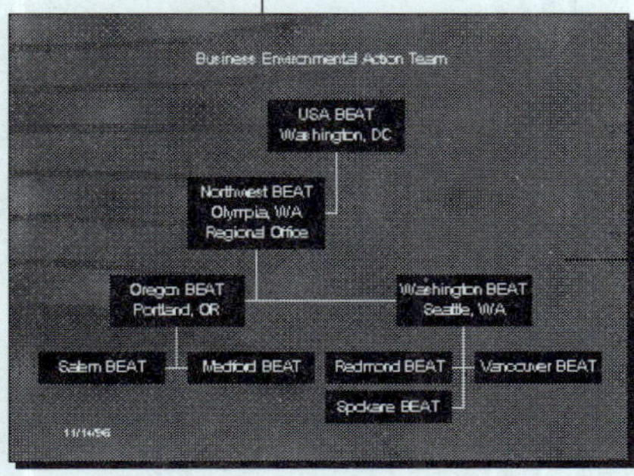

Add as many boxes and levels as you need

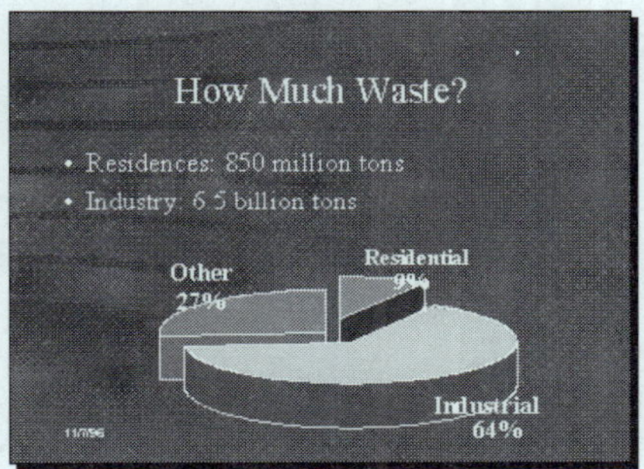

Select the chart type that best suits the data you are plotting

Words and numbers are nice, but visual representations of our words and numbers can really make an audience sit up and take notice. There's nothing like a line graph to show the fluctuations in sales over the past six months or an organization chart to show the current management structure of a corporation. In this chapter, we cover the ins and outs of adding graphs and charts to our presentations, and we also show you how to run an electronic slide show so that you can see a presentation in action on your computer.

Adding Graphs

PowerPoint shares the Microsoft Graph graphing program with other Office members. In this section, we show you how to add a couple of graphs to the 1 Redmond BEAT presentation. We'll use a graph autolayout to add the first graph and the Insert Chart button to add the second graph. We'll also give you a few pointers about working with graph objects and manipulating a graph on a slide.

Using a Graph AutoLayout

Let's add a graph to the 1 Redmond BEAT presentation we created in Chapter 6 by changing the layout of Slide 5:

1. Click the Start button and choose Documents and then 1 Redmond BEAT from the Start menu to start PowerPoint and open the document. Then switch to slide view and move to Slide 5.

The Slide Layout button

2. Click the Slide Layout button on the Standard toolbar, and when the Slide Layout dialog box appears, select the Text & Chart autolayout (the first autolayout in the second row) and click Apply. Slide 5 now looks like this one:

3. Double-click the graph placeholder to start Microsoft Graph. Your screen looks something like this:

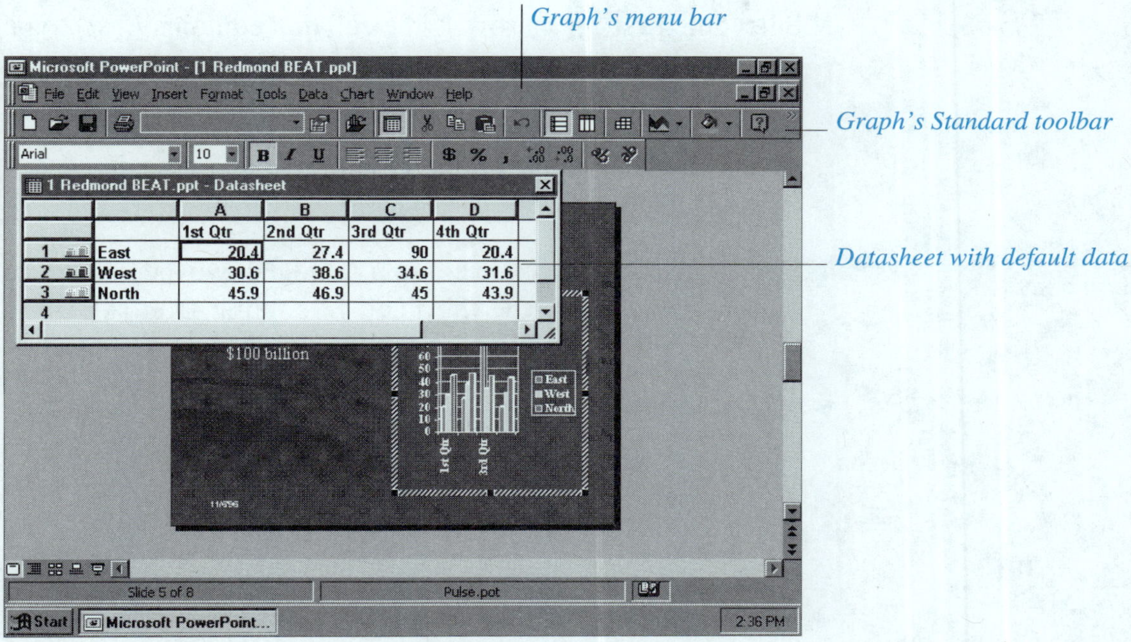

The datasheet

As you can see, Graph first presents its default *datasheet*, which resembles an Excel worksheet. Gridlines divide the datasheet into cells. In the leftmost column and topmost row are column and row headings, or *labels*. We can edit and format these labels like any other text in PowerPoint. Above the column labels and to the left of the row labels are column letter and row number buttons. Depending on whether the data is organized by column or by row (see the adjacent tip), markers appear on the column letter or row number buttons to indicate the current graph type, which by default is a three-dimensional column graph.

> **By row or by column**
>
> You can arrange the data series in your datasheet by row or by column. Graph assumes that the series are arranged by row; but if you have arranged the series by column, you can ensure that Graph will plot your data correctly by clicking the By Column button on Graph's Standard toolbar. If you want to return to the by-row arrangement, click the By Row button. Graph places miniature markers on the row number buttons of the datasheet if the data series are arranged by row and on the column letter buttons if the data series are arranged by column.

Let's replace the "dummy" data in the datasheet with our own information. (By the way, this data is fictitious and is used for demonstration purposes only.) Start with the labels:

1. Select the first cell in column A (the cell that contains *1st Qtr*) by clicking it with the mouse. (Be careful not to click outside the datasheet or graph. If you do, Graph automatically returns you to PowerPoint. You must then double-click the graph on the current slide to start Graph again.)

2. Type *1997*, press Tab to move to the first cell in column B, and type *2000*.

3. Select the first cell in row 1 (the cell that contains *East*), type *US*, press Enter to move to the first cell in row 2, type *Europe*, press Enter again, and type *Japan*.

To speed up the entry of the remaining data in the datasheet, try this technique:

Quick data entry

1. Point to the second cell in column A, hold down the left mouse button, and drag to the third cell in column B to select the block of cells.

2. Now type *10*, press Enter, type *6*, press Enter, type *7.5*, and press Enter again. In the next column, enter the data shown below:

100
57
75

3. Choose Save from Graph's File menu to save your work.

Now you can plot the graph. You don't want to plot the "dummy" data in columns C and D, so first exclude it by doing this:

Excluding data

1. Click column C's letter button, hold down the Shift key, click column D's letter button, and release the Shift key.

2. With both columns selected, choose Exclude Row/Col from Graph's Data menu.

The View Datasheet button

3. Click the View Datasheet button to remove the datasheet and display the new graph, which looks like this:

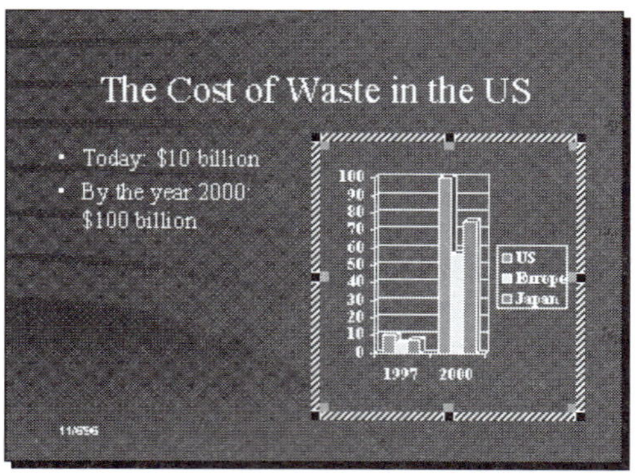

Obviously, we'll have to make some cosmetic adjustments, such as enlarging and repositioning the graph on the slide.

Changing the Graph Type

With Graph, we can easily switch from one graph type to another if we're not satisfied with the way our data is displayed. For clarity, change the type of the graph on Slide 5 by following these steps:

1. Choose the Chart Type command from Graph's Chart menu to display this dialog box, where the current type, a clustered 3-D column graph, is highlighted:

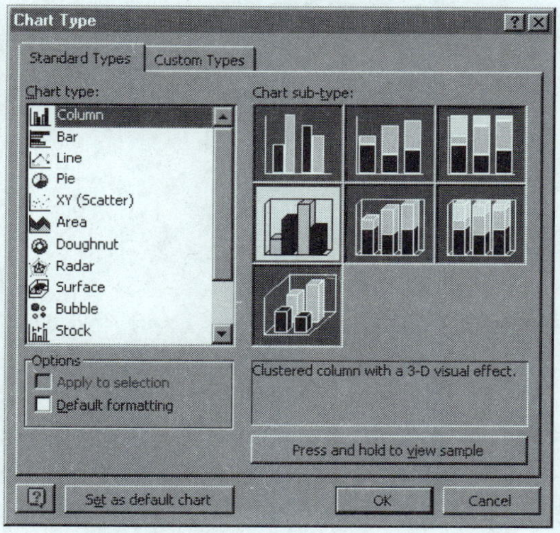

2. Select the first option in the Chart Sub-Type section (a clustered 2-D column graph) and then click OK. Graph inserts a 2-D column graph on Slide 5, like this:

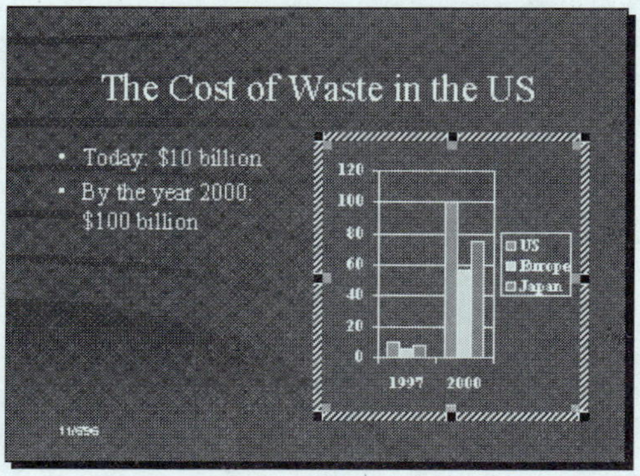

Adjusting column width

To increase or decrease the width of a column in a datasheet, select the column (click the corresponding column letter button), choose Column Width from Graph's Format menu, and enter a number in the Column Width dialog box. Click the Best Fit button in the Column Width dialog box to automatically adjust the column width to fit the longest entry in the column. You can also use the mouse to change the column width. Simply point to the border that separates adjacent column letter buttons, and when the pointer changes to a vertical bar with two arrows, hold down the left mouse button and drag to the left or right. If you double-click the border between two column letter buttons, the width of the column on the left is automatically adjusted to fit the longest entry. You can select multiple columns and use any of the methods described above to change the width of all the selected columns simultaneously.

Adding a Title

We can add a title to the graph as a whole, to the category (x) axis, to the value (y) axis, or to all three. Try adding a title to the column graph in 1 Redmond BEAT now:

1. With the graph still selected, choose the Chart Options command from Graph's Chart menu and click the Titles tab to display these options:

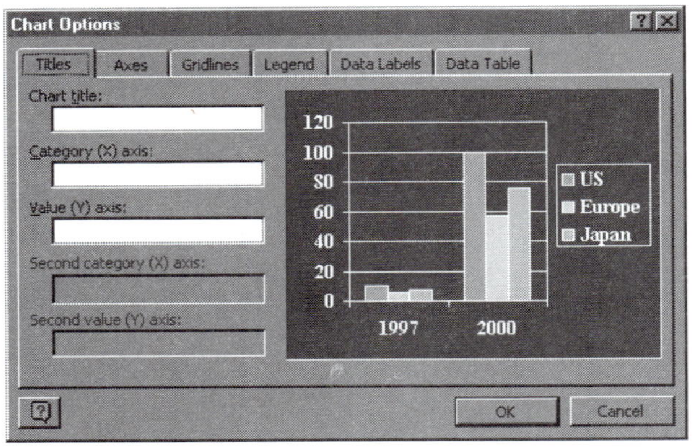

Formatting a graph title

2. In the Chart Title edit box, type *In Billions of Dollars* (the new title appears in the preview box) and then click OK.

3. With the title selected (surrounded by handles), choose Selected Chart Title from Graph's Format menu to display the dialog box shown here:

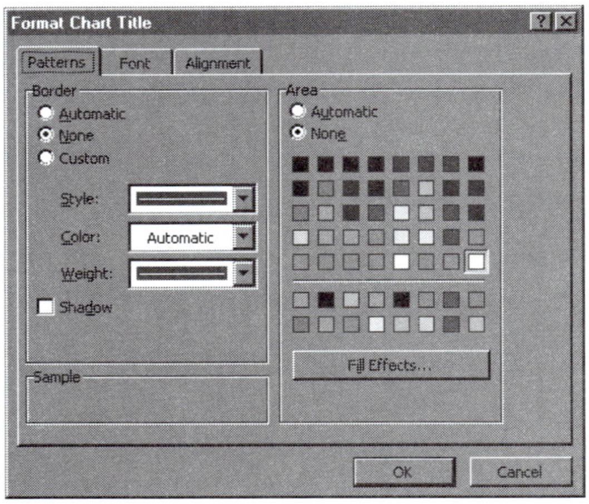

Adding an axis title

To add a title to a graph's axis, choose Chart Options from Graph's Chart menu, enter a title in the appropriate edit box on the Titles tab of the Chart Options dialog box, and click OK. Once the title is in place, you can rotate it by first selecting it and choosing Selected Axis Title from Graph's Format menu. Then click the Alignment tab of the Format Axis Title dialog box and change the Degrees setting in the Orientation section.

4. Click the Alignment tab, select the Top option in the Vertical drop-down list, and click OK. The title shifts upward to give you a little more room.

Positioning and Sizing a Legend

By default, Graph has added a legend to the column graph in 1 Redmond BEAT. (If a graph does not have a legend, we can add one by using the Legend tab of the Chart Options dialog box.) Follow these steps to reposition and resize the legend:

1. Click the legend once to select it. (Be sure the entire legend is selected, not one of the legend entries or keys.)
2. Point to the border surrounding the legend (not a handle) and then drag upward until the legend is positioned just below the graph's title.

Repositioning a legend

3. Click inside the graph's frame to deselect the legend. (Be careful not to click *outside* the graph's frame, or you'll wind up back in PowerPoint.) The graph now looks like this:

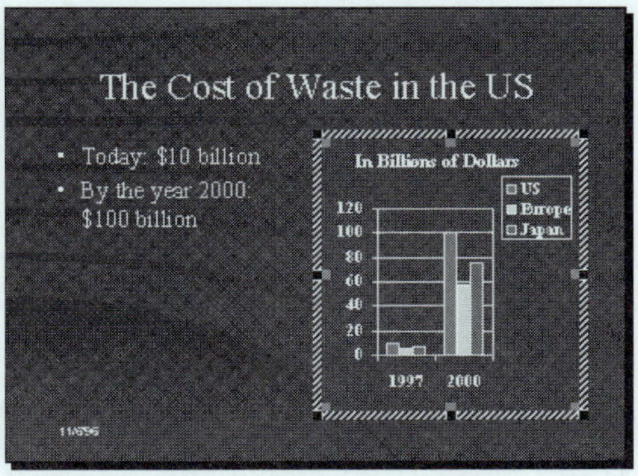

Adding a Border

So that the graph, title, and legend hang together as a unit on the slide, we can surround the chart area with a border. Follow these steps to add a heavy white border to the column graph:

1. Click a blank area of the graph to select the chart area, and choose Selected Chart Area from Graph's Format menu. Graph displays the Format Chart Area dialog box.
2. On the Patterns tab, click the arrow to the right of the Color edit box in the Border section to display the Color palette.

Changing label position

By default, Graph places tick-mark labels—the small marks used to group values or categories—next to their respective axes. You can change the position of the labels by selecting one of the Tick-Mark Labels options on the Patterns tab of the Format Axis dialog box. (To open this dialog box, select an axis and then choose Selected Axis from Graph's Format menu.) Selecting the Low or High option places labels next to the minimum or maximum values of the other axis, respectively. Selecting the None option removes the labels altogether.

3. Select the White box in the palette.

4. Next click the arrow to the right of the Weight edit box, select the last option (heavy), and click OK.

5. Click anywhere outside the chart area to return to PowerPoint.

6. Finally, click anywhere outside Slide 5 to deselect the graph. The results are shown here:

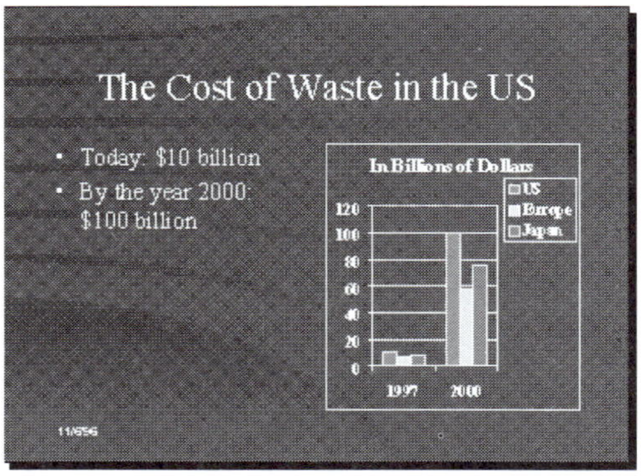

Moving and Sizing Graphs

We don't have to open Graph to move and resize the chart area of a graph. We can accomplish these tasks in PowerPoint, like this:

1. Choose Ruler from the View menu to turn on PowerPoint's rulers. (The rulers will serve as guides when you move and resize the graph.)

2. Click the column graph in 1 Redmond BEAT once to select it.

3. Point inside the graph's border, hold down the mouse button, and when the dashed positioning box appears, drag to the left about ½ inch, using the horizontal ruler as a guide.

As you can see, the bulleted text is crowding the graph a bit. To rewrap the text, follow these steps:

1. Activate the object area by clicking anywhere in the bulleted text. Then click the frame surrounding the object area to select the area.

The Fill Color button

To quickly add color to any graph object, select the object, click the arrow next to the Fill Color button on Graph's Standard toolbar, and select the desired color.

2. Drag the right center handle to the left about 1 inch. When you release the mouse button, the bulleted text rewraps.

Now finish resizing the graph by increasing its width:

1. Click the graph to select it, point to the left center handle, and when the pointer changes to a double-headed arrow, drag to the left ½ inch.

2. Choose Ruler from the View menu to turn off the rulers and then deselect the graph to see the results shown here:

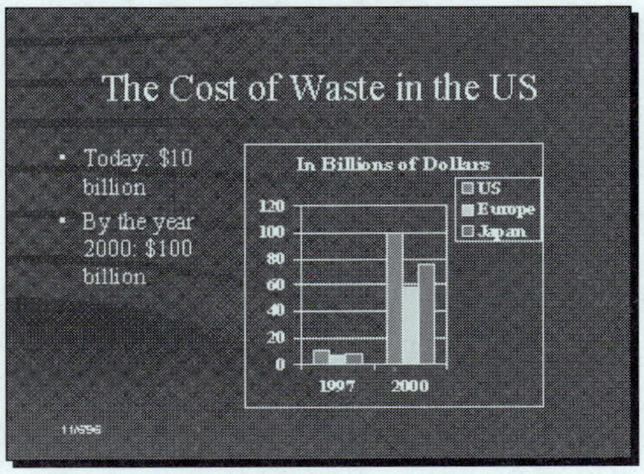

Using the Insert Chart Button

The second method of adding a graph to an existing slide involves using the Insert Chart button on PowerPoint's Standard toolbar. Follow these steps to add a 3-D pie graph to Slide 6:

1. With 1 Redmond BEAT open in slide view, move to Slide 6 and click the Insert Chart button on the Standard toolbar.

The Insert Chart button

2. When the default datasheet appears, complete it as shown here (we used the mouse to widen column A so that the entire Residential heading is visible):

1 Redmond BEAT - Datasheet

		A	B	C	D
		Residential	Industrial	Other	4th Qtr
1	Waste	0.85	6.5	2.65	20.4
2	West	30.6	38.6	34.6	31.6
3	North	45.9	46.9	45	43.9
4					

3. Use the Exclude Row/Col command on Graph's Data menu to exclude rows 2 and 3 and column D from the graph.

Now, instead of using the Chart Type dialog box to change the graph type, try the following:

The Chart Type button

1. Click the arrow to the right of the Chart Type button on the toolbar to display this palette of options:

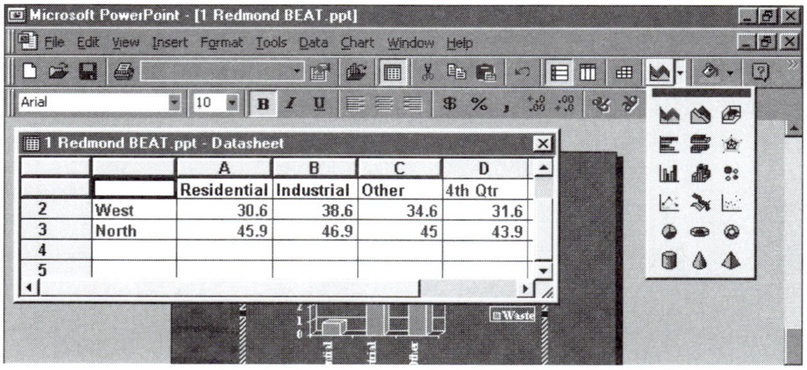

2. Click the 3-D Pie Chart option (the second option in the fifth row).

3. Now click the View Datasheet button. The 3-D pie graph looks like this:

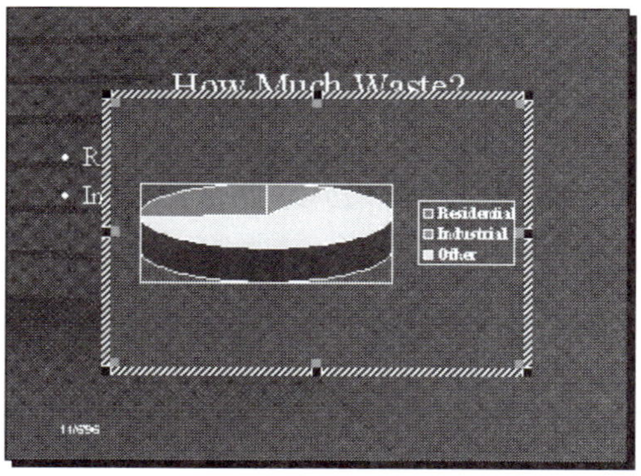

4. Point to the top center handle of the graph's chart area and drag down until the graph no longer obscures the bulleted text of the slide. Then drag the other handles to enlarge the chart area so that it fills the bottom of the slide.

Rotating a pie graph

To rotate a three-dimensional pie graph, choose the 3-D View command from Graph's Chart menu. When the 3-D View dialog box appears, enter the number of degrees you want to rotate the pie in the Rotation edit box and click Apply. A preview of your pie graph is displayed so that you can see the effects of your changes. Click OK to implement your changes.

Adding Data Labels

In addition to the labels along the axes in graphs, we can add labels to the data markers themselves. These labels can even show the value or percent of each marker and can include the legend key. Follow these steps to add data labels to the pie graph:

1. Select the legend and press the Delete key. (The data labels you're going to add will make the legend redundant.)
2. Choose Chart Options from Graph's Chart menu and click the Data Labels tab to display these options:

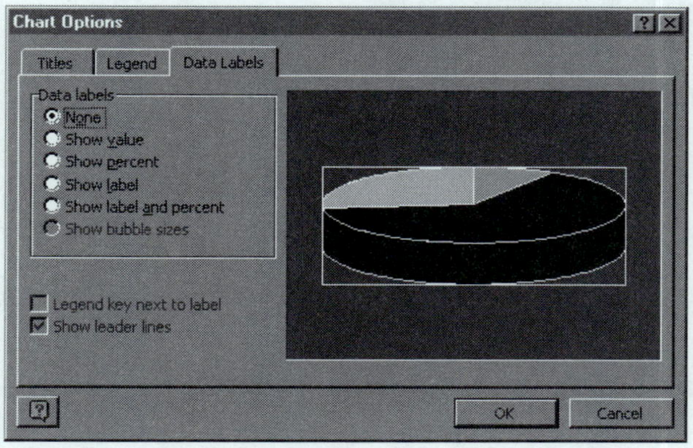

3. Select the Show Label And Percent option and click OK. The plot area of the pie graph shrinks to accommodate the labels, which now appear next to their respective data markers. (Data labels can be tricky. If they don't look right, turn them off by choosing None on the Data Labels tab, adjust the size of the chart area, and try again.)

Now increase the size of the plot area and reposition the data labels by following these steps:

Resizing the plot area

1. Click the plot area—the area occupied by the graph itself—to select it, point to the bottom right handle, and drag downward. Then drag the other corner handles to enlarge the graph without pushing the labels out of view.
2. With the plot area still selected, press Delete to remove the border surrounding the area. (The data labels will be easier to read with this border out of the way.)

Repositioning data labels

3. Now click the Industrial label to select it, point to its frame, and drag the label until it is just touching its marker.
4. Repeat step 3, dragging the other two labels to their respective markers, as shown on the next page.

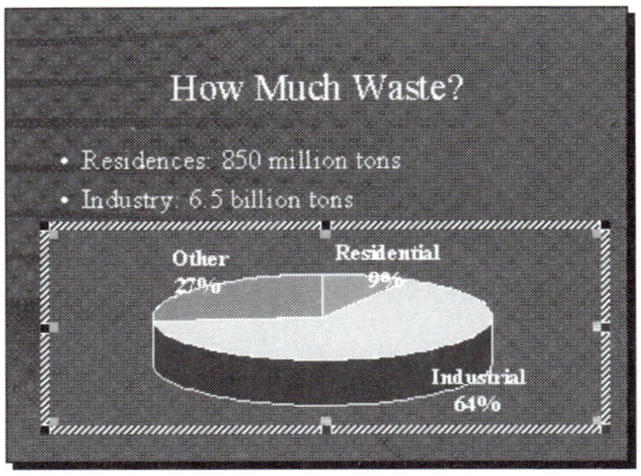

Separating Slices

In pie graphs, we can separate the individual markers, or slices, by simply dragging them with the mouse. As you'll see if you follow these steps, separating the slices helps to distinguish them:

1. Click the Residential marker to select it. (Selecting individual markers is a tricky process. You know that a single marker is selected when it's the only one surrounded by handles.)
2. Point to the marker and drag away from the center of the pie.
3. Repeat step 2 for the Industrial marker and make any necessary adjustments to the graph size and label positions. Here's what the graph looks like after you return to PowerPoint:

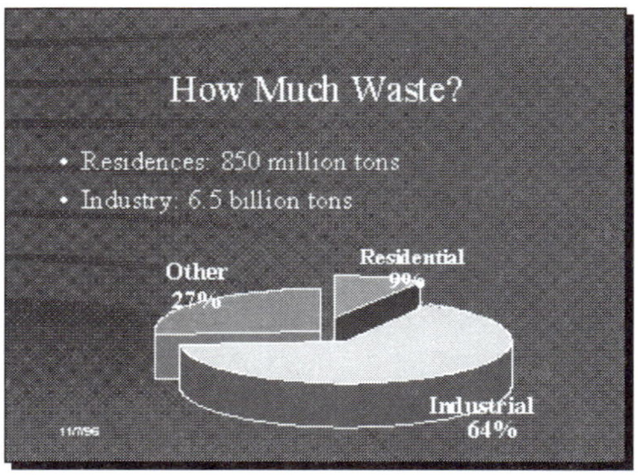

> **Adding an org chart to an existing slide**
>
> You can add an org chart to an existing slide using the Object command on the Insert menu. First move to the slide in slide view and choose Object from the Insert menu. When the Insert Object dialog box appears, be sure the Create New option is selected and then double-click the MS Organization Chart 2.0 option in the Object Type list. When the org chart window opens, you can complete the org chart as usual.

Adding Organization Charts

If you flip back to page 153, you'll see an organization chart on the second slide of the 1 Redmond BEAT presentation. As its name suggests, an organization chart, henceforth known as an *org chart*, shows hierarchy, such as the executive branch of a corporation. With a little imagination, the basic org chart elements can also be used to develop flow charts that illustrate processes.

In this section, we'll create an org chart to depict the structure of USA BEAT, the environmental group from which Redmond BEAT got its start. Follow these steps:

1. With 1 Redmond BEAT open, display Slide 2 in slide view.
2. Click the New Slide button on the Standard toolbar, and when the New Slide dialog box appears, double-click the Organization Chart autolayout (the third autolayout in the second row) to add an org chart slide to the presentation.
3. Double-click the org chart placeholder in the slide's object area to display a window like the one shown here:

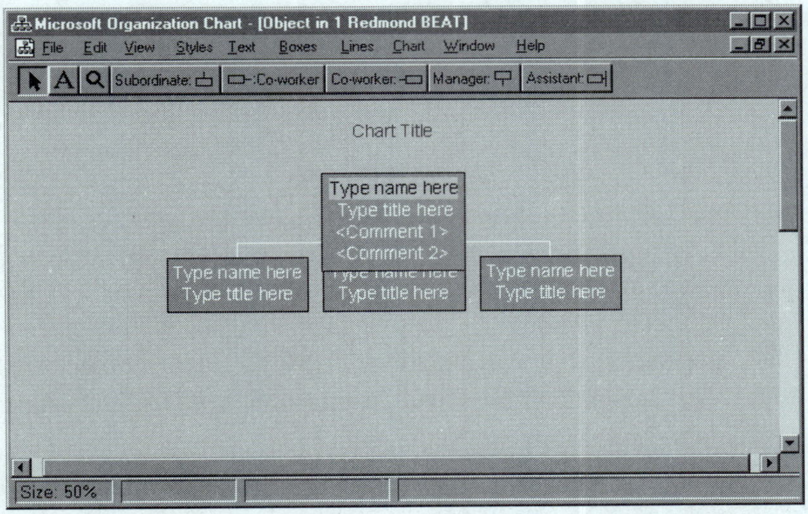

Like Microsoft Graph, Microsoft Organization Chart is a program within a program. As you can see, the org chart window has its own menu bar, toolbar, and status bar.

Microsoft Organization Chart

4. Click the Maximize button at the right end of the org chart window's title bar to maximize the window.

Adding a title

5. Select the text of the chart title placeholder with the mouse (you may have to scroll the window to see this placeholder) and type *Business Environmental Action Team.*

Before we go any further, let's change the interior color of the org chart's boxes so that we can more easily see the contents. (This step is not always necessary; however, this org chart reflects the design template we selected in Chapter 6, and some adjustments are needed here.) Follow these steps:

Changing the color of the boxes

1. Click any of the boxes, hold down the Shift key, and click the remaining boxes to select them.
2. Choose Color from Org Chart's Boxes menu, select black in the top row of the color palette, and click OK.

With this detail out of the way, we're ready to fill in the org chart's boxes:

Filling in the boxes

1. Click the topmost box to select it for editing, replace *Type name here* with *Northwest BEAT*, and press Enter.
2. Type *Olympia, WA* as the title and press Enter, and then type *Regional Office* as the first comment and click outside the box.
3. Click the leftmost subordinate box to select it, replace *Type name here* with *Washington BEAT*, press Enter, type *Seattle, WA*, and click outside the box.
4. Click the second subordinate box, replace *Type name here* with *Oregon BEAT*, press Enter, type *Portland, OR*, and click outside the box. Here are the results:

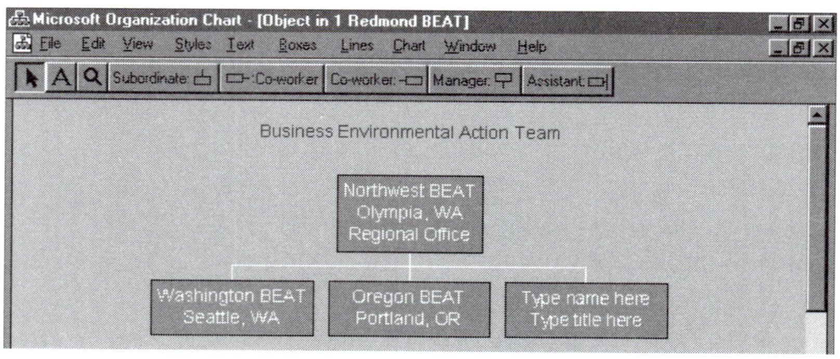

5. Choose Update 1 Redmond BEAT from Org Chart's File menu to update the 1 Redmond BEAT presentation.

Updating a presentation

To actually save the org chart as part of the presentation, we must return to PowerPoint and save it there (see page 171). Again, we won't tell you to update from this point on, but you should remember to do so often.

Saving an org chart

Adding and Removing Boxes

We aren't limited to the four boxes the Org Chart program has provided. We can add and remove boxes with just a few mouse clicks. Follow these steps:

1. To add a box to the top of the org chart, click the Manager button on the Org Chart toolbar, move the mouse pointer (which is now shaped like a manager box) to the topmost box, and click once.

The Manager button

2. The new manager box is active, so type *USA BEAT*, press Enter, type *Washington, DC*, and click outside the box.
3. Next, click the Assistant button on the Org Chart toolbar and then click the Northwest BEAT box to add an assistant box to the org chart.

The Assistant button

4. In the new box, type *Redmond BEAT* and click outside the box.
5. Add two subordinate boxes to Washington BEAT by clicking the Subordinate button on the Org Chart toolbar twice (note that the status bar displays *Create: 2*), moving the mouse pointer (which is now shaped like a subordinate box) to the Washington BEAT box, and clicking once.
6. In the new subordinate boxes, type *Vancouver BEAT* and *Spokane BEAT*, respectively.
7. Repeat step 5 to add two subordinate boxes to Oregon BEAT.
8. In the new subordinate boxes, type *Salem BEAT* and *Medford BEAT*, respectively.

Org chart size

When you create an org chart for a PowerPoint presentation, remember to maintain a reasonable size for the org chart. If your org chart is too small, viewers may not be able to read the contents of the org chart boxes. In addition, if your org chart contains many boxes, you might consider breaking the org chart up and placing it on separate slides so that viewers aren't overwhelmed with information.

9. Remove the "empty" box next to Oregon BEAT by clicking it to select it and pressing Delete. The org chart now looks like this:

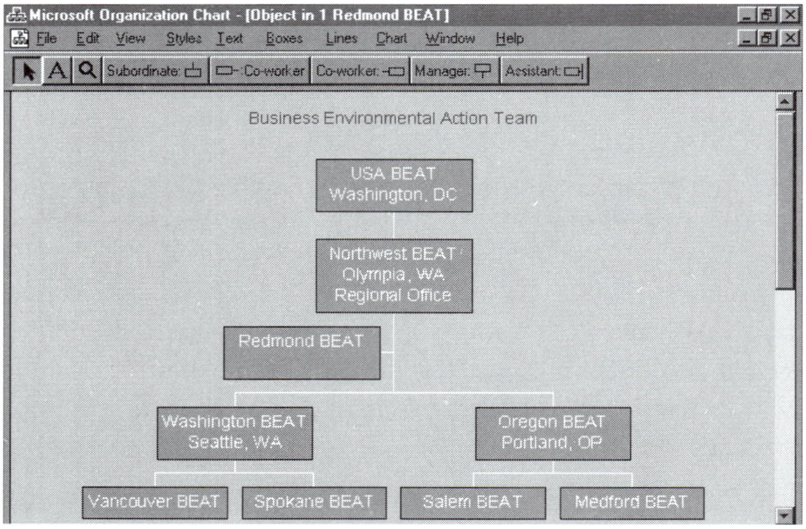

Rearranging Boxes

If we're not happy with the arrangement of boxes in an org chart, we can use the mouse to rearrange them in a variety of ways. Try the following:

1. Point to the Oregon BEAT box, hold down the left mouse button, and drag the box's frame over the Washington BEAT box. The shape of the mouse pointer changes to a left-pointing arrow, indicating that the box will appear to the left of the existing box. (A right-pointing arrow indicates that the box will appear to the right of the existing box, and a subordinate box indicates that the box will appear below the existing box.)
2. With the pointer in the shape of a left-pointing arrow, release the mouse button. The Washington BEAT and Oregon BEAT boxes switch places. (Notice that the subordinate boxes below Oregon BEAT and Washington BEAT move as well.)
3. Now point to the Redmond BEAT box, hold down the left mouse button, and drag the box's frame over the Washington

Magnifying an org chart

You can use the commands on Org Chart's View menu to adjust the magnification of an org chart. The following list describes each command:

- Size To Window displays the entire org chart in the org chart window.
- 50% Of Actual displays the org chart at 50% of Actual Size (see below).
- Actual Size displays the org chart at approximately 50% larger than its printed size.
- 200% Of Actual displays the org chart at 200% of Actual Size.

You can also use the Zoom button on the Org Chart toolbar (the button with the magnifying glass icon) to zoom in on areas of the org chart. To zoom back out, click the Zoom button again (it now displays an org chart icon) and then click anywhere in the org chart.

BEAT box and then downward until the pointer changes to a subordinate box. Release the mouse button.

4. Deselect the Redmond BEAT box by clicking outside it, and then move the box to the left of the Vancouver BEAT box. After all that reshuffling, here are the results:

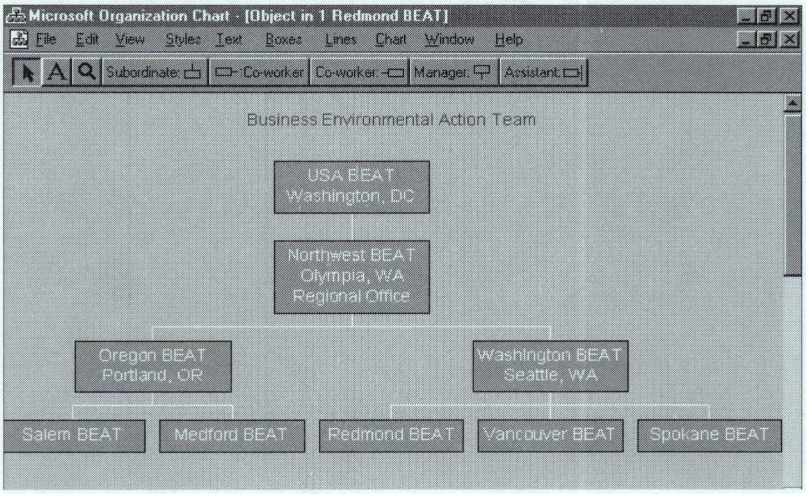

Switching Styles

In Org Chart jargon, a *group* refers to the subordinates under a manager, and a *branch* refers to a manager plus all its subordinates. By default, groups are placed side by side in boxes, as in the sample org chart; however, the Org Chart program offers several style alternatives for both groups and branches. Experiment with some of the other org chart styles by following these steps:

1. Select the Redmond BEAT box and press Ctrl+G to select its group, which consists of all three Washington BEAT subordinate boxes.

2. From Org Chart's Styles menu, choose the second style in the first row. The org chart now looks like the one shown on the next page.

Formatting org charts

You can format the text, boxes, and connecting lines in an org chart by using the commands on Org Chart's Text, Boxes, and Lines menus. All of these commands are self-explanatory, so we don't need to go into a lot of detail here. For example, if you choose the Font command on the Text menu, a Font dialog box similar to other Font dialog boxes appears. You can change the font, style, and size of the org chart text by selecting options in this dialog box. To change the alignment of the org chart text, simply choose Left, Right, or Center from the Text menu. Most of the commands on the Boxes and Lines menus are followed by an arrowhead, which indicates that a drop-down list of options will be displayed when you choose that command. You can then simply click the option you want. Keep in mind that before you can use any of these commands, you must select the text, boxes, and/or lines you want to format. The easiest way to make your selection is to use the Select or Select Levels command on Org Chart's Edit menu. For example, to select all the connecting lines in an org chart, choose Select and then Connecting Lines from the Edit menu.

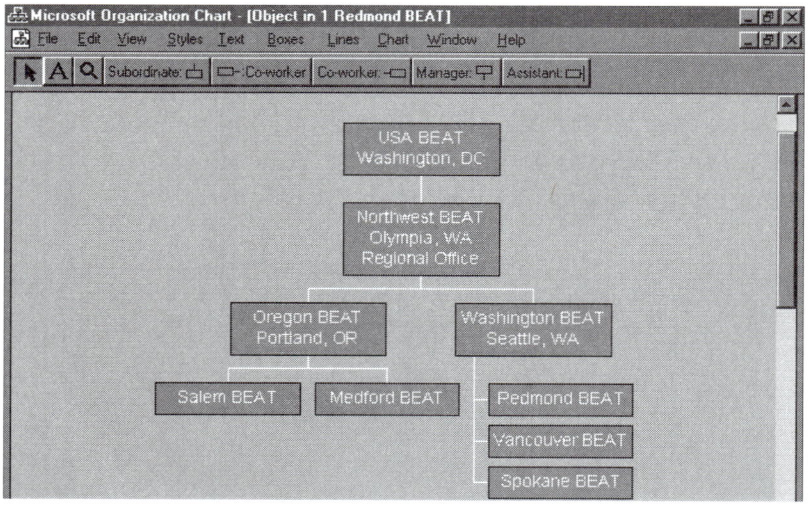

3. Next select the Salem BEAT box and press Ctrl+G.
4. If two or more members of an organization share the same manager as well as the same responsibilities, those members can be designated as comanagers. To designate the selected boxes as comanagers, choose the Co-Manager style from Org Chart's Styles menu by clicking its icon.

To condense the org chart, let's change the style of its main branch:

1. Select the USA BEAT box and press Ctrl+B to select its branch—the entire org chart.
2. From Org Chart's Styles menu, choose the third style in the first row. The results are shown here:

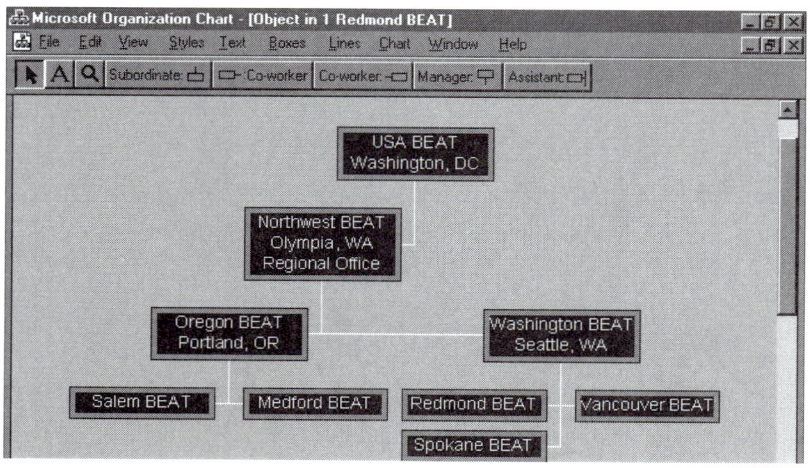

Outputting 35mm slides

The simplest way to output your presentation as 35mm slides is to entrust the imaging procedure to Genigraphics Corporation, a graphics service bureau in Memphis, TN. All you have to do is choose Send To and then Genigraphics from the File menu and follow the instructions in the Genigraphics Wizard dialog boxes. (If the Genigraphics command is unavailable, run Setup and install the Genigraphics Wizard & GraphicsLink option.) If you have a modem, you can send your presentation file electronically; otherwise, you can send the file on disk.

Returning to PowerPoint

After the org chart is complete, quitting Org Chart and returning to PowerPoint automatically adds the org chart to the current slide. Once the org chart is in place, we can use the mouse to reposition or resize it. (We can return to the Org Chart program at any time by double-clicking the org chart on the slide.) Follow these steps to return to PowerPoint:

Quitting Microsoft Organization Chart

1. Choose Update 1 Redmond BEAT from Org Chart's File menu. (If you don't choose this command first, you will be prompted to update the org chart before proceeding.)
2. Choose the Exit And Return To 1 Redmond BEAT command from Org Chart's File menu.

Back in PowerPoint, several adjustments are needed. First, we need to remove the slide's title placeholder because the org chart comes equipped with a title. Second, we need to resize the org chart to fill the current slide. Follow these steps:

1. Click the title area of the slide, press F2 until the title placeholder is surrounded by handles, and then press Delete to remove the placeholder.
2. Click the object area once to select the org chart, point to the top center handle, and when the pointer changes to a double-headed arrow, drag upward a couple of inches (use the rulers as guides).
3. Use the corner and side handles to enlarge the org chart to fit the slide. Here are the final results:

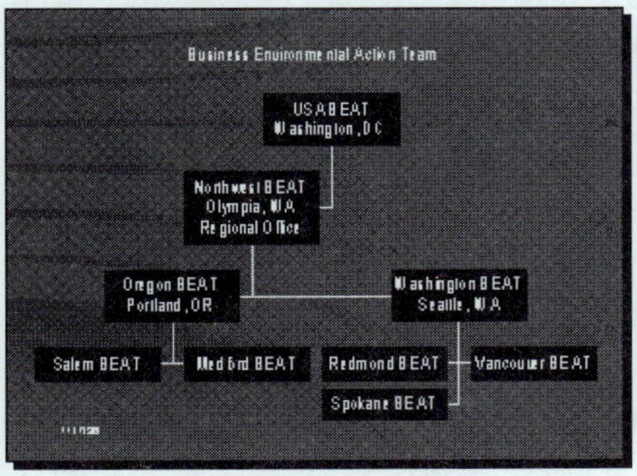

4. Save the presentation.

   If we want to save the org chart as a separate file, we can use the Save Copy As command on Org Chart's File menu.

Running an Electronic Slide Show

To output a PowerPoint presentation on paper or on acetate (to create overhead transparencies), we can use the Print button. We can also send a PowerPoint file to a graphics service bureau if we want to output the presentation as a set of 35mm slides (see the tip on page 170). However, to really impress an audience and simultaneously take advantage of the latest technology, we can turn a presentation into an electronic slide show, complete with special effects. In this section, you'll learn how to view an electronic slide show on your own computer and how to add transitions and builds to the presentation. Let's get going:

The Slide Show button

1. With 1 Redmond BEAT open on your screen, move to Slide 1 and click the Slide Show button at the bottom of the presentation window or choose View Show from the Slide Show menu to display the title slide of the presentation in slide show view, like the one shown here:

Launching slide shows from Explorer

You can automatically launch a slide show by right-clicking a presentation in Windows Explorer and choosing Show from the object menu.

2. Click the left mouse button or press the N key to move to the next slide. Continue moving through the presentation until you reach the slide with the title *Where Do I Start?*.

Moving through a slide show

Notice the "pulse" effect that occurs each time a new slide is displayed. This effect is incorporated in the Pulse design template you selected in Chapter 6. We show you how to add other special effects in the next section.

3. Now move the mouse pointer across the displayed slide. A button with an arrow and a slide icon appears in the bottom left corner. Click the button to display this slide show object menu:

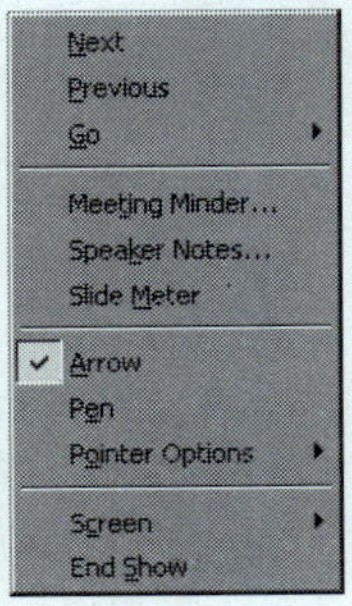

As you can see, the commands on this menu help you control an electronic slide show.

4. Choose Go and then By Title from the object menu to display a drop-down list of slide titles.

5. Select Slide 1's title to return to that slide.

6. Press the Esc key or choose End Show from the slide show object menu to return to slide view.

Adding Special Effects

To spruce up an electronic slide show, we can add special effects such as animation effects and transitions. Animation effects are visual or sound effects that we apply to specific objects on a slide, such as the title. Transitions are visual or sound effects that we apply to an entire slide to help move the audience smoothly from one slide to another. PowerPoint also offers preset animation effects that we apply to the bulleted items on a slide to help keep the audience focused on a

Displaying selected slides

If you only want to show specific slides from a presentation during a slide show, choose the Set Up Show command from the Slide Show menu to display the Set Up Show dialog box. Then, in the Slides section of the dialog box, enter the numbers of the slides you want to show in the From and To edit boxes and click OK. When you click the Slide Show button to view your presentation, only the selected slides are displayed.

particular point. Let's add some special effects to the 1 Redmond BEAT presentation:

The Animation Effects button

1. Display Slide 1 in slide view and click the Animation Effects button on the Formatting toolbar to open this toolbar:

The Laser Text Effect button

2. Click Slide 1's title area to select it, and then click the Laser Text Effect button on the Animation Effects toolbar.

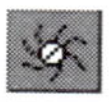

The Camera Effect button

3. Click Slide 1's object area, click the Camera Effect button on the Animation Effects toolbar, and then close the toolbar.

4. Click the Slide Sorter View button at the bottom of the presentation window to switch to slide sorter view, and choose Select All from the Edit menu to select all nine slides.

The Slide Transition Effects box

5. Click the arrow at the right end of the Slide Transition Effects box on the Slide Sorter toolbar and select Blinds Vertical from the drop-down list. PowerPoint demonstrates the effect of this transition on the first selected slide and puts a transition icon below each slide, as shown here (we've reduced the size of the thumbnails):

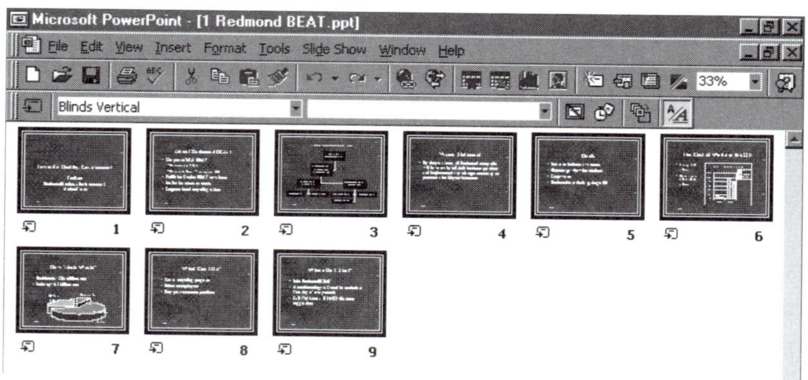

Previewing animation

You can preview an animation effect—from slide or outline view—by choosing Animation Preview from the Slide Show menu. A slide miniature then appears in the presentation window, displaying the effects you selected for the current slide (including transitions and preset animation effects). The Animation Preview command comes in handy when you want to see special effects in action without having to switch to slide show view.

6. Deselect Slides 1, 3, 6, and 7. (Hold down the Shift key as you click the slides to deselect them.)

7. Click the arrow at the right end of the Text Preset Animation box on the Slide Sorter toolbar and select Fly From Right from the drop-down list. Now the bulleted items on each bulleted list slide will "fly in" when you click the left mouse button during the slide show.

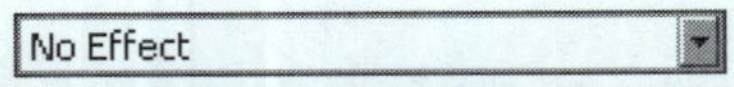

The Text Preset Animation box

Let's check out the special effects we've added by running the show again:

1. Select Slide 1 (to be sure the slide show starts at the beginning of the presentation) and click the Slide Show button.
2. After the title and subtitle appear, press N to move to Slide 2.
3. Click the left mouse button four times to bring each bulleted item into view.
4. Move through all the slides so that you can see the special effects in action.
5. Do a little experimenting with the other animation effects and transitions that PowerPoint offers and then run through the slide show again.
6. When you're ready to leave slide show view, press Esc.

Now that you have an understanding of how PowerPoint works, you can forge ahead on your own to create professional presentations.

Action buttons

PowerPoint's action buttons let you create hyperlinks to other slides, presentations, movies, and so on. To add a button to the current slide, choose Action Buttons from the Slide Show menu and select a button from the available palette. Then drag a frame in the area of the slide where you want the button to appear. The Action Settings dialog box automatically appears so that you can assign an action to the button. For example, add a button to Slide 1 in a presentation and select Last Slide from the Hyperlink To drop-down list in the Action Settings dialog box. Then during an electronic slide show, you can jump to the last slide in the presentation simply by clicking the button on Slide 1.

Custom slide shows

If you plan to give an electronic presentation to several different audiences and you need to vary the presentation slightly in each case, you can use the Custom Shows command to create a custom slide show that you can then branch off to during the presentation. Simply choose Custom Shows from the Slide Show menu, click the New button in the Custom Shows dialog box, and enter a name for the show in the Define Custom Show dialog box. Then select the slides you want to include in the custom show and click the Add button. (You can use the arrow buttons to rearrange the order of the slides.) When you're done, click OK to return to the Custom Shows dialog box, where you can see a preview of the new show by clicking the Show button. To run a custom show from slide show view, choose Go and then Custom Show from the slide show object menu and then select the show you want.

8 Access Basics

Specify an input mask to minimize invalid entries

Set the maximum size for entries, depending on their type

Employees

Emp#	SS#	First Name	Last Name	Address	City	Zip	Phone#	First Day
002	796-29-4473	Carol	Talbot	1109 Emerson Way	Lakewood	98403	334-7625	27-Aug-79
019	228-12-9111	Ron	Westerman	1419 Ivy Drive	Pinedale	98412	335-1326	08-Sep-85
027	854-72-2249	Fred	Anderson	943 Spruce Circle	Lakewood	98403	832-8779	14-Feb-89
033	583-02-1253	Lance	Bright	148 Center St., #B211	Pinedale	98412	334-6683	23-Jun-91
034	477-11-6309	Richard	Talbot	1109 Emerson Way	Lakewood	98403	334-7625	04-Jun-93
035	722-52-2624	Linda	Gardner	8841 Market Street	Lakewood	98403	334-6754	02-May-94
037	455-82-9921	Jefrey	Davis	1171 Simon Heights	Lakewood	98403	334-9297	12-Jun-94
038	241-21-4972	Jonathan	Bray	5941 Hilltop Road	Lakewood	98403	334-0180	17-Jun-94

Substitute captions for cryptic field names

Specify a date format so that entries are displayed consistently

Specify how many digits a field entry must contain

Set a default entry that Access will enter unless you enter something else

Use a wizard to efficiently create database tables and then customize them

You are probably excited but nervous about learning to use a powerful database like Microsoft Access. And you're probably hoping that, like the other Office applications, Access will be simple to use and yet offer you the tools you need to handle complex data. Well, relax. By the end of this chapter, you will be familiar enough with Access to be able to start creating databases to meet most of your needs.

Database tables

Before we load Access, let's discuss the concept of a database. The most basic component of an Access database is a *table*—a collection of information arranged in *records* (rows) and *fields* (columns). A database can consist of several tables of related data. For example, a client database might assign clients a number and list their names and addresses in one table and then list their numbers and credit references in another. Still another table might summarize account transactions for the last three years by client number. All the tables contain information about the clients, but each table has different information that is related by the client number. All the information could be kept in just one table, but if only a few clients have active accounts, the part of the table devoted to account transactions would have only a few entries. So it's more efficient to break the database into separate but related tables.

Other database components

Tables are the basic building blocks of a database. In addition to tables, a database can include queries, forms, reports, and other components, all of which allow us to view and manipulate database information in a variety of ways. As you follow along with our examples, you will create a database for Tip Top Roofing that includes several of these components.

Setting Up a Database

Without any more preamble, let's fire up Access and set up the example database, which is called Roofs. (Please note that we selected the Custom setup option when we installed Access to ensure that certain features, such as the Advanced Wizards, were included in the installation procedure.) Access will then store all the tables, queries, forms, and reports we create as we work our way through Chapters 8 and 9 in the Roofs database file. Follow these steps:

1. Choose Programs and then Microsoft Access from the Start menu to start Access. Then, if necessary, click the Start Using Microsoft Access option to close the Office Assistant.

2. Click the Blank Database option and then click OK to display the File New Database dialog box.

   Note that the File New Database dialog box resembles the Save As dialog box because you must first save your database with a name before you can begin working with it.

3. Type *Roofs* in the File Name edit box and click Create. Access displays the database window shown here:

   Across the top of the window are tabs for each type of database component. Clicking one of these tabs displays in the box below a list of the existing components for that type. Because this is a new database, the Tables option is selected, and the box is empty.

Creating a Table

We can now create the first table in the database, which will be used to store information about Tip Top Roofing's employees. Follow these steps:

1. In the database window, click New. Access opens the dialog box shown on the next page, in which you specify whether

The Table Wizard

you want the Access Table Wizard to help you set up the new table or whether you prefer to do the setup work yourself in either datasheet view or design view.

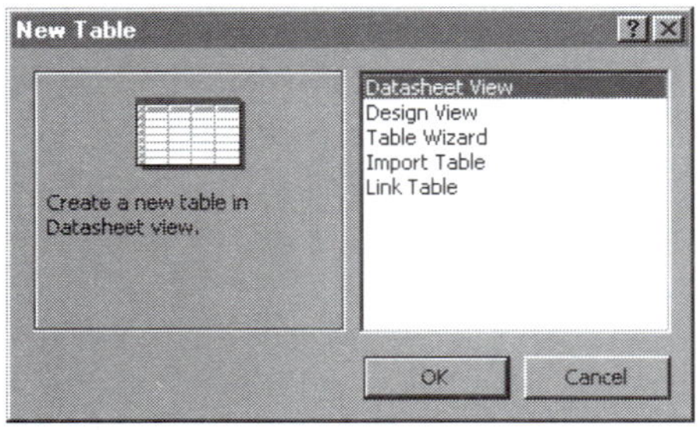

2. Click Table Wizard and click OK to display the first of a series of dialog boxes that lead you through the steps of creating your table's field structure:

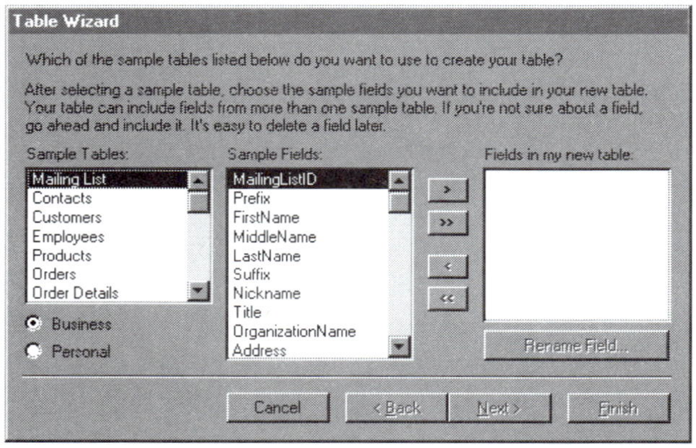

3. In the Sample Tables list, click Employees. The Sample Fields list changes to reflect the kind of information usually stored in an employee database, with DepartmentName selected.

4. Select EmployeeID and then click the > button to add the EmployeeID field name to the Fields In My New Table list.

5. Add the SocialSecurityNumber, FirstName, LastName, Address, City, PostalCode (Zip code), HomePhone, and DateHired field names to the Fields In My New Table list by clicking each name and then clicking the > button. Then click the Next button to display the next wizard dialog box:

Ready-made business and personal tables

The first Table Wizard dialog box provides several Business and Personal options, with Business selected by default. If you click the Personal option, Access displays a list of tables you can create for personal use. You may find some of these sample tables quite useful, so it's worth taking the time to explore the list.

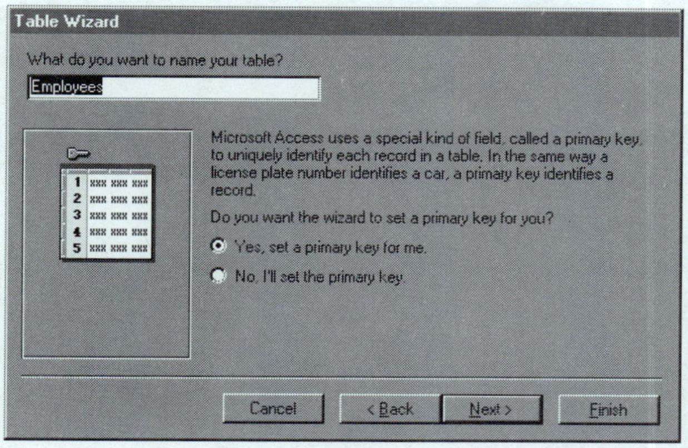

6. The name Access suggests for this database—Employees—is pretty logical, so don't change the entry in the edit box. However, you don't want Access to set the *primary key*, which is a field that distinguishes one record from another. When you enter field values in the table, no two entries in this field can be the same. In keyed tables, if you try to enter the same field value in two records, Access displays an error message and won't let you move to a new record until you change one of the duplicates. Click the No, I'll Set The Primary Key option and then click Next. The next wizard dialog box appears:

The primary key

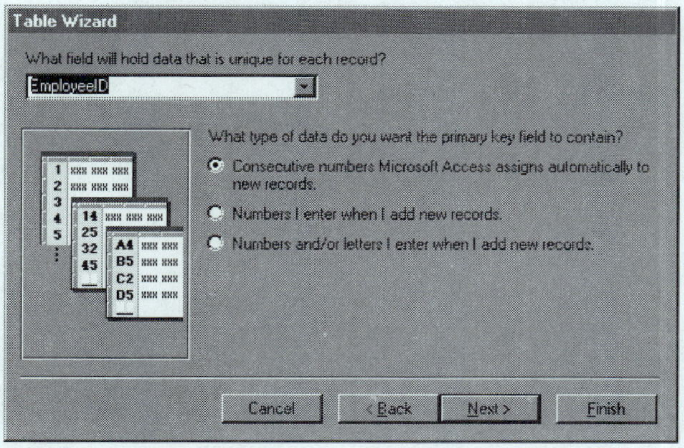

7. Because you want to set up the primary key yourself, you must now tell Access which field you want to use and what type of data that field will contain. You do want to use the default Employee ID as the primary key, but instead of allowing Access to enter consecutive numbers as the primary key, you want to enter the numbers yourself. Click the second option

Allowing Access to create the primary key

If you allow Access to create the primary key, Access inserts an AutoNumber field as the first field of the table, designates that field as the primary key, and automatically enters a consecutive number as that field's value for each record.

button and then click Next. The final wizard dialog box appears:

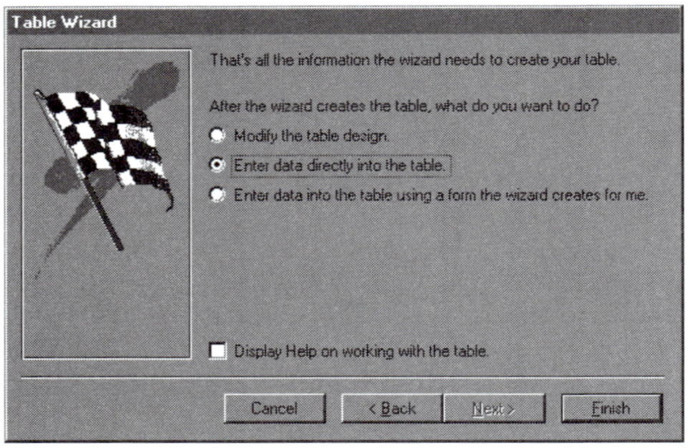

8. Click the Finish button to indicate that you want to enter data directly in the table. Access displays this table window:

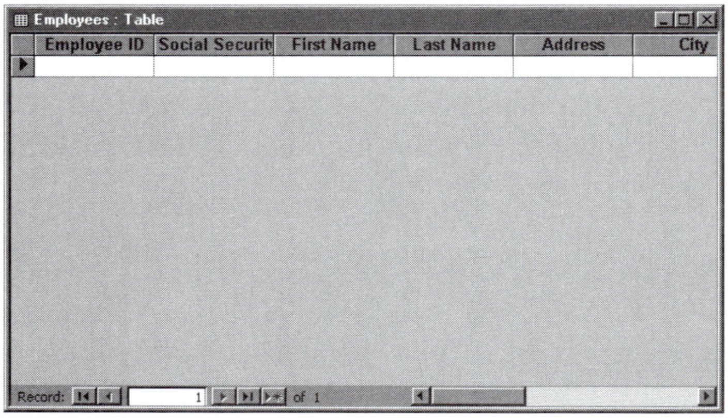

> **Fields and records**
>
> The basic structure of a database is a combination of fields and records. Each field contains bits of similar information—for example, all the phone numbers in the phone book. Each record contains all the bits of information about a particular item such as a person, product, or event—for example, the name, address, and phone number for one person in the phone book.

Entering and Deleting Records

Each record in the Employees table will contain information about one employee. In Access, we can enter and edit records either directly in the table in datasheet view, which displays as many records as will fit on the screen in column/row format, or in a form in form view, which displays one record at a time. We'll look at both methods in this section.

Entering Records in a Table

Because we told the Table Wizard that we wanted to enter data directly in the table, Access has already switched the new table to datasheet view. An insertion point sits blinking in the Employee ID field, ready for you to enter the first item of information, and an arrowhead in the record selector at the left end of the row indicates that the record is ready to receive data. Let's enter the first item now:

1. Type *2* as the first employee number. The arrowhead in the record selector changes to a pencil, indicating that the data in the record has been changed but not yet saved. (Access has added a second record with an asterisk in its record selector, indicating that the record is empty.) Press Enter to move the insertion point to the next field.

2. In the first record, enter the field values shown below, pressing Enter to move from field to field:

Field	Record 1
Social Security Number	796294473 (Access inserts the hyphens)
First Name	Carol
Last Name	Talbot
Address	1109 Emerson Way
City	Lakewood
Postal Code	98403 (Access adds a hyphen)

Don't worry that the data in the Address field doesn't fit within its column; we'll fix that in a minute.

3. Click the Home Phone field, click an insertion point to the right of the area code's closed parenthesis, type *3347625,* and press Enter.

4. In the Date Hired field, type *082779*, and press Enter. (Notice that Access adds the / where appropriate.)

5. Enter records 2 through 5 as shown on the next page, remembering to skip over the area code in the Home Phone field.

Fast navigation

When you are entering and editing data, using the keyboard to move around a window is often faster than using the mouse. You can easily navigate using the Arrow, Tab, Home, End, Page Up, and Page Down keys.

Field	Record 2	Record 3	Record 4	Record 5
Employee ID	19	27	29	33
Social Security Number	228129111	854722249	934218635	583021253
First Name	Ron	Fred	James	Lance
Last Name	Westerman	Anderson	Murray	Bright
Address	1419 Ivy Drive	943 Spruce Circle	7921 Port Avenue	148 Center St, #B211
City	Pinedale	Lakewood	Lakewood	Pinedale
Postal Code	98412	98403	98403	98412
Home Phone	3351326	8328779	8345934	3346683
Date Hired	090885	021489	032291	062391

The Employees table now looks like this:

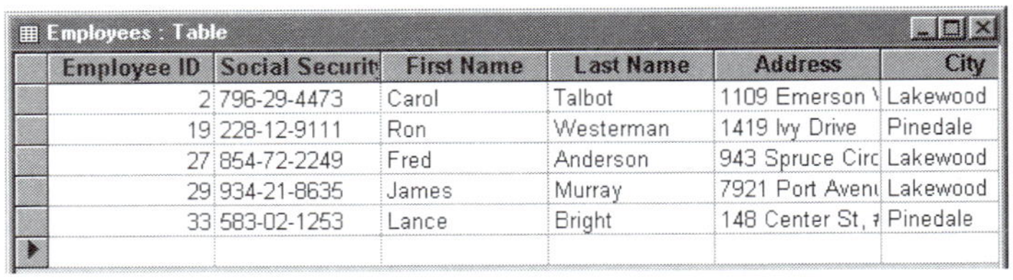
Employees : Table

Employee ID	Social Securit	First Name	Last Name	Address	City
2	796-29-4473	Carol	Talbot	1109 Emerson \	Lakewood
19	228-12-9111	Ron	Westerman	1419 Ivy Drive	Pinedale
27	854-72-2249	Fred	Anderson	943 Spruce Circ	Lakewood
29	934-21-8635	James	Murray	7921 Port Avenu	Lakewood
33	583-02-1253	Lance	Bright	148 Center St, #	Pinedale

Now let's widen the Address field. Follow these steps:

Widening fields

1. Move the pointer to the gridline between the Address and City field names.
2. When the pointer changes to a double-headed arrow, double-click with the left mouse button. Access automatically widens the column to fit the largest entry.

Here's another way to change the widths of fields:

Selecting multiple fields

1. Scroll the table to the right until the last four fields are visible. Move the pointer to the City field name, and when the pointer changes to a downward-pointing arrow, click to select that field in all records. Then move the pointer to the Date Hired field name, hold down the Shift key, and click to add the Postal Code, Home Phone, and Date Hired fields to the selection.
2. Choose Column Width from the Format menu to display this dialog box:

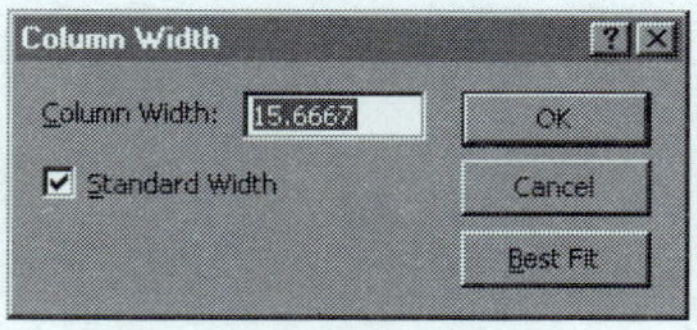

3. Type *15* and press Enter to change the widths of all four fields at the same time.

You might want to take some time to practice resizing the Employees table's fields; for example, try shrinking the fields enough to see all of them at one time.

Entering Records in a Form

Instead of entering information in a table, we can enter it in a *form*. To display a form for the Employees table and see how easy it is to enter records in a form, follow these steps:

1. Click the New Object button to display this form:

The New Object button

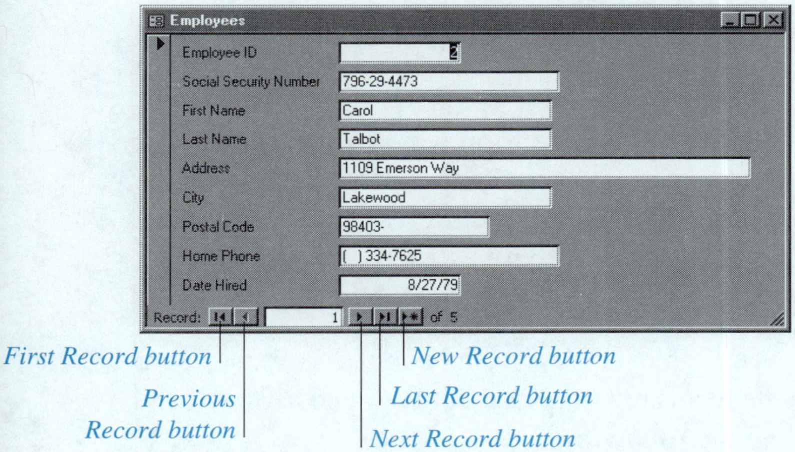

2. Click the Next Record button at the bottom of the form window to display the information for Ron Westerman.

3. Click the Last Record button to move to the last record and then click the New Record button to display a blank record.

4. Enter the record for the sixth employee shown on the next page. After typing the last field value, press Enter to display a new blank record, enter the record for the seventh employee, and then press Enter.

Field	Record 6	Record 7
Employee ID	34	35
Social Security Number	477116309	722522624
First Name	Richard	Linda
Last Name	Talbot	Gardner
Address	1109 Emerson Way	8841 Market Street
City	Lakewood	Lakewood
Postal Code	98403	98403
Home Phone	3347625	3346754
Date Hired	060493	050294

The Employees table is complete for now, and we can view the records in either form view or datasheet view. Here's how to switch back and forth:

The View button

1. Click the down arrow next to the View button at the left end of the toolbar. A list appears that allows you to toggle among the three database views. Click Datasheet View. Instead of the form, you see the table.
2. Click the arrow next to the View button again and click Form View to switch back to the form.
3. Close the form by clicking the form window's Close button, and click No when Access asks whether you want to save the design of the form. (The records themselves are already saved because Access automatically saves each record when you move to another one.)

The Employees table is now visible, but the records we entered via the form are not displayed. We need to update the table by doing the following:

Updating a table

1. Choose the Remove Filter/Sort command from the Records menu. Access updates the table to show the last two records.

Deleting Records

To delete a record, we simply select the record and choose the Delete command. Follow these steps to delete a record from the Employees table:

1. Select James Murray's record by clicking its record selector, and choose Delete from the Edit menu or press the Delete key. Access displays this dialog box:

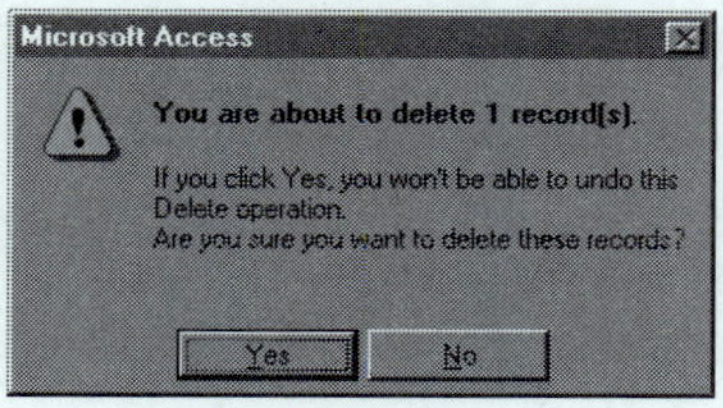

2. Click Yes. Access deletes the record and updates the table.

Be careful when deleting records. If you make a mistake and delete the wrong record, you can't restore the record by clicking an Undo button or choosing Undo from the Edit menu once you've confirmed the deletion.

Delete with caution

Changing a Table's Structure

When we used the Table Wizard to set up the Employees table, Access made a number of decisions about the table's basic design. But those decisions are not cast in stone. Let's examine the existing table structure and see how to change it:

1. Click the arrow to the right of the View button on the toolbar and select Design View. Access displays the structure of the table in this window:

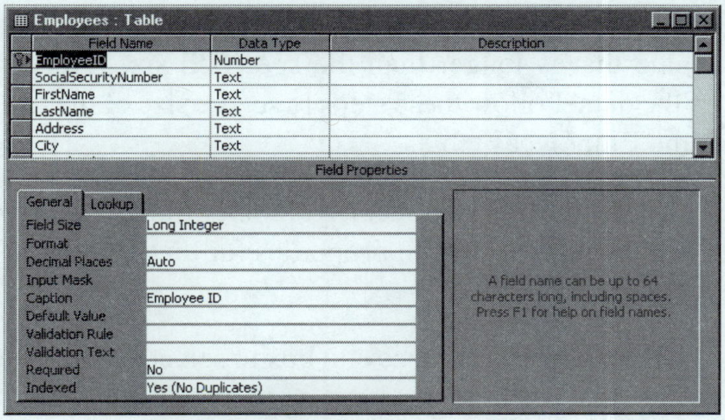

Access data types

As you can see, the window is divided into two sections. The top half lists the table's field names (with no spaces) and their data type. (Specifying the data type determines what kind of information you can put in the field and how Access can work with the information.) The bottom half lists the properties assigned to the field selected in the top half.

2. Press Enter to move to the Data Type column for the EmployeeID field, and click the arrow that appears to display a list of the available data types.

3. Click Number to close the Data Type list without changing its setting, and press Enter to move to the Description column.

4. Type *Unique 3-character number identifies each employee.* When the table is displayed and this field is selected, this description will appear in the status bar.

After we define a field for a table, we can refine our field definitions in the Field Properties section. You will use some of these properties frequently, others rarely. Here, we'll explore the more common properties.

Setting the Field Size

We can set a field size for the text and number data types. For text fields, the size indicates the maximum number of characters we can enter in the field. We can specify up to 255 characters, which can include letters, numbers, and other characters such as &, %, and ?. If we try to enter, paste, or import a field value that is longer than the specified size, Access truncates the data. Follow these steps to set the size of the text fields of the Employees table:

1. Click anywhere in the SocialSecurityNumber field in the top table grid to display the default properties for that field in the Field Properties section.

2. Double-click 30 in the Field Size edit box to select it, and type *11* to indicate that the field can have up to eleven characters.

3. Repeat steps 1 and 2 to assign the following field sizes:

Help with data types

Access is much more rigid about its data types than Excel is about its number formats. For example, specifying a Currency number format for a cell in Excel does not prevent you from entering text in that cell. In Access, you cannot enter text in a field that has been assigned the Number data type. For more information, choose Contents And Index from the Help menu, click the Index tab, enter *data types*, click Display, and then double-click Comparison Of Data Types.

Field	Size	Field	Size
FirstName	10	City	12
LastName	12	PostalCode	10
Address	25	HomePhone	20

For number fields, the size is determined by the complexity of the data type format selected. The options are:

Number field size

Format	Description
Byte	Whole numbers between 0 and 255
Integer	Whole numbers between –32,768 and 32,767
Long Integer	Whole numbers between –2,147,483,648 and 2,147,483,647
Single	Single-precision floating-point numbers between –3.402823E38 and 3.402823E38
Double	Double-precision floating-point numbers between –1.79769313486232E308 and 1.79769313486232E308

Follow these steps to set the size of the table's number field:

1. Click anywhere in the EmployeeID field and then click the Field Size edit box in the Field Properties section.
2. Click the arrow to see a list of available sizes. You don't think the company will ever employ more than 255 employees, so select Byte.

Setting the Format

We use the Format property to specify how the characters entered in a field are to be displayed on the screen. The type of formatting we can perform varies depending on the data type. For example, we can select one of several predefined formats for date/time fields, like this:

1. Click anywhere in the DateHired field and then click the Format edit box in the Field Properties section.

Predefined formats

2. Click the arrow to see a list of predefined formats, and select Medium Date. The dates in the table will now be displayed in dd-mmm-yy format.

In addition to selecting predefined formats, for some data types we can specify custom formats. Follow these steps to tell Access to always display three digits in the EmployeeID field:

Custom formats

1. Click anywhere in the EmployeeID field and then click the Format edit box.

2. Type *000* to tell Access to enter three digits, using zeros unless you enter something else. Now if you enter an EmployeeID of *36*, Access will display the entry as *036*.

Specifying an Input Mask

Formats aren't the only way to control the display of data. We can also specify an *input mask*, or character pattern, that not only determines how our data looks on the screen but also what kind of data can be entered in a particular field. Because we used the Table Wizard to set up the Employees table, Access has already specified input masks for some fields. Let's take a look at a few of these input masks and make any necessary changes:

1. Click anywhere in the SocialSecurityNumber field. The entry in the Input Mask edit box is *000\-00\-0000*. The zeros are placeholders for digits that you must enter, and the backslashes indicate that the hyphens are literal characters that Access will insert for you.

2. Click the PostalCode field in the table grid. The entry in the Input Mask edit box is *00000\-9999*. Again, the zeros are placeholders for digits you must enter. The nines are placeholders for an optional four-digit Zip code extension. Access enters the hyphen whether or not you enter this extension.

3. Click an insertion point after the last 9 and press the Backspace key six times to delete all but the five zeros. Now Access will accept only five digits in this field. We can no longer enter a four-digit extension.

Now let's adjust an input mask with some help from Access:

1. Click the HomePhone field in the table grid. The entry in the Input Mask edit box is !\(999") "000\-0000.

The Input Mask Wizard

2. Click the Input Mask edit box and then click the Build button—the button with three dots to the right of the edit box. Click Yes when Access tells you it must save the table before proceeding, and when another message box warns you that the changes you have made to the field sizes of the table might result in a loss of data (see the tip below), click Yes to proceed. Access displays this Input Mask Wizard dialog box:

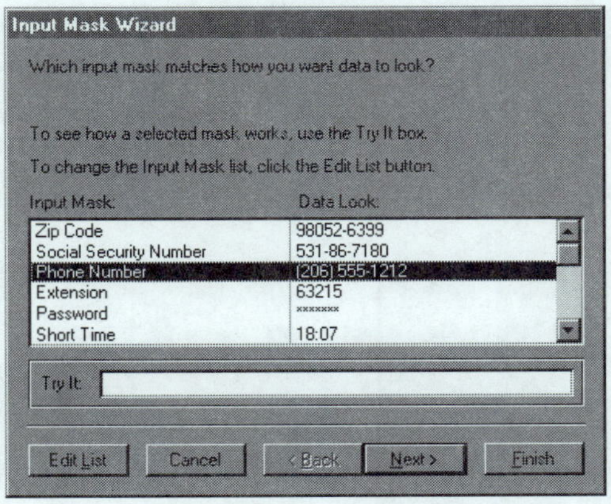

3. Click Next to accept the default Phone Number option and display this dialog box:

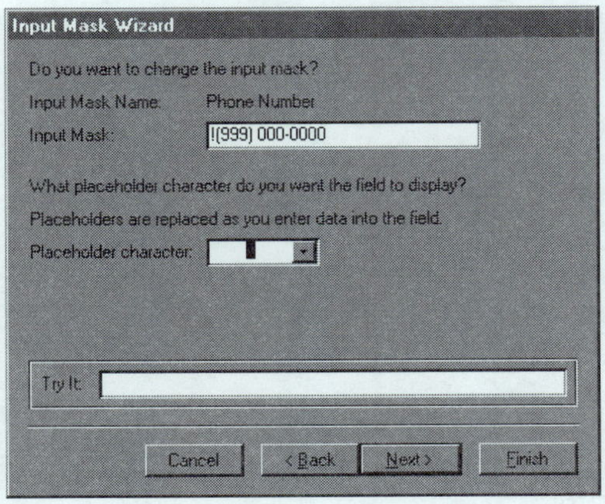

The 9s in the parentheses indicate that a three-digit area code is optional, whereas the seven-digit phone number is required.

Data integrity

Always stop and think before changing the field sizes and input masks for your data. Such changes can result in data losses that will seriously affect the usability of some fields. For example, if you had entered area codes in the HomePhone field, changing the input mask might have resulted in the last three digits of the employees' phone numbers being chopped off.

4. All the employees live in the same area code, so you want to enter only the seven-digit phone number without having to skip over the area code each time. In the Input Mask edit box, click to the left of the first 0 and then press the Backspace key to delete *!(999)* and the extra space.

5. Click the arrow to the right of the Placeholder Character edit box and select the underscore from the drop-down list.

Trying out a mask

6. Now click at the left end of the Try It edit box and type your phone number. Then backspace over the last four digits and try typing *abcd*. Access won't accept letters in the entry because the zeros in the input mask require the entry of digits.

7. Press Esc to clear the Try It entry, and click the Next button to display this dialog box:

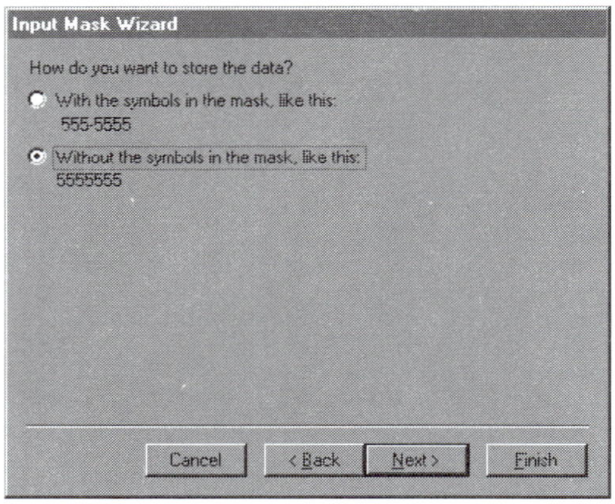

8. Click Finish to accept the default setting in the last wizard dialog box and return to the table window.

Input mask characters

In case you want to experiment further, here's a list of some common characters used in the Input Mask edit box, together with what they mean to Access:

Character	Action
L	Require a letter.
?	Allow any letter; if no letter is entered, leave blank.
&	Allow any character, but no blanks allowed.
0	Require a digit; if no digit is entered, insert 0.
#	Allow any digit; if no digit is entered, leave blank.

Character	Action
<	Convert all following characters to lowercase.
>	Convert all following characters to uppercase.
\	Insert the following character as entered.

You can remove an input mask at any time. For example, let's remove the input mask from the DateHired field:

Deleting an input mask

1. Click anywhere in the DateHired field to display its properties.
2. Select the entry in the Input Mask edit box and press Delete.

Assigning a Caption

The Caption property enables us to substitute text for the field name when we display the table. The caption may simply repeat the field name with spaces added for readability, or it may display something different. Let's change a few of the captions specified by the table wizard when we created the table:

1. Click anywhere in the EmployeeID field to display its properties in the Field Properties section.
2. Click an insertion point to the right of the *p* in *Employee* in the Caption edit box, hold down the Shift key, and press the End key to highlight all but *Emp*. Then type #.
3. Repeat steps 1 and 2 to change the following captions:

   Social Security Number to *SS#*
   Postal Code to *Zip*
   Home Phone to *Phone#*
   Date Hired to *First Day*

When we display the table, the new captions will be displayed as field names above each column of information.

Setting a Default Value

The Default Value property lets us specify a field value that Access is to enter in the table automatically. Because Tip Top Roofing is small and most of the employees live in the same city, we can use this property for both the City and PostalCode fields to speed up data entry. Follow the steps on the next page.

1. Click anywhere in the City field to display that field's properties in the Field Properties section.

2. In the Default Value edit box, click to display an insertion point, and then type *Lakewood* as the default city name.

3. Repeat steps 1 and 2 for the PostalCode field, specifying *98403* as the default value.

Now every record we enter in the new database table will have Lakewood as its City field value and 98403 as its PostalCode field value, unless we replace them with something else.

Requiring Entries

If we leave the table's field structure as it is, it would be possible to create incomplete employee records. To ensure that key information is always entered, we can specify that a field must have an entry. Try this:

1. Click the EmployeeID field, click the Required edit box, click the arrow, and then click Yes.

2. Repeat step 1 for all the other fields.

Other Properties

The Indexed property

When we made the EmployeeID field the primary key for the table, Access changed that field's Indexed property to Yes (No Duplicates), meaning that the field is indexed and no duplicate values will be allowed. Only text, number, currency, and date/time fields can be indexed. When a field is indexed, Access can process queries, searches, and sorts based on the field more quickly. (If a few values will be repeated often in a field, as is the case with the City and PostalCode fields, then indexing the field will not save much processing time.) Data entry and editing may be slower with indexed fields because Access must maintain the index as well as the table.

The Validation Rule property

We set the Validation Rule property for a field when we want Access to allow only specific field values to be entered in the field. The kind of rule we can set up varies with the field's data type. We can specify that a text field should contain one of a set of values—for example, the City field should contain only Pinedale or Lakewood. We can specify that a date field should contain only the current date or a date that falls within a certain range. With number fields, we can specify that Access should accept only a specific value, or we can use the greater than (>) and less than (<) signs to specify that field values must fall within a range. We can also specify that the values in a field must match the values in the same field in another table. When we set a validation rule for a field, we can use the Validation Text property to display a message when an unacceptable value is entered.

The Validation Text property

We will rarely need to use the Allow Zero Length property (available for text fields). When this property is set to Yes, we can enter "" in a field to indicate that the field doesn't apply for this record. For example, we could enter "" to indicate that an employee doesn't have a phone, whereas simply skipping the field indicates that we don't know the phone number.

The Allow Zero Length property

Testing the Changes

Now let's return to the table to see the effects of our changes:

1. Click the arrow next to the View button on the toolbar and select Datasheet View. Access tells you it must save the table before it can switch views.

2. Click Yes. When Access asks whether you want to test the data in the table against the new rules, click Yes. Access displays the table window.

3. Maximize the window and decrease the width of the fields so that you can see more of the employee data at once, as shown below:

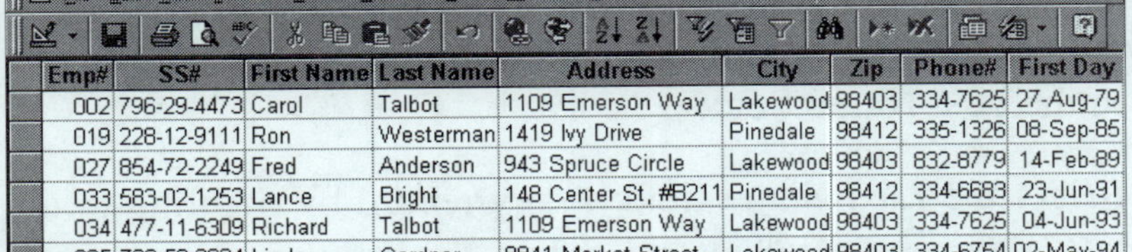

Emp#	SS#	First Name	Last Name	Address	City	Zip	Phone#	First Day
002	796-29-4473	Carol	Talbot	1109 Emerson Way	Lakewood	98403	334-7625	27-Aug-79
019	228-12-9111	Ron	Westerman	1419 Ivy Drive	Pinedale	98412	335-1326	08-Sep-85
027	854-72-2249	Fred	Anderson	943 Spruce Circle	Lakewood	98403	832-8779	14-Feb-89
033	583-02-1253	Lance	Bright	148 Center St, #B211	Pinedale	98412	334-6683	23-Jun-91
034	477-11-6309	Richard	Talbot	1109 Emerson Way	Lakewood	98403	334-7625	04-Jun-93
035	722-52-2624	Linda	Gardner	8841 Market Street	Lakewood	98403	334-6754	02-May-94
					Lakewood	98403		

The table reflects all the visual changes we made to its structure. The Emp# field displays three digits, and *Lakewood* and *98403* have been entered by default in the blank record at the bottom of the table. Let's add more employees to try everything out:

1. Click the Emp# field of the blank record at the bottom of the table, type *38*, and press Enter. Access enters *038* in the field.
2. Type the following information in the indicated fields (press Enter to skip over the City and Zip fields):

Field	Record 7	Record 8
Emp#		37
SS#	241214972	455829921
First Name	Jonathan	Jefrey
Last Name	Bray	Davis
Address	5941 Hilltop Road	1171 Simon Heights
Phone#	3340180	3349297
First Day	06/17/94	06/12/94

3. Press Enter to complete and save Record 8.

As you enter the field values, notice the effect of the field properties specified as part of the table's structure.

Working with Records

In Chapter 9, we show you some fairly sophisticated ways of working with records. Here, we'll cover some simple methods of manipulating data so that we can locate the information we need.

Finding Specific Records

We often need to find either a particular record in a table or all the records that have something in common, so Access provides an easy way to locate records. As a demonstration, let's search the Employees table for a record that has Talbot in the Last Name field:

1. Select the Last Name field of any record by pointing to the left of the field value and, when the pointer changes to a hollow plus sign, clicking to highlight the field.

2. Click the Find button on the toolbar to display the Find dialog box shown here:

The Find button

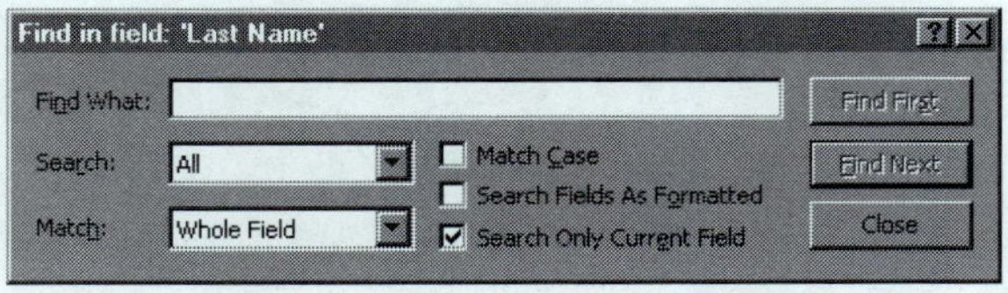

3. Point to the Find dialog box's title bar, hold down the mouse button, and drag the dialog box downward so that you can see the table's records.

4. Type *Talbot* in the Find What edit box and click the Find First button. Access highlights the first field value that matches your specification.

Finding the first record

5. Suppose this is not the employee record you need to examine. Click the Find Next button in the dialog box to display the next record with Talbot in the Last Name field.

Finding subsequent records

6. Click the Close button to close the dialog box.

When dealing with a very large table, we can temporarily focus on a subset of the records in the table by using filters. For example, if we select Talbot and click the Filter By Selection button, Access displays the subset of records that have the value Talbot in the Last Name field. (Choose Remove Filter/Sort from the Records menu to redisplay all the records.) Filters are closely related to *queries*, which you'll learn about in Chapter 9.

The Filter By Selection button

Moving Fields

By default, the fields are displayed in the order in which we entered them when we designed the table. We can change the field order by selecting a field's column and dragging it to a new position. For example, if we want to look up an employee's phone number, it might be useful to see the Phone# field next to the employee names. Follow these steps to move the Phone# field:

1. Click the Phone# field name to select the entire column.

Hiding and unhiding fields

Sometimes you might want to simplify the display by hiding one or more fields. Simply select the field's column and choose Hide Columns from the Format menu. To redisplay the field, choose Unhide Columns from the Format menu, click the check box next to the field(s) you want to redisplay, and then click Close.

2. Point to the Phone# field name, hold down the left mouse button, and drag the field to the left. As you move the field, Access highlights the divider lines between columns to indicate the new position of the Phone# field.

3. When the divider line to the right of the Last Name field is highlighted, release the mouse button. As you can see here, the Phone# field moves to its new position:

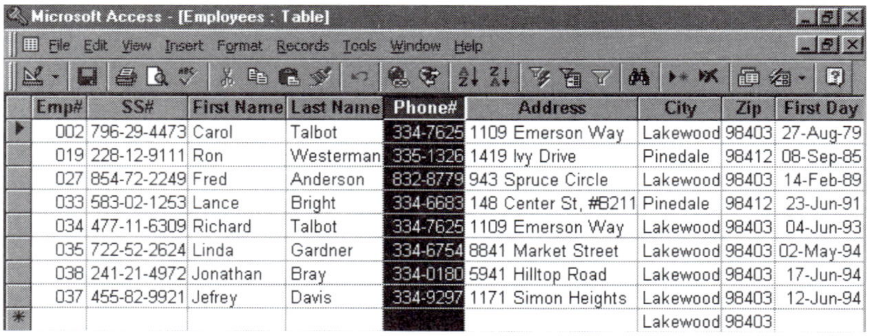

Emp#	SS#	First Name	Last Name	Phone#	Address	City	Zip	First Day
002	796-29-4473	Carol	Talbot	334-7625	1109 Emerson Way	Lakewood	98403	27-Aug-79
019	228-12-9111	Ron	Westerman	335-1326	1419 Ivy Drive	Pinedale	98412	08-Sep-85
027	854-72-2249	Fred	Anderson	832-8779	943 Spruce Circle	Lakewood	98403	14-Feb-89
033	583-02-1253	Lance	Bright	334-6683	148 Center St, #B211	Pinedale	98412	23-Jun-91
034	477-11-6309	Richard	Talbot	334-7625	1109 Emerson Way	Lakewood	98403	04-Jun-93
035	722-52-2624	Linda	Gardner	334-6754	8841 Market Street	Lakewood	98403	02-May-94
038	241-21-4972	Jonathan	Bray	334-0180	5941 Hilltop Road	Lakewood	98403	17-Jun-94
037	455-82-9921	Jefrey	Davis	334-9297	1171 Simon Heights	Lakewood	98403	12-Jun-94
						Lakewood	98403	

4. For more practice, move the Phone# field back to its original position between the Zip and First Day fields.

Moving fields in datasheet view does not affect the data or change the basic structure of the table.

Sorting Records

The Employees table is short enough that we can view all of its records on the screen at one time. But we may need to work with tables, such as mailing lists, that contain several hundred or even several thousand records. In those tables, one way to easily locate a specific record or set of records is to sort the table on a particular field. Try this:

1. Click the Last Name field name to select that column.

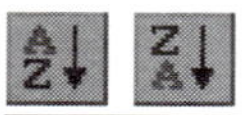

The Sort Ascending and Sort Descending buttons

2. Click the Sort Ascending button on the toolbar to sort starting with A or the lowest digit, or click the Sort Descending button to sort starting with Z or the highest digit.

Sorting on more than one column

To sort the records on more than one column, we must first arrange the columns so that they appear in the table in the order of the sort. For example, to sort a table of invoice data in descending order of sales amount within a region, first move the fields so that they appear side-by-side with the region column to the left of the sales amount column (see page 197). Then select the two columns and click the Sort Descending button. Access sorts the records first into descending order by region and then into descending order by sales amount within each region.

3. To return the data to its original order, choose the Remove Filter/Sort command from the Records menu.

Returning sorted data to its original order

Ending an Access Session

Well, that's a lot of work for one chapter, and you're probably ready for a break. When we finish working with Access, all we have to do is quit. We don't need to worry about saving the information in open database tables; Access updates the table files one record at a time as we enter or edit records. Let's quit Access now:

1. Quit Access by double-clicking the program's Control menu icon—the key in the top left corner. (You can also choose Exit from the File menu.)
2. If Access asks whether you want to save any changes you have made, click Yes.

More About Access

Create forms to facilitate data entry and minimize risk of error

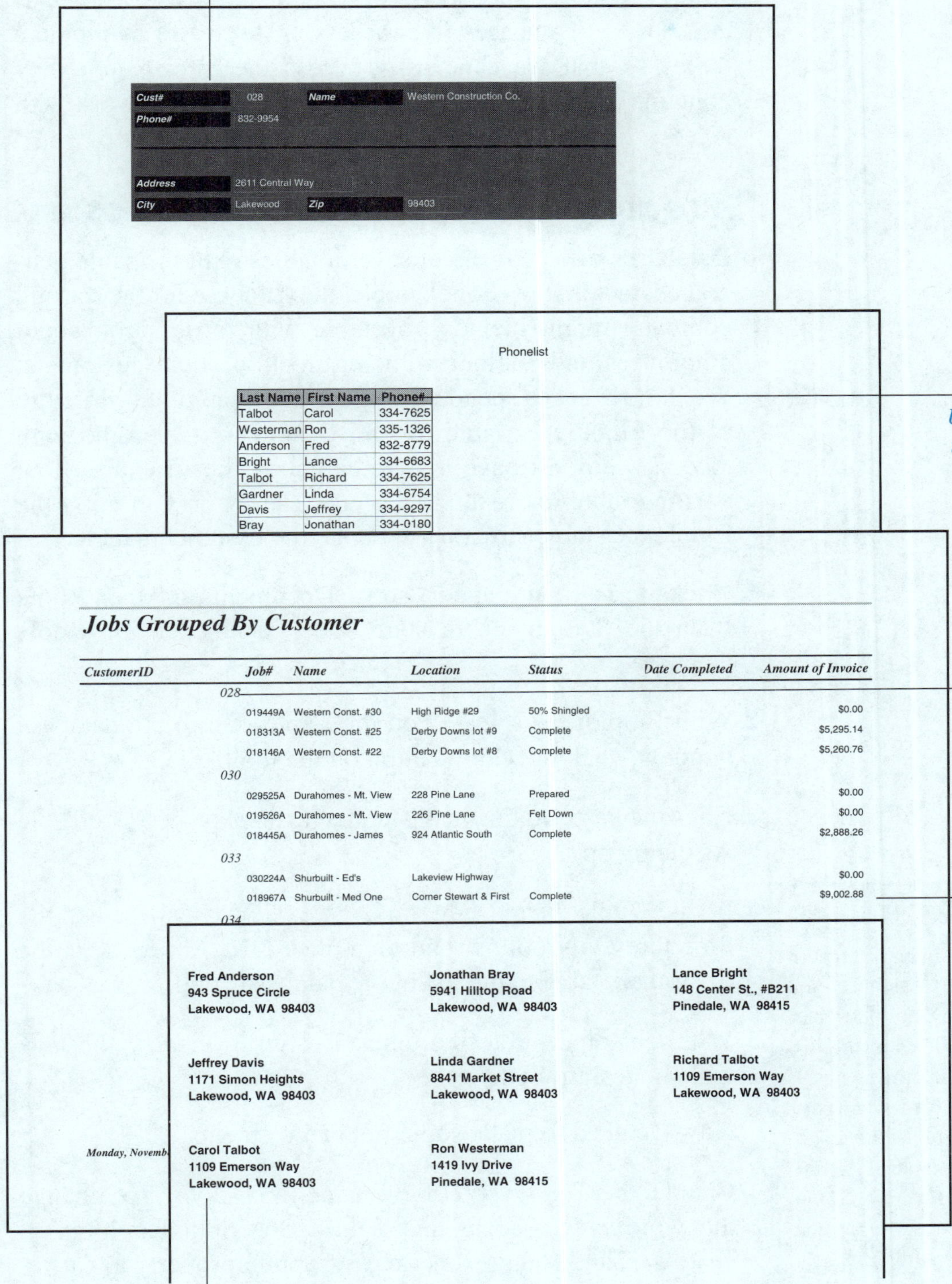

Cust#	028	Name	Western Construction Co.
Phone#	832-9954		
Address	2611 Central Way		
City	Lakewood	Zip	98403

Phonelist

Last Name	First Name	Phone#
Talbot	Carol	334-7625
Westerman	Ron	335-1326
Anderson	Fred	832-8779
Bright	Lance	334-6683
Talbot	Richard	334-7625
Gardner	Linda	334-6754
Davis	Jeffrey	334-9297
Bray	Jonathan	334-0180

Jobs Grouped By Customer

CustomerID	Job#	Name	Location	Status	Date Completed	Amount of Invoice
028						
	019449A	Western Const. #30	High Ridge #29	50% Shingled		$0.00
	018313A	Western Const. #25	Derby Downs lot #9	Complete		$5,295.14
	018146A	Western Const. #22	Derby Downs lot #8	Complete		$5,260.76
030						
	029525A	Durahomes - Mt. View	228 Pine Lane	Prepared		$0.00
	019526A	Durahomes - Mt. View	226 Pine Lane	Felt Down		$0.00
	018445A	Durahomes - James	924 Atlantic South	Complete		$2,888.26
033						
	030224A	Shurbuilt - Ed's	Lakeview Highway			$0.00
	018967A	Shurbuilt - Med One	Corner Stewart & First	Complete		$9,002.88
034						

Monday, Novemb

Fred Anderson
943 Spruce Circle
Lakewood, WA 98403

Jonathan Bray
5941 Hilltop Road
Lakewood, WA 98403

Lance Bright
148 Center St., #B211
Pinedale, WA 98415

Jeffrey Davis
1171 Simon Heights
Lakewood, WA 98403

Linda Gardner
8841 Market Street
Lakewood, WA 98403

Richard Talbot
1109 Emerson Way
Lakewood, WA 98403

Carol Talbot
1109 Emerson Way
Lakewood, WA 98403

Ron Westerman
1419 Ivy Drive
Pinedale, WA 98415

Use queries to select records and fields

Group records in reports in various ways

Calculate totals and other summary statistics

Use a report wizard to create mailing labels

Simple tables like the one we created in Chapter 8 will probably meet many of your needs. However, relational databases like Access enable us to manipulate tables so that we can easily access the information they contain. In this chapter, we look at more ways to work with Access.

Creating One Table Based on Another

Databases often consist of several tables with the same general characteristics. For example, the database for the roofing company might include one table with information about employees and another with information about customers. We don't want to spend a lot of time recreating the structure of the Employees table for the Customers table, and with Access we don't have to. We can copy the structure of an existing table to create a new one. Here's how to copy the Employees table structure to create the Customers table:

1. Click the Start button and choose Documents and then Roofs from the Start menu to start Access and open the Roofs database.
2. With Employees selected on the Tables tab in the database window, click the Copy button on the toolbar.
3. Click the Paste button on the toolbar to display the Paste Table As dialog box.
4. In the Table Name edit box, type *Customers*, select the Structure Only option, and then click OK. Access adds the Customers table to the list in the database window.
5. With Customers selected, click Design to display the new table in design view.

Copying records

When you want to copy a record from one table to another, you can use the Copy and Paste buttons, provided fields in the two tables are of compatible types. If Access has a problem when pasting the record, it puts the record in a Paste Errors table. By scrutinizing the Paste Errors table, you can usually discover the problem and fix it. You can then cut and paste the record from the Paste Errors table into the desired table.

Now we need to make some field adjustments:

1. Change the *EmployeeID* field name to *CustomerID*, change the word *employee* in this field's Description column to *customer*, and change this field's Caption property to *Cust#*.

2. Select the SocialSecurityNumber field by clicking its row selector, and press the Delete key to delete it. Then delete the FirstName and DateHired fields.

3. Change *LastName* to *Name*, change the field size of this field to *30*, and change the Caption property to *Name*.

4. Change the *HomePhone* field name to *Phone*. The table structure now looks like this:

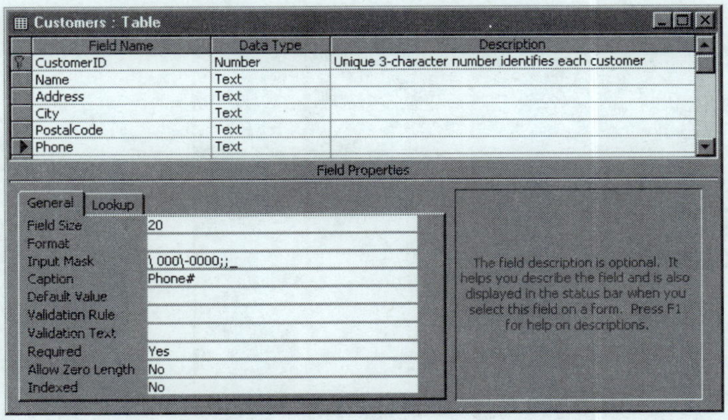

5. Click the View button to switch to datasheet view, and when Access prompts you to save the table, click Yes.

Copy with caution

Copying the structure of simple tables is relatively easy, but as you begin to create more complex tables, you'll need to consider carefully such characteristics as primary keys and validation rules, as well as the applicability of other Access table features such as referential integrity, which we discuss on page 208. In the meantime, you can see that this technique is a great way of streamlining the table-creation process.

Creating Forms

In Chapter 8, you saw how you can use a form to enter and view the information in a database table one record at a time. When we introduced forms, we mentioned that we can create different kinds of forms to accomplish different kinds of tasks. We can also design custom forms. A detailed discussion of customization is beyond the scope of this book, but we do want to give you a taste of it here. Let's create a form for entering information in the Customers table. Follow these steps to set up the form:

1. Close the Customers table, and then with Customers selected in the database window, click the arrow to the right of the New Object button on the toolbar and select Form.

The Form Wizard

2. In the New Form dialog box, select Form Wizard and click OK to display this dialog box:

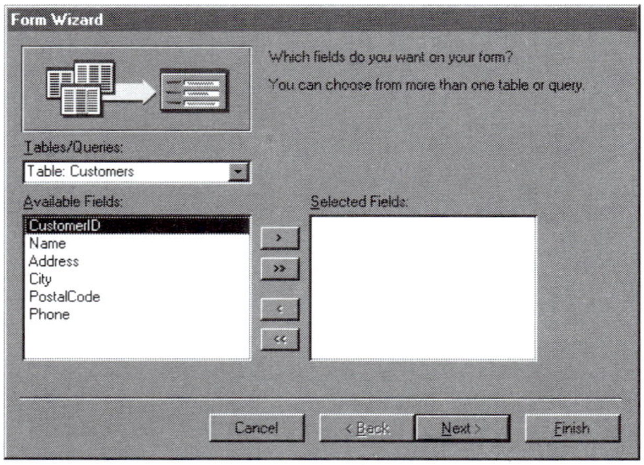

3. With CustomerID selected in the Available Fields list, click the >> button to move all the field names to the list on the right. Then click the Next button to display this dialog box:

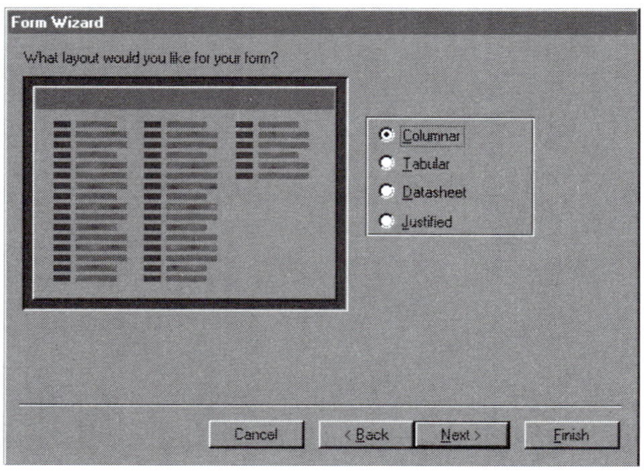

Creating forms from scratch

You can create a blank form by clicking the arrow next to the New Object button on the toolbar, selecting Form, and then double-clicking Design View in the New Form dialog box. Access switches to design view and displays a form containing only the Detail section, ready for you to add the controls you want. To add a Form Header and Footer or a Page Header and Footer, simply choose the corresponding command from the View menu.

4. Be sure Columnar is selected and then click Next to display another dialog box:

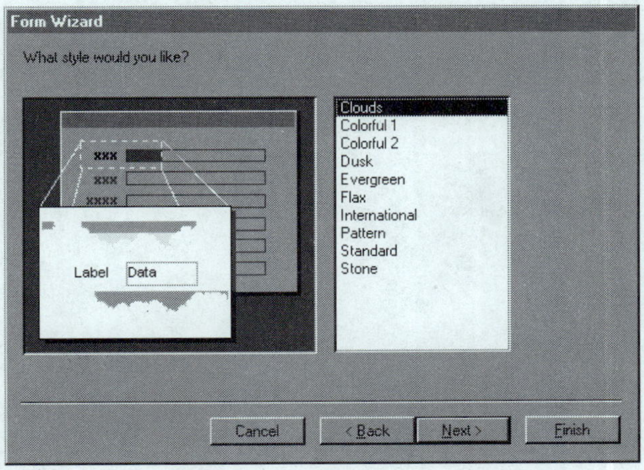

5. Access asks you to choose a style for your form. Select the various styles listed, noticing their effect in the window to the left. Then select Colorful 1 and click Next to display the last dialog box:

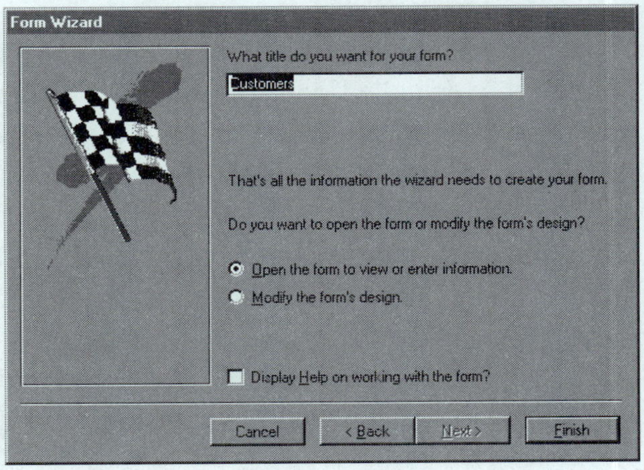

6. Click the Modify The Form's Design option and then click Finish to display the form window shown on the next page.

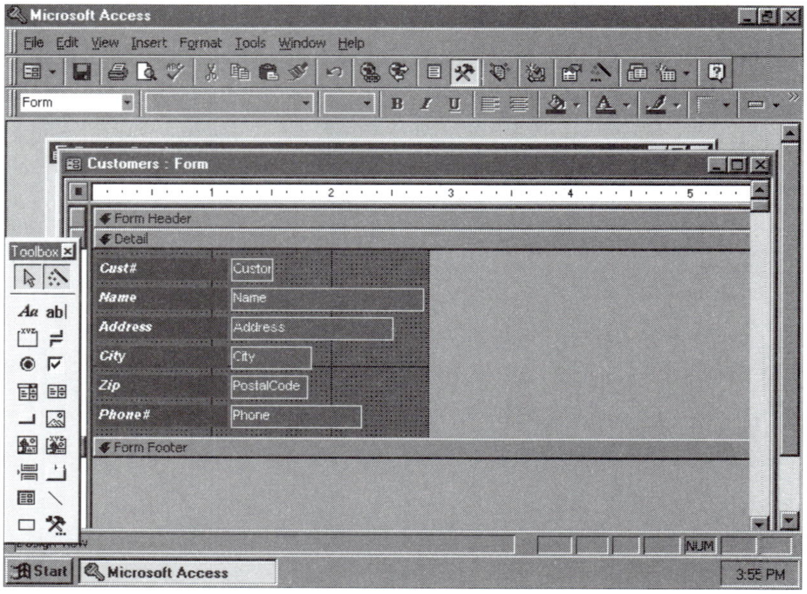

Saving forms

7. Save the form by clicking the Save button on the toolbar.

The form window

Labels and controls

The form window is divided into three sections: the Form Header section, which can contain information such as a title or date that you want to appear at the top of the form; the Detail section, which displays dark blue boxes called *labels* and light-blue framed boxes called *controls* for each of the fields you selected for inclusion in the form; and the Form Footer section, which, like the Form Header, can contain information such as a title or date that you want to appear at the bottom of the form. Two other sections, Page Header and Page Footer, are not visible in the form now on your screen. They contain elements you want to appear on every page of a multi-page form. The window also contains horizontal and vertical rulers and gridlines that help you position controls on the form.

The Toolbox

The Toolbox provides many tools with which you can customize forms. You might want to practice adding elements to forms to explore these tools. If you need help, choose What's This from the Help menu, point to the tool you want to know more about, and click.

Let's customize the Customers form so that its fields are grouped more logically:

1. Click the Name control. Small handles appear around the control's border.
2. Point to the selected control and when the pointer changes to a small open hand, drag the control and its label to the right

of the CustomerID control, shown as *Custo*. (Use the rulers to help align the controls.)

3. Next select and drag the Phone control and its label under the CustomerID control.

4. Drag the City control down into the space formerly occupied by the Phone control, and drag the PostalCode control down to the right of the City control. Then drag the Address control down so that it sits just above the City control. The fields are now arranged in two groups on the form, like this:

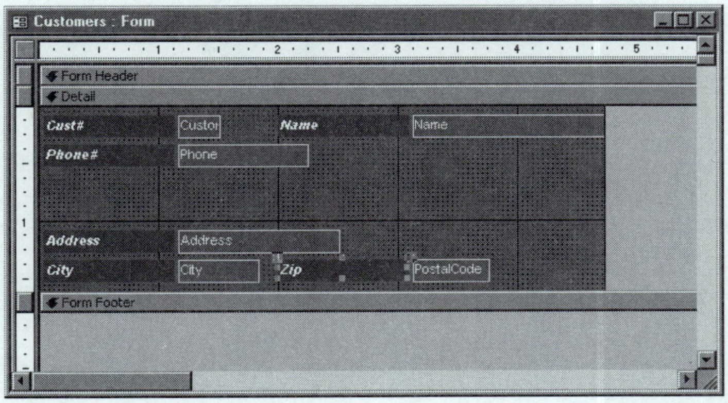

Now let's draw a line to separate the two groups:

The Line button

1. Click the Line button in the Toolbox and position the cross-hair pointer next to the ¾-inch mark on the vertical ruler. (You might have to drag the Toolbox out of the way.)

2. Hold down the left mouse button and drag a horizontal line across the entire width of the window to the 5 ½-inch mark on the horizontal ruler.

3. Click the Save button to save the changes to the form.

4. Click the View button to display the form in form view, as shown on the next page.

Two types of hands

To move a control and its label on a form so that they maintain their relative positions, select the control and drag the black open hand that appears when you point to the control's border. To move a control independently of its label, select the control and drag the black pointing hand that appears when you point to the large handle in the control's top left corner. Similarly, to move a label independently, select the label and drag the pointing hand.

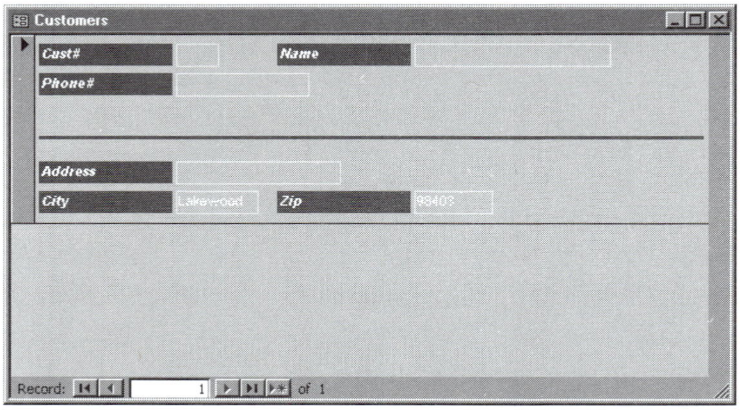

5. Now enter the customer records shown below, pressing Tab to move from field to field and to start a new record:

Cust#	Name	Address	City	Zip	Phone#
28	Western Construction Co.	2611 Central Way			8329954
30	Durahomes	4969 Market St. #211	Pinedale	98412	3347965
33	Shurbuilt	966 8th Street			8848742
34	Lakewood City Const. Dept.	28 Central Way			8327865
35	James Bready	511 Shoreline Drive	Pinedale	98412	3348121
41	Marcus Wilson	1701 Airport Way			8323882
45	Roberts Construction	734 Stewart Road			8321044

6. Close the Customers form.

Establishing Table Relationships

With Access, we can create relationships between tables so that we can combine the data from more than one table in forms, queries, and reports. Usually the relationships involve tables in which the primary key of one table matches a field called the *foreign key* in another table. You can think of the table with the primary key as the *parent* and the table with the foreign key as the *child*. Usually the values in the foreign key field don't have to be unique, but each one must match a value in the parent's primary key field. Access provides a method called *referential integrity* for ensuring that the field values match.

To demonstrate referential integrity, we'll create a new table called Jobs. Follow the steps on the facing page.

Field name rules

The field names in any one table must be unique and cannot be longer than 64 characters. You can use any combination of characters except periods, exclamation marks, and square brackets.

1. Click New in the database window, select Design View, click OK, and create the following table structure:

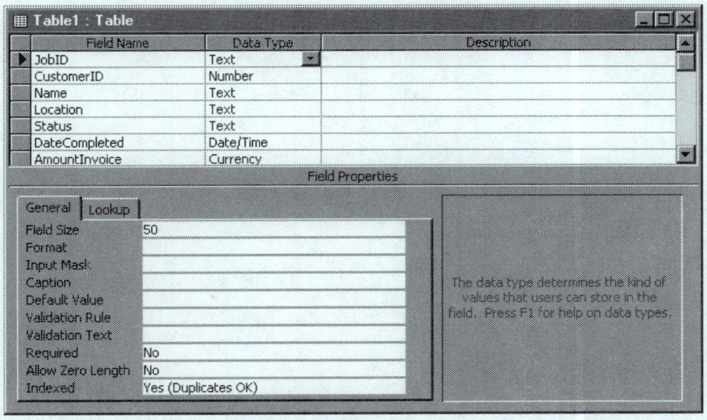

2. Click the row selector of the JobID field and then click the Primary Key button on the toolbar to make this field the table's primary key (see page 181 if you've forgotten what the primary key is).

The Primary Key button

3. Assign the fields these properties:

Field	Field Size	Format	Caption	Required
JobID	8		Job#	Yes
CustomerID	Byte	000	Cust#	Yes
Name	25			
Location	25			
Status	25			
DateCompleted		Short Date	Date Completed	
AmountInvoice		Currency	Amount of Invoice	

4. Double-click the Control menu icon to close the window, and save the new table with the name *Jobs* when prompted.

Now let's create a referential integrity relationship between the Customers and Jobs tables:

1. With the database window active, click the Relationships button on the toolbar to display the dialog box shown on the next page.

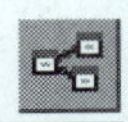
The Relationships button

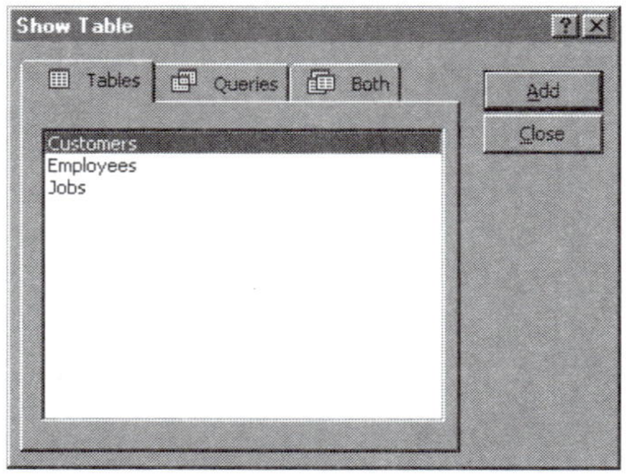

2. In the Tables list, Access has selected the Customers table. Click the Add button to add a Customers box to the blank window behind the dialog box.

3. Click Jobs, click Add, and then click Close. Access displays the relationships window shown here:

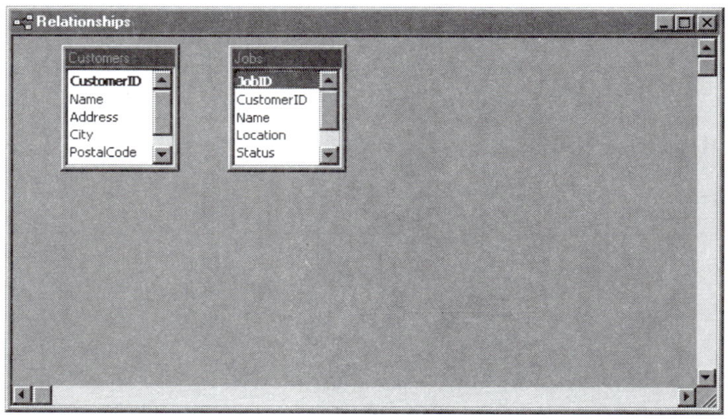

Linking tables

4. In the Customers box, point to the CustomerID field name, hold down the left mouse button, drag the field icon to the CustomerID field name in the Jobs box, and release the mouse button. Access displays this dialog box:

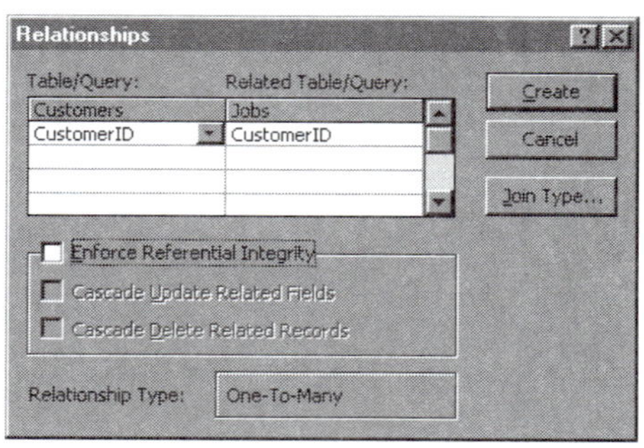

5. Click the Enforce Referential Integrity option to tell Access to require that values in the CustomerID field in the Jobs table match values in the same field in the Customers table. **Enforcing referential integrity**

   At the bottom of the Relationships dialog box, note that the relationship type is listed as One-To-Many, meaning that for each record in the parent table (Customers), there can be many records with a matching field value in the child table (Jobs).

6. Click the Create button to create the new relationship between the tables. Access draws a line connecting the two fields in the relationships window, like this:

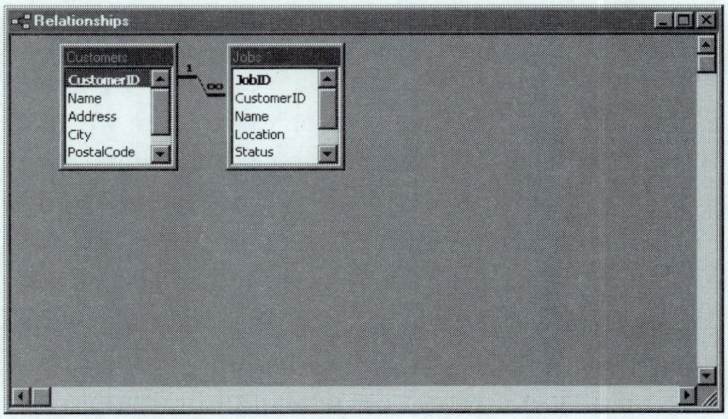

7. Close the relationships window, saving the changes to the database when prompted.

   Here's the acid test:

1. Open the Jobs table and enter the data shown here: **Testing referential integrity**

Jobs : Table

Job#	Cust#	Name	Location	Status	Date	Amount of Invoi
018022A	028	Western Const. #21	Derby Downs lot #7	Complete		$6,908.41
018146A	028	Western Const. #22	Derby Downs lot #8	Complete		$5,260.76
0182730	035	Bready Home	11 Shoreline Drive	Complete		$3,392.57
018313A	028	Western Const. #25	Derby Downs lot #9	Complete		$5,295.14
018445A	030	Durahomes - James	924 Atlantic South	Complete		$2,888.26
018967A	033	Shurbuilt - Med One	Corner Stewart & First	Complete		$9,002.88
0193330	041	Wilson Home	1701 Airport Way	Shingled		$0.00
019449A	028	Western Const. #30	High Ridge #29	50% Shingled		$0.00
019526A	030	Durahomes - Mt. View	226 Pine Lane	Felt Down		$0.00
029525A	030	Durahomes - Mt. View	228 Pine Lane	Prepared		$0.00
0301780	034	City Park Lodge	Main Street Park			$0.00
030224A	033	Shurbuilt - Ed's	Lakeview Highway			$0.00
	000					$0.00

Record: 13 of 13

2. Try entering an incorrect customer number. You can type any number in the field, but Access won't let you leave the record until a correct customer number is in place.

3. When you have entered all the data, close the Jobs table.

Data modeling

Often we will make decisions about the data relationships needed in a relational database before we actually create the tables. Database design involves listing the types of data we want to keep in a database, organizing the data in the most economical way, and then selecting fields such as customer or employee numbers to tie the data in different tables together. This process is called *data modeling*.

Design modification

Even the best database designers don't always get the design right the first time. Sometimes we'll have to make changes after we have created the database or even after we have entered the data. This is the case with the Roofs database. As we create the Jobs table, suppose we realize that we need to track the current job assignments of all employees. We can't add an EmployeeID field to the Jobs table because several employees might be assigned to the same job. Instead, we will have to modify the Employees table to include a JobID field. The process involves changing the design of the Employees table, adding another relationship, and entering job numbers in the Employees table. Follow these steps:

1. In the database window, click Employees and then click the Design button to open the table in design view.

2. Select the FirstName field by clicking its row selector, and press the Insert key to add a new blank row above FirstName.

3. Type *JobID* as the new field name, specify Text as the data type, and assign a field size of 8 and a caption of *Job#*.

4. Close the Employees table, saving the changes when prompted.

Now let's add another relationship to the database:

1. Click the Relationships button on the toolbar.

2. When the relationships window appears, click the Show Table button, select Employees, and click the Add button and then the Close button.

The Show Table button

3. Next drag the JobID field in the Jobs box to the JobID field in the Employees box, click Enforce Referential Integrity in the Relationships dialog box, and then click Create to add this one-to-many relationship to the database.

4. Close the relationships window, clicking Yes to save your changes.

Now all we have left to do is add the job numbers to the Employees table:

1. Open the Employees table and enter the job numbers shown here, leaving the field for Carol Talbot blank because she works in the office:

Employees : Table

Emp#	SS#	Job#	First Name	Last Name	Address	City	Zip
002	796-29-4473		Carol	Talbot	1109 Emerson Way	Lakewood	98403
019	228-12-9111	018445A	Ron	Westerman	1419 Ivy Drive	Pinedale	98412
027	854-72-2249	018445A	Fred	Anderson	943 Spruce Circle	Lakewood	98403
033	583-02-1253	029525A	Lance	Bright	148 Center St., #B211	Pinedale	98412
034	477-11-6309	0193330	Richard	Talbot	1109 Emerson Way	Lakewood	98403
035	722-52-2624	019526A	Linda	Gardner	8841 Market Street	Lakewood	98403
037	455-82-9921	029525A	Jefrey	Davis	1171 Simon Heights	Lakewood	98403
038	241-21-4972	029525A	Jonathan	Bray	5941 Hilltop Road	Lakewood	98403
						Lakewood	98403

Record: 9 of 9

2. Close the table.

Using Queries to Extract Information

In Access, we use queries to ask questions about our database tables, to extract complete or partial records from the tables, and even to edit records. Queries that find and extract information from a database are called *select queries*, and queries that perform an action such as updating or deleting records are called *action queries*.

Select queries

Action queries

Selecting Specific Fields

Suppose Tip Top Roofing's job supervisor has asked us for a list of the phone numbers of company employees. He is not interested in any other information about the employees; all he wants is names and phone numbers. We can create the list by following these steps:

The Simple Query Wizard

1. In the Roofs database window, click the Queries tab and then click New. In the New Query dialog box, select Simple Query Wizard and click OK. Access displays the Simple Query Wizard dialog box shown here:

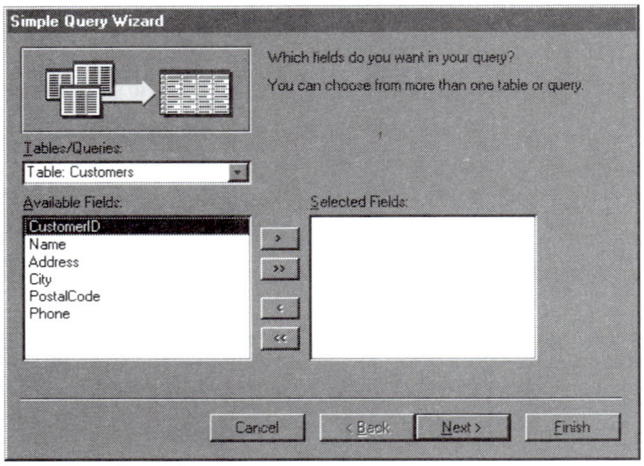

2. Select Table: Employees from the Tables/Queries drop-down list. Access displays the available fields for the Employees table in the list below.
3. Double-click LastName, FirstName, and then HomePhone to move these fields to the Selected Fields list. Then click Next.
4. Save the query with the name *Phonelist* and then click Finish. The result is the datasheet shown at the top of the facing page.

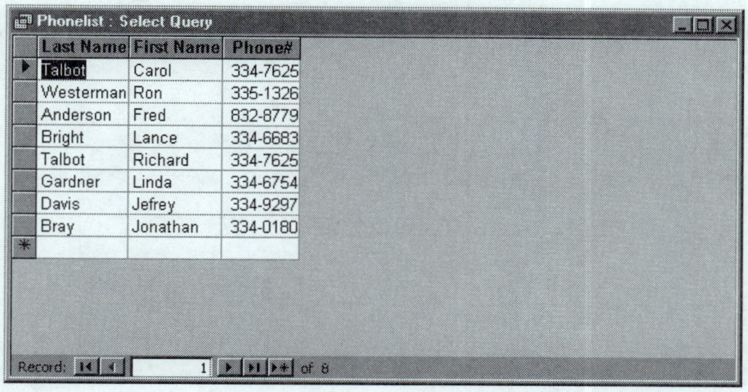

5. Print the query datasheet by clicking the Print button on the toolbar. You can then give the phone-number list to the job supervisor.

Printing the datasheet

6. Close the select query window.

The database window now lists Phonelist as an existing query. Any time we want to access the datasheet of the names and phone numbers of the roofing company's employees, we can select this query and click Open. Access runs the query and opens a datasheet. If we have made changes to the Employees table, these changes will be reflected in the datasheet.

Selecting Specific Records

What if we want Access to select fields only from specific records? For example, suppose that the shingles for job number 029525A are going to be delivered late and we need the employees assigned to that job to report to the office in the morning instead of the job site. Follow these steps to modify the Phonelist query so that Access will include in the query datasheet only the names and phone numbers of the employees assigned to job 029525A:

1. With Phonelist selected in the database window, click the Design button to display the query in design view. Access displays the select query window shown on the next page.

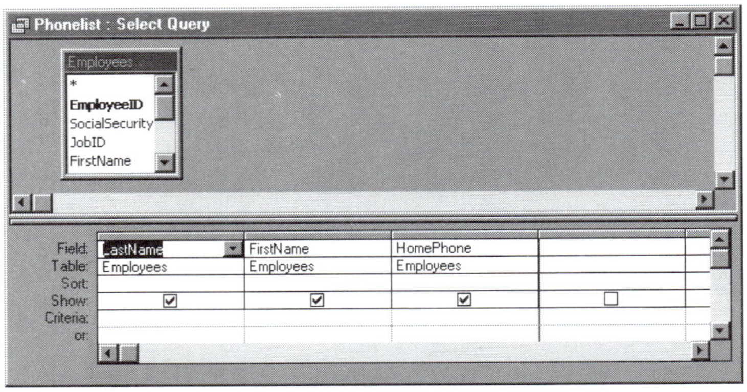

The Employees box lists the fields in the Employees table. (The * at the top of the list represents the entire table.) Below is a table grid called the *query by example (QBE) grid*, in which you can visually structure the query.

Adding fields to queries

2. Double-click JobID in the Employees box to add it to the QBE grid, and click the Show box for the JobID field to deselect it.

3. In the Criteria row of the JobID column, type *029525A*. The query now looks like this:

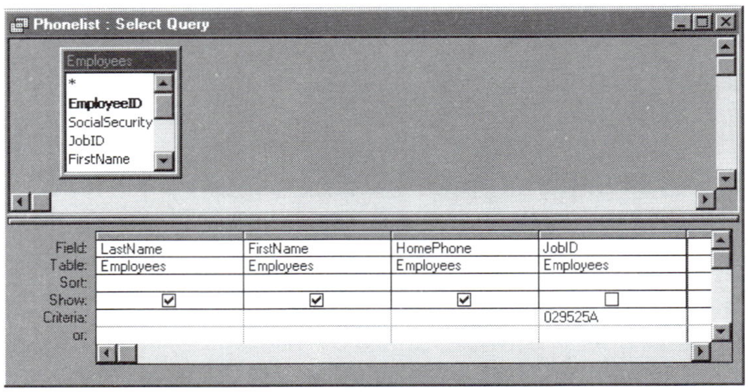

We are telling Access to give us the names and phone numbers from the records that have the value 029525A in the JobID field. (The JobID field value will not appear in the query datasheet because that field's Show box is not selected.)

Using wildcards

When you want to select fields based on only part of their entries, you can use the wildcards * and ? before, after, and between characters as placeholders for unknown or varying characters. For example, to find all entries that include *School* or *Schools*, you can use *School? as the criterion. The * wildcard stands for any number and any type of character, and the ? wildcard stands for any one character of any type. When you use wildcards, Access precedes the criterion with the *Like* operator to indicate that you do not want to look for an exact match.

The Run button

4. Run the query by clicking the Run button on the toolbar. Access displays this new Phonelist datasheet:

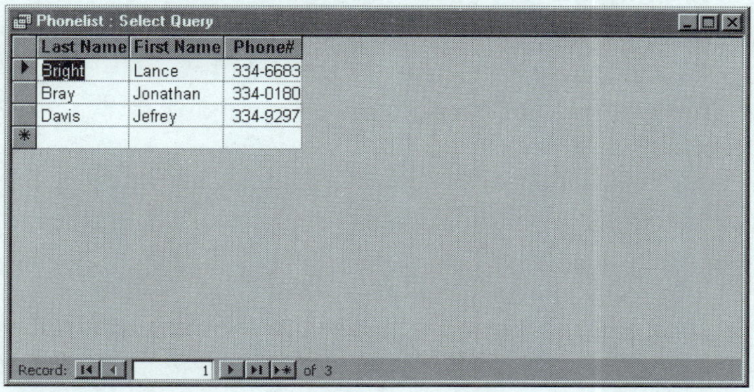

Editing Query Datasheets

If you entered the information for employee number 37 exactly as it is shown on page 190, the datasheet now on your screen indicates a typo in the third record (*Jefrey* should be *Jeffrey*). Correcting the record in the datasheet will automatically correct it in the table. Follow these steps:

1. Click an insertion point to the right of the *f* in *Jefrey*, type *f*, and press Enter to complete the record.

2. Close the select query window without saving the changes to the Phonelist query.

3. In the database window, click the Tables tab, select Employees, and click Open. Employee number 37 now has a First Name field value of *Jeffrey*.

4. Close the table window.

Using Logical Operators

We can narrow down the data Access pulls from a database table by specifying criteria in more than one field of a select query grid. Sometimes we might want to extract records that meet all the criteria in all the fields (this *And* that), and sometimes we might want to extract records that meet any criterion in any field (this *Or* that). Let's look at an example that uses the And operator.

Suppose we need to know which of the Durahomes jobs is complete so that we can bill the customer; that is, we want to see records that are both for Durahomes and complete. In Access, the And operator is implied whenever we use more than one criterion in a single row of the select query window. Follow these steps to extract the required record:

1. In the database window, highlight the Jobs table, click the arrow next to the New Object button on the toolbar, and select Query to open the New Query dialog box.
2. Double-click Design View to display the Jobs box in a select query window.
3. Add the JobID, CustomerID, Location, and Status fields to the QBE grid, type *Complete* as a criterion in the Status field, and type *30* as a criterion in the CustomerID field. The select query window looks like the one shown here:

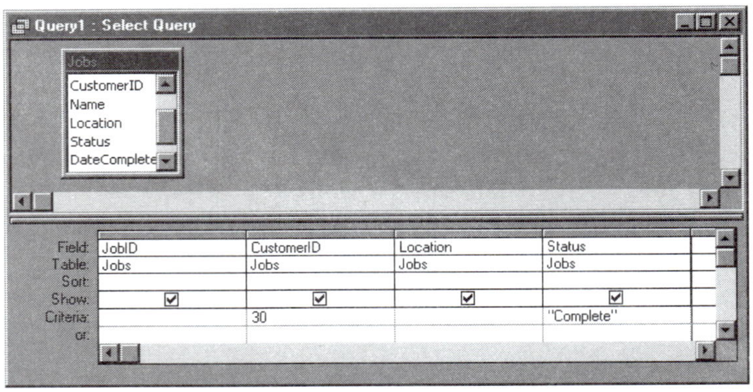

4. Run the query. Access displays the record for the completed Durahomes job:

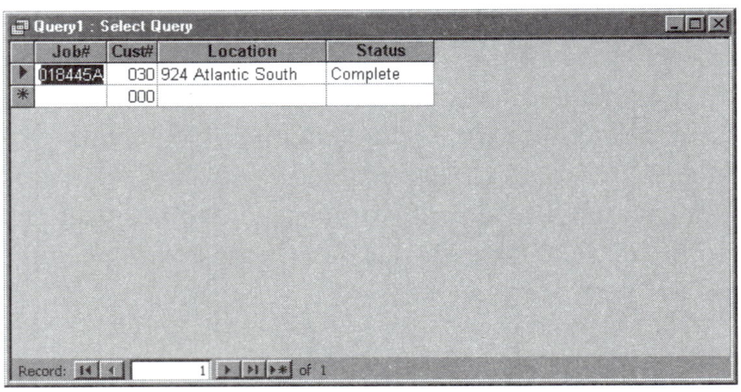

The Or operator

When you want to find records that meet any of two or more criteria, you use the Or operator. Enter the criterion for the first field in the Criteria row and enter all the criteria for the other fields in the Or row. If you want to find records that meet any of two or more criteria in the same field, you enter the criteria under each other in that column of the QBE grid. (Although only one row is designated as the Or row, the Or operator is implied for all the rows below the Or row.)

5. Save the query by clicking the Save button on the toolbar and typing *Complete Jobs* in the Query Name edit box.

If the roofing company has many customers, we might want to include the customers' names in the query results, instead of just their numbers. However, the customers' names are not part of the Jobs table; they are stored only in the Customers table. To get the information we want, we must use both tables in a query, like this:

1. With Complete Jobs still open, use the View button on the toolbar to switch to design view and display the query in the select query window.
2. Click the Show Table button, double-click Customers, and then click the Close button. The select query window now contains boxes for both tables. Because we have created a relationship between these tables (see page 208), Access indicates the relationship in the select query window by drawing a line between the CustomerID fields in the two boxes.
3. In the Customers box, double-click the Name field to add it to the QBE grid.
4. In the QBE grid, deselect the Show box for CustomerID.

Omitting fields from the datasheet

5. Run the query. Access displays the job number, job location, status, and customer name, as shown here:

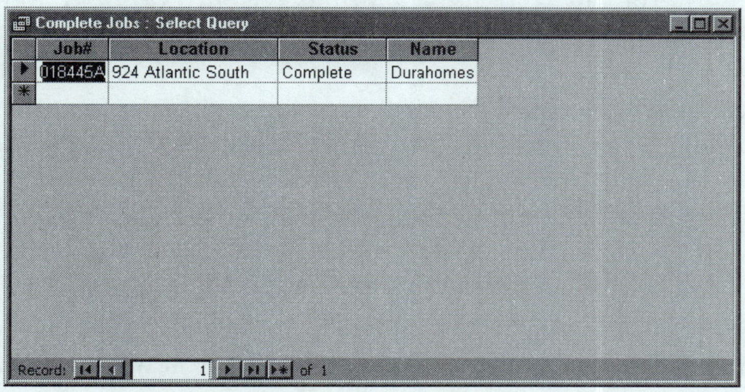

6. Close the select query window, clicking Yes to save the query.

All the queries we've looked at so far have been select queries, which provide information in datasheets. Unless we save this type of query, the information in the datasheet is temporary; it goes away when we close the select query window. Now let's explore action queries, which we can use to modify the information in our tables and even to create new tables.

Updating Records

From time to time, we may want to change a field value in several records in a table. For example, suppose the Post Office has assigned a new Zip code to Pinewood, and we need to update the Employees table to reflect the change. We could update each record in turn, but an easier way is to use an update query. Follow these steps:

1. With the Tables tab displayed in the database window, select Employees, click the arrow next to the New Object button on the toolbar, and select Query.
2. In the New Query dialog box, first double-click Design View and then double-click the PostalCode field to add it to the QBE grid.

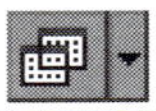

The Query Type button

3. Click the arrow next to the Query Type button on the toolbar and select Update Query to add an Update To row to the QBE grid.
4. In the Update To row, type *98415* in the PostalCode field.
5. In the Criteria row, type *98412* in the PostalCode field and then press Enter.
6. Run the query. Access advises you of the number of records to be updated.
7. Click Yes to complete the changes.

The Database Window button

8. Click the Database Window button on the toolbar and open the Employees table, where the records for the two employees who live in Pinedale have been updated with the new Zip code.

For a small table, it may be faster to make changes like this one manually. For large tables, using an update query is faster and ensures that all the affected records are changed.

Moving Records

The data we keep in tables is rarely static, and it is often easier to work with current data in one table and archive data in another. Tip Top Roofing's Jobs table is a good example. If we keep all the jobs the company has ever worked on in one table, the table will soon become too large to work with on a daily basis. The solution is to have a separate table for the records of jobs that are finished.

To set the stage for the next example, we need to change the Status field values of two records in the Jobs table to *Closed*, indicating not only that the work is complete but that payment has been received. We also need to create a new table to contain the records for closed jobs. Let's get going:

1. To keep your desktop neat, close any query and table windows without saving them. Then open the Jobs table.
2. Change the Status values for the records with job numbers 018022A and 0182730 to *Closed*, enter *2/1/97* and *3/1/97* in the Date Complete field of those records, and close the table, saving any changes if asked.
3. With Jobs highlighted in the database window, click the Copy button on the toolbar.
4. Now click the Paste button on the toolbar, and in the Paste Table As dialog box, name the table *Closed Jobs*, click Structure Only, and then click OK. Access adds the new table to the list in the database window.
5. Open the Closed Jobs table in design view and delete the Status field by clicking its row selector and pressing Delete.
6. Close the table, saving the changes when prompted.

We are now ready to move the closed records from the Jobs table to the Closed Jobs table. Follow these steps:

1. Select the Jobs table in the database window, click the arrow next to the New Object button on the toolbar, and then select Query.

More logical operators

Access allows you to use the following operators as criteria: = (equal to), < (less than), > (greater than), <= (less than or equal to), and >= (greater than or equal to). These operators are often used for such tasks as identifying employees whose salaries fall within a certain range or locating high-volume customers.

2. In the New Query dialog box, double-click Design View.

3. Add all the fields from the Jobs box to the QBE grid by double-clicking the Jobs title bar, pointing to the selection, dragging the image of the fields to the grid, and releasing the mouse button.

4. Scroll the window and type *Closed* in the Criteria row of the Status field.

5. Now click the arrow next to the Query Type button on the toolbar, select Append Query, and when Access displays the Append dialog box, type *Closed Jobs* as the name of the table to which you want to append the results of the query and then click OK.

6. Run the query, and when Access advises you that it will append two rows, click Yes to proceed with the query.

7. Close the append query window, saving the query as *Append Closed Jobs* so that you can run it whenever you need to append records from the Jobs table to the Closed Jobs table.

8. Open the Closed Jobs table to verify that it contains the two closed records, as shown here:

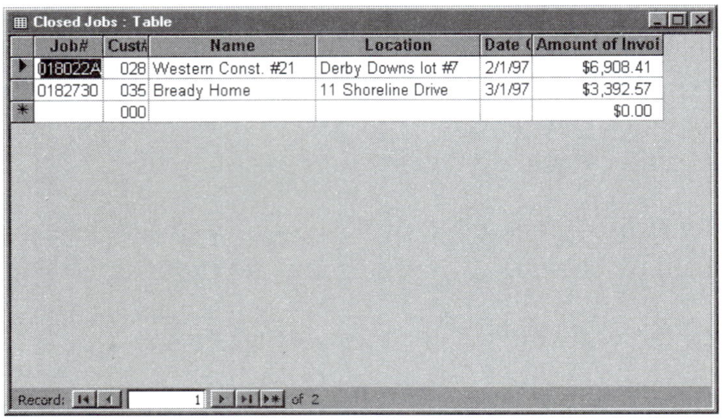

We have copied the closed records to the Closed Jobs table, but the records still exist in the Jobs table. Follow these steps to delete the records:

1. Close the Closed Jobs table and then open the Jobs table. Click the record selector for job number 018022A, press Delete, and click Yes to delete the record.

2. Repeat step 1 for job number 0182730 and close the table window.

Using Reports to Print Information

The purpose of a query is to extract information from a database and display it on the screen. The purpose of a report, on the other hand, is to extract information and show it on the printed page. So when you need a neatly formatted hard copy of sorted and grouped information, consider using a report.

To start exploring reports, follow the steps below to create a single-table, single-column report based on the Jobs table:

1. In the database window, select Jobs in the Tables list, click the arrow next to the New Object button on the toolbar, and click AutoReport. After a few seconds, Access displays this report (we've scrolled the window to show a complete record):

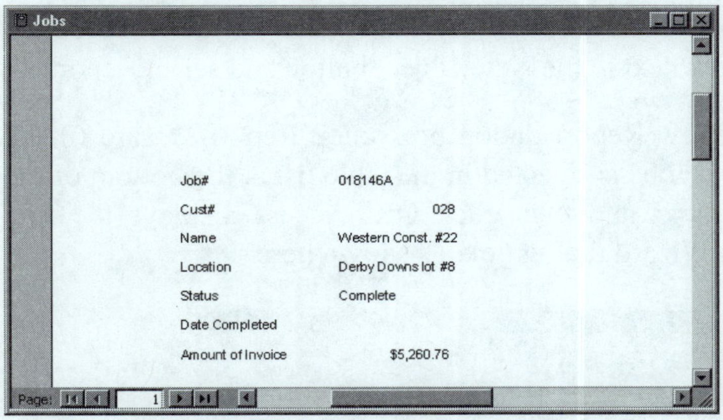

Because reports are usually created to produce printouts, Access displays the report in print preview so that you can see what it will look like on the page.

The Zoom button

2. Click the Zoom button on the toolbar to zoom out for a bird's-eye view, as shown on the next page.

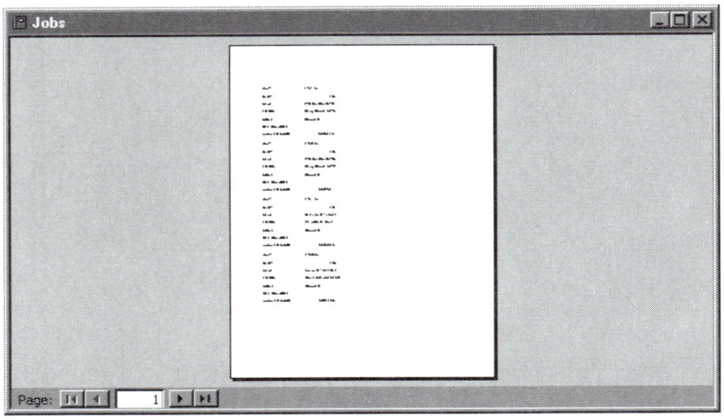

3. Click the Zoom button again to zoom back in and then, using the scroll buttons in the bottom left corner of the screen, scroll the page to see how the report will be printed.

As you scroll, notice that the records will be printed in job order. Suppose we want to sort the records by customer instead of by job. Follow these steps:

1. Double-click the report window's Control menu icon to close the window and click No to discard the report.
2. With Jobs selected in the database window's tables list, click the arrow next to the New Object button and select Report.

The Report Wizard

3. In the New Report dialog box, click Report Wizard (make sure that Jobs is selected in the table list at the bottom of the dialog box) and then click OK. Access displays the first Report Wizard dialog box, as shown here:

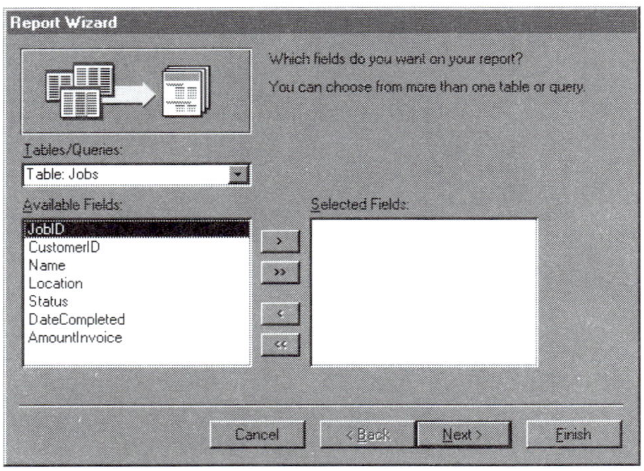

Creating reports from scratch

You can create a blank report by clicking the Reports tab in the database window, clicking New, and then double-clicking Design View in the New Report dialog box. Access opens a new report window containing Page Header, Detail, and Page Footer sections. You can then add controls to design the report.

4. Click the >> button to move all the available fields to the Selected Fields box, and click Next.

5. Click Next in the Report Wizard's second and third dialog boxes without making any selections. (Note that in this case, Access automatically sorts the records by CustomerID.) Access then displays the Report Wizard's fourth dialog box, which looks like this:

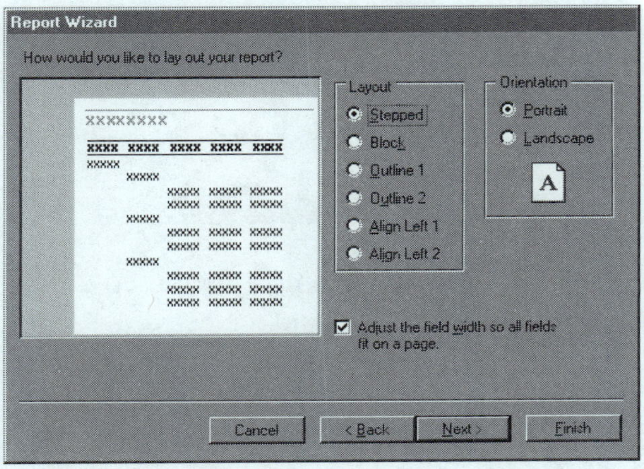

6. Make sure the Stepped and Landscape options are selected and then click Next to display the fifth dialog box:

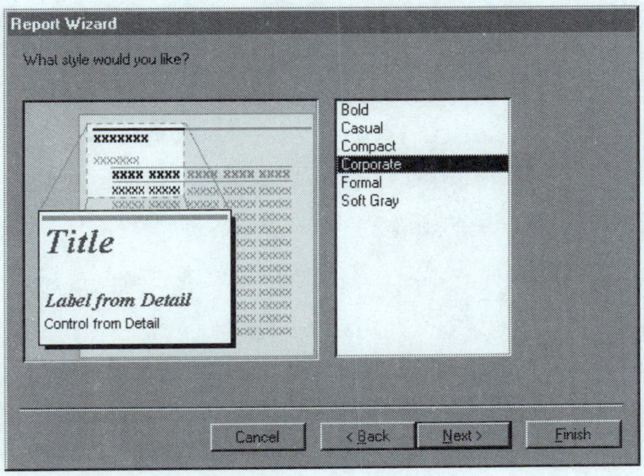

7. With Corporate selected as the style for the report, click Next to display the final Report Wizard dialog box.

Grouping by date or time

In the Report Wizard's second dialog box, you can add grouping levels to your report. If you select a date field to group by and then click the Grouping Options button, Access allows you to group the records in your table or query by units of time from one minute up to a year. Grouping by date or time can be useful when totaling sales for a month or quarter, or for almost any other time-dependent grouping of information.

4. Click the >> button to move all the available fields to the Selected Fields box, and click Next.

5. Click Next in the Report Wizard's second and third dialog boxes without making any selections. (Note that in this case, Access automatically sorts the records by CustomerID.) Access then displays the Report Wizard's fourth dialog box, which looks like this:

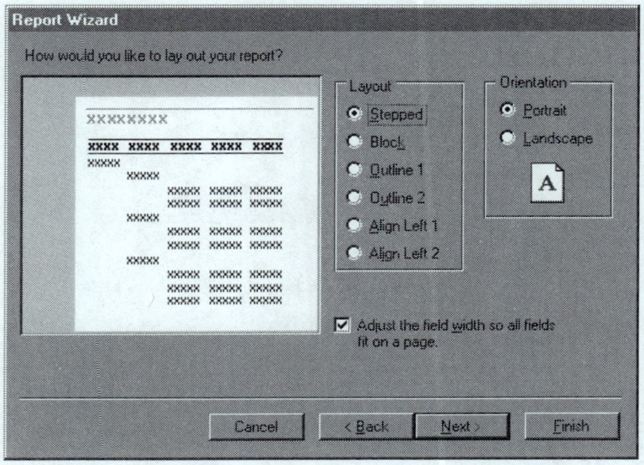

6. Make sure the Stepped and Landscape options are selected and then click Next to display the fifth dialog box:

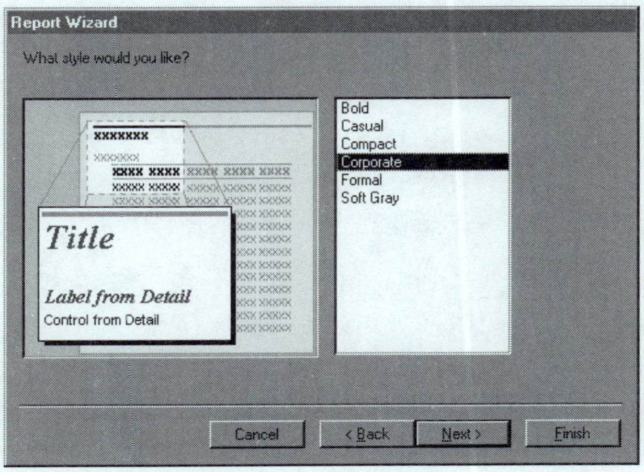

7. With Corporate selected as the style for the report, click Next to display the final Report Wizard dialog box.

Grouping by date or time

In the Report Wizard's second dialog box, you can add grouping levels to your report. If you select a date field to group by and then click the Grouping Options button, Access allows you to group the records in your table or query by units of time from one minute up to a year. Grouping by date or time can be useful when totaling sales for a month or quarter, or for almost any other time-dependent grouping of information.

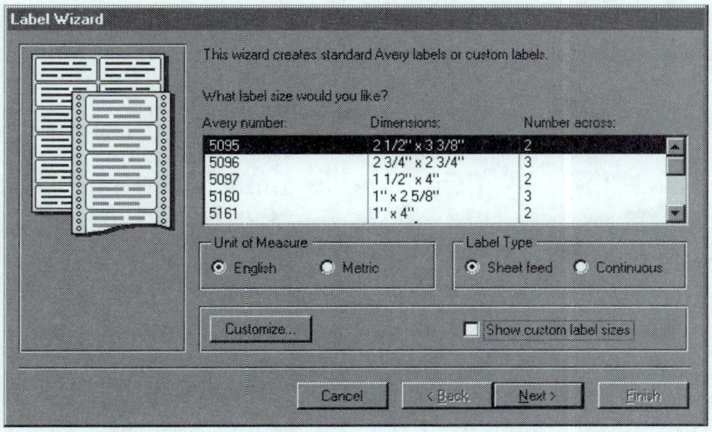

2. If this is not the first screen you see, deselect Show Custom Label Sizes.

   You can select the format by Avery number or by size and number of labels in a row. The list of available formats varies, depending on your printer's capabilities.

3. Select the size you want (we selected Avery 5160) and click Next to display a dialog box where you can format the labels.

4. Change the font size to 10 and the font weight to Bold and click Next. Access displays this dialog box:

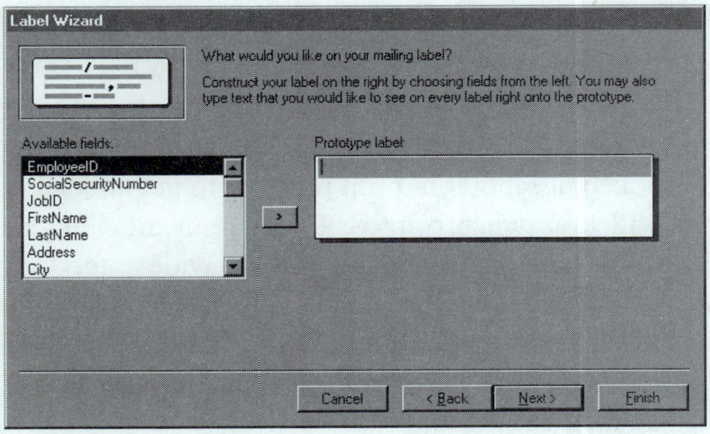

5. The fields are listed for inclusion on the label. Double-click the FirstName field to add it to the first line in the Prototype Label box, and then press the Spacebar.

Graphing Access data

Graphs are sometimes the most logical way to present data because they enable people to quickly make visual comparisons. In Access, you graph data in a form, not a report. You select the table you want to work with, click the arrow next to the New Object button on the toolbar, select Form, and double-click Chart Wizard. The Chart Wizard then helps you plot your data.

6. Double-click the LastName field to add it after the space and then press Enter to create a second line.

7. Double-click the Address field and press Enter.

8. Double-click the City field, type a comma, and press the Spacebar. Then type *WA*, press the Spacebar twice, and double-click the PostalCode field to finish the third line.

9. Click Next, move LastName to the Sort By box, and click Next again.

10. Type Employee Labels as the name for the report and then click Finish to see the labels in print preview (your screen will reflect the label format you selected):

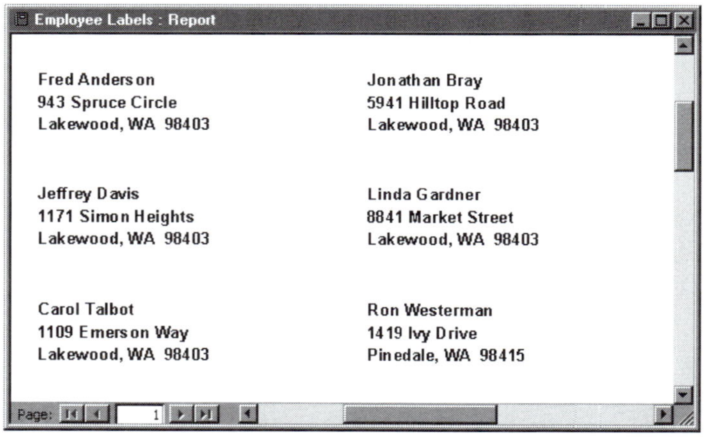

Printing Reports

We have looked at reports in print preview to get an idea of how they will look when printed. Using print preview can save a lot of time and paper. If a report is too wide or too long to fit neatly on a page, we can identify the problems in print preview and change the report's design or modify the page setup before we commit the report to paper. Here we'll look at modifying the page setup:

Basing labels on queries

As with other reports, you can use queries as the information source for labels. For example, to send information to customers in a specific sales area, you could create a query that extracts information by city or Zip code and then use the query as the basis for the mailing labels.

1. With Employee Labels still displayed in print preview, choose the Page Setup command from the File menu to open the Page Setup dialog box, where you can select many print options, including margins, orientation (landscape or portrait), and printer.

2. All the options have been set to print the mailing labels you created in the previous section, so click Cancel to close the dialog box without changing anything.

Now let's give the printer some work to do:

1. Click the Print button on the toolbar.

In Chapters 8 and 9, we have given you only a glimpse of the potential of Access in the expectation that you will learn more about the program as you use it.

Customizing reports

Just as you can create custom forms to tailor the input of data, you can create custom reports to tailor its output. Customizing reports is beyond the scope of this book; however, you might want to create a report and then switch to design view to play around with it. (Choose the Design View command from the View menu to switch to design view.) To get a feel for some of the possibilities, try moving controls around, formatting labels, or using the Toolbox to add new controls. (Use the structure of the existing controls as a guide.)

10

Outlook Basics

Flip between Outlook components with the click of a button

Handle e-mail from various sources in one convenient inbox

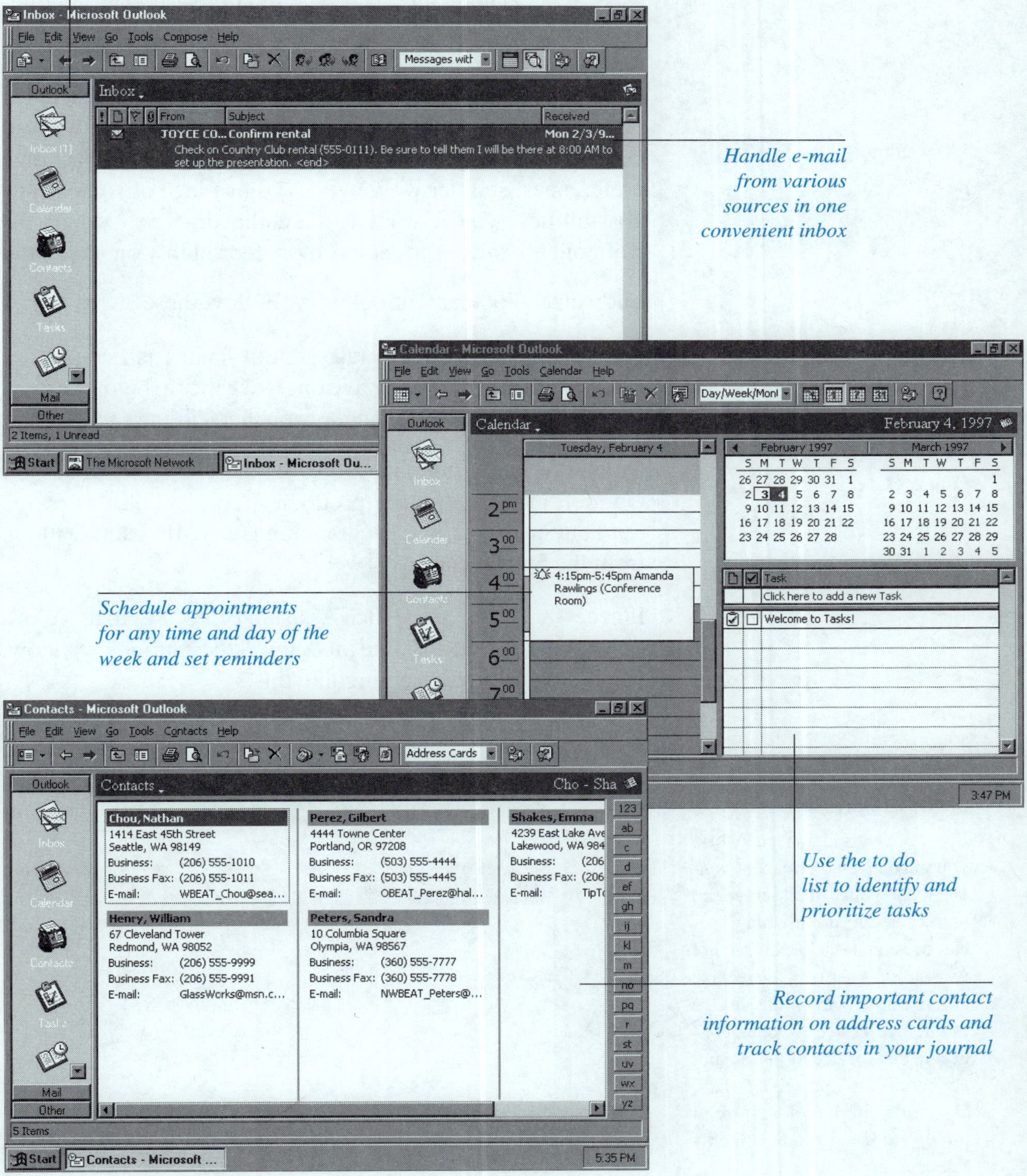

Schedule appointments for any time and day of the week and set reminders

Use the to do list to identify and prioritize tasks

Record important contact information on address cards and track contacts in your journal

We use Microsoft Outlook to manage the crucial personal and business information that we might keep in an assortment of address books, appointment books, and notebooks, as well as to handle e-mail. In this chapter, we briefly cover some key components of Outlook, but we can't possibly discuss all its options in just a few pages. The program is very flexible and offers many ways to tailor its components to meet your personal organizational preferences, so after we've given you an idea of some of the possibilities, you'll want to take the time to explore the components and their features more thoroughly on your own.

Let's take a look at Outlook now. Follow these steps:

1. Because we are going to talk about e-mail first, connect to your e-mail server if you have one. (See the tip below.) If you can, minimize the server window on the Windows 95 taskbar.

Starting Outlook

2. On the Windows 95 desktop, double-click the Microsoft Outlook icon to start the program. (You can also click the Start button and choose Programs and then Microsoft Outlook from the Start menu.)
3. If necessary, close the Office Assistant, click Yes to use Word as your e-mail editor, and maximize the Outlook window, which now looks something like this:

Starting e-mail

If you are working on a network, you may have a permanent connection to your e-mail server and won't need to do anything special to activate it. If you are not working on a network but receive e-mail through an online service or Internet service provider, connect to that service. If you are not yet hooked up to receive e-mail, skip this step and just read through the section on Outlook's Inbox component.

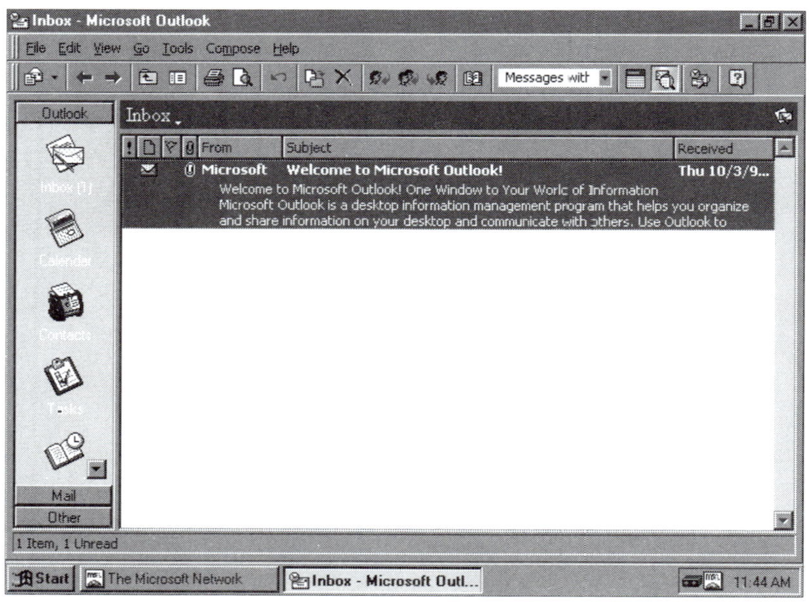

The Outlook bar

The workspace

As you can see, the Outlook window is divided into a vertical bar on the left that displays icons for the various Outlook components, and a workspace on the right. You change the contents of the workspace by clicking the Outlook bar icons. Clicking the down arrow at the bottom of the bar brings more icons into view. Clicking the Mail button displays icons for components of the Inbox, and clicking the Other button displays icons that enable you to quickly find files stored on your computer or jump to specified Web sites.

4. Click various icons and buttons on the Outlook bar to jump from one component to another.

Now that you have a feel for how to move around in Outlook and have a sense of the convenience of working with various types of information in one place, let's look at some of the individual components.

Using the Inbox

Electronic mail

Outlook is set up to work with several popular e-mail (for *electronic mail*) programs, so we can use Outlook's Inbox as an all-purpose e-mail service from which we can send and receive messages to colleagues down the hall or clients on the other side of the world. We can't go into the technicalities of setting up e-mail here, but we'll give you an idea of how Outlook's Inbox works in the following sections.

Sending Messages

As we said, with Outlook, we both send and receive e-mail through the Inbox. We'll look at the sending side of the equation first. For this example, imagine that you are planning a meeting with the local Chamber of Commerce and you want to remind yourself to confirm the rental of the country club first thing tomorrow morning. Follow these steps:

Starting the Inbox

1. If necessary, click the Inbox icon to display your inbox in the workspace.

The New Mail Message button

2. Click the New Mail Message button on the toolbar to display a window like the one shown on the next page.

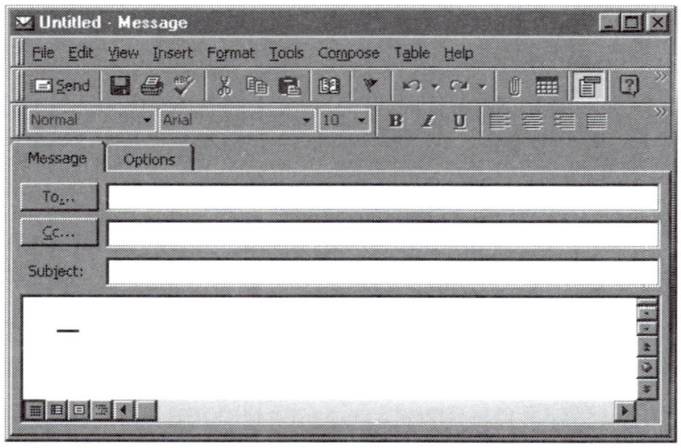

Addressing messages

3. In the To edit box, type your own e-mail address. (To send a message to someone else, enter his or her address. To send the same message to more than one person, enter their addresses one after the other, separated by semicolons.)

4. To send a courtesy copy of the message, you can enter the name of the recipient in the Cc edit box. For this message, leave the Cc edit box blank.

5. In the Subject edit box, type *Confirm rental.*

6. Next, enter the message itself in the blank area at the bottom of the window. Type *Check on Country Club rental (555-0111). Be sure to tell them I will be there at 8:00 AM to set up the presentation.* Your screen now looks like this:

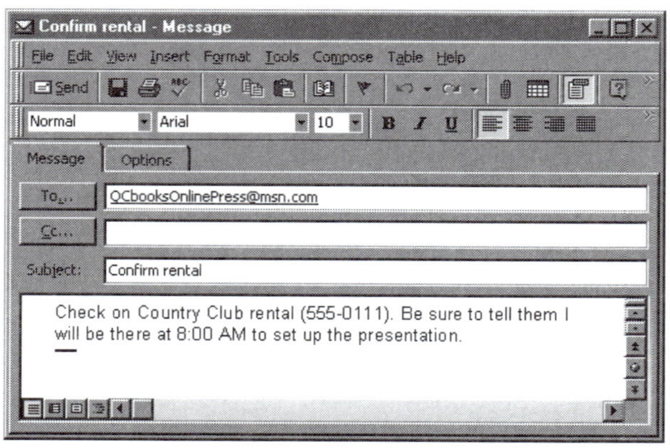

The Send button

7. Send the message by clicking the Send button. The Message window closes, and the message is on its way.

8. Minimize the Outlook window.

Receiving Messages

If we receive a message while we are connected to the e-mail server and Outlook is running, an envelope icon appears to the left of the clock on the Window 95 taskbar. When you see this icon, follow the steps below. (See the adjacent tip if you don't see the icon.)

The envelope icon

1. Double-click the envelope icon on the taskbar to activate the Inbox, which now looks like this (we've deleted the *Welcome to Microsoft Outlook* message; see page 236):

Next to the new message, a closed envelope icon indicates that you have not yet read the message. The sender's name, the subject, and the date and time the message was received are all summarized, and icons to the left of the message header tell you more about the message. (An exclamation point means a message is urgent, and a paper clip indicates that a file is attached to the message.) Below the message header are up to three lines of the message itself. In this case, you can read the message by scanning this summary, but if the message were longer, you could read it by following these steps:

2. Double-click the message to display it in a window, like this:

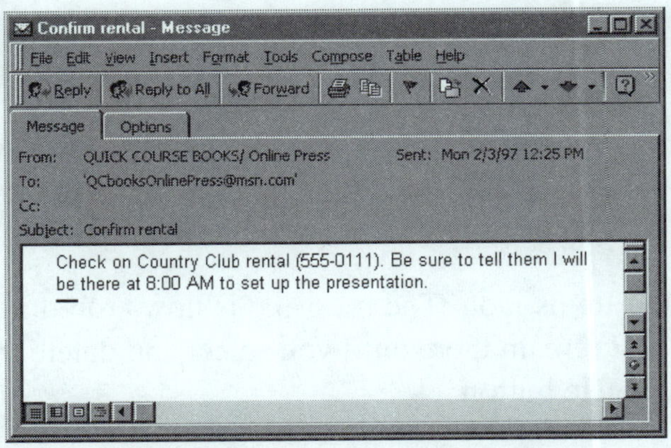

Checking for messages

If you don't see the envelope icon, maximize the Outlook window and choose Check For New Mail from the Tools menu. Your new mail should then appear in the Outlook window.

The Reply button

The Reply To All button

The Forward button

If this message was from a colleague and required a response, you could simply click the Reply button to open a RE: window with the To and Subject edit boxes already filled in. (To send the response to the sender of the message and all recipients of courtesy copies, click the Reply To All button.) Type your reply above the copy of the original message and then send the message with a click of the Send button.

To forward the message to a colleague, first click the Forward button in the window containing the message. When the FW: window opens with a copy of the message already in the message area, enter the name of the person to whom you want to forward the message in the To edit box, and click Send.

3. Click the Close button to close the message window.

Using Folders

In addition to the Inbox, Outlook maintains three "folders" to help organize our messages: Sent Items, Outbox, and Deleted Items. We can move messages between folders and even create new folders by following these steps:

Displaying sent messages

1. To see messages you have already sent, click the Mail button at the bottom of the Outlook bar and then click the Sent Items icon to display its contents in the workspace, like this:

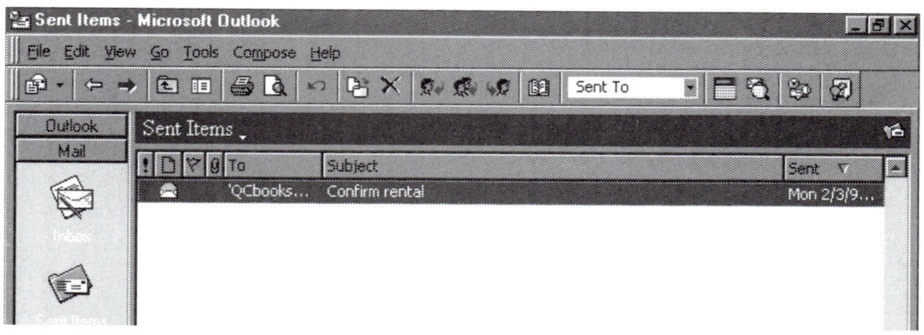

The Delete button

2. With the message you sent earlier selected, click the Delete button on the toolbar. (You can also drag the message to the Deleted Items icon on the Outlook bar.)

Displaying deleted messages

3. Click the Deleted Items icon. The message is now stored in this folder and will remain there until you select and delete it by clicking the Delete button.

To organize your mail, you can create folders for storing related messages. For example, here's how to create a new folder in which to store messages related to the Chamber of Commerce meeting:

Creating new folders

1. Click the Inbox icon on the Outlook bar and choose New and then Folder from the File menu to display this dialog box:

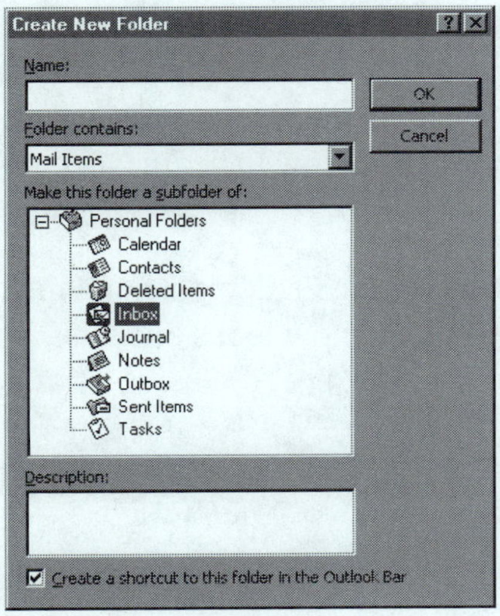

2. In the Name box, type *Chamber of Commerce* and click OK.
3. Scroll the Outlook bar to display the new folder's icon (click the down arrow at the bottom of the bar).
4. Now select the Confirm rental message you sent to yourself earlier and drag it to the new folder on the Outlook bar.
5. If you want, disconnect from your e-mail server. (You will need to reconnect for the exercises on pages 246 and 255.)

We'll leave you to experiment with folders as you receive mail from your colleagues. While you work, you will probably want to minimize Outlook so that it continues to run in the background and you can receive messages as they are sent to you. Alternatively, you can quit the program, knowing that your messages will be stored by your e-mail server until you make your next connection.

Attached files

Suppose you want to send a report to a colleague via e-mail. After composing the e-mail message in a message window, click the Insert File button on the toolbar, locate and select the report's file in the Insert File dialog box, check that the Attachment check box is selected in the Insert As section, and click OK. If you receive a message with an attachment (as indicated in the "paperclip" column of the box), you can print the attachment by selecting the message, choosing Print from the File menu, clicking Memo Style in the Print Style section, selecting Print Attached Files With Item(s), and clicking OK. To save an attachment as a file, choose Save Attachments from the File menu, name the file, and click Save. You can then open the file in the appropriate application.

Using the Calendar

The Calendar component of Outlook is designed to take the hassle out of time management by enabling us to keep track of appointments. When we set up an appointment, we can specify that we want to be reminded of the appointment a few minutes ahead of time. For this reminder feature to work, Outlook must be running when the specified time arrives, so you might want to automatically start Outlook every time you start Windows 95. (All you have to do is add an Outlook shortcut to the StartUp submenu on the Windows Start menu; see the adjacent tip.) Follow the steps below to begin working with the Calendar:

Starting Calendar

1. Click the Outlook button at the top of the Outlook bar and then click the Calendar icon. The workspace now looks like this:

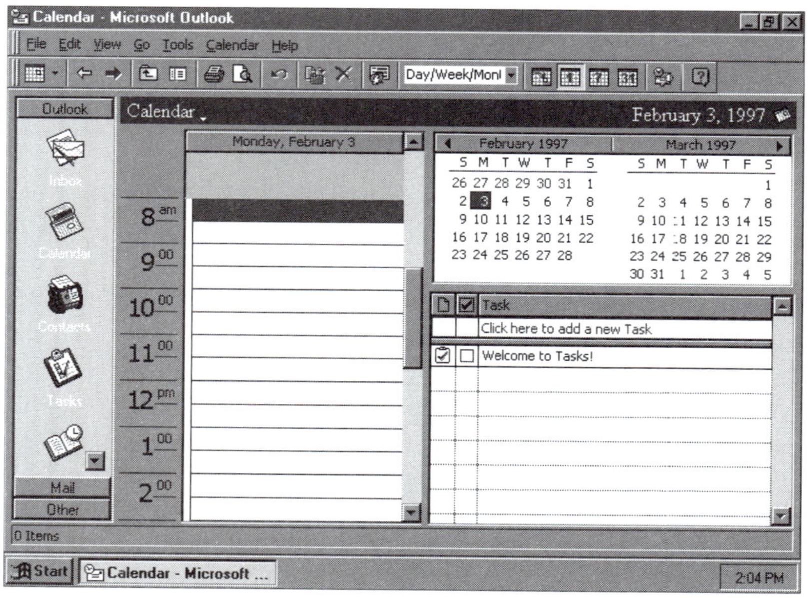

On the left side of the workspace is the appointment area, divided into half-hour intervals. In the top right corner is the Date Navigator, which displays calendars for the current month and next month. (You can cycle through the months by clicking the right and left arrows on the calendar headers.) In the bottom right corner is a small version of the Tasks window, where you keep your to do list (see page 247). By default, Outlook displays your calendar for today.

Automatic Outlook start-up

To have Outlook (or any other program) start automatically every time you start Windows, you can add an Outlook shortcut to the StartUp submenu. First choose Settings and then Taskbar from the Windows 95 Start menu. When the Taskbar Properties dialog box appears, click the Start Menu Programs tab, click the Add button to start the Create Shortcut Wizard, and then click the Browse button in the wizard's first dialog box. Navigate to the Microsoft Office subfolder of the Program Files folder, double-click Microsoft Outlook, and then click Next. In the wizard's second dialog box, select the StartUp folder at the bottom of the list and click Next. Finally, click Finish in the wizard's last dialog box. Click OK to close the Taskbar Properties dialog box. Now the next time you start Windows, Outlook will be ready and waiting for you.

The Week and Month buttons

2. Click the Week button on the toolbar and then click the Month button to see how the calendar view changes.

The Day button

3. Click the Day button to return to the default view.

Entering Appointments

The half-hour intervals in the appointment area designate *time slots*. We use these time slots to schedule appointments for the day. Suppose we have a meeting with a client named Barry Scott at 3:00 this afternoon. We expect the meeting to last half an hour. Follow these steps to enter the appointment:

Simple appointments

1. Scroll the appointment area, click the 3:00 time, type *Barry Scott*, and press Enter.

That's all there is to it. Today's date is now bold in the Date Navigator, indicating that you have an appointment today. The time slot holding the appointment indicates to anyone viewing your schedule that you are unavailable at that time.

Now suppose we need to schedule an interview with a prospective employee named Amanda Rawlings at 4:15 PM tomorrow. The interview will probably last an hour and a half. Follow these steps:

Moving among dates

1. Click tomorrow's date in the Date Navigator. Tomorrow's appointment area is now displayed.

2. Because the Calendar time slots are in half-hour intervals, you need to make a special entry for Amanda Rawlings. Double-click the 4:00 time slot to display this Appointment dialog box, in which you can tailor your appointments:

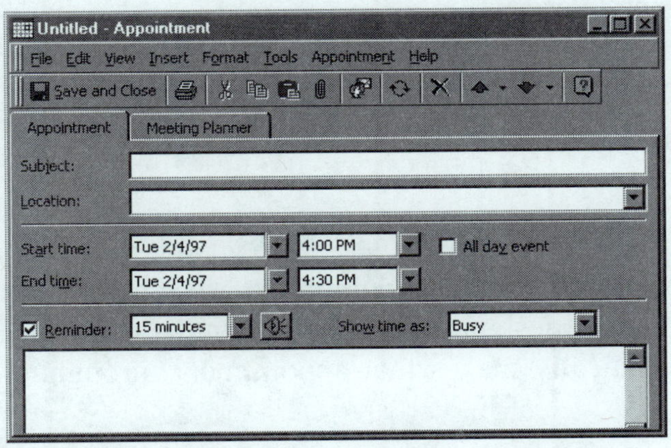

Computer dating

Outlook obtains the date and time from your system clock. If this clock is wrong, Outlook keeps an inaccurate calendar and reminds you of appointments at the wrong time. To set the correct date and time, right-click the clock at the end of the Windows 95 taskbar and choose Adjust Date/Time from the object menu. Then make the appropriate adjustments to the date or time. If Outlook has problems keeping your calendar, suspect problems with your computer's battery, which maintains the system clock.

3. In the Subject edit box, type *Amanda Rawlings*, and in the Location edit box, type *Conference Room*.

Setting reminders

4. To change the Start time, select 00 in 4:00 PM, and type *15*. Then change the End time to 5:45 PM.

5. If necessary, click the Reminder check box to select it, change the amount of warning time from 15 minutes to 10 minutes, and click Save And Close. You return to the Outlook window, which now looks like this:

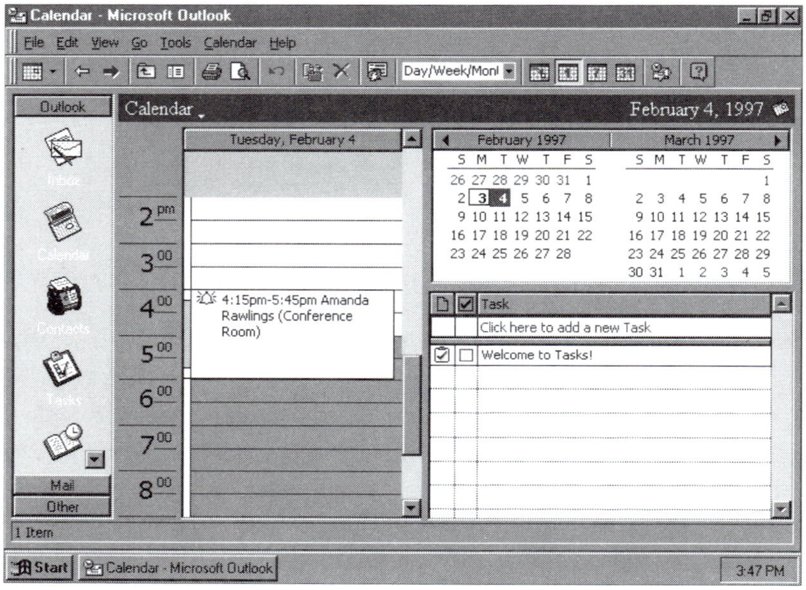

Private appointments

6. If you are working on a network, right-click the appointment and choose Private from the object menu. A key icon in the time slot now indicates that other people viewing your schedule will be told you are busy during this time but won't see the appointment's description.

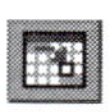

The Go To Today button

7. Click the Go To Today button on the toolbar or click today's date in the Date Navigator to move back to the appointment area for today.

Entering Recurring Appointments

Unless we specify otherwise, appointments we schedule are nonrecurring. If we designate an appointment as recurring, Outlook automatically makes that appointment throughout the appointment book. For example, suppose we meet with the office manager every other Wednesday from 12:00 to 1:00 PM. Here's how to schedule this recurring appointment:

1. Click next Wednesday's date in the Date Navigator and drag through the time slots from 12:00 to 1:00 to select them.
2. Choose New Recurring Appointment from the Calendar menu to display this dialog box:

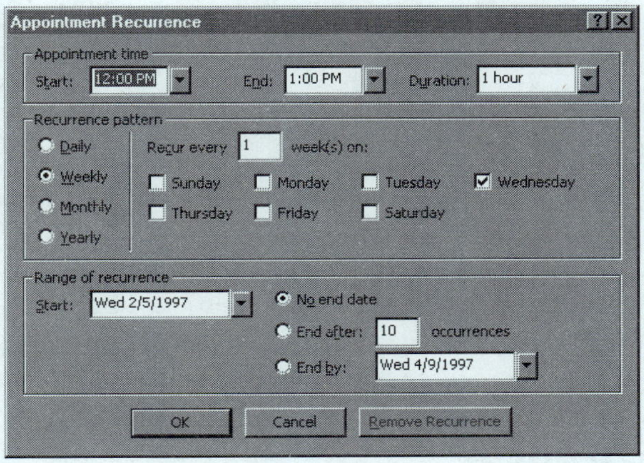

By default, Outlook assumes you want the meeting to occur weekly on the same day of the week, starting and ending at the times you selected, with no end date.

3. In the Recurrence Pattern section, enter *2* in the Recur Every edit box to change the appointment to every other week.
4. To add an end date, click the End By option in the Range Of Recurrence section and then use the drop-down calendar to change the date to July 9, 1997. Then click OK.
5. In the Appointment dialog box, type *Progress report* in the Subject edit box. Change the reminder time for the appointment to 30 minutes and then click Save And Close. The result is shown on the next page.

Canceling appointments

To cancel an appointment, select the appointment and click the Delete button on the toolbar. When you delete a recurring appointment, Outlook displays a dialog box in which you can specify whether the program should delete just this occurrence of the appointment or all occurrences.

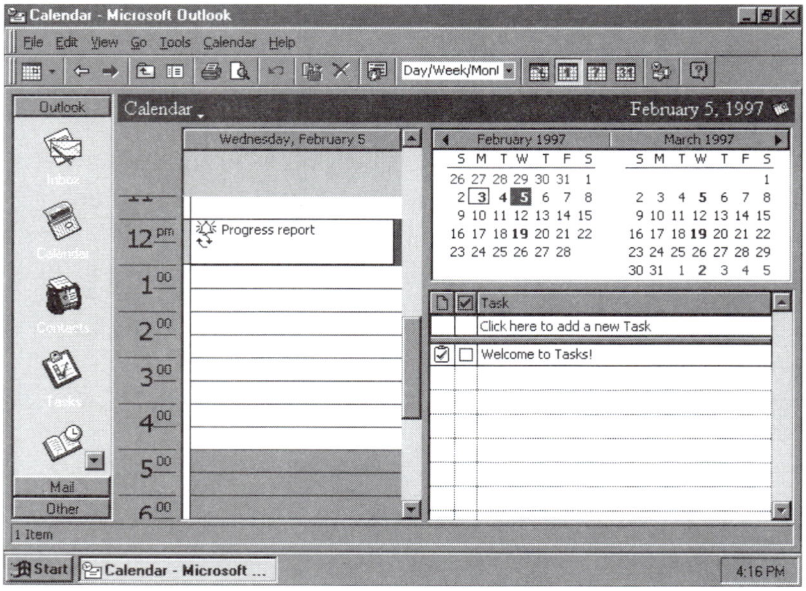

Outlook has entered the recurring appointment in the specified time slot for next Wednesday and for every other Wednesday thereafter, designating it with a circle icon.

Planning Meetings

The Plan A Meeting button

Those of you who are working on a network might want to explore the Calendar's meeting-planning capabilities. Clicking the Plan A Meeting button displays a dialog box like this one, in which you can specify who should attend the meeting and identify a mutually convenient time slot:

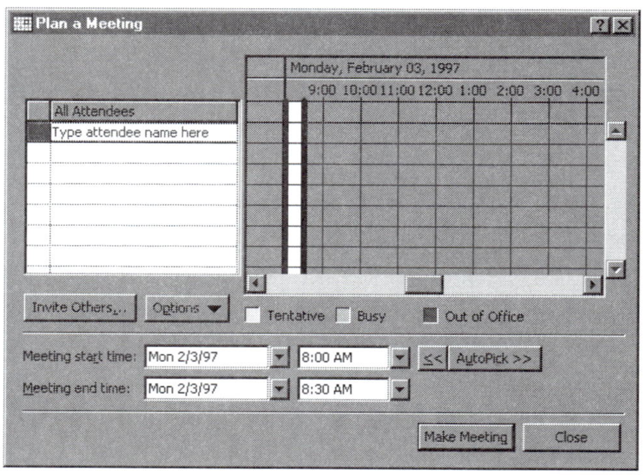

Printing calendars

To print a calendar, choose Print from the File menu or click the Print button on the toolbar, select a print layout (and any other options) in the Print dialog box, and click OK. If you're not sure what type of layout you want to print, select one of the layout options and click the Preview button. You can also specify the dates you want to print in the Print Range section of the Print dialog box.

You can then have Outlook send invitations to those you want to attend the meeting. These invitations will show up as meeting requests on the calendars of those you have invited. Obviously for the meeting planner to achieve its full potential, all members of a networked workgroup must keep their calendars up-to-date in Outlook and must stay signed onto e-mail throughout the day.

Managing Contacts

The Contacts component of Outlook lets us keep important addresses, e-mail addresses, and phone numbers handy at all times. We can look up addresses when sending e-mail (or regular letters in Word) and we can even have our computer dial a selected phone number for us. What's more, we can designate important contacts for automatic journal tracking, which logs all activities related to that contact (see page 251 for more information about the Journal component of Outlook). In this section, we'll take a quick look at Contacts and leave you to explore how you might put it to work for you.

Creating Address Cards

Follow these steps to make some entries in your contact list:

Starting Contacts

1. Click the Contacts icon on the Outlook bar to display a contact list like this one in the Outlook workspace:

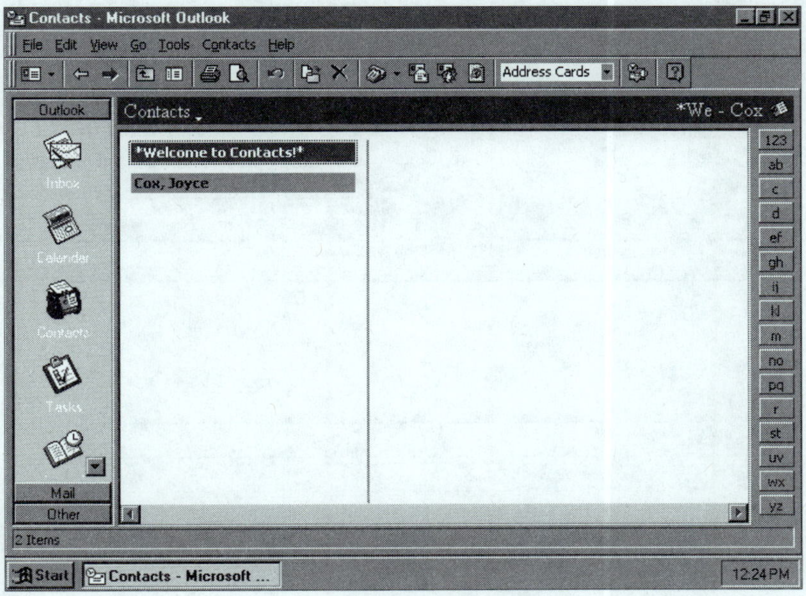

Address cards

Because we have not used Contacts before, our list consists of two entries, called *address cards*, that have been created by Outlook: one labeled *Welcome to Contacts* and one labeled with the name of the person licensed to use Office on this computer.

The New Contact button

2. Click the New Contact button on the toolbar to display this address-card window:

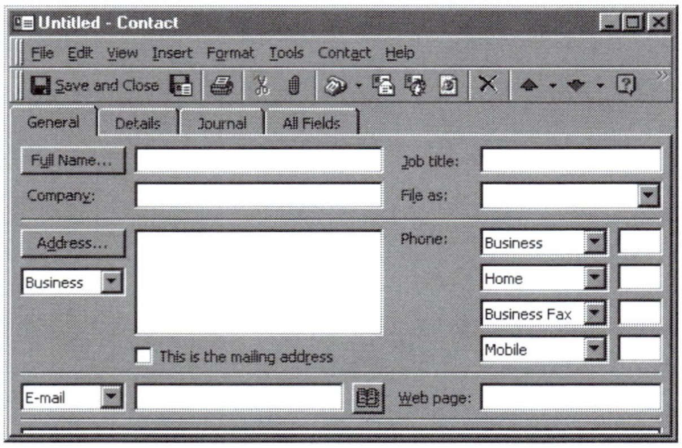

3. Maximize the window and enter the information shown here, entering the phone numbers without parentheses or hyphens (Outlook adds them):

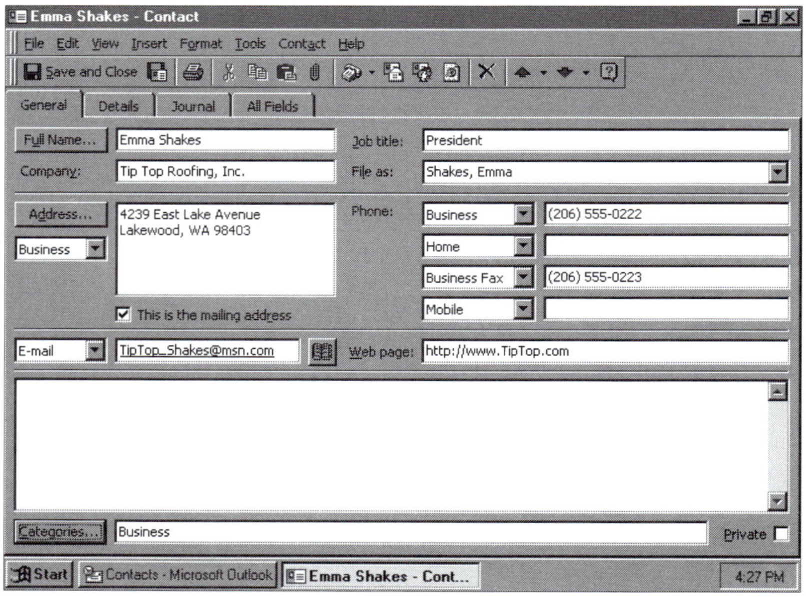

Address books

Your contact list is one of the "address books" available when you click the Address Book button on the toolbar. These address books store e-mail and fax information for use when sending electronic mesages. (Other information included on contact-list address cards is not available in the Address Book dialog box.) The other available address books might include the Global Address List (created & maintained by your company) and a Personal Address Book, where you keep the information you use most frequently (particularly if you regularly send the same message to a group of people).

4. Click the Save And New button to save the current address card and display a blank address-card window.

The Save And New button

5. Create address cards for these people, assigning them to the Business category (click Save And Close after the last one):

Name	Job Title	Company	Address	Business Phone	Business Fax	E-mail
Sandra Peters	Director	Northwest BEAT	10 Columbia Square Olympia, WA 98567	360 5557777	360 5557778	NWBEAT_Peters@ netcom.com
Gilbert Perez	Coord-inator	Oregon BEAT	444 Towne Center Portland, OR 97208	503 5554444	503 5554445	OBEAT_Perez@ halcyon.com
Nathan Chou	Coord-inator	Washington BEAT	1414 East 45th Street Seattle, WA 98149	206 5551010	206 5551011	WBEAT_Chou@ seanet.com
William Henry	President	Creative GlassWorks	67 Cleveland Tower Redmond, WA 98052	206 5559999	206 5559991	GlassWorks@ msn.com

Looking over the address cards in the Contacts window, suppose you discover an error in the Gilbert Perez card. Here's how to edit existing contact information (and add additional information):

1. Double-click Perez, Gilbert to display his address card.

Editing address cards

2. Change *444 Towne Center* to *4444 Towne Center*, and then click Save And Close.

Deleting Contacts

To keep your contact list up to date, you may need to delete address cards. Try this:

1. If your contacts list includes a Welcome to Contacts address card, click its header to select it, and then click the Delete button.
2. Delete any other contacts shown in the list when you first displayed the Contacts window, leaving only the five you just entered. The Contacts list now looks like the one shown on the next page.

More contact details

On the Details tab of the address-card window you can supply additional information for each contact, including personal information important to maintaining good client relations.

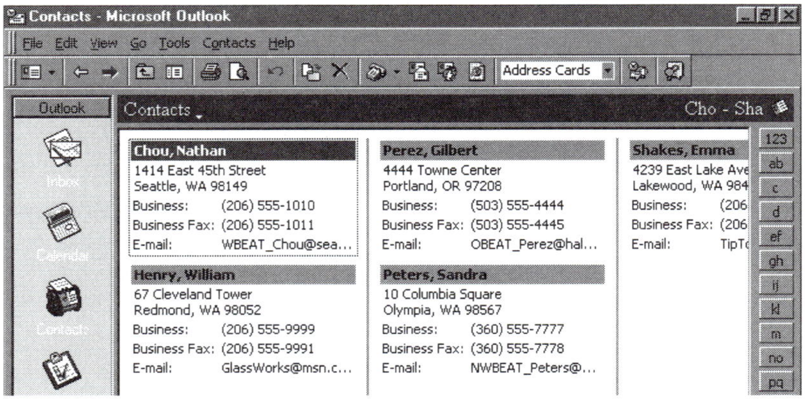

Using Your Contact List with E-mail

As an example of one way you might use your contact list, follow these steps to send an e-mail message to one of the people on your list:

1. Add a new address card for yourself to your contact list, entering your e-mail address in the appropriate edit box.

The New Message To Contact button

2. Select your address card in the Contacts window and click the New Message To Contact button on the toolbar. Outlook displays a Message window like the one shown on page 234, with your e-mail address already entered in the To edit box.

3. Send yourself a message by completing the edit boxes in the Message window and then clicking the Send button. If you are connected to your e-mail server, you will soon see an envelope icon in the notification area of the Windows 95 taskbar, announcing the arrival of your message.

We'll leave you to explore other ways to use the Contacts component of Outlook on your own.

Organizing Tasks

Using the Tasks component of Outlook, we can create and manage a to do list, "scheduling" time for specific tasks in our calendars if necessary. Other people will then know that we are unavailable during the time we plan to work on a task.

Adding Tasks

Let's start by adding a couple of tasks, first a simple one and then one with a deadline and high priority:

Starting Tasks

1. Click the Tasks icon to open this to do list (check that Simple List is the setting in the Current View box on the toolbar):

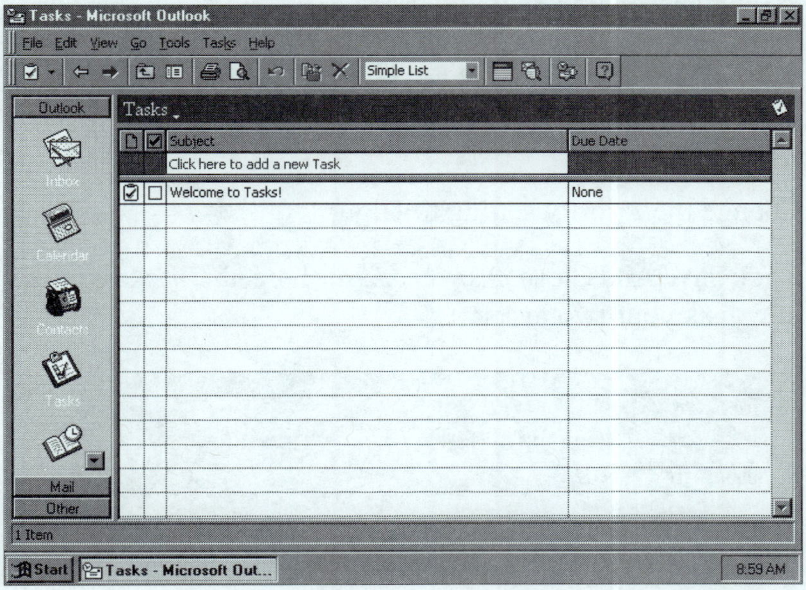

2. Click the task slot marked Click Here To Add A New Task, type *Pick up dry cleaning*, click None in the Due Date column, click the down arrow, select tomorrow's date from the drop-down calendar, and press Enter.

The New Task button

3. To add the second task, click the New Task button on the toolbar to display this window:

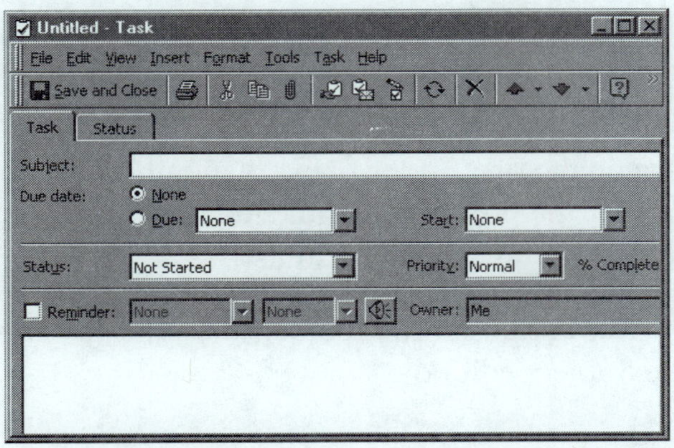

4. Type *Prepare for presentation* in the Subject edit box of the Task tab.

   By default, the task has no due date and has not yet started. You can enter start and due dates and assign a priority level. For example, suppose this task is very important and must be completed by tomorrow afternoon. Follow these steps to assign dates and change the priority:

1. Click the Due option button, then click the down arrow next to the current date and when the calendar appears, click tomorrow's date.
2. Change the Priority setting to High.
3. Click Save And Close. As you can see here, the Tasks window now lists your two tasks:

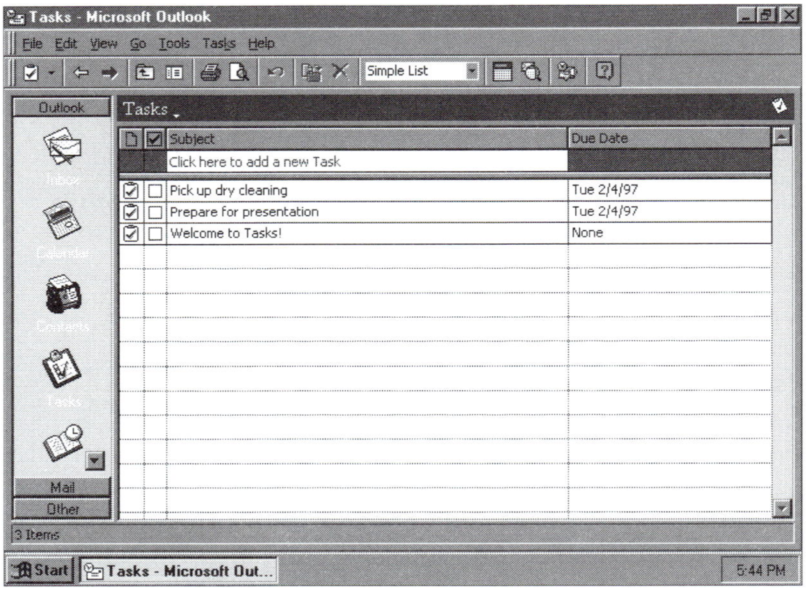

Sorting tasks

To sort tasks (in ascending order) by their description, priority, percent complete, and so on, right-click the appropriate column header above the Tasks list and choose Sort Ascending or Sort Descending from the object menu. Outlook then sorts the tasks accordingly. If you want to sort the tasks on a different category or on multiple categories (or in descending order), choose Sort from the View menu and make your selections from the drop-down lists in the Sort dialog box.

Adding Recurring Tasks

Now suppose that on the first Friday of every month, we have to review a report of the previous month's activities. Here's how we add a recurring task to the to do list:

1. Click the New Task button on the toolbar and type *Review last month* in the Subject edit box.

The Recurrence button

2. Click the Recurrence button on the Task window's toolbar to display a dialog box similar to the one shown on page 241.

3. Select Monthly and change the entries in the adjacent section to the first Friday of every month. The dialog box now looks like this:

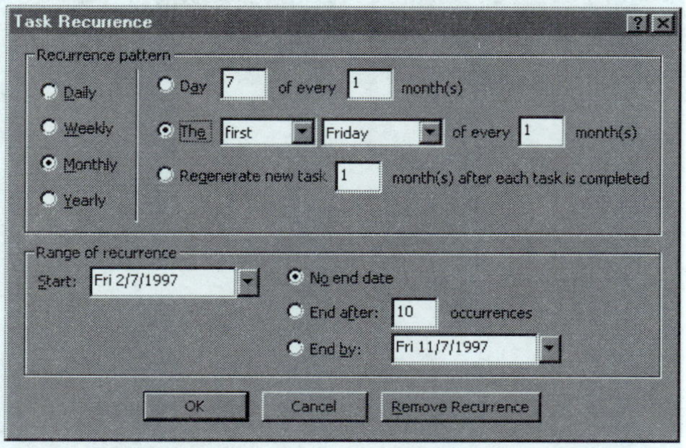

4. Click OK to close the Recurrence dialog box.

Setting reminders

5. Back in the Tasks window, change the Reminder time to 1:00 PM, and click Save And Close.

Deleting Tasks

Follow these steps to see how to designate a task as completed and how to remove a completed task from the list:

Completed tasks

1. In the Tasks list, click the check box in the second column of the Welcome To Tasks entry. (If you don't have such an entry, quickly create a task you can experiment with.) Outlook checks the box and draws a line through the task to indicate that it is complete.

2. With the completed task selected, click the Delete button on the toolbar to remove the task from the list.

Categorizing Tasks

With Outlook, you can assign tasks to categories for easier organization. Follow the steps on the next page.

The Current View box

1. Click the arrow to the right of the Current View box on the toolbar and select Detailed List from the drop-down list. The Tasks window changes to look like this:

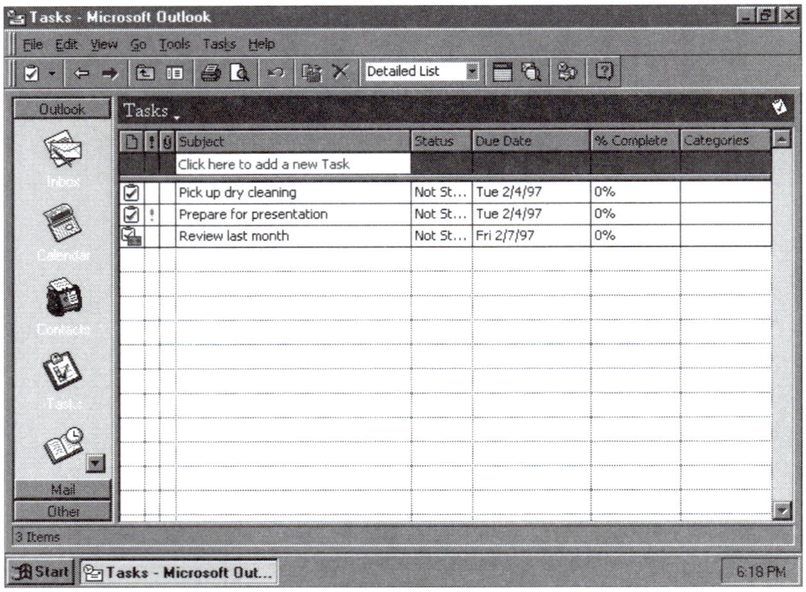

Notice that the important preparation task is flagged with an exclamation mark.

2. Select the Pick Up Dry Cleaning task and choose Categories from the Edit menu to display this dialog box:

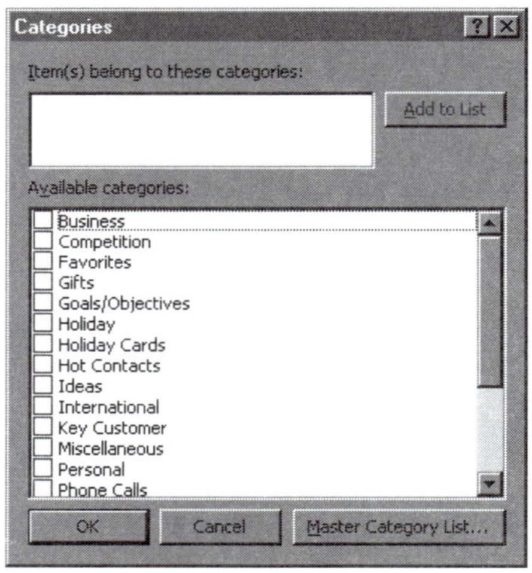

3. Click the Personal check box and click OK.

Adding new categories

The Categories dialog box includes many ready-made categories, but if none of these meets your needs, click Master Category List to display a dialog box where you can add new categories and delete ones you know you'll never use.

4. Repeat steps 2 and 3 to assign the two remaining tasks to the Business category.

5. Select By Category from the Current View box's drop-down list and if necessary, click the + buttons adjacent to the Categories headers to display the tasks by category, as shown here:

Displaying tasks by category

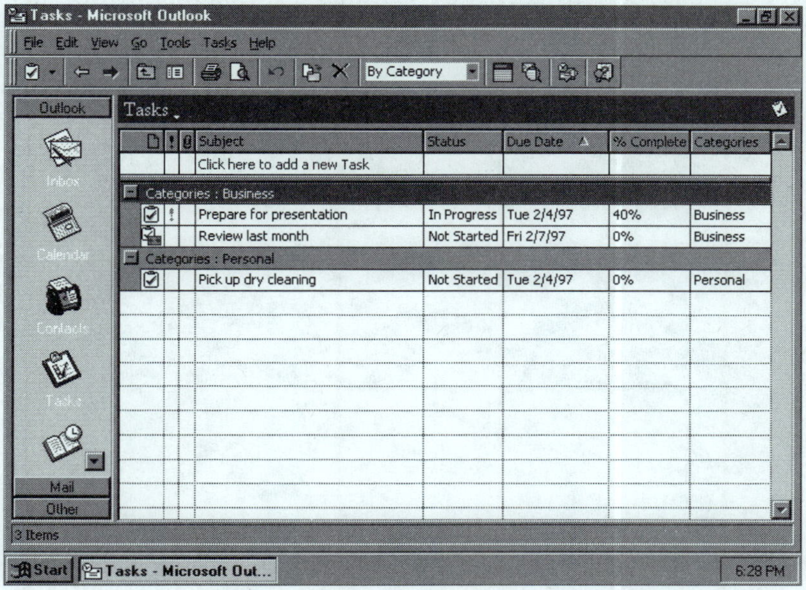

(We edited the Status and %Complete columns of the first task directly in the Tasks window, and we also widened the Status column by dragging its header border to the right.)

The usefulness of the Tasks component of Outlook is augmented by the fact that a small version of the Tasks list is displayed in the Calendar, making it easy to allocate time slots for specific tasks so that nothing slips through the cracks.

Customizing the Outlook window

You can hide the Outlook bar by right-clicking it and choosing Hide Outlook Bar from the object menu. Then to move from one Outlook component to another, click the arrow to the right of the component name (for example, Tasks in the screen above) and select the desired component from the drop-down list. (You can also cycle through the components you have worked with in this session by clicking the Back and Forward buttons on the toolbar.) Redisplay the Outlook bar by choosing it from the View Menu.

Keeping a Journal

As you work with Office, the Journal component of Outlook is active behind the scenes, logging the tasks you perform with your computer. As you'll see, you can also make your own journal entries and you can have Outlook track your interactions with designated contacts. Let's take a look at the Journal and then see what we can do with it.

Creating Journal Entries

Here's how to display the Journal and create a journal entry for the interview with Amanda Rawlings:

Starting Journal

1. Click the Journal icon on the Outlook bar to display the current month's journal in the Outlook workspace (check that By Type is the setting in the Current View box on the toolbar):

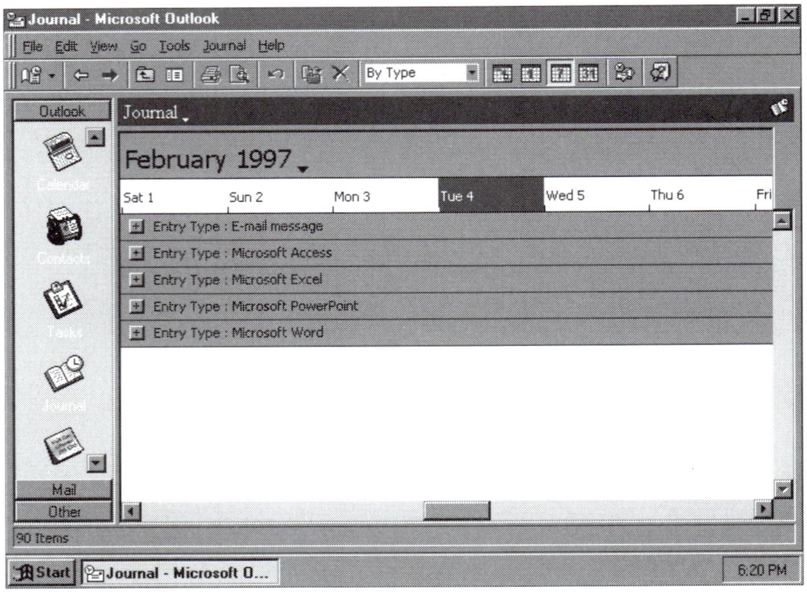

The New Journal button

2. Click the New Journal button to display a blank Journal Entry window, and then fill in the journal entry so that it looks like this, clicking Save And Close when you're done:

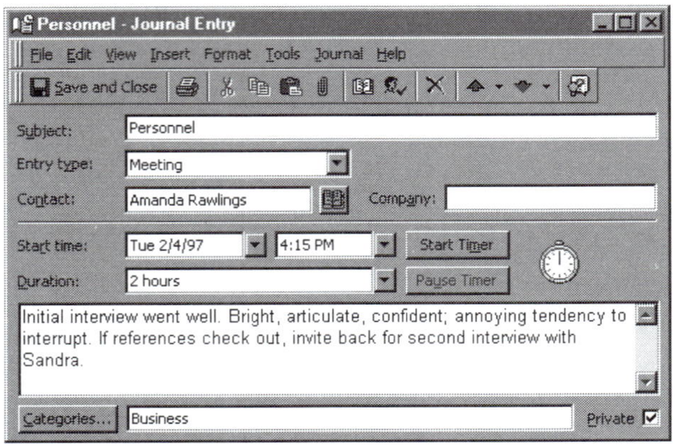

Types of journal entries

Outlook automatically records certain types of activities in your journal, including e-mail messages, meetings scheduled using the Calendar, and documents created with the Office applications. You can also select from a list of entry types by clicking the arrow to the right of the Entry Type box in the Journal Entry window.

Tracking phone calls

Notice that you can use the Journal Entry window to track phone calls, including their length (for billing purposes). All you have to do is open the Journal Entry window, fill in the edit boxes, dial the phone number, and click the Start Timer button when you make the connection. Click Pause Timer when you hang up the phone and then click Save And Close.

Now let's display the journal entry in the workspace:

Displaying journal entries by contact

1. Click the arrow to the right of the Current View box on the toolbar and select By Contact. (If a warning message appears, click OK with the Discard The Current View Settings option selected.)

2. If necessary, click the + button adjacent to the Amanda Rawlings header. The workspace now looks like this:

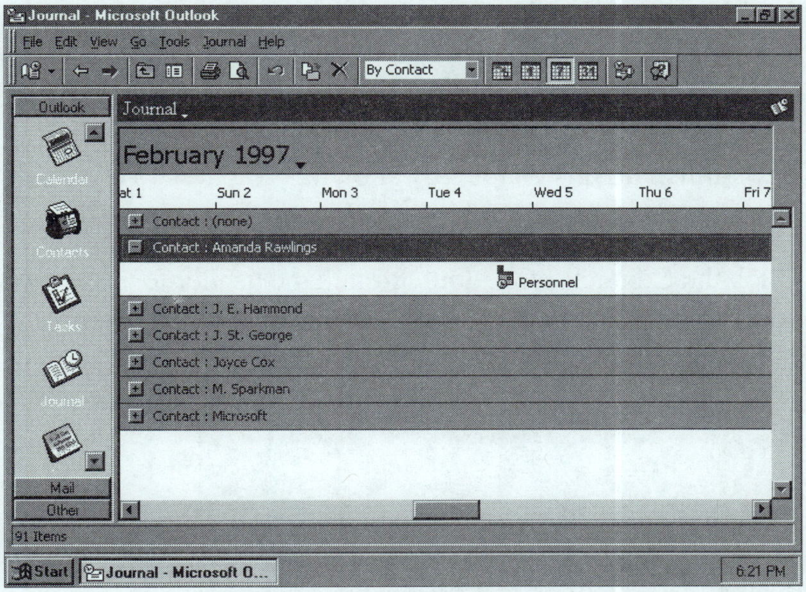

3. Double-click the Personnel entry to redisplay the Journal Entry window shown earlier, and then click its Close button.

4. Select Entry List from the Current View box's drop-down list to see a log of tasks you've performed with your computer, similar to the one shown on the next page.

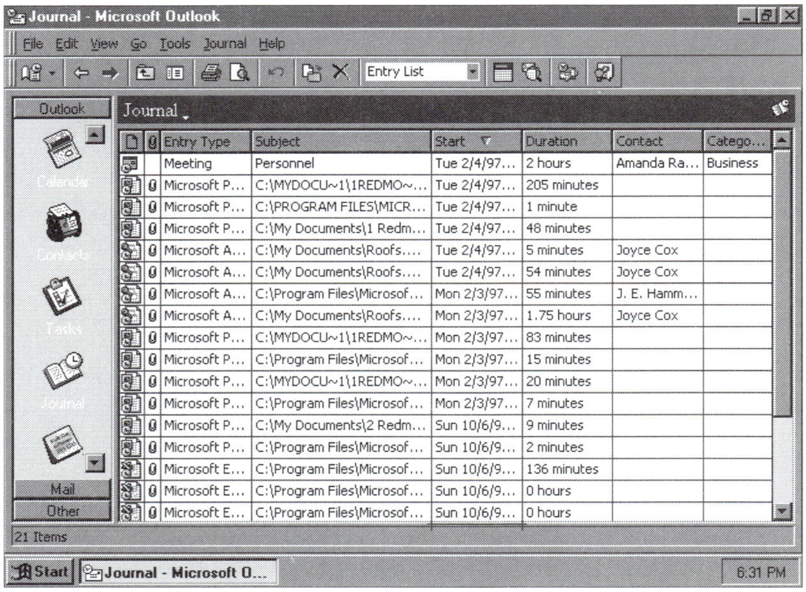

As you can see, you can not only track what you did when but also how long it took you.

Tracking Contacts

Let's finish up this chapter by showing you how to designate a contact for journal tracking. Follow these steps:

1. Click the Contacts icon, double-click the header for your own address card, and in the Contact window, click the Journal tab to display these options:

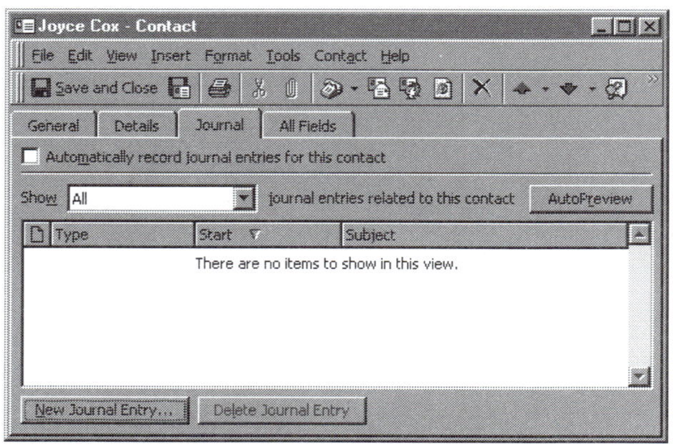

2. Click the Automatically Record check box and click Save And Close.

Jotting down notes

The Notes component of Outlook is a place to record simple reminders or ideas that don't fit in any other component. After clicking the Notes icon on the Outlook bar, you create a note by clicking the New Note button on the toolbar. Then simply type your note and click the Close button to close it. You can right-click the note to assign it to a category or color-code it. Then you can view notes by category or by color by selecting those options from the Current View box's drop-down list. You can also view notes as icons or in a list, and you can restrict the display to notes created in the previous seven days.

3. Choose options from the Tools menu, click the Journal tab, check that E-mail Message is selected in the Automatically Record These Items section, and click OK.

4. Make sure you are connected to your e-mail server, and then check that your address card is selected.

5. Click the New Message To Contact button to display a Message window, and send yourself a message.

6. Double-click your address card in the workspace and click the Journal tab of the Contact window, where Outlook has recorded your e-mail message.

7. Close the Contact window.

Well that's it for a quick tour of the Outlook components. To quit Outlook, click its Close button. As we mentioned earlier, because the reminder and meeting planner features can work only when Outlook is running, those of you who are working on a network might want to start Outlook and then minimize it at the beginning of each work session, quitting the program only when you're ready to quit for the day.

11

Using the Office Tools Together

Print form letters using information from a database

Use Excel worksheet data to plot a graph on a slide

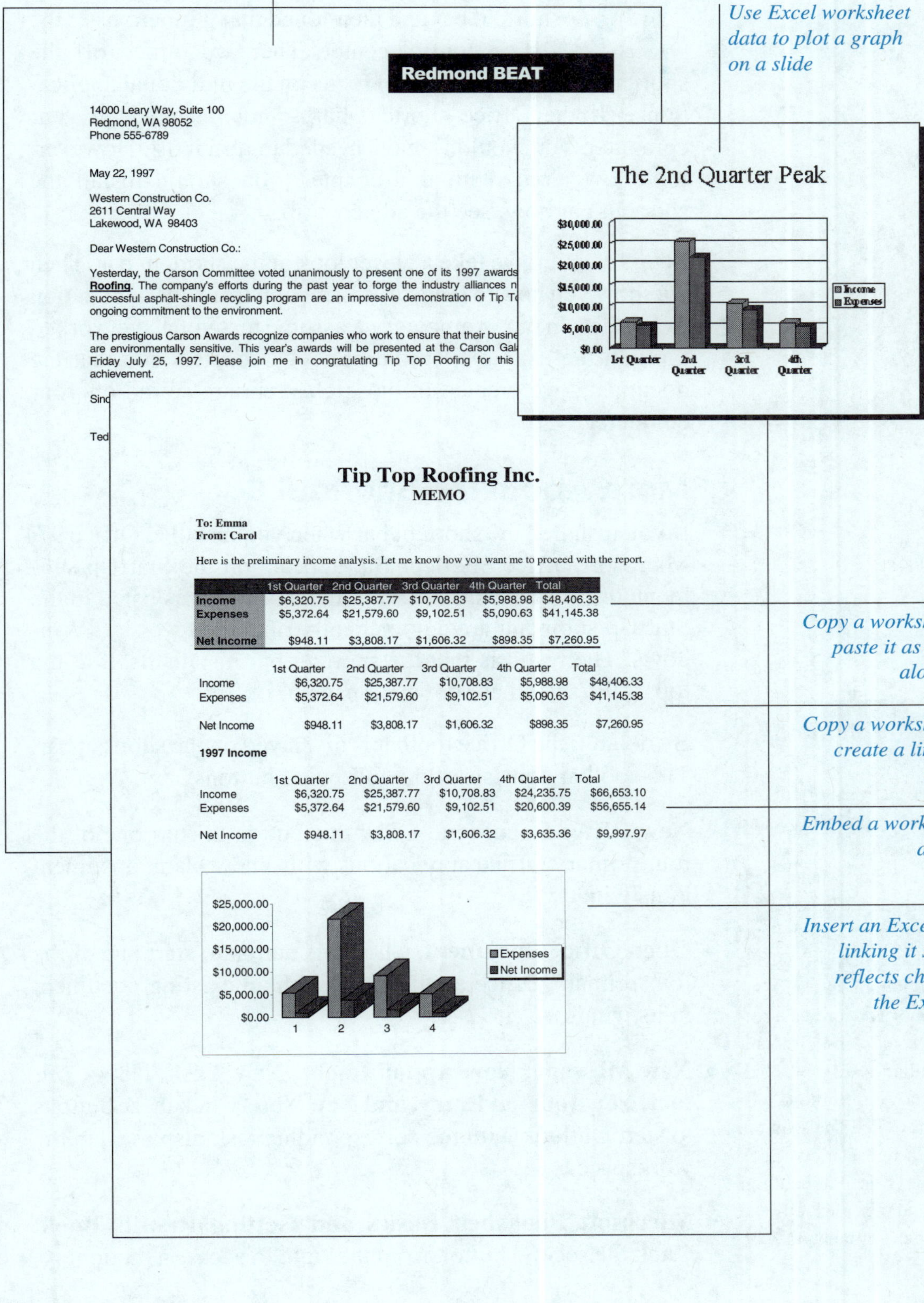

Redmond BEAT

14000 Leary Way, Suite 100
Redmond, WA 98052
Phone 555-6789

May 22, 1997

Western Construction Co.
2611 Central Way
Lakewood, WA 98403

Dear Western Construction Co.:

Yesterday, the Carson Committee voted unanimously to present one of its 1997 awards **Roofing**. The company's efforts during the past year to forge the industry alliances n successful asphalt-shingle recycling program are an impressive demonstration of Tip T ongoing commitment to the environment.

The prestigious Carson Awards recognize companies who work to ensure that their busine are environmentally sensitive. This year's awards will be presented at the Carson Gal Friday July 25, 1997. Please join me in congratulating Tip Top Roofing for this achievement.

Sinc

Ted

Tip Top Roofing Inc.
MEMO

To: Emma
From: Carol

Here is the preliminary income analysis. Let me know how you want me to proceed with the report.

	1st Quarter	2nd Quarter	3rd Quarter	4th Quarter	Total
Income	$6,320.75	$25,387.77	$10,708.83	$5,988.98	$48,406.33
Expenses	$5,372.64	$21,579.60	$9,102.51	$5,090.63	$41,145.38
Net Income	$948.11	$3,808.17	$1,606.32	$898.35	$7,260.95

	1st Quarter	2nd Quarter	3rd Quarter	4th Quarter	Total
Income	$6,320.75	$25,387.77	$10,708.83	$5,988.98	$48,406.33
Expenses	$5,372.64	$21,579.60	$9,102.51	$5,090.63	$41,145.38
Net Income	$948.11	$3,808.17	$1,606.32	$898.35	$7,260.95

1997 Income

	1st Quarter	2nd Quarter	3rd Quarter	4th Quarter	Total
Income	$6,320.75	$25,387.77	$10,708.83	$24,235.75	$66,653.10
Expenses	$5,372.64	$21,579.60	$9,102.51	$20,600.39	$56,655.14
Net Income	$948.11	$3,808.17	$1,606.32	$3,635.36	$9,997.97

Copy a worksheet and paste it as a stand-alone table

Copy a worksheet and create a link to the original

Embed a worksheet as an object

Insert an Excel graph, linking it so that it reflects changes to the Excel data

Way back in Chapter 1, we introduced the Office shortcut bar and mentioned that it functions as the Office control center. Then we turned off the shortcut bar so that we could focus on the individual applications. (If the Office shortcut bar is not installed on your computer, you wouldn't have needed to turn it off. However, to follow along with this chapter, you should install the shortcut bar now; see the adjacent tip.)

In this chapter, we take a closer look at the shortcut bar. Then we show you how to recycle information from one application to another. In our examples, we assume that you have worked through the examples in the previous chapters and that the documents we created in those chapters are stored on your computer.

More About the Shortcut Bar

If you installed the shortcut bar when you installed Office 97, Microsoft Office Shortcut Bar appears on the StartUp submenu of Programs on the Start menu. Programs listed in the StartUp submenu are automatically run when we start Windows. The result is that the shortcut bar installs itself at the top of the screen as shown on page 5.

By default, the Office toolbar is displayed on the shortcut bar. This toolbar consists of the following buttons:

- **New Office Document.** Click this button to start one of the four primary Office applications with a new blank document in its window.
- **Open Office Document.** Click this button to start one of the four primary Office applications with an existing document in its window.
- **New Message, New Appointment, New Task, New Contact, New Journal Entry, and New Note.** Click these buttons to start Outlook with the corresponding task displayed in the workspace.
- **Microsoft Bookshelf Basics and Getting Results Book.** Click the second button from the right to access a dictionary,

Installing the shortcut bar

To install the Office shortcut bar, close any open applications and choose Settings and then Control Panel from the Start Menu. Next double-click the Add/Remove Programs icon in the Control Panel window, select Microsoft Office 97 in the Add/Remove list and click the Add/Remove button at the bottom of the Install/Uninstall tab. Insert the installation disk and click OK. Click the Add/Remove button, select the Office Tools option, and click Change Option. Click the Microsoft Office Shortcut Bar check box and then click OK and proceed with the installation.

a thesaurus, and a book of quotations; and click the rightmost button to access the *Getting Results* documentation.

Also by default, the shortcut bar hovers at the top of the screen over any open programs. But in this location, it is hard to appreciate the flexibility of the shortcut bar. Follow these steps to move it:

Moving the shortcut bar

1. Point to a blank area between the buttons on the shortcut bar and drag the bar to the middle of your screen. When you release the mouse button, the shortcut bar becomes a floating window like this one:

As you can see, the shortcut bar now displays a button for the Office toolbar, in addition to the familiar buttons.

Docking the shortcut bar

2. Point to the shortcut bar's title bar and drag all the way to the right side of the screen, releasing the mouse button when the outline of the shortcut bar indicates that it will be *docked* as a strip down the edge of the screen.

3. Try docking the bar at the bottom and left sides of the screen, and then finish up with the small floating window shown earlier.

When the shortcut bar is floating on the screen, we can use its Minimize button to tuck it out of sight on the taskbar. Try this:

Minimizing the shortcut bar

1. Click the shortcut bar's Minimize button.

2. Click the Microsoft Office Shortcut Bar button on the taskbar to redisplay its window.

Customizing the Shortcut Bar

The Control menu

When the shortcut bar is a floating window, it has a Control menu icon at the left end of its title bar, just like other windows. (When the shortcut bar is docked, the Control menu icon is at the top or left end of the bar.) Although the Control menu provides access to several features, we are most likely to use it to customize the bar. Let's take a look:

The Control menu icon

1. Click the Control menu icon to display the Control menu. The first set of commands on this menu duplicate the sizing buttons at the right end of most title bars. The second set of commands customizes the look and content of the shortcut bar. The commands in the third set change the Office installation and provide help. And the lonely command in the fourth set removes the shortcut bar from the screen.

2. Choose the Customize command to display this dialog box:

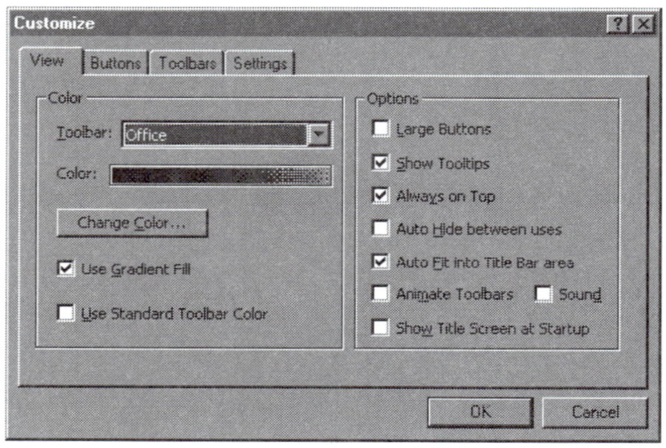

The options on the View tab control the way the Office shortcut bar looks and behaves on the screen. You might want to experiment with these options later, after you understand a bit more about how the shortcut bar works.

Displaying and Hiding Toolbars

As we've said, by default the shortcut bar displays the Office toolbar, but you can display other toolbars at any time. Follow these steps:

1. Click the Toolbars tab of the Customize dialog box to display a list of the toolbars you can display on the shortcut bar:

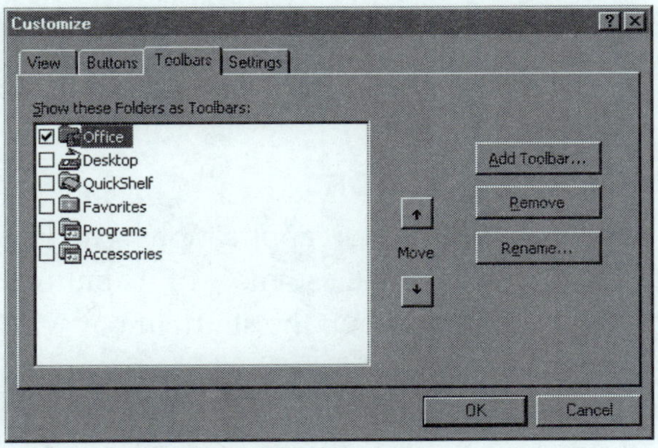

2. Click the Programs check box and then click OK. The shortcut bar now looks like this:

As you can see, the Office toolbar is hidden below its button on the left side of the shortcut bar, and the buttons on the Programs toolbar are now displayed.

3. Click the Office button. The Programs toolbar shrinks under its button, and the buttons on the Office toolbar are once again displayed.

4. Choose Customize from the Control menu, click the Toolbars tab, select Desktop, QuickShelf, and Accessories, and click OK. Here's the result:

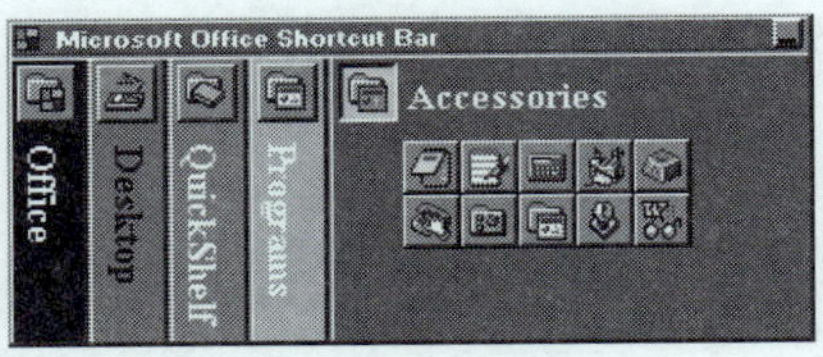

5. Dock the shortcut bar at the bottom of the screen to see how the toolbars look in this configuration, and then switch from one toolbar to another by clicking the toolbar buttons.

Creating custom toolbars

To create a custom toolbar to add to the Office shortcut bar, start by choosing Customize from the Control menu. Then, when the Customize dialog box appears, click the Add Toolbar button on the Toolbars tab; select the Create A New, Blank Toolbar option; enter a name for the toolbar; and click OK. Next click the Buttons tab of the Customize dialog box, be sure the name of the custom toolbar appears in the Toolbar box, and then click the Add File or Add Folder button to add files and/or folders to the new toolbar. When you're ready, click OK to add your customized toolbar to the Office shortcut bar.

6. Hide all the toolbars except the Office toolbar by deselecting their check boxes in the Customize dialog box. Then refloat the shortcut bar.

Displaying and Hiding Buttons

The Programs toolbar enables us to start applications with just the click of a button. However, if we use most of its buttons only rarely, it's not worth cluttering up the shortcut bar with an entire toolbar. Instead, we can add buttons for the programs we use most often to the Office toolbar. (We don't need to add buttons for Word, Excel, PowerPoint, and Access because we can click the New Office Document or Open Office Document button to simultaneously start one of these programs and open a document.) As a demonstration, we'll add two buttons to the Office toolbar. Let's get going:

Displaying buttons

1. Choose Customize from the Control menu and click the Buttons tab to display these options:

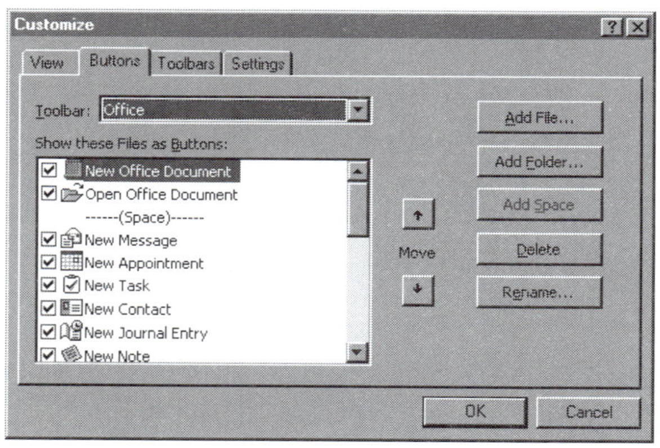

Changing toolbar order

Changing the order of the toolbars on the Office shortcut bar is similar to changing the order of buttons on a particular toolbar. Simply choose Customize from the Control menu, click the Toolbars tab, select the name of the toolbar you want to move, click the Move Up or Move Down button, and then click OK.

2. Scroll the Show These Files As Buttons list and click the check box to the left of Microsoft Binder to add its button to the toolbar.

3. Click Microsoft Binder's name to highlight it and then click the Move Up button—the upward-pointing arrow above the word *Move*—until Microsoft Binder is at the top of the list, above New Office Document. Click OK. As you can see at the top of the facing page, the Office toolbar now includes instant access to Binder.

Here's how to hide a button:

Hiding buttons

1. Choose Customize from the Control menu and click the Buttons tab.

2. Scroll the Show These Files As Buttons list, deselect the Getting Results Book check box, and click OK. This button no longer appears on the toolbar.

Adding buttons for unlisted applications

Suppose we want to add a button for the Character Map program, which is not listed in the Customize dialog box. Here's what we do:

1. Choose Customize from the Control menu, click the Buttons tab, and click the Add File button to display this dialog box:

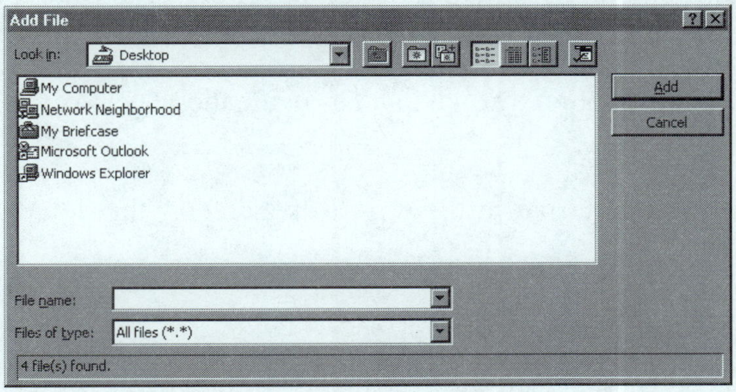

2. Navigate to the Windows folder (for example, double-click My Computer, the C: drive, and the Windows folder in succession), and then scroll Charmap (or Charmap.exe) into view.

3. Click Charmap to select it, and then click the Add button. In the Customize dialog box, Charmap now appears in the Show These Files As Buttons list, and its check box is selected.

4. Click OK to close the dialog box and display the shortcut bar with its new button.

5. Next, adjust the position of the Charmap button by displaying the Buttons tab of the Customize dialog box, selecting Charmap at the bottom of the Show These Files As Buttons list, and clicking the Move Down button—the downward-pointing arrow below the word *Move*. Because Charmap can't move down any further, it jumps to the top of the list.

6. Click OK. Here are the results:

Suppose we decide we don't need Character Map on the shortcut bar any more. We could hide the button by deselecting its check box in the Show These Files As Buttons list, but if we're really sure we won't need it again, we can delete it like this:

Hiding vs. removing

A good rule of thumb to remember when you're working with the Office shortcut bar is to hide rather than remove the default toolbars and buttons so that you can easily restore them. To hide toolbars or buttons, choose the Customize command from the Control menu, click the Toolbars or Buttons tab of the Customize dialog box, and deselect the toolbars or buttons by clicking their check boxes. (Before you can hide a button, you must use the Toolbar drop-down list on the Buttons tab to select the toolbar on which the button resides.) When you create custom toolbars or add custom buttons to the Office shortcut bar, you might want to enlist the Remove button on the Toolbars tab or the Delete button on the Buttons tab to remove toolbars and buttons that have become obsolete.

1. Choose Customize from the Control menu, click the Buttons tab, select Charmap, click the Delete button, and click OK.

2. Confirm the deletion by clicking Yes in the message box that appears.

3. Dock the shortcut bar at the top of the screen—the default position.

Using Microsoft Binder

Having added the Microsoft Binder button to the Office toolbar on the shortcut bar, we may as well see how to use it. Microsoft Binder is a very useful program that enables us to group related files created in different applications. How is a binder different from a folder? Let's create a new binder so that we can explore:

1. Click the Microsoft Binder button on the shortcut bar to start the program and open the binder window shown on the facing page. (If necessary, click the Start Using Microsoft Binder option to close the Office Assistant.)

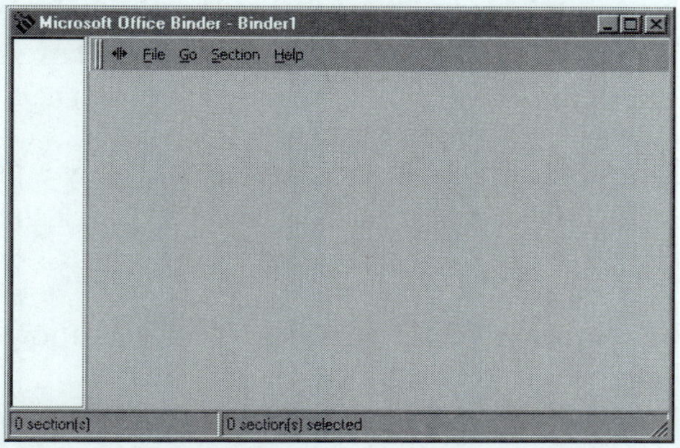

2. Choose Save Binder As from the File menu, name the new binder *Examples*, and click the Save button to save the binder in the My Documents folder.

An empty binder is not very useful, so let's add some sections to it. Sections can contain existing documents that are stored as separate files on disk, or they can be created as part of the binder file, meaning that they don't exist outside the binder. Follow these steps to add existing documents to the binder:

Adding existing documents as sections

1. Choose Add From File from the Section menu to display this dialog box:

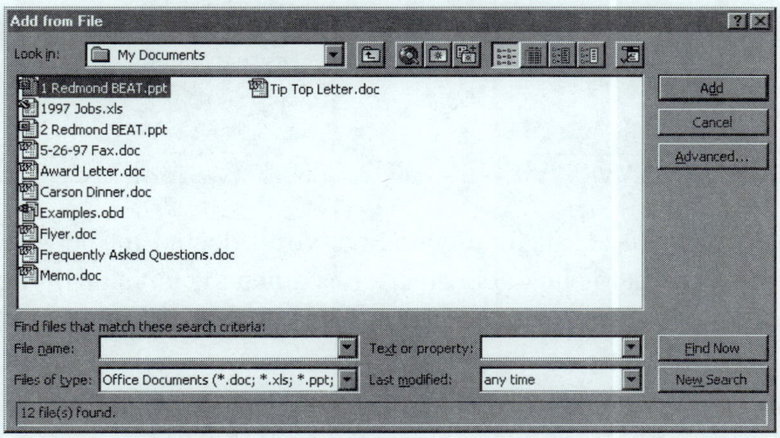

The list of documents in the My Documents folder includes those created with Word, Excel, and PowerPoint. Access databases cannot be added to a binder, so the Roofs database we created in Chapters 8 and 9 does not appear in the list even though it is stored in this folder.

2. Select all the documents by holding down the Shift key and clicking the last document in the list box, and then click the Add button.
3. Choose Save Binder from the File menu to save the additions as part of the binder.
4. Click the Maximize button to expand the binder window to look like this:

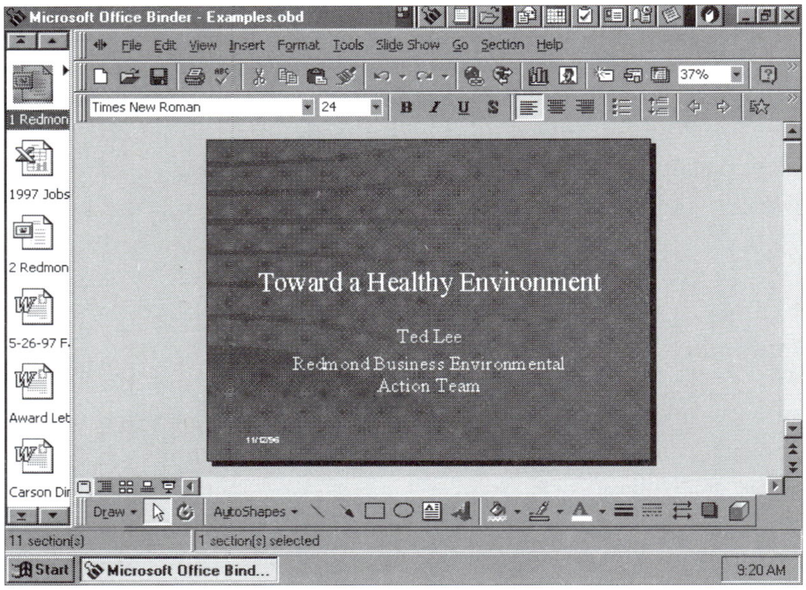

As you can see, all the documents you selected in the Add From File dialog box appear as icons down the left side of the window. The active document—the presentation we created in PowerPoint in Chapters 6 and 7—is displayed in the window to the right with PowerPoint's menus and toolbars available so that you can work on the presentation.

5. Click the 1997 Jobs icon. After a few seconds, the window on the right looks like this:

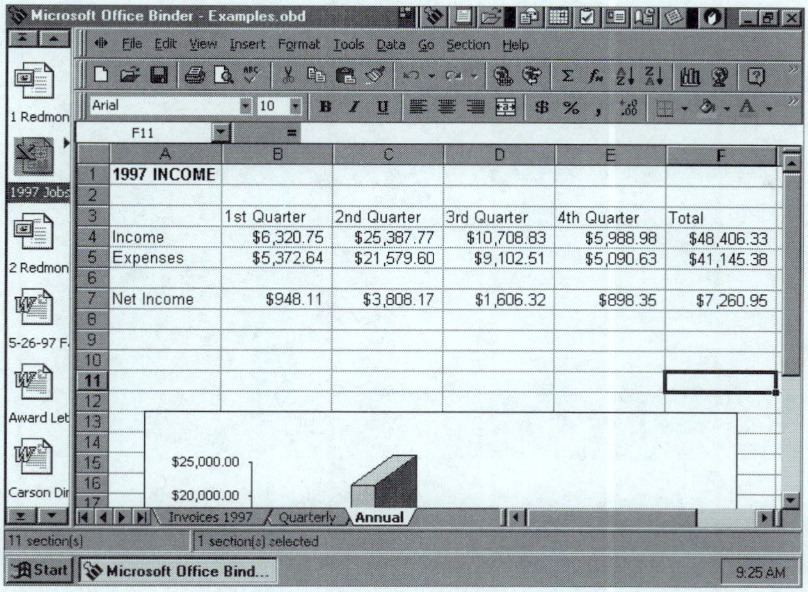

Not only has the selected worksheet replaced the presentation, but Excel's menus and toolbars have replaced PowerPoint's.

6. Switch to other documents, using the arrows at the top and bottom of the icon area to scroll out-of-sight documents into view.

We are going to use the Examples binder later in this chapter, but we don't need all these sections. Here's how to delete the sections we don't need (the actual files will still be on your hard drive):

Deleting sections

1. Select the 5-26-97 Fax icon and choose Delete from the Section menu.
2. Click OK to confirm the deletion.
3. Repeat steps 1 and 2 to remove all the documents except 1 Redmond BEAT, 1997 Jobs, Flyer, and Memo.

As well as adding existing documents to a binder, you can create binder sections from scratch. Follow these steps:

Creating new sections

1. Activate Memo and then choose Add from the Section menu to display the dialog box shown on the next page.

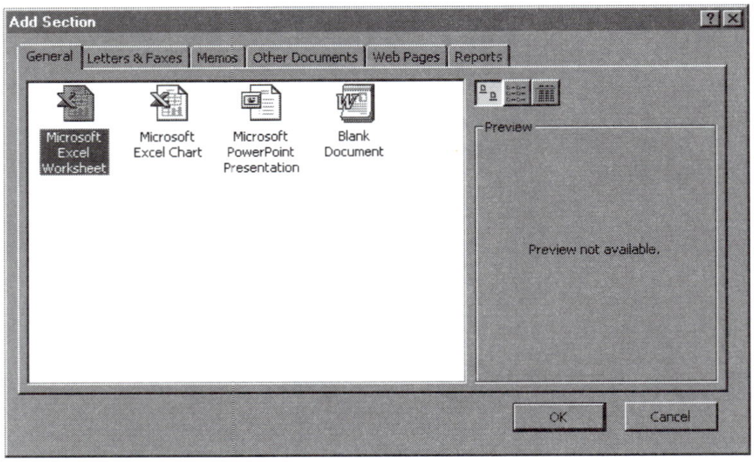

2. Select Blank Document and click OK. A new icon labeled *Section 1* is added to the list on the left below Memo, and a new blank Word document opens in the window on the right.

3. With the Section 1 icon selected, choose Rename from the Section menu to select the icon's name, type *Income Memo*, and press Enter.

4. Click the Normal View button at the left end of the status bar and check that the ruler is turned off.

Saving new binder sections as documents

When you create a new binder section and choose Save Binder or Save Binder As from the File menu to save it, Office saves the section as part of the binder only. The section does not exist as a separate file outside the binder. To save a binder section as a separate file, choose Save As File from the Section menu, specify where you want to store the file, enter a name, and then click Save. You can then open the file in the application in which it was created just like you would load any other file. Keep in mind that when you make changes to a document outside the binder, those changes will not be reflected in the original binder section.

5. Then type the memo shown here, formatting the first four lines (the memo header) to make them stand out and pressing Enter twice after the last line:

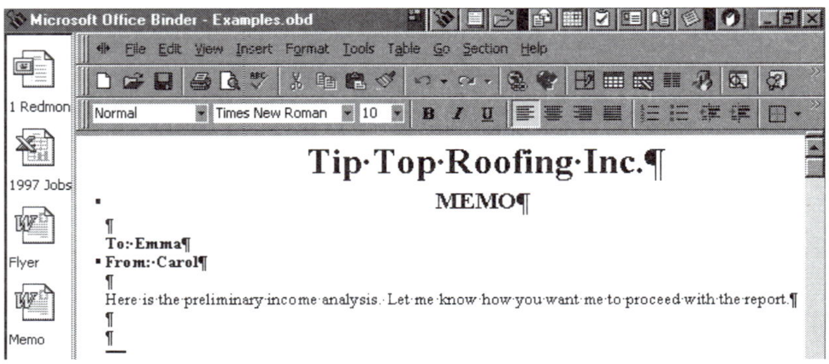

6. Click the Save button to safeguard this new section.

Leave the Examples binder and the Income Memo section open on your screen so that we can use them in our discussions of recycling information from one Office document to another.

Recycling Office Information

We'll start this discussion with a demonstration of the simplest way to recycle information: copying and pasting. Follow these steps:

1. Press Ctrl+End to make sure the insertion point is at the bottom of the Income Memo document, and click the 1997 Jobs icon.
2. With the Annual sheet active, select A3:F7, and click the Copy button on the toolbar.
3. Click the Income Memo icon to switch back to the memo section, and with the insertion point at the end of the document, click the Paste button on the toolbar to insert the copied range as a Word table.
4. As a finishing touch, click anywhere in the table and choose Select Table from the Table menu. Then choose Table AutoFormat from the Table menu and double-click Classic 2. Here are the results:

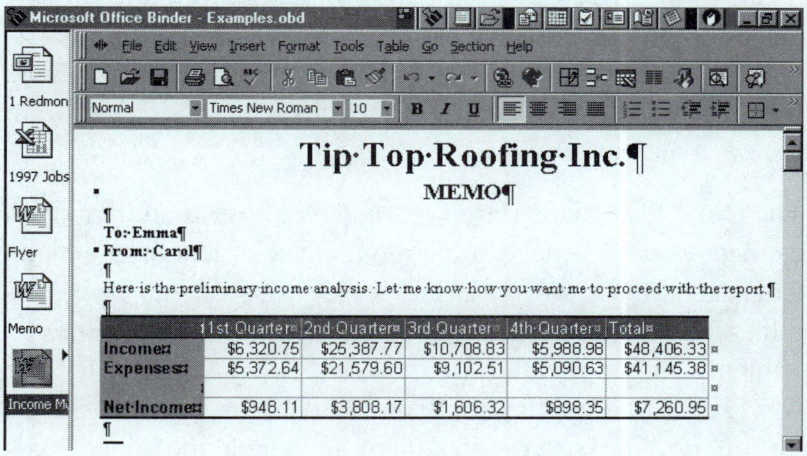

5. Save the binder.

Difficulty working in Binder?

Not surprisingly, Binder tends to be a memory hog. If you experience difficulties while working through our examples in a binder, you might want to use the individual applications instead. For example, you can create Income Memo in Word and then import the information you need from the 1997 Jobs worksheet in Excel.

As you have just seen, when we simply paste information from a worksheet into a Word document, the information is translated into a Word table. We could create the information in Word and get the same result, but when the data already exists in Excel, we can save ourselves a lot of typing by recycling the information instead. However, the power of the Office applications far exceeds this simple kind of copy-and-paste recycling. With Office, we can create documents that are a patchwork of pieces created in the different Office applications.

These patchwork documents allow us to maintain information in files that can be manipulated by the application that created them but also use that information in files created by other applications. For example, if we want to use an Excel worksheet that relies on an IF function in a Word report, copying and pasting the worksheet would freeze the results of the function. If we later updated the worksheet so that the IF function produced new results, we would have to copy and paste the worksheet again to update the Word report. With Office, we can recycle the information in a way that ensures the report always reflects the latest results of the worksheet's IF function.

What Is OLE?

In Office, recycling information in different types of documents is made possible by OLE, which is pronounced *olay*. We don't have to be OLE experts to recycle information, but understanding a bit about the concept of OLE helps us decide which of a couple of different recycling methods to use. So here is a quick rundown.

Objects

The O in OLE stands for *object*, and an object is an item or an element of a document. It can be a block of text, a graphic, a table, a chart, and so on. Each object consists of data that determines how the object is displayed and data that determines its content. The application that creates the object is called the *server*, and the application that receives the object is called the *client*. The server document in which the object was created is called the *source document*, and the client document in which the object is used is called the *container document*.

Linking vs. embedding

To create a patchwork document, we can *link* an object to the container document (the *L* in *OLE*), or we can *embed* the object (the *E*). When we link information stored in a source document to a container document, we need both the source document and the container document in order to be able to display the object. When we embed information, the information becomes part of the container document, and we no longer need the source document.

When to link

When to embed

So how does all this influence how we go about recycling information? If the object we want to use in a container document is likely to change and we want to be sure that every instance of the object in every container document where the information is used reflects the changes, it is best to create the information in its own source document and then link the object where it's needed. If the information is not going to change, embedding might be the best way to go because embedded information can be edited in the container document without the source document having to be present. Bear in mind, however, that documents that contain embedded objects can get very large.

So that's the scoop on OLE. Now let's see how we might go about using it.

Recycling Excel Worksheets

You have seen how to add an Excel worksheet to a Word document when you don't need to maintain a link to the worksheet information in Excel. In this section, we'll look at other ways to recycle Excel worksheets. The techniques you'll learn here also apply to the other Office applications, which we'll briefly cover in later sections.

Adding Excel Worksheets to Word Documents

To demonstrate a couple of ways of creating container documents, we'll use the memo now on your screen and the Annual worksheet in the 1997 Jobs workbook. Follow the steps on the next page to link the worksheet information.

1. Press Ctrl+End to move to the end of the memo and then press Enter to add some space.

Linking an Excel worksheet

2. Click the 1997 Jobs icon to switch to the Annual sheet of this Excel workbook, be sure A3:F7 is still selected, and click the Copy button.

3. Click Income Memo to switch back to the memo, and choose Paste Special from the Edit menu to display this dialog box:

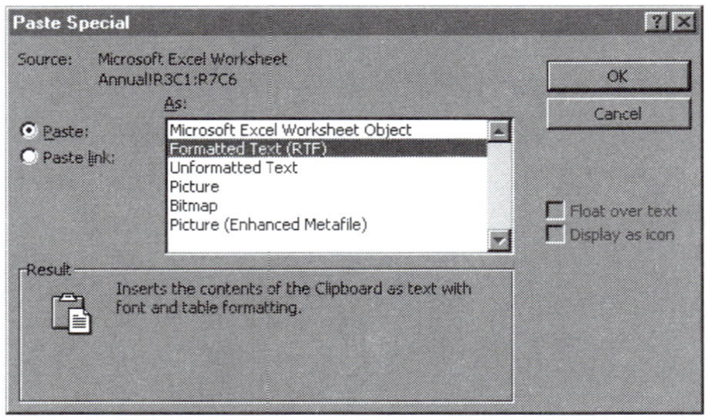

4. Select the Paste Link option, select Microsoft Excel Worksheet Object in the As list, and click OK. Word switches to page layout view and pastes a copy of the worksheet selection in the memo, linking the copy to the original worksheet.

5. Save the binder.

We'll test the worksheet link in a moment. For now, let's embed a copy of the same range so that we can explore yet another technique. This technique will embed the entire active sheet of the selected workbook, so to avoid embedding the Annual worksheet's graph as well as the income statement, first move the graph to a different sheet and save the workbook with the Annual sheet active:

1. Click the 1997 Jobs icon and insert a new sheet by choosing Worksheet from the Insert menu.

2. Next move the graph to the new sheet by clicking the graph to select it, clicking the Cut button, clicking the Sheet1 tab, and then clicking the Paste button. Deselect the graph and rename Sheet1 as *Graph* (see page 114).

More about linking

By default, when you open a document that contains a link to another file, Word automatically udates the linked information. It also updates the information if the source file changes while the linked document is open. The source file does not have to be open for this updating to happen, but it does have to be available to your computer and it does have to be stored exactly where it was when you established the link. If the source file is moved or renamed, the link will be broken. To reestablish the link, choose Links from the Edit menu, select the link, click the Change Source button, select the source file, and click OK.

3. Move to cell A1 on the Annual sheet and save the binder.

4. To update the workbook file stored on disk, choose Save As File from the Section menu. In the Save As dialog box, select 1997 Jobs from the My Documents list and click Save. Click Yes to overwrite the existing version, saving the workbook with the new Graph sheet and with the Annual sheet active.

Now for the embedding operation:

1. Switch to Income Memo, press Ctrl+End, and press Enter to add some space.

2. Choose Object from the Insert menu and then click the Create From File tab to display these options:

Embedding an Excel worksheet

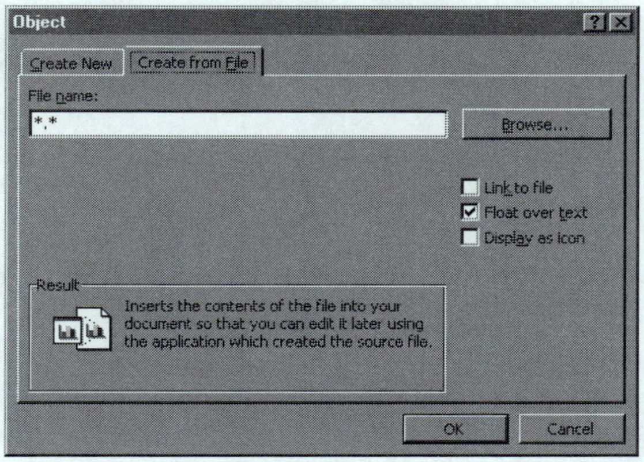

3. Click the Browse button, double-click 1997 Jobs in the Browse dialog box, and click OK to close the Object dialog box.

4. Save the binder.

To see the effects of the different types of objects, let's make a change to the worksheet:

1. Click the 1997 Jobs icon to switch back to Excel, move to the Invoices 1997 sheet, and change the amount in cell E26 to $20,000. Then move back to the Annual sheet, which because of the links you created in Chapter 5, has been updated to reflect the changed amount.

2. Choose Save As File from the Section menu and save the 1997 Jobs workbook.

Embedding documents as icons

The Display As Icon option in the Object dialog box allows you to embed an object as an icon. You might use this option, for example, if you want to include supporting information with a report but don't want to clutter up the report itself with information that not everyone would want to read. When you select this option, the object appears in the document as a small graphic, and double-clicking the graphic displays the actual object.

3. Click the Income Memo icon and scroll the document until you can see the "bottom line" for each worksheet, as shown below. (If you don't see all of the embedded worksheet, see the tip on the facing page.)

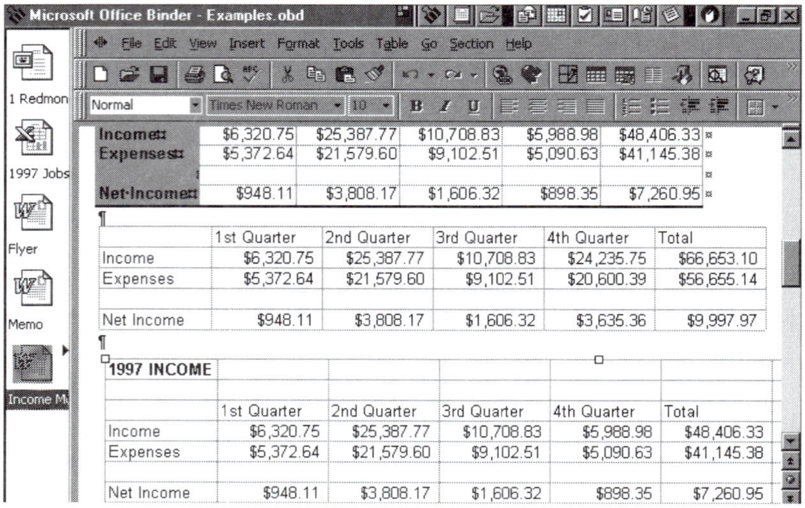

Word has updated the linked table (the second table) to reflect the invoice change in the source document. (If the table hasn't been updated, see the adjacent tip.) To update the first table, we can use regular Word editing techniques, but to update the embedded table, we have to work through Excel, the application that created the object. Try this:

Updating an embedded table

1. Double-click the embedded table. Excel's menus and toolbars replace Word's, and the table now appears as a worksheet with a grid of lettered columns and numbered rows, as shown here:

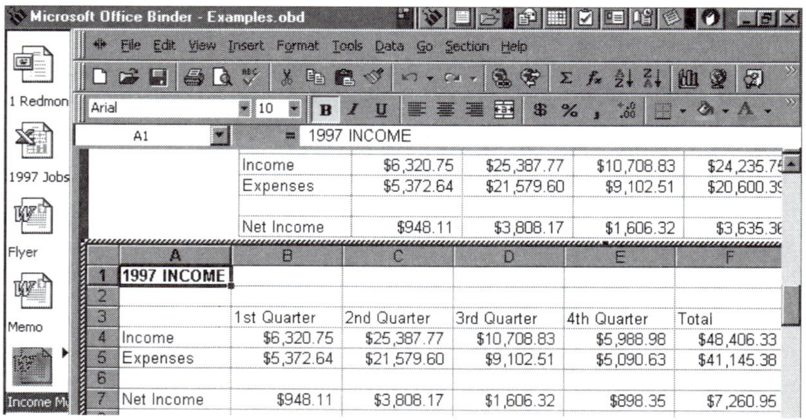

Updating linked tables

If the linked table does not update correctly, select the table by clicking it, choose Links from the Edit menu, click the Update Now button, and then click Close.

2. Type *24235.75* in cell E4 and click the Enter button on the formula bar. The values in the remaining cells in the 4th Quarter and Total columns are automatically updated because the formulas in those cells remained intact during the embedding procedure.

3. Click outside the worksheet's frame to return to the memo, where the embedded table now matches the linked table:

Returning to Word

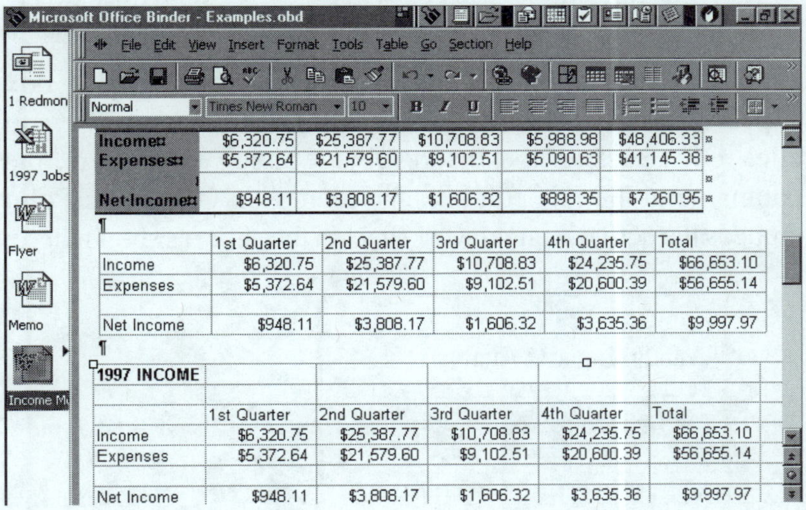

4. Save the binder to save the changes to the memo.

After working through these examples, you should have some idea of the advantages and disadvantages of the various ways of using Excel worksheets in Word documents. Let's move on to see how to use worksheets in other applications.

Displaying specific cells

When you embed a worksheet in a document, too many or too few cells may be displayed. To control what you see, double-click the embedded worksheet to activate Excel, and then increase or decrease the size of the frame surrounding the worksheet to display specific cells. (You can also select the rows or columns you don't want to display and choose Row or Column and then Hide from Excel's Format menu.) Click outside the Excel frame to return to the document. This can be a tricky process and you may need to play around to get it right.

Adding Excel Worksheets to PowerPoint Slides

Suppose we want to use the information in the 1997 Jobs Annual worksheet in a PowerPoint presentation to Tip Top Roofing's management. Follow these steps to embed the worksheet in a slide:

1. Choose Add from Binder's Section menu and double-click Microsoft PowerPoint Presentation in the Add Section dialog box. A blank title slide appears.

Creating an object slide

2. Change the slide type by clicking the Slide Layout button on the Standard toolbar and double-clicking the Object autolayout (the fourth autolayout in the fourth row).

3. Click the title area, type *Annual Income Analysis*, and double-click the object area to display the Insert Object dialog box.

4. Select Microsoft Excel Worksheet as the object type and then select the Create From File option to display a dialog box in which you specify the file to be used.

5. Click the Browse button, and when the Browse dialog box appears, select 1997 Jobs in the My Documents folder and click OK. Back in the Insert Object dialog box, check the pathname in the File edit box and then click OK. PowerPoint embeds the active Annual worksheet in the slide, as shown here:

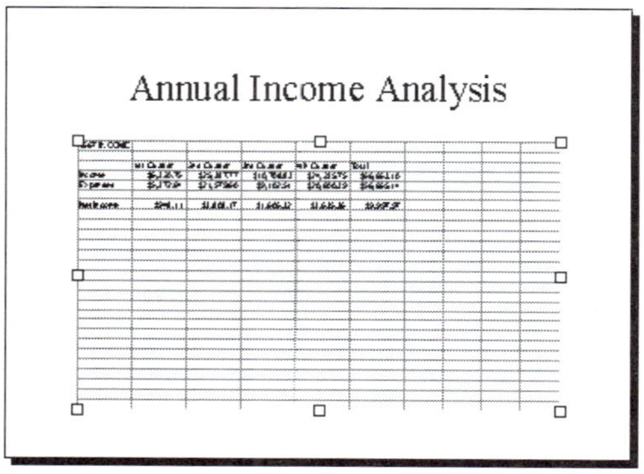

6. Choose Rename from the Section menu, type *Income Presentation* as the section name, and press Enter.

7. Save the binder.

As with the embedded worksheet in Word, we can edit the slide worksheet through Excel by double-clicking the worksheet to display the grid and Excel's menus and toolbars. We can also display specific cells by adjusting Excel's frame. (See the tip on page 275.)

WordArt

WordArt is a great little program that ships with Office and that helps you produce striking text effects with almost any printer. You can insert a WordArt object in a Word, Excel, or PowerPoint document by first clicking the Insert WordArt button on the Drawing toolbar to display the WordArt Gallery. Then select a style, click OK, enter a word or phrase in the Edit WordArt Text dialog box, and click OK. WordArt arranges your word(s) in the style you have selected, inserts the word(s) in your document as an object, and displays the WordArt toolbar so that you can change the object if necessary. You can resize the WordArt object and copy it just like any other object.

Importing Excel Worksheets into Access

In the past, many people used spreadsheet applications like Excel to store databases of information. Now that easy-to-use database applications like Access are available, it makes sense to switch to Access to take advantage of its many database management features. If we have current data in a worksheet that could be better maintained in a database, we can import the data to avoid having to recreate the records. Because Access is not compatible with Binder, we'll use the primary applications for this exercise. Follow these steps:

1. Close Binder, saving any changes when prompted, click the Open Office Document button on the shortcut bar, and double-click 1997 Jobs.

2. Move to the Invoices 1997 worksheet, select A14:E26, and choose Convert To MS Access from the Data menu to display the dialog box shown below. (If this command does not appear on the Data menu, you need to install the AccessLinks add-in program, see the tip below.)

Selecting an import range

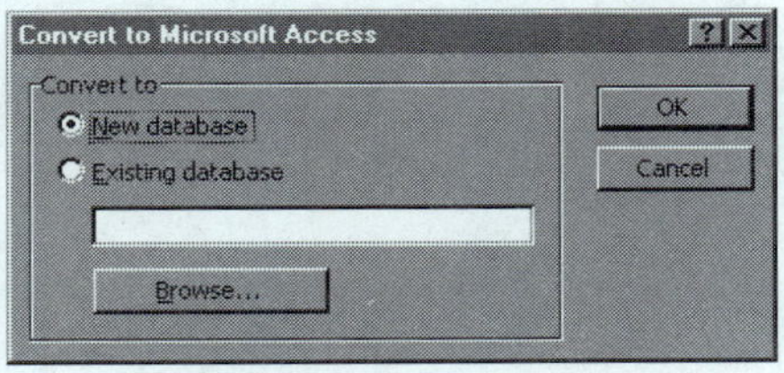

3. Select the Existing Database option, click the Browse button, double-click Roofs in the Choose Database dialog box, and then click OK. After a few seconds, Access opens and you see the first of the Import Spreadsheet Wizard's dialog boxes, as shown here:

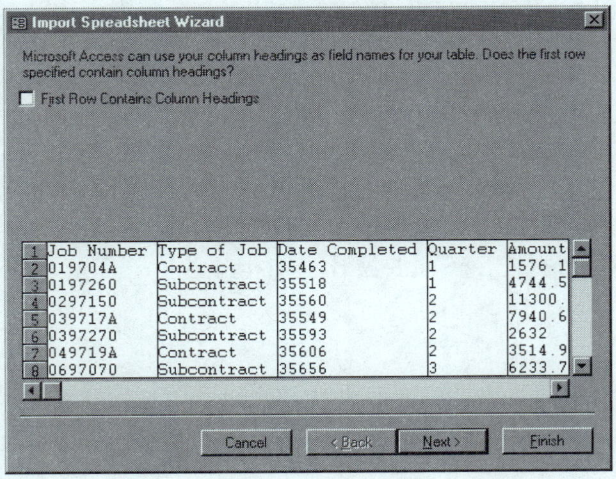

Installing the AccessLinks add-in program

If you want to convert an Excel spreadsheet file to an Access database, you need to install the AccessLinks add-in program. To do so, choose Add-Ins from Excel's Tools menu. In the Add-Ins dialog box, click the Microsoft AccessLinks Add-In check box and then click OK. (If this option is not listed, you may need to run setup and select the AccessLinks option in the Add-Ins section of the Microsoft Excel component.) After a few moments, Excel completes the add-in process. You should now be able to choose the Convert To MS Access command from the Data menu.

4. Select the First Row Contains Column Headings option and click Next.

5. Accept the default settings in the wizard's second, third, and fourth dialog boxes by clicking Next in each one.

6. In the final dialog box, change the suggested table name to *Invoices* and then click Finish. When the wizard displays a message that it has finished importing the worksheet, click OK. Access displays the new Invoices table in the database window.

7. Now open the Invoices table to check the results of the import operation (you might want to maximize the Access window first), and then quit Access and Excel.

Recycling Excel Graphs

The techniques used for recycling Excel graphs are very similar to those used for worksheets. For practice, let's link a graph to both a Word document and a PowerPoint slide.

Adding Excel Graphs to Word Documents

Without any preamble, here are the steps for linking the 1997 Jobs graph to the Income Memo document:

1. Open the Examples binder, click the 1997 Jobs icon, move to the Graph sheet, and with the chart area of the graph selected, click the Copy button.

2. Click the Income Memo icon, move to the end of the document, and press Enter a couple of times to create some space. (So that the memo would fit on one page, we adjusted the embedded worksheet's frame to hide the blank rows at the bottom of the table; see the tip on page 275.)

3. Now choose Paste Special from the Edit menu, select Microsoft Excel Chart Object, select the Paste Link option, and click OK. Here is the result:

Graphing Word tables

You can use Microsoft Graph to plot graphs of the data in Word tables. First select the data and click the Copy button. Then choose Object from the Insert menu and double-click Microsoft Graph 97 Chart in the Object Type list to open Graph. Graph inserts the data you have copied into the datasheet and displays the plotted data in a graph. Click outside the graph to close Graph and view the results.

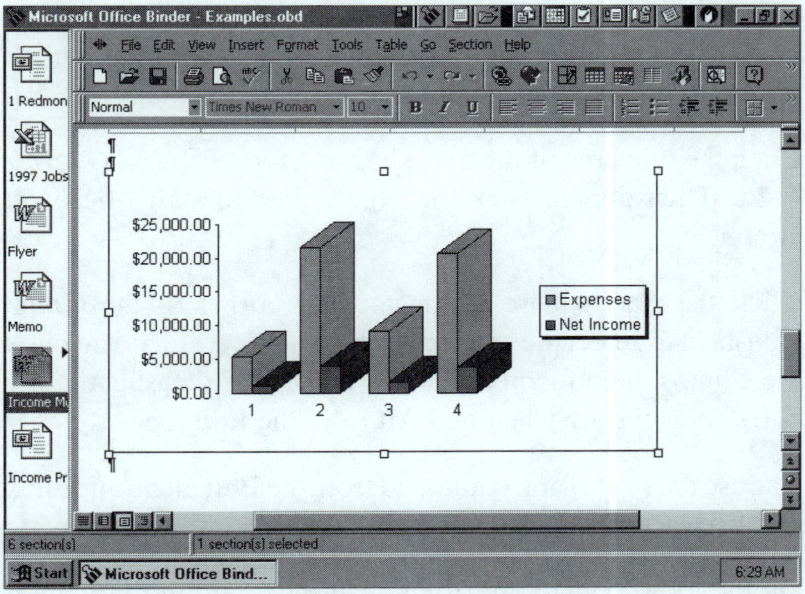

4. Save the binder to save the changes to the memo, click the 1997 Jobs icon, move to the Invoices 1997 worksheet, and change the entry in E26 back to $1,753.23.

5. Click the Income Memo icon to open the memo where the linked table and the graph have been updated to reflect the change you made to the worksheet.

6. Save the binder.

Adding Excel Graphs to PowerPoint Slides

If a graph has been created on its own chart sheet, we can add that graph to a slide by activating the Graph program, clicking the Import File button, and identifying the graph's file. In Chapter 5, we created an embedded worksheet graph and even though we have moved this graph to its own sheet, Graph cannot import it the way it could if we had created it on a separate chart sheet. All is not lost, however. Here's how to recreate the graph in PowerPoint by using its underlying Excel data:

The Import File button

1. Click the 1997 Jobs icon, move to the Annual sheet, select A3:E5, and click the Copy button.

2. Click the Income Presentation icon, click the New Slide button on PowerPoint's Standard toolbar, and double-click the Chart autolayout (the fourth one in the second row).

3. Click the title area of the new slide and type *The 2nd Quarter Peak*. Then double-click the object area to start Microsoft Graph.

4. Click the gray square in the top left corner of the Graph datasheet to select the entire datasheet. (Be careful not to click the Control menu icon at the left end of the datasheet's title bar.) Then choose Clear and All from the Edit menu.

5. Choose the Paste Link command from the Edit menu and click OK to overwrite the datasheet.

6. On the toolbar, click the View Datasheet button to toggle it off. Click outside the chart area to see these results:

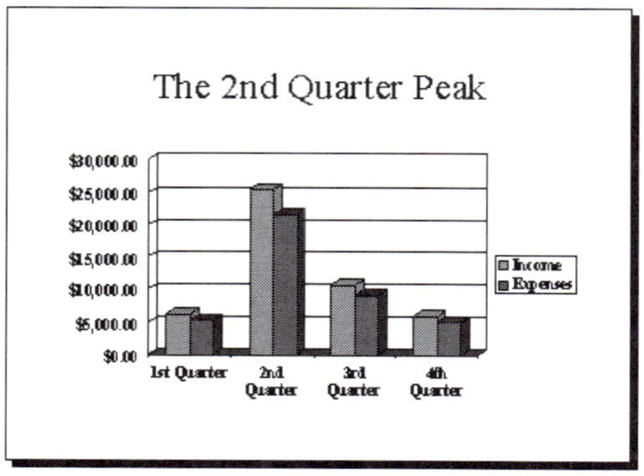

Recycling Word Tables

In Chapter 3, we created a simple Word table to show you how easy it is. As we discuss in this section, Word's powerful table-making feature can be used to build tables in PowerPoint. In addition, we can import the data in our Word tables into both Excel and Access.

Formatting embedded Excel graphs

To format an Excel graph that has been embedded on a PowerPoint slide, you simply double-click the graph to start Microsoft Graph, click the View Datasheet button to hide the datasheet, and then double-click the graph object you want to format to open the corresponding Format dialog box.

Adding Word Tables to PowerPoint Slides

When information needs to be displayed in tabular format but does not need the number-crunching power of Excel, we can embed a Word table in a slide to keep it neat and tidy. Follow these steps:

Creating a table slide

1. With Income Presentation open on your screen, click the New Slide button and add a table slide (use the fourth autolayout in the top row).

2. Click the title area of the slide and type *Contract vs. Subcontract*, and then double-click the object area.

3. When the Insert Word Table dialog box appears, change both the Number Of Columns and Number Of Rows settings to 3 and click OK. Word's menus and toolbars replace PowerPoint's so that you can work with the table.

4. Click the second column in the first row, type *# of Jobs*, press Tab, type *Contribution to Bottom Line*, and press Tab again. Then enter the following information to complete the table:

Contract	*4*	*$15,941.73*
Subcontract	*8*	*$32,464.14*

5. Select the entire table, choose Table AutoFormat from the Table menu, and double-click Classic 4.

6. Increase the size of the frame around the table and make any cosmetic adjustments you want, and then click outside the frame to see these results:

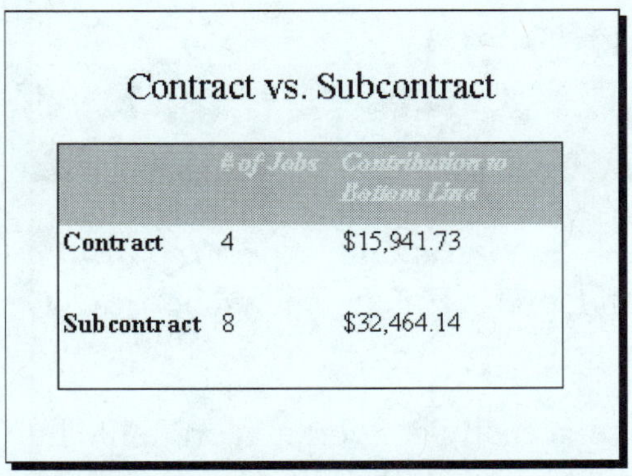

7. Save the binder to save the changes to the presentation.

Converting Word Tables to Excel Worksheets

We've seen how to add Excel worksheets and graphs to Word documents. Now let's see how to import a Word table into an Excel worksheet. Follow the steps on the next page.

Formatting tables

Using the buttons on Word's Formatting toolbar and the commands on its Format menu, you can format tables on slides just as you would format a table in a Word document. You can format the text of individual table entries; or you can add a border, gridlines, or shading to the table as a whole.

1. Click the Flyer icon and move to the table at the top of the second page.

2. Select the title, the subtitle, and all the rows of the table by dragging the pointer in the selection bar, and then click the Copy button.

3. Choose Add from the Section menu, double-click Microsoft Excel Worksheet, and with cell A1 of the new worksheet selected, click the Paste button. Excel imports the table as a worksheet, which you can then reformat to look something like the worksheet shown here:

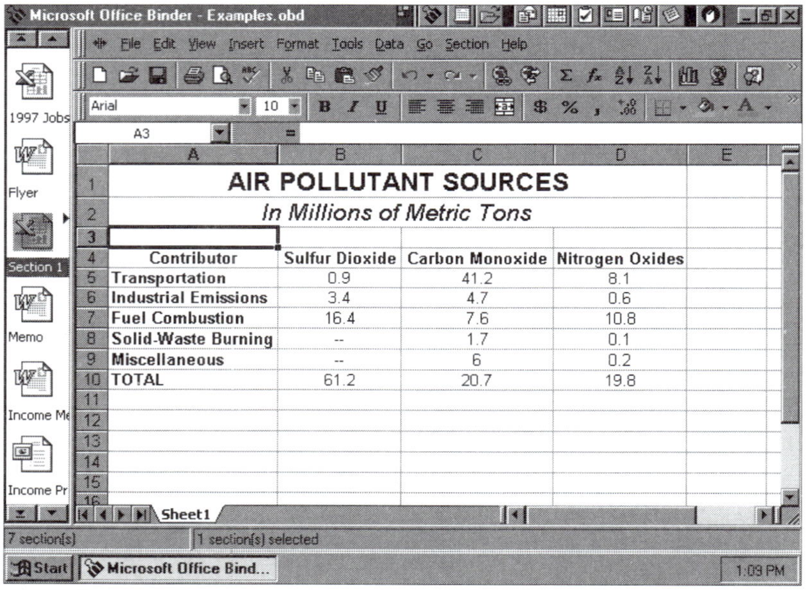

4. Choose Rename from the Section menu, type *Air Pollution* as the section name, and press Enter. Then choose Save Binder from the File menu.

As you have seen, Excel can easily convert a Word table into a worksheet that you can manipulate using familiar Excel techniques. If preserving the table's existing Word formatting is critical, instead of using the Paste button, you can use the Paste Special command on the Edit menu to paste the table into Excel as a Word object.

Clip art

Office ships with a wide variety of clip art files, which you can insert into your documents to give them some pizzazz. The technique for inserting clip art images varies between applications, so consult the Help menu for more information. However, once you insert a graphic, you can resize it the same way you would a graph (see page 126).

Importing Word Tables into Access

Before we can import a Word table into Access, we have to strip it of all Word's formatting. After we convert the table into a text-only file, Access can handle it just like any other delimited file. (A *delimiter* is a character that indicates where one field ends and another begins.) Follow the steps below to set up the pollutants table created earlier in Word so that it can be imported as an Access table:

Delimiters

1. Close the Examples binder. (We don't need the binder for the remaining examples.) Then click the Open Office Document button on the shortcut bar and double-click Flyer. (Maximize the Word document window, if necessary.)
2. Move to the second page of the flyer, select only the table, and click the Copy button. Then close the flyer.
3. Click the New button on Word's Standard toolbar to open a new document, click the Paste button to paste in the table, and then switch to normal view by clicking the button at the left end of the horizontal scroll bar. (Page layout view was activated when you opened the Flyer document.)
4. Because Access requires that the data types within a given field must be consistent (all text or all currency, for example), change both sets of dashes in the Sulfur Dioxide column of the table to 0 (zero).
5. Now to convert the table to plain text, select the table, choose Convert Table To Text from the Table menu, and click OK to accept Tabs as the Separate Text With option. Word converts the table to regular text paragraphs with tab characters where the columns used to be.

   Converting a table to text

   Using tab separators
6. Choose Save As from the File menu, type *Pollutants* in the File Name edit box, select Text Only from the Save As Type drop-down list, click Save, and click Yes in the warning box.
7. Close the Pollutants document and then quit Word.

Now let's move to Access:

1. Click the Open Office Document button on the shortcut bar and double-click Roofs.

2. Choose Get External Data and then Import from the File menu. In the Import dialog box, select Text Files from the Files Of Type drop-down list and then double-click Pollutants. Access displays the first Import Text Wizard dialog box:

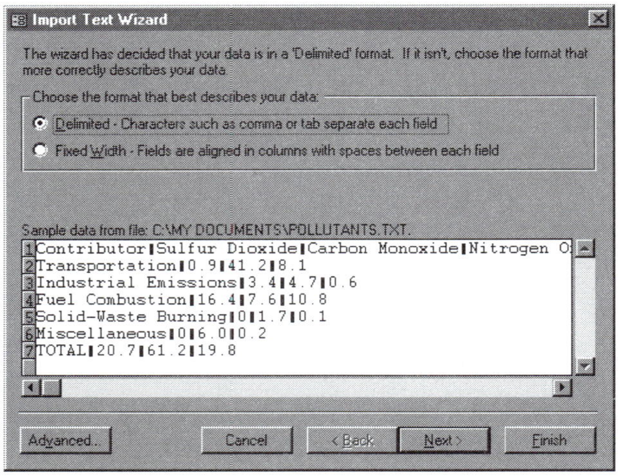

3. Be sure the Delimited option is selected and then click Next.

4. In the wizard's second dialog box, be sure Tab is selected as the delimiter, select the First Row Contains Field Names option, and click Next.

5. Accept the default settings in the wizard's next three dialog boxes by clicking Next in each one.

6. In the wizard's final dialog box, click Finish to accept the suggested table name. When the wizard displays a message that is has finished the importing procedure, click OK. Access adds a Pollutants table to the Roofs database window.

7. Examine the Pollutants data in its table window and then quit Access.

Text delimiters

In some text files that are destined to be imported into a database program, fields are enclosed in delimiter characters, such as double quotation marks. The fields in Pollutants have no delimiters; they are simply separated by tab characters. Because these characters serve no other purpose, they can be designated as field separators. If, however, the fields were separated by a character such as a comma and commas also occurred as regular punctuation within fields, the fields would need delimiters in order for the database program to know which commas were punctuation and which were field separators.

Recycling PowerPoint Slide Shows

Once we have invested effort in creating a presentation, we can recycle the presentation text to create an outline that can be used as the basis for a Word document. Here's how:

1. Click the Open Office Document button on the shortcut bar and double-click 1 Redmond BEAT.
2. Display Slide 1 in slide view and choose Send To and Microsoft Word from the File menu to display the Write-Up dialog box.
3. Select the Outline Only option and click OK. (You may want to explore the other options later on your own.) After a few seconds, Word starts and displays the text of the presentation in a document window, like this:

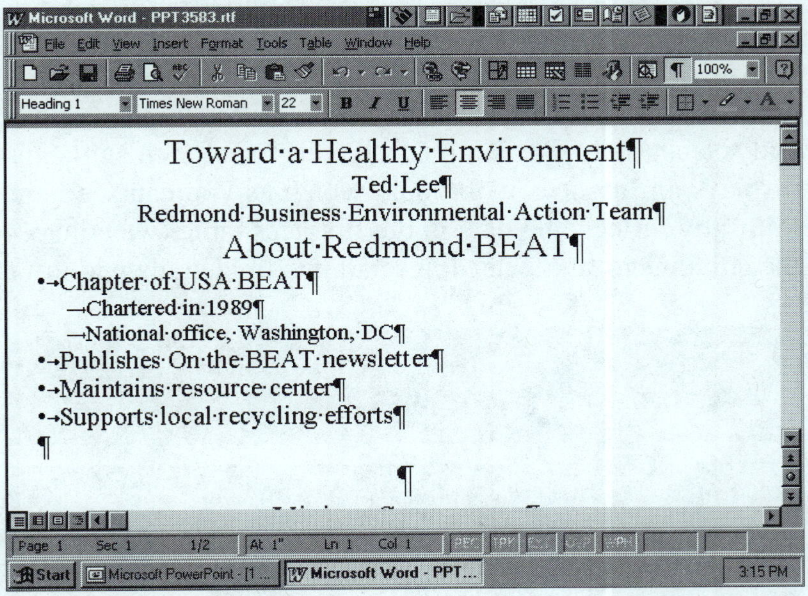

Note that Word designates the new document with the letters *Ppt* (for *PowerPoint*) and a number.

4. Choose Save As from the File menu, select Word Document from the Save As Type drop-down list, and save the document with the name *3 Redmond BEAT* in the My Documents folder.

You can now reformat the document as appropriate to the task at hand.

Embedding a presentation in a Word document

You can embed a presentation in a Word document just like any other object. For example, you could send a letter to clients about a new product and embed in the letter a presentation that reinforces your sales pitch. Simply choose Object from the Insert menu, click the Create From File tab, select the filename of the presentation and either click OK to insert the first slide of the presentation as a graphic or select the Display As Icon option and click OK to embed the entire presentation as an icon. In the latter case, clients who have PowerPoint can double-click the icon to view the presentation.

Recycling Access Tables

We've seen how to get Excel worksheets and Word tables into Access, but what if we want to get part of a database table out of Access and into another application? This section discusses Access export procedures.

Exporting Access Tables as Excel Worksheets

Earlier we imported invoice information into Access from Excel, but in fact we are much more likely to maintain this kind of log in Access and then export it to Excel for any necessary analysis. Let's export the Invoices table from the Roofs database as a demonstration:

1. Quit Word and PowerPoint. Then click the Open Office Document button on the shortcut bar and open the Roofs database.

The OfficeLinks button

2. Select Invoices from the Tables list in the database window, click the arrow next to the OfficeLinks button on the toolbar, and select Analyze It With MS Excel. Excel then starts and displays an Invoices workbook, which as you can see here, faithfully reflects the data in the Invoices table (we adjusted the columns to fit the headings and maximized the window):

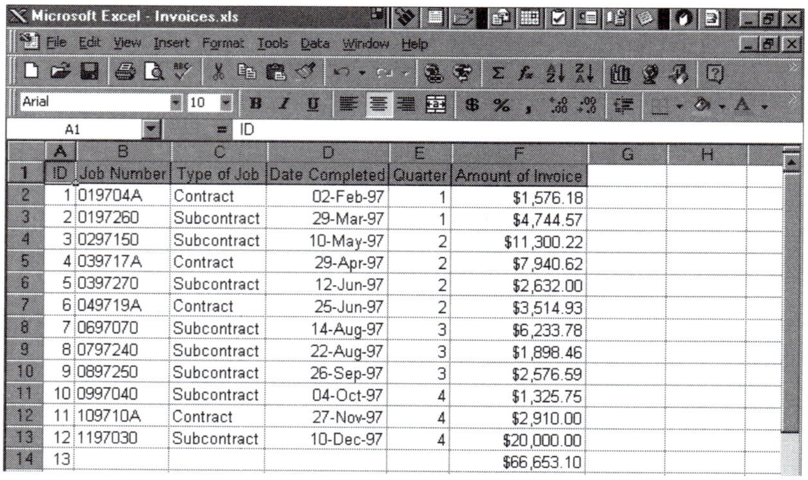

	A	B	C	D	E	F	G	H
1	ID	Job Number	Type of Job	Date Completed	Quarter	Amount of Invoice		
2	1	019704A	Contract	02-Feb-97	1	$1,576.18		
3	2	0197260	Subcontract	29-Mar-97	1	$4,744.57		
4	3	0297150	Subcontract	10-May-97	2	$11,300.22		
5	4	039717A	Contract	29-Apr-97	2	$7,940.62		
6	5	0397270	Subcontract	12-Jun-97	2	$2,632.00		
7	6	049719A	Contract	25-Jun-97	2	$3,514.93		
8	7	0697070	Subcontract	14-Aug-97	3	$6,233.78		
9	8	0797240	Subcontract	22-Aug-97	3	$1,898.46		
10	9	0897250	Subcontract	26-Sep-97	3	$2,576.59		
11	10	0997040	Subcontract	04-Oct-97	4	$1,325.75		
12	11	109710A	Contract	27-Nov-97	4	$2,910.00		
13	12	1197030	Subcontract	10-Dec-97	4	$20,000.00		
14	13					$66,653.10		

3. Save the Invoices workbook clicking Yes to save it in Excel 97 format. Then quit Excel, leaving Access open.

Exporting Access Tables as Word Documents

We can easily print database tables from Access, but those tables are not formatted in any way. If we want a table to include formatting, we can export it to Word as a delimited text file and convert it into a table before printing it. This process is essentially the reverse of the importing process (see page 283). Follow the steps below:

1. With the Roofs database window open in Access, select Customers in the Tables list.
2. Click the arrow next to the OfficeLinks button on the toolbar and select Publish It With MS Word. Word then starts and displays the Customers table in a document window.
3. Adjust the columns to fit the headings. Here are the results:

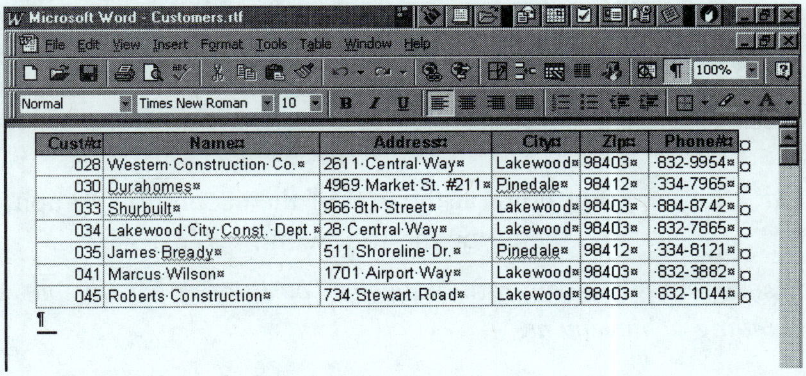

Cust#	Name	Address	City	Zip	Phone#
028	Western Construction Co.	2611 Central Way	Lakewood	98403	832-9954
030	Durahomes	4969 Market St. #211	Pinedale	98412	334-7965
033	Shurbuilt	966 8th Street	Lakewood	98403	884-8742
034	Lakewood City Const. Dept.	28 Central Way	Lakewood	98403	832-7865
035	James Bready	511 Shoreline Dr.	Pinedale	98412	334-8121
041	Marcus Wilson	1701 Airport Way	Lakewood	98403	832-3882
045	Roberts Construction	734 Stewart Road	Lakewood	98403	832-1044

As you can see, Word automatically formats the table during the importing process.

4. Save the Customers document. Then quit Word and Access.

Creating Form Letters

In Chapter 9, we briefly covered the process for creating mailing labels from an Access database of names and addresses. In Word, we can use a process called *mail merge* to create form letters for bulk mailings to the names and addresses in an Access database. Mail merge is the printing of a bunch of similar documents by merging the information

Mail merge

in one document, called the *main document*, with a database of variable information in a second document, called the *data source*. The main document contains the information that does not change from document to document—the text of a form letter, for example—along with placeholders called *merge fields* for the variable information.

As a demonstration, follow the steps below to set up a form letter and mail merge a copy for each of the customers who have records in the Customers table:

1. Click the Open Office Document button, double-click Memo in the My Documents folder to open the memo you created in Chapter 3, and click the Normal View button.
2. At the top of the memo, select the word *Memo*, the five header lines, and the title. Then press Delete.
3. Type *14000 Leary Way, Suite 100*, press Enter, type *Redmond, WA 98052*, press Enter, type *Phone 555-6789*, and press Enter three times.
4. Type *May 22, 1997* and press Enter twice more.
5. Click an insertion point at the end of the second paragraph, type a space, and then type the following:

   Please join me in congratulating Tip Top Roofing for this outstanding achievement.

   Sincerely,

   Ted Lee

The letter now looks like the one shown at the top of the facing page (we've temporarily turned off the toolbars so that you can see the entire letter).

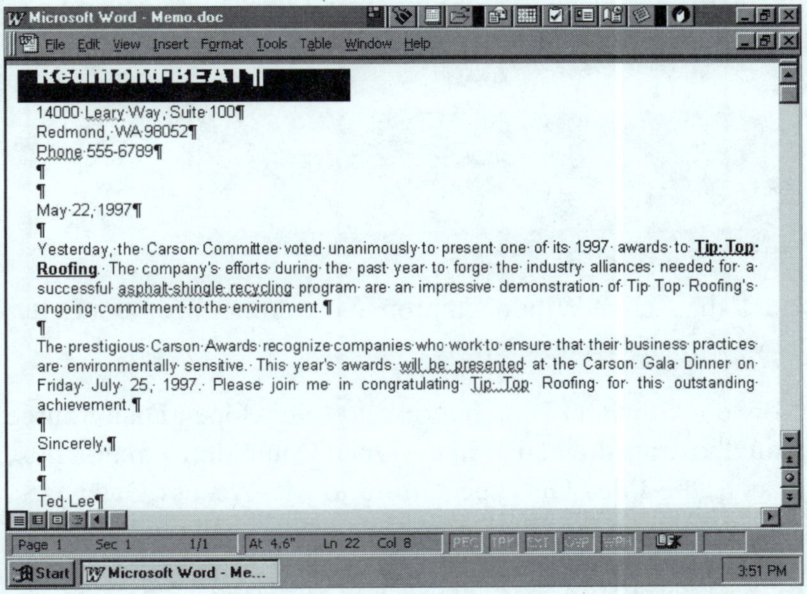

6. Save the letter with the name *Announcement Letter*.

Now let's add the information that will turn this simple letter into a form letter:

1. Choose Mail Merge from the Tools menu to display the dialog box shown here:

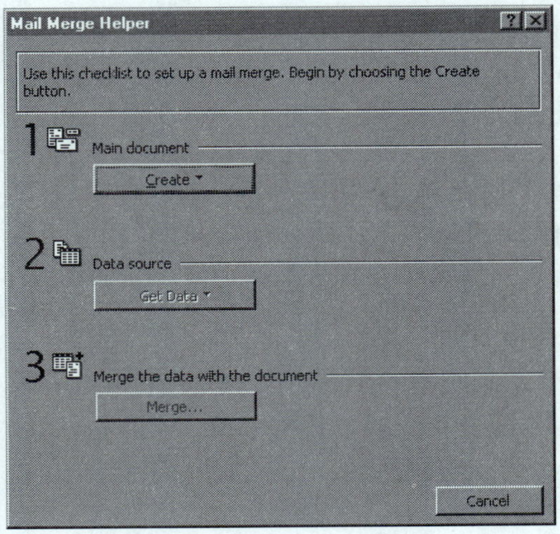

An entire sheet of the same label

Sometimes you may need to print an entire sheet of the same label—for example, for your return address. In Word, choose Envelopes And Labels from the Tools menu. Click the Labels tab and type the desired information on the label in the Address box. Click the Full Page Of The Same Label option in the Print section, click Options to select the label style you are using, and click OK. Finally, click Print to send the sheet of labels directly to the printer, or click New Document to insert the label information in a document that you can edit, format, and save just like any other Word document.

2. Click the Create button and select Form Letters from the drop-down list. Word displays the dialog box shown here:

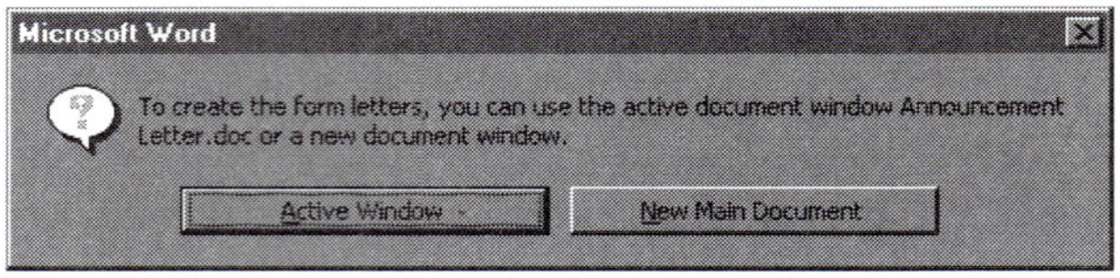

3. Click the Active Window button to use Announcement Letter as your main document.
4. Now click the Get Data button and select Open Data Source from the drop-down list. In the Open Data Source dialog box, change the Files Of Type setting to MS Access Databases, select Roofs in the My Documents folder, and click Open.
5. In the Microsoft Access dialog box that appears, select Customers in the Tables list and click OK. You see the dialog box shown here:

6. Click Edit Main Document to close the Mail Merge Helper dialog box and display the Mail Merge toolbar, which helps you complete the process.
7. Click an insertion point two lines below the date, click the Insert Merge Field button to drop down a list of available fields, and click Name. Word inserts a Name placeholder surrounded by chevrons.
8. Press Enter and insert a merge field for Address. Then press Enter and insert a merge field for City; type a comma, a space, *WA*, and two more spaces; and finally, insert a merge field for PostalCode.
9. Press Enter twice, type *Dear* and a space, insert a Name merge field, type a colon, and press Enter twice. If necessary, close the Office Assistant. Here are the results:

Creating a new main document/data source

If your main document does not already exist, you can click the New Main Document button. Word then opens a new document and adds an edit button to the Mail Merge Helper dialog box that allows you to go to the main document at any time and type or edit it. If your data source does not already exist, you can select Create Data Source instead of Open Data Source, and Word will walk you through the steps of setting up a table of fields (columns) and records (rows) to be used as the source of the variable mail-merge information.

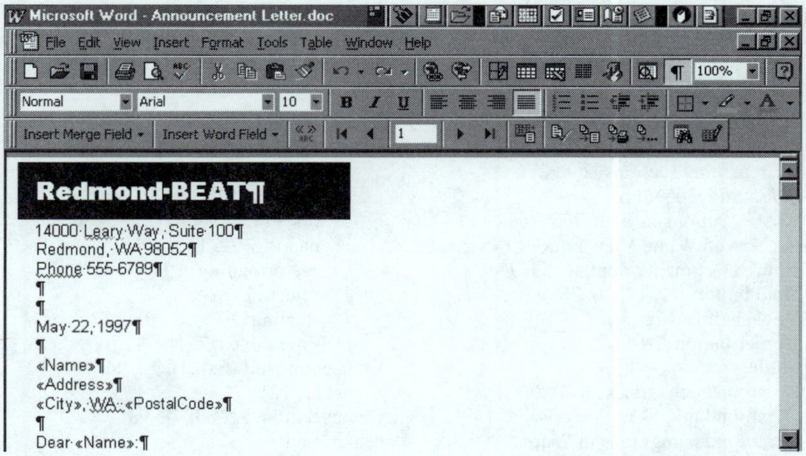

10. Before you go any further, click the View Merged Data button to check that you have entered the merge fields correctly. Word displays the data from the first Customers record, like this:

The View Merged Data button

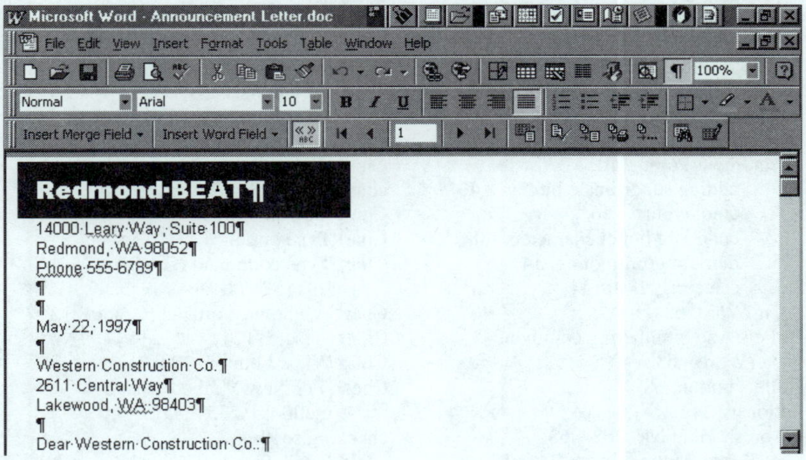

You can cycle through all the records by clicking the Next Record button on the Mail Merge toolbar.

The Next Record button

11. Now for the acid test. Click the Merge To Printer button and then click OK in the Print dialog box to print one copy of the letter for each customer. An example is shown at the beginning of the chapter.

The Merge To Printer button

This very simple example barely scratches the surface of Word's mail merge capabilities. You might want to experiment with other options to see some of the possibilities.

Index

D

E

F

T